G000056769

BANK FRAGILITY AND REGULATION: EVIDENCE FROM DIFFERENT COUNTRIES

RESEARCH IN FINANCIAL SERVICES: PRIVATE AND PUBLIC POLICY

Series Editor: George G. Kaufman

RESEARCH IN FINANCIAL SERVICES: PRIVATE
AND PUBLIC POLICY   VOLUME 12

BANK FRAGILITY AND REGULATION: EVIDENCE FROM DIFFERENT COUNTRIES

EDITED BY

GEORGE G. KAUFMAN

Loyola University Chicago, Chicago, IL, USA

2000

JAI
An Imprint of Elsevier Science

Amsterdam – London – New York – Oxford – Paris – Shannon – Tokyo

ELSEVIER SCIENCE Inc.
655 Avenue of the Americas
New York, NY 10010, USA

© 2000 Elsevier Science Inc. All rights reserved.

This work is protected under copyright by Elsevier Science, and the following terms and conditions apply to its use:

Photocopying
Single photocopies of single chapters may be made for personal use as allowed by national copyright laws. Permission of the Publisher and payment of a fee is required for all other photocopying, including multiple or systematic copying, copying for advertising or promotional purposes, resale, and all forms of document delivery. Special rates are available for educational institutions that wish to make photocopies for non-profit educational classroom use.

Permissions may be sought directly from Elsevier Science Global Rights Department, PO Box 800, Oxford OX5 1DX, UK; phone: (+44) 1865 843830, fax: (+44) 1865 853333, e-mail: permissions@elsevier.co.uk. You may also contact Global Rights directly through Elsevier's home page (http://www.elsevier.nl), by selecting 'Obtaining Permissions'.

In the USA, users may clear permissions and make payments through the Copyright Clearance Center, Inc., 222 Rosewood Drive, Danvers, MA 01923, USA; phone: (978) 7508400, fax: (978) 7504744, and in the UK through the Copyright Licensing Agency Rapid Clearance Service (CLARCS), 90 Tottenham Court Road, London W1P 0LP, UK; phone: (+44) 207 631 5555; fax: (+44) 207 631 5500. Other countries may have a local reprographic rights agency for payments.

Derivative Works
Tables of contents may be reproduced for internal circulation, but permission of Elsevier Science is required for external resale or distribution of such material.
Permission of the Publisher is required for all other derivative works, including compilations and translations.

Electronic Storage or Usage
Permission of the Publisher is required to store or use electronically any material contained in this work, including any chapter or part of a chapter.

Except as outlined above, no part of this work may be reproduced, stored in a retrieval system or transmitted in any form or by any means, electronic, mechanical, photocopying, recording or otherwise, without prior written permission of the Publisher.
Address permissions requests to: Elsevier Science Global Rights Department, at the mail, fax and e-mail addresses noted above.

Notice
No responsibility is assumed by the Publisher for any injury and/or damage to persons or property as a matter of products liability, negligence or otherwise, or from any use or operation of any methods, products, instructions or ideas contained in the material herein. Because of rapid advances in the medical sciences, in particular, independent verification of diagnoses and drug dosages should be made.

First edition 2000

Library of Congress Cataloging in Publication Data
A catalog record from the Library of Congress has been applied for.

ISBN: 0-7623-0698-X

∞ The paper used in this publication meets the requirements of ANSI/NISO Z39.48-1992 (Permanence of Paper).
Printed in The Netherlands.

CONTENTS

LIST OF CONTRIBUTORS

David Aadland	Department of Economics, Utah State University
James R. Barth	Lowder Eminent Scholar in Finance, Auburn University
Harald A. Benink	Professor of Finance, Rotterdam School of Management, Erasmus University Rotterdam
Steven B. Caudill	Department of Economics, Auburn University
Marsha J. Courchane	Principal Economist, Freddie Mac
Drew Dahl	Department of Business Administration, Utah State University
Robert DeYoung	Senior Economist and Economic Advisor, Federal Reserve Bank of Chicago
Douglas D. Evanoff	Vice President, Federal Reserve Bank of Chicago
R. Alton Gilbert	Vice President, Federal Reserve Bank of St. Louis
Thomas Hall	Economist, Milken Institute, California
George G. Kaufman	John F. Smith Professor of Finance and Economics, Loyola University
Karel Lannoo	Senior Fellow, Centre for European Policy Studies, Brussels
David T. Llewellyn	Professor of Money and Banking, Loughborough University, U.K.

Jose A. Lopez	Economist, Federal Reserve Bank of San Francisco
Paolo Marullo Reedtz	Director, Banking and Financial Supervision, Bank of Italy, Rome
Andrew P. Meyer	Economist, Banking Supervision and Regulation, Federal Reserve Bank of St. Louis
Donald P. Morgan	Economist, Federal Reserve Bank of New York
John O'Keefe	Section Chief, Division of Research and Statistics, Federal Deposit Insurance Corporation
Marc R. Saidenberg	Senior Economist, Federal Reserve Bank of New York
Reinhard H. Schmidt	Wilhelm Merton Professor of International Banking and Finance, Goethe University, Germany
Steven A. Seelig	Financial Sector Advisor, International Monetary Fund
Alan Stephens	Department of Business Administration, Utah State University
Maurizio Trapanese	Banking and Financial Supervision, Bank of Italy
Mark D. Vaughan	Senior Manager and Economist, Banking Supervision & Regulation, Federal Reserve Bank of St. Louis
Larry D. Wall	Vice President, Federal Reserve Bank of Atlanta
Glenn Yago	Director of Capital Studies, Milken Institute, California

INTRODUCTION

The papers in this volume were presented at three invited sessions at the annual meeting of the Western Finance Association in Vancouver, Canada on July 2, 2000. The comments by the discussants were also presented at these sessions and are included in the volume.

As did many of the past volumes in this series, this volume focuses on current problems in banking that have the potential not for only disrupting the smooth provision of banking and other financial services, but also for adversely affecting domestic and even international macroeconomic activity. Because serious banking problems have been experienced by most countries in recent years, the papers both focus on fragility and regulation in different countries and are authored by leading financial economists in six different countries, including Belgium, Germany, Italy, the Netherlands, the United Kingdom, and the United States. By providing an international perspective, the papers provide insights into the commonality of banking problems in different countries and the role of regulation both in attempting to prevent and in potentially, albeit unintentionally, encouraging banking crises. As such, the papers and add to our storehouse of knowledge on the causes, symptoms, and consequences of banking problems across countries.

PART I

CROSS-COUNTRY EVIDENCE ON BANKING CRISES: DO FINANCIAL STRUCTURE AND BANK REGULATION MATTER?

James R. Barth, Steven B. Caudill, Thomas Hall and Glenn Yago

ABSTRACT

This chapter examines the effect of bank regulation and financial structure on both the likelihood and cost of banking crises in a diverse group of countries around the world. Bank regulation refers to the allowable activities and ownership arrangements of banks, while financial structure refers to the importance of securities markets relative to banks in the financial intermediation system. After controlling for other important variables previously identified in the literature, we find that financial structure does not matter with respect to either the likelihood or cost of banking crises. Preliminary evidence indicates, however, that stricter bank regulation increases both the probability and the cost of banking sector crises.

I. INTRODUCTION

More than two thirds of the member countries of the International Monetary Fund (IMF) have experienced either banking crises or significant banking

Bank Fragility and Regulation: Evidence from Different Countries, Volume 12, pages 3–23.
2000 by Elsevier Science Inc.
ISBN: 0-7623-0698-X

problems over the past twenty years.[1] Some countries, moreover, have experienced more than one disruptive episode during this relatively short time period. Furthermore, the crises have occurred in countries at all levels of economic development and in all parts of the world.

The occurrence of banking crises or significant banking problems merits special attention because they can lead to severe disruptions in both a country's payment mechanism and its credit system. Indeed, the estimated costs of such crises have been enormous in many instances, ranging as high as 41% of GDP in Chile and 55% in Argentina in the early 1980s to 60% in South Korea and 80% in Indonesia in the late 1990s.[2] The fact that banking crises can be so costly poses difficult challenges and choices not only for countries experiencing crises but for countries everywhere. Many are concerned that a banking crises in one country may spread beyond that country's own borders as the financial systems of individual countries increasingly become integrated into the global financial system.

The obvious solution to this extremely troubling situation is for countries to take appropriate action to reduce the likelihood of banking crises and to lessen the costs of banking crises when they occur. This, of course, requires an understanding of the determinants of both the likelihood of a banking crisis and the cost of a banking crisis. Recently, as relevant data have become available for a relatively large and diverse group of countries, studies have been conducted to enhance our understanding of just these issues. Of the relatively few cross-country, econometric studies, the analysis by Demirgüç-Kunt and Detragiache (1998) is particularly noteworthy for its thoroughness and comprehensiveness. Based upon a large and diverse sample of countries, they find that banking crises are more likely to occur ". . . when the macroeconomic environment is weak, particularly when growth is low and inflation high." They also find that " . . . high real interest rates are clearly associated with systemic banking sector problems . . ." and ". . . countries with an explicit deposit insurance scheme were particularly at risk" (p. 81). Furthermore, they find that ". . . the variables that are significantly correlated with the probability of a crisis are also significantly correlated with the cost of a crisis . . ." (p. 102). These findings are especially important because they indicate that banking crises are not inexplicable, random events for which no corrective, preventive action can be taken. Governments can indeed influence the macroeconomic environment in which banks operate as well as determine the structure of any deposit insurance scheme in which banks participate. Such findings should therefore help policymakers determine the most appropriate action to take to reduce the likelihood of banking crises and to lessen the costs of banking crises should they occur.

The purpose of this work is to update and to extend the existing empirical research on banking crises, with special attention given to the work of Demirgüç-Kunt and Detragiache (hereafter DD). This will be done by taking into account more recent data on banking crises and by examining the effect of two additional and important variables on both the likelihood of a banking crisis and the cost of a banking crisis. These variables are the tightness of the restrictions placed on the activities and ownership arrangements of banks as well as the degree to which the financial structure of a country is "bank-based" rather than "market-based". Both of these variables can either be controlled or influenced by governmental action. Equally important, both variables are currently receiving considerable attention by both researchers and policy-makers in countries around the world. Yet, bank regulation and financial structure have received relatively little attention in the empirical research on banking crises.[3] It therefore seems quite timely to assess whether or not these variables have any significant effect on the likelihood of a banking crisis, or the cost of a banking crisis, or both.

The remainder of the study proceeds as follows. The next section discusses the two new variables in more detail and their potential relationship to banking crises. The third section discusses the sample of countries, selection of variables and model specifications that will be used to assess the effects of the two variables on the likelihood of a banking crisis and the cost of a banking crisis. The fourth section discusses the empirical results. The fifth section discusses several issues that merit further comment. The final section provides the summary and conclusions.

II. BANK REGULATION AND FINANCIAL STRUCTURE

It seems important that a study of the likelihood and the cost of a banking crisis consider bank regulation and financial structure as potential explanatory variables. First, consider bank regulation. The United States enacted the Gramm-Leach-Bliley Act (GLBA) in late 1999 to broaden the powers of banking firms.[4] By repealing several federal laws and overriding numerous state laws, GLBA specifically permits the creation of new financial holding companies that may establish separate but affiliated subsidiaries to engage in commercial banking, investment banking and insurance activities. At the same time, however, GLBA not only retains certain restrictions on real estate activities but actually tightens the restrictions on the mixing of banking and commerce (i.e. the ability of banks to own non-financial firms and vice-versa).

Despite the enactment of GLBA, there is a lingering controversy over whether the new law expanded bank powers too much or failed to expand their powers enough. Some argue that such activities as the underwriting of securities and insurance expose banks to too much risk. Some further argue that the mixing of banking and commerce generates various conflicts of interest that also expose banks to too much risk. Based upon such reasoning one would expect tighter restrictions on banking activities and ownership arrangements to reduce the likelihood and lessen the cost of a banking crisis. Others argue, however, that broader powers provide banks with greater diversification opportunities, thereby contributing to a more stable banking environment. These competing views indicate that the effect of the restrictiveness or permissiveness of bank regulation on banking crises is ambiguous.[5]

Second, consider financial structure. Financial structure refers to the type of financial system within a country, whether it is a bank-based or market-based. Germany and Japan, for example, are widely referred to as having bank-based financial systems, whereas the United Kingdom and the United States are referred to as having market-based financial systems. The distinction being made is whether firms obtain external funds mainly from banks in the form of loans or from capital markets by issuing securities.[6] Since banks and markets channel funds from savers to borrowers, some argue that a financial system that is predominately bank-based better enables banks to extract rents from borrowers.[7] Based upon this reasoning a bank-based financial system should provide for a more profitable and thus stable banking environment. However, banks have relatively long-term illiquid assets on the one hand and short-term liquid liabilities on the other. This makes them susceptible to liquidity shocks. The occurrence of such shocks, in turn, could create a banking crisis. But markets might be able to assist banks by allowing them to hedge these and other risks that make them financially fragile. Based upon this reasoning a market-based financial system should contribute to a more stable banking environment. Given these competing views, it remains unclear as to which type of financial structure is more likely to reduce the likelihood of a banking crisis.[8]

In the event a banking crisis does occur, it seems reasonable to argue that the associated cost will be higher for a bank-based than a market-based financial system. The reason is that when banks become seriously troubled a credit crunch might occur. Indeed, in a study of 26 countries, Kaminsky and Reinhart (1999) find that ". . . at around the peak of the banking crisis . . . the lending/ deposit ratio [decreases below] its level in tranquil times, as banks become increasingly unwilling to lend" (p. 484). Substantial credit can still flow from savers to borrowers through the markets, however, so long as banks do not dominate a country's financial system. The cost of a banking crisis, in other words, is likely to be greater in a predominately bank-based system even though this type of financial structure might not increase the likelihood of a crisis.

To the extent that bank regulation and financial structure matter with respect to bank fragility, countries can take appropriate action to alter regulations and to promote the particular type of structure that enhances overall bank stability. Of course, bank regulation may affect neither the likelihood nor the cost of a banking crisis. If this is the case, some arguments for regulation might have to be reconsidered. Also, banks and markets may be complements, not substitutes, in which case neither type of structure, *per se*, should be promoted for the purpose of decreasing bank fragility. Indeed, White (2000) states that "perhaps the only thing that is clear is that financial systems having both strong markets and strong intermediaries are likely to be more stable than systems based on only one pillar" (p. 3). Recently available measures for both of these variables will enable us to address these timely and important issues, albeit in a preliminary and tentative manner.

III. SAMPLE COUNTRIES, SELECTION OF VARIABLES AND MODEL ESTIMATION

Sample Countries

DD graciously and readily provided us with the data they used in Demirgüç-Kunt and Detragiache (1998). We used this data for our empirical work on the likelihood of a banking crisis. According to DD, the largest group of countries that they used in their empirical work on the likelihood of a crisis was 65. This group included 29 countries that experienced a banking crisis over the time period of their study, which was 1980 to 1994. Various attempts were made to replicate DD's reported results. Although we were not successful in exactly duplicating their results, we did obtain signs and significance levels that were generally similar. We therefore proceeded to rely on those observations that yielded replication results closest to DD's reported results. This provided us with a group of 64 countries, including 32 countries that experienced a banking crisis during the 1980–1994 time period. The specific countries included in our sample are provided in the Appendix.

As regards our empirical work on the cost of a banking crisis, we supplemented the data provided by DD with more recent data. More specifically, in Demirgüç-Kunt and Detragiache (1998) the costs of banking crises were obtained from Caprio and Klingebiel (1996). This particular source enabled DD to obtain cost figures (as a share of GDP) for 24 of the 31 crisis episodes in their sample. We supplemented this sample with more recently available cost data from Caprio and Klingebiel (1999) and Kaufman (1999). This enabled us to enlarge the number of crisis episodes for which cost data were available to 31. The specific countries included in our sample are provided in the Appendix.

Selection of Variables

The purpose of our study is to assess the effect of two variables – bank regulation and financial structure – that are currently receiving widespread attention by researchers and policymakers on both the likelihood and the cost of a banking crisis. We now proceed to discuss the selection of the banking crisis variables, the measurement of the two new variables, and the control variables to be used in our empirical work. The crisis variables include a dummy variable indicating whether or not a crisis occurred in a country and, if so, a variable measuring the cost of the crisis. As to whether or not a crisis occurred, we relied entirely upon the data supplied to us by DD in our work on the likelihood of a crisis. They, in turn, relied upon several previous studies to identify and to date the crises. More specifically, they decided that a country experienced a banking crisis if at least one of four conditions was satisfied. The four conditions are as follows. First, the ratio of nonperforming-assets-to-total-assets in the banking system had to exceed 10%. Second, the cost of resolving the banking problems had to exceed 2% of GDP. Third, the banking sector problems had to result in a large-scale nationalization of banks. Fourth, extensive bank runs had to have taken place or emergency measures such as deposit freezes, prolonged bank holidays, or generalized deposit guarantees had to have been enacted by the government in response to the banking crisis. Based upon these criteria and our replication efforts, the 32 countries listed in Table 1 are countries that had experienced banking crises between 1980 and 1994. Of these countries, Mexico and Turkey each experienced two crisis episodes. We therefore include 34 observations designating crises in our empirical work on the likelihood of a banking crisis.

As regards the cost of a banking crisis, DD relied upon Caprio and Klingebiel (1996) for their data. In doing so, they obtained cost figures (as a share of GDP) for 24 of the 31 crisis episodes in their sample. Subsequent to the study by DD, more recent data have become available on the costs of banking crises for a larger sample of countries. By relying upon this more recent data, we are able to enlarge the number of episodes of banking crises to 31 for our work on the cost of a banking crisis.[9]

The two new variables considered here have only recently become available for empirical work. The bank regulation variable is obtained from Barth, Caprio and Levine (2000). This variable is constructed based upon the degree to which national regulatory authorities permit banks to engage in the following activities:

Table 1.   Countries Experiencing Banking Crises and Dates

Country	Date
Chile	1981–83
Columbia	1982–95
El Salvador	1989
Finland	1991–94
Guyana	1993–95
India	1991–94
Indonesia	1992–94
Israel	1983–84
Italy	1990–94
Japan	1992–94
Jordan	1989–90
Kenya	1993
Malaysia	1985–88
Mali	1987–89
Mexico	1982, 1994
Nepal	1988–94
Nigeria	1991–94
Norway	1987–93
Papua New Guinea	1989–94
Peru	1983
Philippines	1981–87
Portugal	1986–89
Senegal	1983–88
South Africa	1985
Sri Lanka	1989
Sweden	1990–93
Tanzania	1988–94
Thailand	1983
Turkey	1991, 1994
Uruguay	1981–85
USA	1981–92
Venezuela	1993–94

Securities (R1): the ability of commercial banks to engage in the business of securities underwriting, brokering, dealing, and all aspects of the mutual fund industry.

Insurance (R2) :the ability of banks to engage in insurance underwriting and selling.

Real Estate (R3): the ability of banks to engage in real estate investment, development, and management.

Each country in our sample was assessed regarding these activities and then rated with respect to the regulatory restrictiveness for each activity from 1 to 4, with larger numbers representing greater restrictiveness. The specific definitions of the 1 through 4 designations are as follows:

(1) Unrestricted. A full range of activities in the given category can be conducted directly in the commercial bank.
(2) Permitted. A full range of activities can be conducted, but all or some must be conducted in subsidiaries.
(3) Restricted. Less than a full range of activities can be conducted in the bank or subsidiaries.
(4) Prohibited. The activity cannot be conducted in either the bank or subsidiaries.

In addition, two measures of the degree of regulatory restrictiveness on the mixing of banking and commerce have been constructed. Again, the regulatory restrictiveness for each variable was rated from 1 to 4. The variable definitions and the definitions of the 1–4 designations are as follows:

Non-financial Firms Owning Banks (R4): the ability of non-financial firms to own and control banks.

(1) Unrestricted. A non-financial firm may own 100% of the equity in a bank.
(2) Permitted. Unrestricted with prior authorization or approval.
(3) Restricted. Limits are placed on ownership, such as a maximum percentage of a bank's capital or shares.
(4) Prohibited. No equity investment in a bank.

Banks Owning Non-financial Firms (R5): the ability of banks to own and control non-financial firms.

(1) Unrestricted. A bank may own 100% of the equity in any nonfinancial firm.
(2). Permitted. A bank may own 100% of the equity in a nonfinancial firm, but ownership is limited based on a bank's equity capital.
(3). Restricted – A bank can only acquire less than 100% of the equity in a nonfinancial firm.

(4). Prohibited – A bank may not acquire any equity investment in a non-financial firm.

The measure of bank regulation employed here is based upon the numerical ratings assigned to the above five variables. Specifically, RESTRICT is the average of the five ratings (R1 through R5) for restrictions placed on bank activities and ownership arrangements. The higher the value for this variable the greater the restrictiveness of bank regulation. The average value of RESTRICT for the countries in our sample is 2.2, with a low of 1.0 and a high of 3.4. The United States has a value of 3.2.

The financial structure variable is obtained from Demirgüç-Kunt and Levine (mimeo). We rely upon what they describe as a conglomerate index based on measures of size, activity, and efficiency of a country's financial system. This index enables one to rank countries along a bank-based versus market-based continuum. Briefly, it is constructed as follows. Size is measured as the domestic assets of deposit money banks relative to domestic stock market capitalization. Activity is measured as the ratio of private credit by deposit money banks relative to the total value of stock transactions on domestic exchanges. Efficiency is measured as the value of stock market transactions relative to GDP multiplied by the overhead cost of banks. After subtracting the means from each measure, they are summed and the average is taken to be the conglomerate index. This is the variable we employ for the type of financial structure in a country, or MKTvBANK. Higher values of MKTvBANK indicate a more market-based financial system relative to a bank-based financial system. The average value of MKTvBANK for the countries in our sample is 0.03, with a low of –0.87 and a high of 2.93. The United States has a value of 1.96.

In addition to these two variables, there are obviously other variables that should be included as control variables when attempting to explain both the likelihood of a banking crisis and the cost of a banking crisis. Given the nature of our study and the fact that there are relatively few cross-section, econometric studies in this area, we follow DD and include their variables in our study. These variables are therefore our control variables. They include macro-economic variables, financial variables and institutional variables, which are described in Table 2.

Model Estimation

There are two basic empirical models to be estimated, each of which has several specifications. The first model involves the estimation of the likelihood or probability of a banking crisis. As in the case of DD, we estimate a logit model. The dependent variable takes the value one if there is a banking crisis, zero otherwise. When interpreting the results for this particular model it is important to note that while the signs of the estimated coefficients indicate the direction of change, the magnitude of change depends on the values of all the explanatory variables and their estimated coefficients. The second model involves the estimation of the cost of a banking crisis. As in the case of DD again, we estimate the model using ordinary least squares (OLS).

Table 2.   Description of the Explanatory Variables and Sources

Variable	Definition	Source
GROWTH	Rate of growth of GDP	Demirgüç-Kunt and Detragiache (1998)
TOTCHANGE	Change in the terms of trade	Demirgüç-Kunt and Detragiache (1998)
DEPRECIATION	Rate of change of the exchange rate	Demirgüç-Kunt and Detragiache (1998)
RLINTEREST	Nominal interest rate minus the contemporaneous rate of inflation	Demirgüç-Kunt and Detragiache (1998)
INFLATION	Rate of change of the GDP deflator	Demirgüç-Kunt and Detragiache (1998)
SURPLUS/GDP	Ratio of Central Government budget surplus to GDP	Demirgüç-Kunt and Detragiache (1998)
M2/RESERVES	Ratio of M2 to foreign exchange reserves of the Central Bank	Demirgüç-Kunt and Detragiache (1998)
PRIVATE/GDP	Ratio of domestic credit to the private sector to GDP	Demirgüç-Kunt and Detragiache (1998)
CASH/BANK	Ratio of bank liquid reserves to bank assets	Demirgüç-Kunt and Detragiache (1998)
CREDITGRO	Rate of growth of real domestic credit	Demirgüç-Kunt and Detragiache (1998)
DEPOSITINS	Dummy variable for the presence of an explicit deposit insurance scheme	Demirgüç-Kunt and Detragiache (1998)
DURATION	Length of any previous banking crisis	Demirgüç-Kunt and Detragiache (1998)
LAW & ORDER	An index of the quality of law enforcement	Demirgüç-Kunt and Detragiache (1998)
RESTRICT	Summary index of overall bank restrictiveness	Barth, Caprio and Levine (2000)
MKTvBANK	A conglomerate index of financial structure based on size, activity and efficiency	Demirgüç-Kunt and Levine (1999)

-

IV. EMPIRICAL RESULTS

The empirical results are reported in Tables 3–6. There are two sets of tables. The first set of tables pertains to the likelihood of a banking crisis, Table 3 represents our attempt to reproduce the original DD results, while Table 4 supplements these results with our two new variables. The second set of two tables pertains to the costs of a banking crisis. Table 5 represents our attempt to reproduce the original DD results, while Table 6 supplements these results with our two new variables. Each of these tables will now be discussed in turn.

Table 3 presents our attempt to reproduce the results originally reported by DD in Demirgüç-Kunt and Detragiache (1998). Although DD supplied their data to us, differences between what they report and what we obtained did occur. Nonetheless, the overall results are close. Our empirical results, moreover, are based upon more observations than DD. Equations (1a) through (4a) are DD's original results, while equations (1b) to (4b) are our replication results. As may be seen, based upon the four specifications in Demirgüç-Kunt and Detragiache (1998), we were able to obtain results comparable to those reported by DD. In one of the specifications, moreover, we were able to obtain the same signs and significance levels for the same variables as DD. We therefore believe our results at replicating those reported by DD are reasonable enough to use their data and basic empirical models as the basis for our work.[10] In particular, their variables are used as control variables in our work to assess the effect of our two new variables on the likelihood of a banking crisis.

Table 4 presents the empirical results after re-estimating the four specifications reported in Table 3 with the inclusion of the two new variables, RESTRICT and MKTvBANK. The significance of the control variables remains broadly unaffected when these two variables are included. The coefficient on RESTRICT is positive and significant in three of the four specifications. These results provide some evidence that tighter restrictions on activities and ownership arrangements increase the likelihood of a banking crisis. On average, the marginal probability of a crisis approximately doubles when RESTRICT increases by one unit. This is equivalent to going from the bank regulatory environment in Norway, which has a value of 2, to the environment in Indonesia, which has a value of 3. At the same time, the results indicate that the type of financial system (i.e. whether bank-based or market-based) does not matter with respect to the likelihood of a banking crisis.

Turning next to the determinants of the cost of a banking crisis, Table 5 presents our results compared to those reported in Demirgüç-Kunt and

Table 3.   Determinants of Banking Crises
(Dependent Variable: Likelihood of Crisis)

Variable	(1a)	(1b)	(2a)	(2b)	(3a)	(3b)	(4a)	(4b)
GROWTH	-0.076***	-0.080***	-0.149***	-0.131***	-0.254	-0.212***	-0.226***	-0.187***
	(0.024)	(0.024)	(0.040)	(0.035)	(0.059)	(0.049)	(0.056)	(0.052)
TOTCHANGE	-0.027	-0.016	-0.025	-0.019	-0.034	-0.023	-0.035	-0.029
	(0.019)	(0.017)	(0.020)	(0.018)	(0.027)	(0.022)	(0.028)	(0.026)
DEPRECIATION	0.008	0.009*	0.006	0.007	0.006	0.007	0.001	0.001
	(0.006)	(0.005)	(0.006)	(0.005)	(0.007)	(0.006)	(0.007)	(0.007)
RLINTEREST	0.067***	0.051***	0.072***	0.051***	0.106***	0.066***	0.083***	0.073***
	(0.020)	(0.015)	(0.022)	(0.016)	(0.034)	(0.021)	(0.028)	(0.026)
INFLATION	0.023**	0.013	0.035***	0.024**	0.037**	0.017	0.043**	0.038**
	(0.012)	(0.010)	(0.013)	(0.011)	(0.018)	(0.013)	(0.020)	(0.018)
SURPLUS/GDP	-0.016	-0.000	-0.009	0.003	-0.032	0.004*	-0.008	0.004
	(0.030)	(0.002)	(0.032)	(0.002)	(0.049)	(0.003)	(0.043)	(0.003)
M2/RESERVES			0.016***	0.015***	0.016***	0.018**	0.021***	0.018**
			(0.006)	(0.005)	(0.007)	(0.008)	(0.009)	(0.009)
PRIVATE/GDP			0.013	0.004	0.024*	0.004	-0.001	-0.004
			(0.013)	(0.011)	(0.015)	(0.013)	(0.011)	(0.011)
CASH/BANK			-0.013	-0.018	-0.004	-0.010	-0.046*	-0.050*
			(0.019)	(0.016)	(0.025)	(0.018)	(0.031)	(0.029)
CREDITGRO$_{t-2}$			0.011	0.020*	0.024***	0.035***	0.007	0.013
			(0.010)	(0.012)	(0.009)	(0.013)	(0.014)	(0.020)
GDP/CAP	-0.032	-0.049	-0.089*	-0.075	-0.126*	-0.079		
	(0.033)	(0.033)	(0.056)	(0.050)	(0.071)	(0.055)		
DEPOSITINS					1.130**	0.523		
					(0.630)	(0.500)		
LAW & ORDER							-0.389*	-0.375*
							(0.218)	(0.203)
DURATION	0.157***	0.123***	0.180***	0.140***	0.119*	0.089	0.219**	0.188**
	(0.053)	(0.047)	(0.059)	(0.050)	(0.075)	(0.059)	(0.089)	(0.085)

Table 3. Continued

Variable	(1a)	(1b)	(2a)	(2b)	(3a)	(3b)	(4a)	(4b)
No. of Crises	31	34	29	34	23	28	20	22
No. of Observations	645	741	581	716	483	595	350	429
Chi-Square Statistics	42.63***	39.25***	55.54***	53.65***	64.15***	58.38***	37.86***	34.53***
AIC	224	255	201	246	149	195	141	165

Note: The dependent variable takes a value of one if there is a crisis and a value of zero otherwise. Standard errors are in parentheses. *, ** and *** indicate significance levels of 10, 5 and 1%, respectively.

Table 4. Determinants of Banking Crises
(Dependent Variable: Likelihood of Crisis)

Variable	(1)	(2)	(3)	(4)
GROWTH	−0.223***	−0.246***	−0.244***	−0.312***
	(0.053)	(0.055)	(0.055)	(0.083)
TOTCHANGE	−0.007	−0.001	−0.001	0.005
	(0.025)	(0.028)	(0.028)	(0.034)
DEPRECIATION	0.013	0.011	0.011	0.012
	(0.008)	(0.009)	(0.009)	(0.015)
RLINTEREST	0.064***	0.069***	0.068***	0.094**
	(0.023)	(0.023)	(0.023)	(0.044)
INFLATION	0.004	0.011	0.011	0.019
	(0.015)	(0.016)	(0.016)	(0.033)
SURPLUS/GDP	0.004	0.006*	0.006*	0.009**
	(0.003)	(0.003)	(0.003)	(0.004)
M2/RESERVES		0.019**	0.019**	0.024
		(0.009)	(0.009)	(0.016)
PRIVATE/GDP		0.005	0.006	0.005
		(0.014)	(0.014)	(0.014)
CASH/BANK		−0.004	−0.003	−0.043
		(0.026)	(0.027)	(0.056)
CREDITGRO$_{t-2}$		0.037***	0.036**	0.041**
		(0.014)	(0.014)	(0.020)
GDP/CAP	−0.032	−0.061	−0.059	
	(0.040)	(0.055)	(0.056)	
DEPOSITINS			−0.114	
			(0.565)	
LAW & ORDER				−0.296
				(0.284)
DURATION	0.092	0.096	0.099	0.066
	(0.063)	(0.069)	(0.070)	(0.125)
RESTRICT	1.056**	0.965*	1.006*	0.852
	(0.499)	(0.516)	(0.517)	(0.614)
MKTvBANK	0.663**	0.540	0.524	0.031
	(0.296)	(0.331)	(0.333)	(0.545)
No. of Crises	24	24	24	15
No. of Observations	505	494	479	320
Chi-Square Statistics	51.71***	62.18***	61.21***	37.40***
AIC	163	160	161	114

Note: The dependent variable takes a value of one if there is a crisis and a value of zero otherwise. Standard errors are in parentheses. *, ** and *** indicate significance levels of 10, 5 and 1%, respectively.

Detragiache (1998). We specifically focus on two of the four specifications considered by DD, given the limited number of observations and relatively large number of explanatory variables employed. Once again, equations (1a) and (2a) are DD's original results, while equations (1b) and (2b) are our results. Two of the variables, RLINTEREST and INFLATION, enter significantly as originally reported by DD. However, DEPRECIATION entered significantly negative in our case, whereas it was either insignificant or significantly positive as reported by DD. Also, CASH/BANK yielded different results in the specification in which it was included. It was not significant in our case, but significant in the case of DD.[11] The other explanatory variables are generally similar in terms of significance to those reported by DD. The difference in the number and composition of countries in our sample as compared to DD's sample undoubtedly explains the differences in empirical results. In any event, we will use the variables in the two specifications in Table 5 as our control variables when considering the effects of our two new variables on the cost of a banking crisis.

Table 5. Determinants of the Costs of Banking Crises
(Dependent Variable: Cost of Crisis)

Variable	(1a)	(1b)	(2a)	(2b)
GROWTH	0.580	0.328	0.313	0.345
	(0.407)	(0.587)	(0.279)	(0.600)
TOTCHANGE	−0.215	−0.291	−0.025	−0.301
	(0.223)	(0.248)	(0.200)	(0.256)
DEPRECIATION	0.016	−0.224**	0.083*	−0.201**
	(0.077)	(0.094)	(0.049)	(0.100)
RLINTEREST	0.466***	0.164**	0.564***	0.147**
	(0.143)	(0.068)	(0.129)	(0.073)
INFLATION	0.454***	0.217**	0.533***	0.194*
	(0.142)	(0.092)	(0.129)	(0.098)
CASH/BANK			−0.338***	−0.168
			(0.112)	(0.218)
GDP/CAP	0.531	−0.391	0.281	−0.494
	(0.311)	(0.365)	(0.337)	(0.394)
R^2	0.32	0.29	0.40	0.29
No. of Observations	24	31	24	30

Note: The dependent variable is the cost of a banking crisis as a share of GDP. Standard errors are in parentheses. *, ** and *** indicate significance levels of 10, 5 and 1%, respectively.

Table 6 contains the results when RESTRICT and MKTvBANK are added to the two empirical models reported in Table 5. The significance of the control variables remains essentially unchanged. Although the coefficient on MKTvBANK is negative, as expected, it is not significant. With respect to RESTRICT, there is limited evidence that tighter restrictions on the activities and ownership arrangements of banks increase the cost of a banking crisis. Based on the estimated coefficient of RESTRICT in the second specification, on average, the marginal cost of a banking crisis increases by 19 percentage points with a one unit increase in this variable. This means that if regulatory tightness were to increase from its mean value of 2.2 to 3.2., the marginal cost of a crisis would increase from its mean value of 14% to 33%.

There are several issues regarding these empirical results that merit further comment. These issues are considered in the next section.

Table 6.   Determinants of the Costs of Banking Crises
(Dependent Variable: Cost of Crisis)

Variable	(1)	(2)
GROWTH	0.469	0.119
	(0.773)	(0.785)
TOTCHANGE	−0.482	−0.518
	(0.366)	(0.372)
DEPRECIATION	−0.278**	−0.263**
	(0.117)	(0.113)
RLINTEREST	0.204**	0.192**
	(0.085)	(0.082)
INFLATION	0.272**	0.259**
	(0.115)	(0.111)
CASH/BANK		−0.152
		(0.298)
GDP/CAP	−0.402	−0.577
	(0.444)	(0.504)
RESTRICT	7.560	19.348*
	(7.691)	(10.000)
MKTvBANK	−3.193	−5.313
	(3.818)	(4.023)
R^2	0.44	0.53
No. of Observations	23	22

Note: The dependent variable is the cost of a banking crisis as a share of GDP. Standard errors are in parentheses. *, ** and *** indicate significance levels of 10, 5 and 1%, respectively.

V. SOME ADDITIONAL COMMENTS

A few comments should be made about the way in which our findings contribute to the existing literature. As mentioned earlier, there are three other studies that examine the effect of bank regulation on the likelihood – but not the cost – of a banking crisis. These studies, however, employ a slightly narrower measure of regulatory restrictiveness than employed here. Specifically, they take the average value of R1 through R4 as their measure, whereas we take the average value of R1 through R5. In other words, our measure encompasses completely the three activity powers and the mixing of banking and commerce. These other studies, allowing for this difference, reach the same conclusion as our study, however. In particular, Barth, Caprio and Levine (1999), based upon a cross-section, econometric study of about 50 countries, find that ". . . restricting the ability of banks to diversify their activities influences their fragility in an economically important manner." Also, Barth, Caprio and Levine (2000), based on a cross-section, econometric study of more than 60 countries, find that "regulatory restrictiveness is positively linked with financial fragility" (p. 21). Lastly, Demirgüç-Kunt and Detragiache (2000), based upon a cross-section, econometric study of 61 countries, find that restrictions "tend to increase crisis probabilities" (p. 23).

The fact that these three studies and our own study use different samples of countries, different explanatory variables, different time periods, and different estimation techniques but yet reach the same conclusion about bank regulation is reassuring. Such consistency across studies is essentially a robustness check. There may be benefits in collectively restricting the securities, insurance and real estate activities of banks as well as the mixing of banking and commerce, but one benefit does not appear to be a reduction in bank fragility.

As regards financial structure, the only study that has examined its effect on the likelihood of a banking crisis is Barth, Caprio and Levine (2000). They find that "the degree to which the financial system is primarily bank-based or market-based" . . . "did not enter the crises regressions significantly" (p. 23). In an interesting and related paper, moreover, Levine (2000), based upon a cross-section, econometric study of 48 countries for the 1980–1995 time period, finds that "Distinguishing countries by financial structure does not help in explaining cross-country differences in long-run economic performance" (p. 35). He concludes on the basis of this evidence that "policymakers should resist the desire to construct a particular financial structure" (p. 36). Our findings, together with those just discussed, suggest that this may not only be good advice with respect to economic growth but also with respect to bank fragility.

To our knowledge, this study is the only one that examines the effect of bank regulation and financial structure on the cost of a banking crisis. Indeed, there are relatively few cross-country, econometric studies of the severity of banking crises. We are aware of only three such studies, apart from our own. These are the recent studies by Demirgüç-Kunt and Detragiache (1998), Frydl (1999) and Honohan and Klingebiel (2000). This is an unfortunate situation, because in many respects understanding the determinants of the cost of a banking crisis is more important than understanding the determinants of the likelihood of a banking crisis. This is particularly the case when the determinants of the former are not the same as the determinants of the latter and it is acknowledged that banking crises will inevitably occur in the future. The fact that costs range from less than 5% to over 50% of GDP suggests there is substantial room for action to contain such costs should crises occur. A major problem in this regard, however, is the relative paucity of data. More specifically, in the four studies of costs, the number of banking crisis episodes for which cost data are available ranges from a low of 24 to a high of 41. When conducting empirical work, the number of available observations declines still further from even these already relatively low figures due to missing data for other relevant variables. Given the limited degrees of freedom that results from this situation, one must be cautious in placing too much reliance on the findings obtained from such studies. Instead, one should consider the findings as preliminary and tentative.

VI. SUMMARY AND CONCLUSIONS

Using recently available measures of bank regulation and financial structure to examine their effects on both the likelihood and the cost of a banking crisis, we found that the more restrictive is bank regulation, the greater is the likelihood of a banking crisis. In contrast, whether the type of financial structure is bank-based or market-based does not seem to matter.

There is more limited evidence that the more restrictive bank regulation the greater the cost of a banking crisis. No evidence, however, was found that the type of financial structure affects the cost of a crisis.

Much more empirical work, of course, should be done to better understand the role of bank regulation and financial structure in banking crises. This work should be broadened to encompass an examination of a wider range of legal and institutional factors than considered here.[12] It should also be broadened to encompass other aspects of bank regulation as well as bank supervision. Lastly, the timing of and reasons for changes in bank regulation and financial structure merit a thorough and separate analysis. We hope our study helps motivate others to pursue this important work.

APPENDIX

Sample Composition

The countries included in the empirical models for estimating the likelihood of a banking crisis are the following: Austria, Australia, Burundi, Belgium, Bahrain, Canada, Chile, Congo, Colombia, Cyprus, Denmark, Ecuador, Egypt, Finland, France, Germany, Greece, Guatemala, Guyana, Honduras, Indonesia, India, Ireland, Israel, Italy, Jamaica, Japan, Jordan, Kenya, Korea, Malaysia, Mali, Mexico, Netherlands, Nepal, New Zealand, Niger, Nigeria, Norway, Papua New Guinea, Paraguay, Peru, Philippines, Portugal , Senegal, Seychelles, Singapore, South Africa, Sri Lanka, Sweden, Swaziland, Switzerland, Syria, Tanzania, Thailand, Togo, Turkey, United Kingdom, United States, Uruguay, Venezuela, Zaire and Zambia.

The countries included in the empirical models for estimating the cost of the banking crisis are the following: Argentina, Benin, Bolivia, Brazil, Chile, Colombia, Côte d'Ivoire, Egypt, Finland, Indonesia, Israel, Japan, Jordan, Malaysia, Mauritania, Mexico, Norway, Paraguay, Philippines, Senegal, Sri Lanka, Sweden, Tanzania, Thailand, Turkey, United States, Uruguay, Venezuela.

NOTES

1. Lindgren, Garcia and Saal (1996) survey the experiences of 133 countries from 1980 to 1996. More recently, Caprio and Klingebiel (1999) survey 112 episodes of systemic banking crises in 93 countries and 51 borderline crises in 46 countries since the late 1970s.

2. See Caprio and Kleingebiel (1996 and 1999) and Kaufman (1999). It should also be noted that these costs do not take into account all the adverse effects on economic and social activity.

3. To our knowledge, only three other studies [Barth, Caprio and Levine (1999 and 2000) and Demirguc-Kunt and Detragiache (2000)] have examined the effect of banking regulation on the likelihood of a banking crisis. We know of no other study that has examined the effect of bank regulation on the cost of a banking crisis. As regards the effect of financial structure on the likelihood of a banking crisis, we know of only one other study [Barth, Caprio, and Levine (2000)]. We know of no study of its effect on the cost of such a crisis. These few studies will be discussed later.

4. See Barth, Brumbaugh and Wilcox (2000) for a discussion of the new law.

5. Barth, Brumbaugh and Wilcox (2000) provide a fuller discussion of these and related arguments.

6. The exact measure of bank structure employed by us in our empirical work is discussed later.

7. See Weinstein and Yafeh (1998). They find that "Underdeveloped capital markets endow financial institutions, or suppliers of capital, with monopoly power" (p. 666).

8. For a thorough theoretical analysis of the relative merits of bank-based versus market-based financial systems, see Allen and Gale (2000). Levine (2000) provides a thorough empirical examination of the effects of these two types of systems on economic growth.

9. See Caprio and Klingebiel (1996 and 1999) and Kaufmann (1999)for more information about the cost figures.

10. We found the inflation variable to be significant in only two specifications, whereas DD found this variable to be significant in all four of their specifications. This does not trouble us greatly because in a more recent and closely related paper DD do not find this particular variable to be significant in any specification. As is the case for us, moreover, the more recent paper is based upon a different number of crisis countries and crisis episodes than their earlier paper (see Demirguc-Kunt and Detragiache (2000, p.42)).

11. It is not significant, however, for two other cost specifications of DD and generally insignificant in the case of their probability specifications.

12. This should include the recent studies by Davis and Trebilcock (1999), Johnson, McMillan and Woodruff (1999), La Porta, Lopez- de- Silanes, Shleifer and Vishny (1997 and 1998), and Mehrez and Kaufmann (1999).

ACKNOWLEDGMENTS

The authors are extremely grateful for the excellent assistance provided by Cindy Lee and Sevilay Özdemir.

REFERENCES

Allen, F., & Gale, D. (2000). *Comparing Financial Systems*. Cambridge, MA: MIT Press,.

Barth, J. R., Caprio, G., & Levine, R. (1999). Financial Regulation and Performance: Cross-Country Evidence. In: L. Hernandez & K. Schmidt-Hebbel (Eds), *Banking, Financial Integration, and Macroeconomic Stability*. Central Bank of Chile (Santiago, Chile).

Barth, J. R., Caprio, G., & Levine, R. (2000). *Banking System around the Globe: Do Regulation and Ownership Affect Performance and Stability?*, in Prudential Supervision: Why Is It Important and What Are the Issues?, F. S. Mishkin (Ed.). University of Chicago Press (Forthcoming). Also issued as Milken Institute Policy Brief (Santa Monica, CA) July 24.

Caprio, G. Jr., & Klingebiel, D. (1996). *Bank Insolvencies: Cross-Country Experience*. The World Bank (Washington, D.C.).

Caprio, G. Jr., & Klingebiel, D. (1999). *Episodes of Systemic and Borderline Financial Crises*. The World Bank (Washington, D.C.) mimeo.

Davis, K., & Trebilcock, M. (1999). *What Role do Legal Institutions Play in Development?* University of Toronto Working Paper.

Demirgüç-Kunt, A., & Levine, R. (1999). *Bank-Based and Market-Based Financial Systems: Cross-Country Comparisons*. The World Bank (Washington, D.C.) mimeo.

Demirgüç-Kunt, A., & Detragiache, E. (1998). *The Determinants of Banking Crises: Evidence from Developing and Developed Countries*. IMF Staff Papers (Washington, D.C.), March, 81–109.

Demirgüç-Kunt, A., & Detragiache, E. (2000). *Does Deposit Insurance Increase Banking System Stability? An Empirical Investigation*. The World Bank Working Paper (Washington, D.C.), April.

Frydl, E. (1999). *The Length and Cost of Banking Crises, International Monetary Fund*. Monetary and Exchange Affairs Division Working Paper (Washington, D.C.), March.

Johnson, S., McMillan, J., & Woodruff, C. (1999). *Property Rights, Finance and Entrepreneurship*. MIT Sloan School of Management Working Paper (Boston, MA).

Kaminsky, G. L., & Reinhart, C. M. (1999). The Twin Crises: The Causes of Banking and Balance-of-Payments Problems. *American Economic Review* (Nashville, TN), June, 473–500.

Kaufman, G. G, (1999). *Banking and Currency Crises and Systemic Risk: A Taxonomy and Review*. Federal Reserve Bank of Chicago (Chicago, IL) Working Paper No. 12.

La Porta, R., Lopez-de-Silanes, F., Shleifer, A., & Vishny, R. W. (1997). Legal Determinants of External Finance. *Journal of Finance* (Pittsburgh, PA) July, 1131–1150.

La Porta, R., Lopez-de-Silanes, F., Shleifer, A., & Vishny, R. W. (1998). Law and Finance. *Journal of Political Economy* (Chicago, IL) December, 1113–1155.

Levine, R. (2000). *Bank-Based or Market-Based Financial Systems: Which is Better?* The World Bank (Washington, D.C.) mimeo.

Lindegren, C., Garcia, G., & Saal, M. (1996). *Bank Soundness and Macroeconomic Policy*. International Monetary Fund (Washington, D.C.).

Mehrez, G., & Kaufmann, D. (1999). *Transparency, Liberalization and Financial Crises*. Georgetown University Working Paper, August.

Weinstein, D. E., & Yafeh, Y. (1998). On the Costs of a Bank- Centered Financial System: Evidence From the Changing Main Bank Relations in Japan. *Journal of Finance* (Pittsburgh, PA), April, 635–672.

White, W. R. (2000). *What Have We Learned From Recent Financial Crises and Policy Responses?* BIS Working Papers, No. 84 (Basel, Switzerland) January.

TOWARDS A REGULATORY AGENDA FOR BANKING IN EUROPE

Harald A. Benink and Reinhard H. Schmidt

ABSTRACT

Although the world of banking and finance is becoming more integrated every day, in most aspects the world of financial regulation continues to be narrowly defined by national boundaries. The main players here are still national governments and governmental agencies. Until recently, they tended to follow a policy of shielding their activities from scrutiny by their peers and members of the academic community rather than inviting critical assessments and an exchange of ideas.

The turbulence in international financial markets in the 1980s, and its impact on U.S. banks, gave rise to the notion that academics working in the field of banking and financial regulation might be in a position to make a contribution to the improvement of regulation in the United States, and thus ultimately to the stability of the entire financial sector. This provided the impetus for the creation of the "U.S. Shadow Financial Regulatory Committee". In the meantime, similar shadow committees have been founded in Europe and Japan.

The specific problems associated with financial regulation in Europe, as well as the specific features which distinguish the European Shadow Financial Regulatory Committee from its counterparts in the U.S. and Japan, derive from the fact that while Europe has already made substantial progress towards economic and political integration, it is still primarily a collection of distinct nation-states with differing institutional

Bank Fragility and Regulation: Evidence from Different Countries, Volume 12, pages 25–51.
2000 by Elsevier Science Inc.
ISBN: 0-7623-0698-X

set-ups and political and economic traditions. Therefore, any attempt to work towards a European approach to financial regulation must include an effort to promote the development of a European culture of co-operation in this area, and this is precisely what the European Shadow Financial Regulatory Committee (ESFRC) seeks to do. In this chapter, Harald Benink, chairman of the ESFRC, and Reinhard H. Schmidt, one of the two German members, discuss the origin, the objectives and the functioning of the committee and the thrust of its recommendations.

I. INTRODUCTION AND OVERVIEW

Inspired by the example of the U.S. Shadow Financial Regulatory Committee (SFRC), the European Shadow Financial Regulatory Committee (ESFRC), as well as a similar Japanese body, were founded two years ago. All three shadow committees consist of academics and other independent experts. At their regular meetings, they develop recommendations regarding fundamental issues and approaches, as well as topics of current interest, in the fields of banking and financial market regulation and supervision. Through their work, the committees try to "shadow" the work of the relevant national or, as the case may be, supranational regulatory and supervisory authorities. That is, they observe, examine and critically assess the evolution and implementation of the strategies and policies of the regulatory and supervisory authorities.

The work of the ESFRC is based on the assumption that scrutiny and critical, but constructive comments by independent researchers working in relevant fields can make a positive contribution to the quality of the ongoing discourse in Europe regarding banking and financial regulation, to the quality of regulatory and supervisory policies and practices, and ultimately also to the stability and efficiency of national and supranational financial systems.

In this chapter, we first provide background information on the circumstances which led to the creation of the ESFRC and discuss its objectives, composition and structure, and procedures. Then, we give a brief overview of the statements which have been issued so far by the ESFRC. In presenting the structure and the work of the committee, we attempt to demonstrate the presence of an interesting parallel between the ESFRC and its field of inquiry: incentive compatibility is, in our view, every bit as crucial for the smooth functioning of the committee as it is for the effectiveness of financial regulation and supervision. The study concludes with a brief look at planned future activities of the ESFRC and some remarks on how we view the potential, and the inherent limits, of this attempt by a group of academics and other independent experts from different countries to make a meaningful contribution both to the overall culture of economic policy discourse and to the quality of European financial regulation.

II. BANKING AND FINANCIAL MARKET REGULATION IN EUROPE

Today, there is general agreement that it is necessary to regulate and supervise financial institutions – particularly banks – and financial markets. As regards the objectives of financial regulation and supervision, the common view is that they are needed to protect the financial system against systemic risks, which are encountered in a very specific, and potentially very threatening, form in the financial sector. The more integrated the European financial landscape becomes, the more important systemic aspects become, and the more important it is to view them from a regional, European perspective and to address the problem of systemic risk at a regional level. In this respect, developing a European approach to financial regulation and supervision is a complement to the equally important task of identifying and addressing potential systemic risks at a global level. A second objective of financial regulation is to protect consumers who are not sufficiently well-informed to protect themselves, and who would find it overly costly to obtain the information they would need to safeguard their own interests.[1] There is also widespread agreement as to the necessity of regulatory action in this area. Here, though, there would seem to be less of a need for transnational strategies and solutions than there is in the fields of regulatory activity that deal with systemic risk.

Traditionally, and in particular in Europe, banks and financial markets have also been regulated to promote other objectives. One goal has been to secure the access of national, state and local governments to cheap, flexible and reliable sources of funding; another has been to foster national banking and financial services industries; and regulatory instruments have also been used to shape the development of the non-financial sectors of economies by allocating or withholding credit according to political criteria. Given the nature of these objectives, it is clear why the financial sector has historically been, and in many cases still is, the most strongly regulated part of the entire economy in most countries. And, at least to a certain extent, the desire to further these goals also explains why, despite the adoption of a common currency, the creation of a single market and the trend towards European integration and globalisation, financial regulation is still seen essentially as a national undertaking in Europe.

The strong vested interest of governments in maintaining control over their own national financial sector gives rise to the concern that in the regulation and supervision of the financial sector, the transnational – or pan-European – dimensions of ensuring the safety and soundness of financial systems may not be receiving the attention they deserve. One might object to this assessment by pointing to the ongoing co-ordination and co-operation at the European level, the results of which are reflected in pertinent EU directives; the co-operation among the members of the Basel Committee of banking regulators and supervisors; and the efforts of the analogous group of capital market regulators and supervisors (IOSCO). But the existence of these supranational forums is not enough to allay doubts about whether a sufficiently pan-European approach is being taken to financial regulation and supervision. After all, these groups are composed of, and in fact also dominated by, representatives of national governments whose thinking can be assumed to reflect those governments' traditional interests.[2]

That being said, there are good reasons not to call for the creation of a new supranational agency which would be responsible for regulating and supervising the financial industry. One reason for reservations regarding the concentration of authority in such an agency is the fear that it would be plagued by the problems which are typical of big bureaucracies, e.g. that it would in many cases be too far removed from the place at which a specific problem arises to be in a position to act quickly and in an appropriate manner on the basis of reliable first-hand information. Another reason is that concentrating responsibility within a centralised regulatory agency might take too much responsibility away from the national supervisors who would still have a role to play in any centralised system, and thus undermine their commitment to the system's objectives and their willingness to rigorously enforce its standards. Furthermore, the centralisation of authority in a field in which national interests are as strong as they are in banking and finance would in all likelihood lead to politically motivated compromises embodying the proverbial "lowest common denominator" and also stifle innovation in the areas of regulation and supervision.[3] Finally, and perhaps most importantly, centralisation implies the significant problem of addressing and enforcing very different national legal systems. Given that there are sound arguments both for and against the centralisation of financial regulation at the European level, the ESFRC has not taken a stand in favour of institutional concentration or centralisation. And while the European Shadow Committee seeks to provide a central forum for the discussion and critical assessment of regulatory policies and practices, it would be wrong to assume that those who created this unique European initiative see its role as that of a lobby for the idea of *institutional* centralisation. Instead, the ESFRC takes the present decentralised institutional structure as a given and endeavours to evaluate other forms and means of European and global co-operation and co-ordination and, wherever feasible and necessary, to promote their adoption.

III. THE ORIGIN, COMPOSITION, OBJECTIVES AND PROCEDURES OF THE ESFRC

Origin and Composition

The idea to set up a European Shadow Financial Regulatory Committee was strongly promoted by George Kaufman, one of the initiators and most prominent spokesmen of the U.S. Shadow Financial Regulatory Committee, which was itself modelled on the Shadow Open Market Committee.[4] The U.S. SFRC comprises many U.S. academics who have made important contributions to the literature on financial regulation.[5] The ESFRC follows the model of the U.S. SFRC quite closely. This has proven to be a great advantage, as it has meant that the ESFRC has not had to spend much time on discussions regarding basic objectives and procedures.

The ESFRC was founded at a meeting in Brussels in March 1998. The initial members were selected on the basis of a vaguely defined, but decidedly nonpolitical criterion: a large number of European countries were targeted, and in each country one or two academics were approached who could be assumed to be experts in the field of financial regulation, and would presumably also be interested in taking part in a co-operative international effort over an extended period of time. Currently, the ESFRC has 13 active members from 11 countries.[6] The range of countries which are represented is not confined to the EU, and it is most certainly not limited to the euro zone. One member is from Switzerland, and one is an American who, however, studied in the UK and has done research there for many years.

Another factor in the selection of members, besides ensuring the representation of a sufficiently broad range of countries, was the idea that each individual member should be in a position to contribute competence in a specific field such as monetary economics, financial economics or derivatives in addition to his or her knowledge of banking regulation and supervision. One member was on the board of a major international bank before becoming a university professor. While the majority of the members are economists, some are legal scholars who specialise in banking and financial market law. Thus, in terms of both the nationalities and the areas of professional specialisation which are represented, the members of the ESFRC are a heterogeneous group. They hold positions at universities, research institutes and think tanks. If members worked in the financial sector or as members of a legislative body or as regulators or supervisors, this would be seen as compromising the independence of the ESFRC, which forms the basis of its credibility.

At least from a European perspective, it appears that the U.S. SFRC advocates a very specific point of view regarding regulatory issues. Its statements very often embody a radically "liberal" position – in the sense of the word as it is generally used outside the U.S. – which implies a deep-seated scepticism concerning government-imposed regulation, and indeed concerning government intervention in the economy in general. Given the way the European Shadow Financial Regulatory Committee came into existence, it is appropriate to ask whether it shares the orientation of its U.S. counterpart, and if it does not, whether its members have some other common "regulatory philosophy". The answer to both parts of this question is clearly "No". Even though many individual ESFRC members have studied or been a (visiting) professor in one of the Anglo-Saxon countries for an extended period of time, and have certainly also been strongly influenced by this experience, the ESFRC has not adopted the fundamental point of view of the U.S. committee. Nor can it be said, as a group, to be advocating a specific approach to regulatory matters. It would appear that the influence of European heterogeneity is stronger than the members' shared familiarity with the relevant U.S. discussions of, and positions on, regulatory and supervisory issues, and this in fact makes the meetings of the group rather interesting. The heterogeneity of the group, which is an outgrowth of its members' differing national backgrounds, has also shaped the selection of topics on which the ESFRC has so far issued statements, and its influence can even be seen in the statements themselves. Topics on which it would be plainly impossible, or perhaps just very difficult, to reach a consensus are simply not put on the agenda. As will be explained below, this cautious approach has played a constructive role in the work of the ESFRC.

Objectives

The ESFRC has defined three roles for itself: to observe, and comment critically upon, current regulatory policy and practice; to serve as a bridge between academia and "the real world"; and to provide a European forum for the discussion of regulatory and supervisory issues. The first of these three functions is the most important one. This "shadow function" does not imply an adversarial attitude, but it does oblige the ESFRC to maintain a certain distance between itself and the agencies whose activities it seeks to evaluate. However, while it is essential to maintain the critical distance required for objectivity, the committee must at the same time make a sufficient effort to appreciate the problems which must be addressed by those who make regulatory and supervisory policy, and the constraints faced by financial regulators at the level of policy implementation. Under no circumstances should the committee engage in gratuitous or glib criticism of regulators or adopt a patronising attitude towards them.

At least in comparison to the situation in the United States, the exchange of information and ideas in Europe between practitioners in the field of financial regulation and supervision and researchers in relevant fields was very limited in scope until quite recently. At the same time, the financial sector and regulatory challenges and practices have changed dramatically, as have the views of academics on regulatory and supervisory issues. The turbulence and crises that have been experienced in the financial sectors of many countries since the beginning of the 1980s[7] strongly suggest that a solid bridge should be built between theory and practice. There would seem to be sufficient ground for assuming that conventional regulatory approaches are no longer suitable for meeting the challenges posed by today's financial markets. The old capital adequacy rules of the Basel Committee, and also the new proposal for their revision, are good examples of this point.[8] An exchange of ideas between academics and practitioners can help to identify regulatory problems that call for innovative solutions and highlight effective ways of addressing them. What does this imply for the tasks which the ESFRC has set for itself?

There are, of course, many academics who prefer to remain in their ivory towers instead of making the results of recent academic research – which is often quite sophisticated in terms of the theories and methodologies it employs – accessible to politicians and practitioners. This usually involves "advertising" the importance and relevance of these results, and thus the possibility that they will be criticised as erroneous, irrelevant or impossible to apply in practice. However, the ESFRC feels that its job is to do precisely this, i.e. to attempt to derive strategies for practical action from academic theories and at the same time to test those theories with respect to their relevance and practicability.

Issuing statements aimed at politicians, policymakers and practitioners with the expectation that they will be taken seriously is indeed a way of testing the theories which underlie the statements. Although a given statement might be well founded from a purely academic point of view, its authors will be forced to conclude that it was not as sound as they thought it was if it turns out that those to whom it was primarily addressed, i.e. the relevant group of practitioners, reject it as inappropriate or useless. A consistently negative reaction to the statements of a shadow committee would not only undermine the credibility of this committee, but would also make the relevant group of policymakers generally less willing to accept advice from the academic community. The ESFRC is aware of how important it is to avoid this outcome. This it why it endeavours to take the problems faced by practitioners seriously. And if it is clear to them that the committee understands their problems and realises how difficult it is to solve these problems in the real world, then this means that the first section of the bridge between academics and practitioners has already been built. Important insights produced by advances in economic theory such as the recognition that explicit and implicit guarantees for financial institutions serve to increase risk, or the insight that adherence to the "principle" that some banks are too big to fail has adverse consequences,[9] will only be accepted – and will only begin to shape regulatory policy and practice – if a serious effort is made to show how they can be implemented in the real world.

Procedures

The ESFRC meets on three weekends per year, and its meetings are held in various cities in Europe. The immediate objective is to prepare a statement on a topic selected at an earlier meeting. Before the group convenes, one or two members will have prepared a draft statement. After a short general discussion of the subject of the planned statement, the draft is then discussed – "pulled to pieces" would be a more accurate way of putting it – for almost an entire day, and then it is usually rewritten completely. On Monday morning, the new draft is presented to the group, discussed again and put into its final form, after which it is presented at a press conference which will have been arranged well in advance.[10]

This procedure is informal, but nevertheless very strict. It entails an unusual challenge for a group of university professors, as they are not normally subject to the pressure of having to meet an absolutely firm deadline and nonetheless produce something which is good enough to present to an audience which is also thoroughly familiar with the subject matter. In working towards this goal, the opinions of a dozen strong-willed people from very different backgrounds have to be accommodated. Given the problems this invariably creates, achieving a consensus is by no means easy. Thus, we find it particularly gratifying that so far it has always been possible to arrive at a position that, while it clearly represents a compromise between the group members, is not simply the "lowest common denominator".

The next step is to disseminate the statement. The ultimate objective is to attract the attention of the European regulatory community. A crucial channel of dissemination is the financial press, represented by journalists working for leading financial newspapers.[11] Thus, it is essential to ensure that the statements are not dull, i.e. that they are not so diplomatic and well-balanced that they do not really say anything that is worth reporting. On the other hand, the statements must be more than just a collection of provocative, "flashy" pronouncements, because while the immediate goal is to attract journalists to the press conferences, the ultimate goal is of course to get the committee's message across to the members of the regulatory community. And this means that they must take that message seriously, which in turn means that the statements must be well-conceived and present a well-founded case using sound arguments. However, if the statements simply said what the regulators believed anyway, they would probably regard them as sound and well-reasoned, but not consider them very interesting.

As we have seen, the mode of dissemination is part of the incentive system that has been created for the committee, and the goal of this system is to ensure that the ESFRC issues statements which not only present sound arguments based on accurate information, but are also interesting and relevant to the practical work of regulators in the various European countries. As a result, the European Shadow Financial Regulatory Committee must seek to meet various criteria when drafting its statements, which invariably involves achieving a balance among differing objectives. The give-and-take involved in this process makes its meetings extremely stimulating, and this in turn appears to provide a strong incentive for the members to participate in the meetings.

The second channel of dissemination consists of e-mail messages by which the statements are sent directly to politicians, regulators and regulatory authorities, and to fellow academics.[12]

Needless to say, use of the procedure we have adopted for the production and dissemination of our statements cannot guarantee that the positions taken in them will be correct. However, the built-in system of incentives and checks and balances ensures that all views submitted for the group's consideration are subjected to critical scrutiny, and this in turn makes it highly improbable that an erroneous position will be adopted in an uncritical manner and promulgated "in the name of academic wisdom".

To date, one joint meeting with a subgroup of members from the U.S. and Japanese Shadow Financial Regulatory Committees has taken place. The statement which resulted from this meeting was one of the first comments on the new capital adequacy framework which the Basel Committee had issued only days before.[13]

IV. THE STATEMENTS OF THE ESFRC

Since its founding meeting in Brussels in March 1998, the ESFRC has produced, issued and disseminated eight statements. All statements are similar in terms of their length and style. They are no more than five pages long and are written in a style which avoids economic and regulatory jargon as far as possible so that they can be understood by most educated readers. In the following, the eight statements are briefly summarised and certain common themes identified.

Dealing with Problem Banks in Europe[14]

The first statement seeks to identify ways in which regulation and supervision can take preventive action to help ensure that a bank does not eventually find itself in a situation in which its entire capital is absorbed by losses and it becomes technically insolvent. As things currently stand, the relevant authorities of the country in which a problem bank is domiciled select one of the following two forms of intervention. Either the bank is saved by a capital injection, which typically comes from the ministry of finance, or from other banks which are pressured to undertake the rescue operation, or it is simply closed by the supervisory agency. Even though in almost all cases the closing of a bank does not mean that its depositors will lose their money (a considerable portion of bank deposits are now formally or informally insured in all European countries), and even though the failure of a single institution will not necessarily endanger the stability of the entire banking system, it will lead to social losses, i.e. losses which affect not only the owners of the failed bank. Interventions typically come too late, and when they are undertaken they are usually not sufficiently well-structured. Moreover, if a bank is already in serious difficulties, all of the available intervention options will necessarily be heavy-handed. This is the main reason why there are so many attempts to avoid intervention altogether – or to delay taking appropriate action. In a nutshell, the lack of a differentiated set of instruments that can be employed selectively – and in time to keep banks from becoming distressed in the first place – leads to regulatory forbearance and bail-outs.

The solution recommended by the ESFRC is an approach which it calls "structured early intervention and restructuring". It entails the definition of a series of trigger points for the capital ratio – and certain other operational indicators of an emerging problem situation at an individual bank – and of specific responses in case these trigger points are reached. If the capital ratio falls to a level defined as a trigger point, the supervisory authority has the strict, e.g. legally stipulated, obligation to take action according to the pre-specified list of measures. These measures serve to restore bank solvency. If the bank's situation continues to deteriorate in spite of the early intervention, more rigorous measures have to be taken. Ultimately, a point may be reached at which the supervisors *must* either restructure or close the bank.

Creation of a strict obligation to act – whether it be legally stipulated or based on some other form of commitment – which causes the supervisors to intervene in certain well-defined cases in specific, but differentiated ways, would have several advantages. Firstly, it would lead to certainty for all concerned regarding the timing of intervention, i.e. an early response by the supervisors would be assured. Secondly, it would reduce the opportunities, and the incentives, of the owners and managers of troubled banks to take overly risky positions in order to "gamble for resurrection" or to speculate that their banks will ultimately be bailed out. Thirdly, it would reduce the incentives for banks to take the kinds of imprudent actions that are likely to get them into trouble in the first place.

The fourth advantage is that it would make a big difference in terms of combating the practice of regulatory and supervisory forbearance, which has been frequently observed in recent years and which too often aggravates the problems. The strict obligation for the supervisors to take action would mitigate the time-inconsistency problem that plagues supervisory practice. This inconsistency is not a consequence of laxity or incompetence or of moral hazard behaviour on the part of bank supervisors. Rather, it is a "rational" consequence of the fact that, in a crisis situation, the imposition of sanctions that they have said they will implement if a crisis materialises, is simply not an attractive prospect for supervisors. Finally, if regulators and supervisors had an array of "softer" instruments in addition to the authority to close a bank which they could, and indeed were obliged to, use, it would also increase their willingness to take the appropriate form of action in a given situation.

EMU, the ECB and Financial Supervision[15]

The topic of the second statement is the institutional structure of banking supervision in Europe. The present structure is an outgrowth of the Single European Act of 1986 and the 1989 second banking co-ordination directive. This directive combines a minimum degree of harmonisation in the field of banking regulation with the principles of mutual recognition and home country control. All EU member states have in the meantime implemented the directive, with the consequence that the relevant regulation is largely similar in all member states and banking supervision can, and indeed must, be restricted to that which is exercised by the authorities of the respective home country.

The European Shadow Committee is well aware of the advantages of this approach to banking regulation and supervision. But it feels that the decentralised approach should be complemented by a certain degree of co-ordination at the European level, and that there must be an institutional basis for this co-ordination. Therefore, the ESFRC recommends the creation of a "European Observatory of Systemic Risk", which might or might not be a part of the ECB. An important function of this observatory would be to improve the flow of information which might be relevant to the task of assessing systemic risk within the emerging pan-European financial system and specifically between the various countries and their national regulatory and supervisory authorities, and, by so doing, to help the national regulators and supervisors carry out their functions more effectively.

The EU principle of home country control is based on the assumption that the various national bank regulators and supervisors have the same legal standing. This assumption of formal equality suggests that the national authorities are also equal in terms of their professional expertise and ability to perform their assigned functions and with respect to the degree of political independence which they enjoy. In fact, however, the various national agencies are probably not all equally competent, or equally independent. Evidence drawn from specific cases in various countries shows that supervisors in the EU are not all equally well prepared to take appropriate action in a national banking crisis, and that they are not all equally free from the kind of political pressure that can limit the scope for such action. The ESFRC feels that the mere existence of a European Observatory of Systemic Risk with the right to request relevant information from the national supervisory authorities would help to make the conditions under which they operate more uniform, and thereby strengthen these agencies' independence and powers and contribute to a harmonisation of the practice of banking supervision in Europe.

In this context, the ESFRC also recommends that national practices in relation to lender-of-last-resort operations should be harmonised within the euro zone and that responsibilities in this area should be clearly allocated between the ECB and the national central banks.

Towards Safer Derivatives Markets[16]

Since the beginning of the 1980s, there has been a spectacular increase in derivatives trading. The extremely rapid growth in the markets for derivatives contracts has raised concerns regarding their potential to undermine the stability of financial systems. The ESFRC's third statement addresses this issue, and deals primarily with the risk in over-the counter (OTC) markets for derivatives.

OTC derivatives are not standardised with respect to volumes, currency denominations or terms to maturity. Therefore, they are not traded on exchanges, which means that trading in these instruments is not regulated and supervised and transactions in OTC derivatives are not protected by the involvement of clearing houses, which would eliminate most of the transaction and counterparty risk. This is why the clearing and settlement of OTC transactions very often leads to problems. For instance, if a clearing house is not used, there is the danger that one bank might believe that it has hedged a risky position through a derivative contract with another bank, only to find that, due to the latter's default, the position is not hedged. If they involve large amounts, cases like this can lead to a systemic crisis.

The European Shadow Committee drafted a series of recommendations which would make the OTC derivatives market safer. One of theses recommendations concerns the capital requirements which banks have to meet with respect to derivatives. The ESFRC feels that the capital requirements for positions in OTC derivatives should be higher than for exchange-traded derivatives. This would have two advantages. One advantage lies in the fact that higher capital requirements would correctly reflect the fact that the risks involved – in particular, clearing and settlement risk – are indeed higher. The ESFRC sees a second, and possibly even greater, advantage in the fact that higher capital requirements for OTC derivatives would presumably encourage financial institutions to switch from OTC to exchange-traded derivatives wherever possible.

Improving the Basel Committee's New Capital Adequacy Framework[17]

The fourth statement issued by the ESFRC was drafted and published as a joint statement by members of the Shadow Committees of the U.S., Japan and Europe. This statement was the first formal response to the draft version of a "New Capital Adequacy Framework" which the Basel Committee on Banking Supervision had issued only a few days earlier to initiate a discussion of its position and elicit comments from members of the regulatory community, academics and other knowledgeable observers of the global banking scene.[18] The fourth statement deals with the following question: What is the best *fundamental* approach to the problem of defining capital adequacy and determining capital requirements for banks? And the fact that this issue was addressed only days after the publication of the Basel Committee's new draft framework meant that, in this case, the fulfilment of one of the tasks which the ESFRC had defined for itself – namely that of observing, and commenting critically upon, the work of international regulatory authorities – was greatly assisted.

At the heart of the new proposal put forth by the Basel Committee is a revision of the risk weights for individual asset classes that are employed in the determination of the credit-risk capital requirement for an internationally active bank.[19] The other side of the "equation", i.e. the definition of what constitutes the capital of a bank and the percentage of the risk-weighted assets which has to be available in the form of capital, is not specifically modified by the new Basel proposal, and is therefore also not discussed at great length in the statement of the Shadow Committees.

As is by now well known, the first version of the Basel Committee's New Capital Adequacy Framework outlined an innovative approach that would permit borrowers' external credit ratings, as provided by rating agencies, and the internal ratings established by "sophisticated banks" – the term used in the Basel proposal – to be employed to determine the risk weights for loans.

It appears to the Shadow Committees that, compared with the current system which is based on an arbitrary set of risk classes,[20] the approach set forth in the new proposal represents a step in the right direction. However, it fails to eliminate the central drawback of the current method of determining a bank's capital requirement, as the new proposal maintains the present system's "crude additive approach to measuring the risk of a portfolio", as it is characterised by the Basel Committee itself. This "additive approach" is extremely "crude", not only because of the concept of portfolio risk on which it is based, but also because it is an unsuitable means of achieving what capital regulation is intended to accomplish. The risk in a portfolio of any kind – including one consisting of loans – is not simply equal to the sum of the risks associated with the individual assets in the portfolio. And while a more sophisticated, differentiated approach is clearly needed, it would be highly problematic to permit each individual bank to evaluate the level of risk in its portfolio completely on its own. This might create strong incentives for the banks to misrepresent risk-related information and it would also place an excessive burden on bank supervisors, who would, in effect, be given the task of monitoring the quality of the institutions' internal risk assessment systems.

Given these problems, the statement issued by the three Shadow Committees contains an innovative – and, in our view, very useful – alternative proposal which is based to an important extent on earlier academic contributions by

Charles Calomiris, a member of the U.S. Shadow Committee. This proposal outlines an approach that enables the information which market participants have, and the financial self-interest of well-informed market participants, to be utilised for the purposes of banking regulation.

Of the various economic agents that operate in financial markets, professional investors can be assumed to have the best information. If these market participants lend money to a bank in the form of subordinanted debt which cannot be called in whenever the lender wants to get its money back, *and* must be rolled over or replaced with new lendings at short intervals, then the interest spread on the subordinated debt can be taken as an indicator of the solvency of the bank as it is assessed by the market. The spread is a risk premium and thus also an indicator of risk.

The implication of this insight for solvency regulation is straightforward. Instead of defining an upper limit for subordinated debt as a component of the so-called tier-two capital, which is what the current Basel Accord does, the capital adequacy framework should require international banks and banks domiciled in countries with an active interbank market to have a certain minimum amount of subordinated debt at all times. Imposition of such a requirement would create an efficient incentive mechanism: The providers of subordinated debt would have strong incentives to reveal their information on the borrowing bank by requiring a spread which adequately reflects the riskiness of its assets; and they would be motivated to monitor the solvency of the borrower closely so as to safeguard their funds and ensure that they would be well informed when the time came to renew the loan. The borrowers would have an equally strong incentive to minimise the spread or risk premium on the subordinated debt, which they would be required to take on. They could accomplish this by ensuring that they had a sufficient amount of equity, which is, of course, exactly what bank regulators and supervisors want them to do in any case. But this is not the only advantage of the proposed arrangement. Bank supervisors could also easily observe the spread on the subordinated debt of a given bank, which lenders would require. And they would interpret an increase in the spread or risk premium – or, in extreme cases, the observed inability of a bank to obtain subordinated loans at any price – as a signal that something had happened which deserves their attention. Alternatively, bank supervisors could define events of this type as triggers for on-site inspections or other measures from the arsenal of early and structured intervention discussed above. If supervision made use of this opportunity, its interventions could be relatively limited in scope because they would be undertaken quickly and in a timely fashion.

A New Role for Deposit Insurance in Europe[21]

The fifth statement addresses the question of whether the deposit insurance systems that are in place in Europe need to be modified to take account of the fact that the European financial system is currently undergoing a process of rapid integration. The changes in the financial system that have focused attention on this issue arise from increased competition and a wave of restructuring in national financial sectors, and they are likely to lead to a higher incidence of bank insolvencies in the coming years. As a result, the ESFRC concludes that changes to deposit insurance systems are indeed required and specifies the kinds of action that should be taken. The European Shadow Committee recommends that the EU's 1994 Deposit Guarantee Directive be clarified and modified as follows:

(1) Financial institutions should be permitted to advertise that their depositors' funds are insured under certain conditions and up to a certain, i.e. precisely defined, limit. As the insurance coverage differs between countries, the increased transparency created by this change to the regulations would seem desirable.
(2) In the case of a bank failure, the guarantee institutions should reimburse eligible depositors immediately, and not wait for three months to do so. This change would reduce the likelihood of bank runs.
(3) It should be made very clear to depositors that there is no difference between the declared scope of deposit guarantees and the effective extent of such guarantees; in other words, steps should be taken to ensure that the relevant authorities never exceed the formal guarantee limits. Unless this commitment is binding, it will be impossible for the kind of market pressure to develop which is needed to discipline banks and give them an incentive to limit their risk-taking.
(4) Risk-dependent insurance premiums should be used. These premiums should be set on the basis of observable market indicators of solvency risk such as those proposed in the fourth statement, and payments into the insurance fund should be made before and not after a case of insolvency occurs.

All of these proposals are motivated by the concern that deposit guarantee systems, which the ESFRC regards as politically and economically unavoidable, may have strong negative incentive effects, *and* by the conviction that such systems need not have such effects if they are properly designed. The above recommendations are furthermore based on the insight that in the real world the alternative to having a formal deposit guarantee system in place is not simply doing without deposit guarantees, but rather employing informal or implicit guarantees. Given this situation, the proposals of the ESFRC would serve two purposes: For one thing, they would make it both possible and desirable for national authorities to liquidate insolvent banks instead of bailing them out, which is what supervisors have often done in the past; for another, they would make it unattractive for banks to take on an excessive amount of risk.

Banking Mergers and Acquisitions in Europe[22]

The sixth statement of the ESFRC deals with mergers and acquisitions involving financial institutions from different European countries. It proceeds from the plausible assumption that in the future there will be many more cross-border M&A transactions involving European banks, and acknowledges the fact that at present national regulations and policies pose specific obstacles to cross-border mergers and acquisitions in the banking industry. Moreover, policies in this area differ between countries, and they are not sufficiently transparent. Thus, cross-border mergers and acquisitions in the banking sector are subject to a specific "political" risk, i.e. the risk that relevant national policies and attitudes will prevent these capital transactions between countries from being carried out, and thus make it impossible to realise the efficiency gains which can be produced by such transactions.

The ESFRC is of the opinion that the relevant national authorities should continue to have, and exercise, the right to express their opinion on aspects of a planned or proposed cross-border merger or acquisition which have to do with solvency and governance. However, any discretionary action which would prevent an envisaged cross-border M&A transaction from taking place should be strictly limited to cases in which there are concerns relating to anti-trust issues or fears regarding the safety and soundness of the respective financial system. This limitation of the scope for action on the part of national authorities would increase transparency and make it easier for European financial institutions to engage in long-term planning, and to conclude the agreements needed to achieve strategic goals in the European market. At the same time, the ESFRC recommends that the European Commission take steps to harmonise and liberalise the various national policies and regulations concerning cross-border mergers and acquisitions.

Internal Ratings Capital Standards and Subordinated Debt[23]

In its seventh statement, the ESFRC returns to the New Capital Adequacy Framework proposed by the Basel Committee in 1999 and to the joint statement of the three Shadow Committees discussed above, which explains how the introduction of a subordinated debt requirement could facilitate capital regulation.

One key feature of the original proposal was that it attached great importance to external ratings in the determination of risk weights. From a European perspective, this proposal must necessarily be regarded as problematic. External ratings are not widely used in Europe, and, as a result, such an approach would create an inappropriate competitive disadvantage for European banks. This criticism has in the meantime been expressed very clearly by many participants in the ongoing discussion of options for the reform of the capital adequacy framework. The Basel Committee has responded to these concerns by assigning a larger role to internal ratings. In its statement, the ESFRC welcomes this shift of emphasis because internal ratings may at least offer some scope to incorporate portfolio aspects in the measurement of banks' risk exposure, and because their use is much more compatible with the economic logic of banking than the employment of external ratings. But the ESFRC also reiterates its concern that the use of internal ratings as a basis for determining how much capital a bank must have might encourage banks to manipulate and misrepresent information, and that bank supervisors would scarcely be in a position to prevent them from doing so. These problems cannot be eliminated by simply requiring banks to subject their internal rating systems to the scrutiny of bank supervisors. What is needed instead is an incentive mechanism which would induce banks to reveal their information to the supervisors in a truthful manner.

One such mechanism is the requirement that banks have a minimum proportion of "credibly uninsured liabilities", i.e. subordinated debt, which is recommended in statement No. 4 and discussed above. The use of internal ratings in conjunction with a requirement mandating a certain level of subordinated debt is a particularly attractive option, and it is therefore strongly endorsed by the ESFRC. Despite the fact that a compulsory subordinated debt scheme would give rise to certain problems in the case of small banks, such a scheme is an essential part of any capital standard based on internal ratings. Indeed, it is a necessary element of a standard of this type, for without such a scheme a standard based on internal ratings is not likely to work, and without an internal ratings standard, capital requirements are not likely to serve their overall purpose of improving the safety and soundness of the banking system.

Towards a Single Market in European Securities Trading[24]

Over the past decade, the development of the European securities exchanges has been a remarkable success story. Owing directly to the force of cross-border competition, European exchanges have implemented major reforms in trading systems and internal governance which have significantly improved their efficiency and reduced investor trading costs. Yet the exchanges are now facing enormous pressure from the major international trading houses to cut costs much further by consolidating trading and settlement operations on far fewer platforms. This has led to a wave of dramatic merger and alliance proposals which augur a fundamental restructuring of the competitive landscape in trading operations and the re-allocation of market regulation authority across EU national securities commissions.

The European Commission is currently conducting a major review of the 1993 Investment Services Directive (ISD) as part of its "Financial Services Action Plan", with the aim of proposing wide-ranging reforms. In its most recent statement the ESFRC urges the European Commission to address a key weakness of the ISD – the so-called "regulated markets" concept – which, as things stand, may be used by national authorities as a protectionist weapon.

Article 15.4 of the ISD provides for a "single passport" for EU trading systems, allowing a system authorised by the competent authority in one national jurisdiction to provide remote services in all the others. This single passport is a manifestation of the concepts of "mutual recognition" and "home country control", utilised in a number of Single Market Programme directives to facilitate market integration without the need for prior harmonisation of laws and regulations across the Union. Home country control provides a major stimulus to market integration by negating the natural protectionist tendencies of host state authorities, which may attempt to hinder the operations of foreign competitors when they threaten the franchises of domestic incumbents.

The ISD single passport, however, only applies to so-called "regulated markets". The definition of such markets was the source of enormous controversy within the EU Council of Ministers during the original ISD negotiations, which began in 1988. If an exchange or trading system was not legally a "regulated market", then it was obliged to seek explicit authorisation to operate in each and every national jurisdiction in which it wished to provide services, even if only by remote cross-border electronic link. Local protectionism was therefore a real threat to any trading system operator which could not satisfy the "regulated market" criteria.

The ISD unnecessarily conflates the regulation of corporate disclosure with the regulation of trading systems. "Listing" of securities in conformance with basic standards is held to be a hallmark of a "regulated market", and acquisition of a single passport is therefore made contingent on it. As SEAQ International did not list the continental stocks which it traded in the late 1980s and early 1990s, a formal listing requirement was clearly a threat to its cross-border operations at the time. A North-South split emerged in the Council of Ministers during the ISD negotiations over the appropriateness of a listing requirement, leading to a compromise around a deliberately ambiguous text. Article 1.13 therefore specifies that a "regulated market" must satisfy the requirements of the Listing Particulars Directive (79/279/EEC) *where [the Directive] is applicable*. Failure to identify who ultimately determines applicability leaves considerable room for protectionism by host state authorities on behalf of their own domestic exchange operators.

The European Shadow Financial Regulatory Committee would like to see a competitive market emerge for listing services in Europe, with non-exchanges competing directly with exchanges for establishing standards appropriate to the age and size of the companies which wish to be publicly traded. Market forces can only improve on the current situation by allowing specialisation between listing service provision and trading service provision (de-linking listing and trading). To move us in this direction, the ISD should be revised to make clear: (a) that whereas "regulated markets" *may* be obliged by home state authorities to deal only in formally "listed" stocks, the actual listing function may be performed by *any* exchange or other body (such as an accounting firm, rating agency or government institution) duly authorized to provide listing services in any EU national market; and (b) that it is the home state authority which is authorised to decide whether the Listing Particulars Directive is applicable in any given case. This would ensure that a trading system operator designated as a "regulated market" in one jurisdiction is not denied single passport rights in another jurisdiction on the basis that that particular operator does not itself "list" the securities which it trades.

Another potential weakness of the ISD relates to the so-called concept of "new markets". Article 15.5 states that article 15 "shall not affect the Member States' right to authorise or prohibit the creation of new markets within their territories". This clause is clearly unnecessary if its true intent was merely to reinforce home state discretion in designating "regulated markets". But the intent was actually to furnish host states with an escape clause from the single passport provision for screen-based trading systems. By declaring a foreign trading system to be a "new market", a host state could deny it single passport rights. In order to prevent such actions, the ESFRC recommends to eliminate article 15.5.

Common Features of All Statements

So far, there has not been a clearly discernible logical sequencing of, or connection between, the various *topics* that have been selected for discussion in the statements of the European Shadow Financial Regulatory Committee. There are so many problems in the field of financial regulation which should be addressed from a European perspective that there does not seem to be much of a need for the ESFRC to choose its topics on the basis of a particular strategy. However, in terms of the fundamental *approach* they take to regulatory and supervisory issues, the various statements have a great deal in common, and this is certainly not a coincidence. In all of the statements, problems of financial regulation and supervision are viewed and discussed as incentive problems; and in each case the recommendations are intended primarily to bring a specific incentive problem more clearly into focus and to devise better, i.e. more incentive-compatible, solutions to the this problem.

There are always incentive problems at two levels: At the level of the economic units that are subject to a given regulatory standard or scheme, there will be incentives for such entities to act in ways which are contrary to the interests of the regulating and supervising agencies, or at least contrary to their declared objectives. For instance, individual banks might be inclined to issue too many loans with highly correlated risks. At the same time, there is typically also an incentive for the regulating agency, or for individual people working there, to act in ways which are contrary to its overall interests as an institution and to its declared aims in a given situation. Regulatory forbearance, the view that some banks are "too big to fail", and various types of interventions in problem banks are manifestations of this problem of misaligned incentives and time inconsistency.

The incentive problems at both levels are aggravated, or caused in the first place, by information problems. This sheds light on an additional layer of incentive problems: In many relevant contexts, the incentives to produce, reveal, collect and disseminate the required information are not structured in an optimal way. Incentive and information problems are intertwined and they tend to be mutually exacerbating. The recommendations of the ESFRC are invariably based on the premise that if regulation is to be effective, it must address the web of interdependent incentive and information problems at both levels and also mitigate those problems at both of the levels at which they are encountered.[25] The statements of the ESFRC tend to confirm that such a comprehensive approach, which is also in line with the theory of optimal financial system design, is useful and that it can be put into practice.

V. ASSESSMENT AND OUTLOOK

As we have tried to argue, the task of financial regulation is essentially one of solving incentive problems, and, more specifically, it is one of creating the right

incentives for both regulated institutions and regulators to produce, communicate and use the right kind of information in the right way. Every kind of
regulation that is undertaken at the European level has to cope with the
additional problem that the various European countries, and particularly their
financial systems, differ widely and in important respects.[26] These differences
cannot be ignored, as the European Community had correctly recognised by the
early 1980s. Therefore, producing, communicating and using the right kind of
information in the right way may mean different things in different countries,
and if financial regulation at the European level is to be both effective and
appropriate, it must be designed in such a way as to be compatible with the
legal, cultural, economic and social systems of the individual countries in
which it is to be applied. In practice, though, this means that there are indeed
issues in financial regulation for which an optimal Europe-wide policy cannot
be devised,[27] or for which a policy that might be considered optimal could not
be successfully implemented. But the fact that there will not always be a first-
best solution that can be implemented at the European level should not be used
as a pretext to stop looking for optimal regulatory strategies for Europe as a
whole. Indeed, while it is important to bear in mind the constraints faced by any
attempt to arrive at a common solution to concrete problems, it is equally
important to recognise the potential benefits of a transnational approach.
Giving due consideration to both aspects constitutes, in our view, a contribution
to the development of a specifically European "regulatory culture".

In its own work, the European Shadow Committee faces problems that are
analogous to those which it tries to address in its statements. Indeed, in the
activities of the ESFRC incentive and information problems and issues of
heterogeneity are intertwined in a complex way, and they make certain things
difficult and others quite simply impossible. Nevertheless, the attempt to
overcome these problems seems well worth the effort it entails. Almost by
necessity, the European Shadow Committee is a bold, perhaps even audacious,
undertaking. After all, it involves the operation of a group which has no formal
mandate from any body or institution, whose members cannot be obliged to
attend its meetings regularly, and whose meetings are in any case relatively
brief and infrequent, but whose purpose is to produce meaningful statements
and issue recommendations on important and difficult problems. Only time will
tell, and others will have to judge, whether this kind of undertaking is in fact
feasible and useful and whether the ESFRC can achieve the goals it has set for
itself.

The incentive and information problems which the ESFRC faces in its work
are probably the most serious potential obstacles to the success of its activities.
There are two main issues here: First, there is the question of whether it is

feasible to mobilise the information which the committee members are assumed to have and to communicate, process and transform it within the group and disseminate the outcome, and the related question of where the incentives to reveal information come from. Second, there is the simple fact that the statements of the ESFRC can only reach the regulatory community if the information which they contain is sufficiently interesting to motivate journalists, who are needed as intermediaries and "multipliers" in the dissemination process, to come to the press conferences, listen to what is said at these presentations, read the statements on their own, and then write about them. But they obviously cannot be forced to play this role. Finally, the statements must be sufficiently useful to regulators to make them want to read what the ESFRC has to say and to consider its recommendations. And this means that they also need information and incentives, which must be provided by the statements.

Thus, information and incentive problems are relevant on various levels. Like financial regulation, the "ESFRC project" itself can usefully be regarded as a problem of mechanism design. Obviously, the production of uninteresting, irrelevant or simply erroneous statements would be a reason for the various parties whose co-operation is required to achieve the committee's objective – the members, the "multipliers" and the regulators – to stop playing their respective roles. Only time will tell whether they will continue to co-operate in this undertaking over the long term, but based on the experience of the ESFRC so far, we are fairly optimistic that this will be the case.

Heterogeneity is also an important potential constraint for the ESFRC, given the diversity of its members' specific areas of interest and academic backgrounds and the broad range of countries from which they come. To a certain extent, however, this heterogeneity is clearly a positive feature: a – fictitious – member from Norway would be able to draw upon different kinds of experience, and would give priority to different issues, than one from Portugal. This ensures that a great deal of information is presented for consideration at the committee meetings. Also, the fact that, at least to a certain extent, each member must expect to be held accountable for the statements of the ESFRC is clearly positive. It strengthens the members' incentive to reveal information and to become actively involved in candid, and sometimes rather heated, discussions of controversial issues, and it ensures that the group does not issue statements precipitously or adopt unsound positions.

The next joint meeting of the three Shadow Committees will be held in Tokyo in the autumn of 2000. Given the proposed topic – "Market Discipline in Different Parts of the World" – the meeting can be expected to produce highly interesting discussions, results and insights, not least because it will show whether the important differences in attitudes and approaches that undeniably exist between the U. S., Europe and Japan are so profound that they make it impossible for the participants to draft a meaningful joint statement and joint recommendations.

NOTES

1. For discussions of the rationale for banking regulation, see Bhattacharya et al. (1998), Burghof and Rudolph (1996), and Dewatripont and Tirole (1994), and for a presentation of the rationale for the regulation of capital markets, see Pagano and Röell (1992).

2. On this point, see the instructive discussions presented in Herring and Litan (1995) and in Burghof and Rudolph (1996).

3. With respect to the Basel Committee, this negative aspect of international co-operation between regulatory and supervisory agencies is discussed in detail by Herring and Litan (1995, pp.132 ff).

4. Since 1973, this group has regularly issued assessments of U.S. monetary policy, and its statements have invariably attracted a great deal of attention in the press and in other media.

5. The U.S. SFRC is currently co-chaired by George Kaufman, Loyola University, Chicago, and Robert Litan, the director of research at the Brookings Institution in Washington. Litan has produced a sizeable body of work on regulatory and supervisory issues; of greatest interest in the present context is the monograph on the international co-ordination of financial regulation which he co-authored with Richard Herring, who is also a member of the SFRC; cf. Herring and Litan (1995).

6. The members are: Harald Benink, Erasmus University, Rotterdam; Christian de Boissieu, University of Paris I (Sorbonne); Franco Bruni, Bocconi University, Milan; Jordi Canals, IESE, Barcelona; Richard Dale, University of Southampton; Hans Geiger, University of Zurich; Friedrich Kübler, Johann Wolfgang Goethe University, Frankfurt/ Main, and Clifford Chance; Karel Lannoo, Centre for European Policy Studies, Brussels; Rosa Lastra, University of London; Reinhard H. Schmidt, Johann Wolfgang Goethe University, Frankfurt/Main; Benn Steil, Council on Foreign Relations, New York; Niels Thygesen, University of Copenhagen; and Clas Wihlborg, University of Gothenburg.

7. See, for example, Demirgüc-Kunt and Detragiache (1997) and Caprio (1997).

8. Cf. Basel Committee on Banking Supervision (1988, 1996, 1999a) and Deutsche Bundesbank (1998).

9. For a discussion of these effects, see Bhattacharya et al. (1998), Burghof and Rudolph (1996, pp. 46 ff), Demirgüc-Kunt and Huizinga (1999), and Freixas and Rochet (1997, chap. 9).

10. So far, there have been several cases in which draft statements on two different topics were prepared for a meeting of the ESFRC, but there has been only one case in which two statements were actually issued. Whenever draft statements have been prepared on more than one subject, the decision as to which topic, or topics, should be addressed at the press conference is always one of the first items on the agenda of the meeting.

11. So far, interest on the part of the relevant newspapers and periodicals has been strong: among other publications, the *Financial Times, The Banker*, the *Frankfurter Allgemeine Zeitung* and the *Handelsblatt* have reported on the statements in detail.

12. The statements are also published on the web site of the Brussels-based Centre for European Policy Studies: www.ceps.be, click "research programmes", and on the web site of the American Enterprise Institute: www.aei.org.

13. This meeting was very important and productive in terms of its output. However, it was also important because it highlighted certain constraints faced by groups such as the ESFRC which are an outgrowth of their organisational structure and procedures: the group that met in New York – which consisted of the U.S. SFRC, the ESFRC and members of the Japanese Shadow Committee – was too large to permit the kind of intensive deliberation needed to produce a joint statement more or less "from scratch". The process of establishing a consensus was greatly facilitated by a draft paper prepared by the U.S. Shadow Committee, which provided a starting point for the group's discussions.

14. This is the title of the first statement issued at a meeting in London, June 1998.

15. This is the title of the second statement issued at a meeting in Frankfurt, October 1998. For further reading see the conference book "Which Lender of Last Resort for Europe?", Edited by Charles Goodhart (2000), in particular the chapters by Bruni and De Boissieu (2000) and Lasgra (2000).

16. This is the title of the third statement issued at a meeting in Paris, March 1999.

17. This is the title of the fourth statement of the ESFRC, which was prepared at a joint meeting of members of the U.S., Japanese, and European Shadow Committees (New York, June 1999).

18. Cf. Basel Committee on Banking Supervision (1999b). This preliminary draft version of a new capital adequacy framework was published on 3 June 1999, and the Basle Committee indicated that it would produce a revised version in approximately one year's time. Persons and institutions wishing to make their views on the preliminary draft known to the Committee were invited to submit their comments during this period.

19. The procedure for calculating the minimum capital level which was established in the 1988 Basel Accord defined the minimum capital requirement as a function of the amount of banks' risk-weighted assets. Originally, this procedure was intended to be employed only in the case of internationally active banks. In the meantime, though, it has been adopted in almost all countries, and the national regulatory agencies that employ this procedure require it to be used for all banks. A number of authors have pointed out that this "one-size-fits-all" approach does not always make sense, and that it can have particularly unfavourable consequences in developing countries; on this point, see in particular Dziobek et al. (1995), who provide a broad overview of the relevant issues, and Schmidt (2000), who addresses certain key topics in greater detail. It can be expected that, like the existing "Basel standard", the revised version of the capital adequacy framework will be almost universally adopted and applied by national regulatory agencies, and this is why the preliminary draft prepared by the Basel Committee last year has attracted so much attention and has been subjected to such intense scrutiny.

20. The current risk weighting system is biased in favour of loans to OECD countries and loans to certain financial institutions. Moreover, all loans to the private sector are put in the same risk category.

21. This is the title of the fifth statement issued at a meeting in Milan, October 1999.

22. This is the title of the sixth statement issued at a meeting in Brussels, February 2000.

23. This is the title of the seventh statement, which was also issued at the Brussels meeting in February 2000.

24. This is the title of the eighth statement issued at a meeting in London, June 2000.

25. This is also the position taken by Bhattacharya et al. (1998) and Boot and Thakor (1993).

26. For an analysis of key structural differences between the financial systems of various countries, see Hackethal and Schmidt (2000).

27. In Hellmann et al. (2000), convincing arguments are advanced to show that a uniform system of regulation can prove to be problematic at a fundamental level if there are significant differences in the operating environments of the banks it covers.

ACKNOWLEDGMENT

The views expressed in this chapter are the authors' personal opinions and do not necessarily represent the views of the European Shadow Financial Regulatory Committee. Richard Dale provided helpful comments. An earlier version was published in German in Vol. 1, No. 3 of *Perspektiven der Wirtschaftspolitik* (copyright by Verein fuer Sozialpolitik and Blackwell Publishers).

REFERENCES

Basel Committee on Banking Supervision (1988). *International Convergence of Capital Measurement and Capital Standards*. Basel.

Basel Committee on Banking Supervision (1996). *Amendment to the Capital Accord to Incorporate Market Risks*. Basel.

Basel Committee on Banking Supervision (1999a). *Capital Requirements and Bank Behaviour: The Impact of the Basel Accord*. Basel.

Basel Committee on Banking Supervision (1999b). *A New Capital Adequacy Framework*. Basel.

Bhattacharya, S., Boot, A., & Thakor, A. (1998). The Economics of Bank Regulation. *Journal of Money, Credit and Banking, 30*, 744–770.

Boot, A., & Thakor, A. (1993). Self-Interested Bank Regulation. *American Economic Review, 83*, 206–212.

Bruni, R., & De Boissieu, C. (2000). Lenging of Last Resort and Systematic Stability in the Eurozone. In: C. Goodhart (Ed.), *Which Lender of Last Resort in Europe?* (pp. 175–196). London: Central Bank Publications.

Burghof, H.-P., & Rudolph, B. (1996). *Bankenaufsicht: Theorie und Praxis der Regulierung*. Gabler Verlag, Wiesbaden.

Caprio, G. (1997). Safe and Sound Banking in Developing Countries: We're Not in Kansas Anymore. *The World Bank Working Paper*. Washington, D.C.

Demirgüc-Kunt, A., & Detragiache, E. (1997). Banking Crises Around the World: Are There Any Common Threads?. *IMF Working Paper.* Washington, D.C.

Demirgüc-Kunt, A., & Huizinga, H. (1999). Market Discipline and Financial Safety Net Design. *The World Bank Working Paper.* Washington, D.C.

Deutsche Bundesbank (1998). Bankaufsichtrechtliche Risikosteuerungsmodelle und deren bankaufsichtliche Eignung. *Monatsbericht*, October 1998, pp. 69–84.

Dewatripont, M., & Tirole, J. (1994). *The Prudential Regulation of Banks.* Cambridge, Massachusetts: MIT Press.

Dziobek, C., Frecuat, O., & Nieto, M. (1995). Non-G–10 Countries and the Basle Capital Rules: How Tough a Challenge Is It to Join the Basel Club? *IMF Paper on Policy Analysis and Assessment*, 95(5). Washington, D.C.

Freixas, X., & Rochet, J.-C. (1997). *Microeconomics of Banking.* Cambridge Massachusetts: MIT Press.

Goodhart, C. (Ed.) (2000). *Which Lender of Last Resort for Europe?* London: Central Bank Publications.

Hackethal, A., & Schmidt, R. H. (2000). Finanzsysteme und Komplementarität. *Kredit und Kapital*, Beiheft Nr. 15: Neue finanzielle Arrangements: Märkte im Umbruch, forthcoming.

Hellmann, Th., Murdock, K., & Stiglitz, J. (2000). Liberalization, Moral Hazard in Banking and Prudential Regulation: Are Capital Requirements Enough? *American Economic Review*, 90, forthcoming.

Herring, R., & Litan, R. (1995). *Financial Regulation in the Global Economy.* Washington, D.C.: Brookings Institution.

Lasgra, R. (2000). The Role of the European Central Bank with regard to Financial Stability and Lender of Last Resort Operations. In: C. Goodhart (Ed.), *Which Lender of Last Resort in Europe?* (pp. 197–212). London: Central Bank Publications.

Pagano, M., & Röell, A. (1992). Self-Regulation of Financial Markets. In: P. Newman, M. Milgate & J. Eatwell (Eds), *The New Palgrave Dictionary of Money and Finance* (Vol. 3). London: Macmillan Press.

Schmidt, R. H. (2000), Banking Regulation *contra* Microfinance. *Savings and Development*, 24, 111–121.

U.S. Shadow Financial Regulatory Committee (2000). *Reforming Bank Capital Regulation: A Proposal by the U.S. Shadow Financial Regulatory Committee*, Statement No. 160, March 2.

SUBORDINATED DEBT AND BANK CAPITAL REFORM

Douglas D. Evanoff and Larry D. Wall

ABSTRACT

In recent years there has been a growing realization that there are significant problems with the current bank risk-based capital guidelines. As financial firms have become more sophisticated and complex they have effectively arbitraged the existing capital requirements. They have become so good at avoiding the intent of capital regulation that the regulations have essentially ceased being a safety and soundness issue for supervisors and have become more a compliance issue. There is also a growing realization that bank regulation must more effectively incorporate market discipline to encourage prudent risk management. One means recommended to accomplish this is to increase the role of subordinated debt in the bank capital requirement. Arguments have been made that this could lead to improvements in both market and supervisory discipline. Although a number of such proposals have been made, there appears to be significant misunderstanding of how bank capital requirements would be modified and what might be accomplished by the modification. The goal of this article is to provide a comprehensive review and evaluation of subordinated debt proposals, and to present a regulatory reform proposal that incorporates the most desirable characteristics of subordinated debt.

Bank Fragility and Regulation: Evidence from Different Countries, Volume 12, pages 53–119.
Copyright © 2000 by Elsevier Science Inc.
All rights of reproduction in any form reserved.
ISBN: 0-7623-0698-X

I. INTRODUCTION AND OVERVIEW

In the early 1980s Paul Horvitz recommended that mandatory bank capital requirements, which had been introduced in the U.S. only a few years previously, be modified to increase the amount held in the form of debt. Since then several proposals have recommended that banks increase reliance on subordinated debt (sub-debt) to serve the role of bank capital. Recent responses to those recommendations include the expressed interest by financial regulatory authorities in the U.S. [see Ferguson (1999) and Meyer (1999)], recommendations by academics and regulatory scholars [see U.S. Shadow Regulatory Committee (2000) and Benink and Schmidt (2000)], and the introduction of a bank regulatory framework in Argentina which has characteristics similar to those suggested in recent sub-debt proposals [see Calomiris and Powell (2000)]. More importantly, in the U.S. the 1999 U.S. Financial Services Modernization Act (Gramm-Leach-Bliley Act) requires large U.S. national banks to have outstanding debt that is highly rated by independent agencies to fund expansion of financial activities into areas not previously allowed. The Act also instructs the Board of Governors of the Federal Reserve System and the Secretary of the Treasury to conduct a joint study of the potential use of sub-debt to protect the financial system and deposit insurance funds from "too big to fail" institutions.[1]

The argument behind proposals to increase the role of sub-debt in the bank capital structure is the potential improvement in market and supervisory discipline over bank risk-taking activities. Although a number of such proposals have been made, there appears to be significant misunderstanding of how bank capital requirements would be modified and what might be accomplished by the modification. On the one extreme, some discussions of sub-debt seem to imply that merely requiring banks to issue some debt would solve all safety and soundness related concerns. At the other extreme, are a series of questions that raise doubts as to whether any change in the role of sub-debt could contribute toward safety and soundness goals.

The goal of this article is to provide a comprehensive review and evaluation of bank capital reform proposals that incorporate a mandatory sub-debt component, and to present a new proposal that we believe incorporates the most desirable characteristics of sub-debt.

As general background, in the basic model of financial intermediation, bankers purchase short-term funds in the marketplace and transform them into risky earning assets. The risk of these assets derives both from their maturities and from default prospects. Absent the safety net (particularly deposit insurance) the providers of this funding are at risk. Uninsured depositors as providers of these funds can reduce their risk by evaluating the banks' activities to insure that the portfolio generated is of acceptable risk. If the quality of the portfolio declines, or the capital, which serves to absorb variations in income, decreases, the depositors will demand a higher return on their investment commensurate with the increased risk; or will simply withdraw their funds. Banks, needing a steady flow of reasonably priced funds, have an incentive to maintain high quality portfolios.

For numerous reasons, policymakers moved away from this market-driven environment and introduced a bank safety net. However, the presence of this safety net can sever the investor relationship between the depositor and the bank, weakening market discipline. Without this discipline, the risk-taking incentives of bank management and investors are distorted and increased risk is likely to be incurred.

For years, industry scholars argued that industry risk-taking was too far removed from this market-driven model. The resulting distortions were labeled moral hazard problems.[2] The arguments intensified during the 1980s as substantial public funds were used to recapitalize the S&L sector following depletion of its deposit insurance fund. Indeed, during this period numerous alternative means to increase reliance on market forces and market discipline were proposed.[3]

To maintain social welfare, discipline not provided by the marketplace must be supplemented or replaced via the supervisory process. During the 1990s, discipline was imposed primarily through supervisory oversight and through risk-based capital requirements. In many cases, however, depository institutions have employed methods that weaken the relationship between capital levels and risk.[4] Indeed, in today's markets there is little doubt that, particularly at larger institutions, there has been a significant deterioration in this relationship. As the bank's ability to measure and manage their risk exposures improved, their ability to avoid binding capital requirements also improved. At the same time, as banks became more complex, supervising and regulating banking organizations became more difficult.[5] Thus, once again there has been a call for increased reliance on market discipline to augment supervisory discipline, particularly in overseeing the activities of large financial conglomerates.

With the growing interest in increasing market discipline, there have been a number of proposals to increase the role of sub-debt in the bank capital structure. Although the specifics of these proposals differ, all rely on one or both of two arguments that sub-debt has desirable properties for regulatory purposes. One argument is that expanded use of sub-debt allows regulators to require banks to have more private funds at risk without mandating that they adopt ratios of debt-to-equity that place them at a competitive disadvantage. Bankers have long complained that regulatory equity capital requirements placed them at a competitive disadvantage because, for example, the interest on debt is deductible but dividends to equity-holders are not. Expanded use of sub-debt may allow banks to choose their debt-to-equity ratios while assuring regulators that at least a minimal amount of private funds are outside the safety net and are at risk. The other argument for sub-debt is that the risk signals from this debt more closely follow the needs of the regulators. That is, both are concerned more with guarding against the potential for bank failure than they are with the potential for higher profits from taking on additional risk. In contrast, equity-holders may gain from increased risk taking since they reap all of the profits and do not bear all of the costs because the current pricing of the safety net is insufficiently sensitive to changes in risk exposure. Thus, sub-debt yields are likely to be more informative about a bank's risk exposure.

Authors of reform proposals generally agree that increasing the role of sub-debt in the bank capital structure should result in greater discipline over the risk-taking activities of banks, decrease potential losses to the deposit insurance funds, and, by having the debt-holders gradually apply increasing pressure to the bank as its condition deteriorates, help manage the failure resolution process when larger banks encounter difficulties. However, there are differences in the proposals based on the specific goals and objectives of the author. Some attempt to supplant supervisory oversight while others strive to provide supervisors with an additional tool to enable them to better supervise banks. Some rely on pressure being exerted on the bank by increasing its cost of funding while others rely more on the signal sent by changing debt prices in the secondary market.

A requirement for these proposals to be effective as a regulatory tool is that the debt-holders be capable of distinguishing between banks with different risk profiles. Studies dating back to the 1970s have evaluated whether various holders of bank liabilities price differences in banks' risk. The majority of this literature suggests that liability holders do effectively price such risk in the expected manner. The exception to this finding concerns debt-holders at large U.S. banks during the 1980s. This too, it is argued, can be explained by rational, informed behavior. During this period it was commonly believed that these investors fell under an implicit too-big-to-fail guarantee.[6] Investors rationally expected to be protected from bank problems. Thus, the literature suggests that investors behave rationally and demand higher compensation from banks when they are at risk of loss.

After a discussion of the relevant issues, we present a new sub-debt proposal that incorporates many of the characteristics, and resulting advantages, of earlier proposals, but offers some new characteristics that address specific regulatory concerns. The timing seems particularly good for consideration of such a plan as the U.S. Congress has expressed interest in the potential merits of sub-debt as a regulatory tool. Additionally, recognizing problems with the current Basel Capital Accord, the Basel Committee on Banking Supervision is currently evaluating alternative means to improve capital regulation to make capital more reflective of banks' actual risk levels. In the U.S., banks as a group are relatively healthy which allows time for a carefully thought out plan instead of quickly imposing a plan in response to a financial crisis. Worldwide, there seems to be the realization that regulators need to find means to avoid the financial crises seen in recent years, and increased reliance on market discipline is gaining acceptance as a means to regulate banks.[7] Sub-debt proposals seem to be gaining support as a preferred means to impose this discipline.

In the remaining pages we provide a comprehensive review of issues associated with sub-debt proposals. The article is intended as a reference piece from which readers new to the topic may find a thorough review of the issues, and others can draw on specific aspects of the debate. Readers most familiar with the topic may want to go directly to the new regulatory reform proposal. The chapter is organized as follows: in the next section we discuss the characteristics of sub-debt that make it attractive for imposing market and supervisory discipline on banks and explain how current regulatory arrangements do not allow these features to be fully utilized. We emphasize the role of debt markets, equity markets and supervision in disciplining firm behavior, and show how the use of sub-debt avoids many of the problems associated with alternative regulatory proposals (such as elimination or significant reductions in deposit insurance). Since the effectiveness of sub-debt proposals rely on the market's effectiveness in influencing firm behavior, in Section III we review the evidence on the extent of market pricing and disciplining of risk imposed by holders of bank liabilities. Section IV summarizes some of the existing sub-debt proposals emphasizing their differences and the reasoning for those differences. Our regulatory reform proposal which increases the role of sub-debt is presented in Section V. Finally, for completeness, in Section VI we address some of the standard questions raised about the sub-debt proposals and, when appropriate, explain how our proposal addresses these concerns. The last section summarizes.

II. SUBORDINATED DEBT AS THE PREFERRED MECHANISM FOR RE-IMPOSING MARKET DISCIPLINE

The problem of disciplining firm risk taking is not unique to banks. Ordinarily the focus in evaluating risk taking is on the equity-holders' incentives. Limited liability, however, may provide equity-holders with an incentive to have the firm take excessive risk, particularly when equity is low. This occurs because limited liability gives equity-holders almost all of the gains if the risky investment pays off, whereas their losses are limited to the extent of their investment. Losses in excess of their investment are borne by the firm's creditors. This asymmetry in the sharing of risks leads equity-holders to demand excessive risk.[8] Similarly, it leads debt-holders to be more risk adverse.

If the desire is to rely on equity holders to impose discipline, the most straightforward means to insure they do not have an incentive to take excessive risk is to require that the firm have sufficient equity to absorb *any* potential losses. In this case, the equity-holders would obtain all of the benefits and, similarly, bear all of the costs of risks undertaken by the firm. The costs of all-equity financing, however, are typically too high, and a firm will choose to issue debt to help finance activities. The U.S. tax code heightens the advantages of debt financing by allowing the interest expenses to be deducted as a business expense.[9] An important characteristic of debt in determining the degree of discipline that debt-holders can exert on the issuing firm is its maturity structure. The shorter the maturity, the more discipline that can be imposed by either requiring higher yields to rollover the debt or simply by refusing to roll it over.[10] Flannery (1994) and Calomiris and Kahn (1991) argue that portfolio composition, particularly, the opaqueness and information intensiveness of the assets (particularly loans), leads banks to rely on lower capital ratios and more short-term debt. This results from the dynamic characteristic of bank portfolios; that is managers have the ability to quickly change risk profiles by altering asset composition. Flannery emphasizes that high debt levels constrain managerial discretion in making investment decisions. However, the high debt levels also afford managers a chance to own a larger fraction of the equity, which increases their incentive to maximize shareholder wealth by increasing risk. The combination of high debt levels with long-term debt would induce a strong preference for risky projects on the part of management. Shortening the maturity of the debt can reduce this incentive. Thus, banks typically issue the shortest-term debt possible, debt that must be repaid upon demand.

The extensive use of short-term debt raises concerns about the stability of the financial system.[11] Depositors, lacking full information about the quality of a bank's assets may demand repayment and make a bank illiquid even though it remains solvent. Policy makers responded to this concern and introduced a safety net in the form of deposit insurance, the discount window, and payments system guarantees. While the bank safety net addresses liquidity concerns, it also distorts behavior and alters the effectiveness of market discipline as it reduces incentives for depositors to discipline banks through higher interest rates. In the absence of closure by the regulatory agencies, depositories could, as some did in the 1980s, continue to operate and be primarily funded by deposits even though they were insolvent; e.g. see Kane (1989). Thus, instead of depositors discouraging excessive risk-taking, they were essentially indifferent to it. Equity-holders at poorly capitalized banks were put in a position that can be summarily described as "heads, I win; tails the deposit insurer covers most of the losses".[12]

Losses can continue to accumulate in this environment as long as the bank is allowed to operate once it becomes insolvent. This was a somewhat common occurrence in the U.S. in the 1980s, particularly in the Savings and Loan industry, as regulatory forbearance allowed losses to grow and be passed on to the deposit insurance funds. In response, in 1991 Congress adopted prompt corrective action as part of the Federal Deposit Insurance Corporation Improvement Act (FDICIA). The goal is to require banks to adhere to capital requirements by having progressively stricter supervisory action as the ratio of capital to portfolio risk declines. This action is triggered in a stepwise fashion by declining bank capital-to-risk-weighted-asset ratios.[13] However, weaknesses in both the numerator and denominator of this ratio raise concerns that, as currently structured, prompt corrective action may be inadequate.

One major problem with the current procedures, but one that can be relatively easily fixed, is that the "triggers" are based on capital valued at book rather than at market-value. A more fundamental problem exists however in accurately measuring the riskiness of the bank and having meaningful triggers to initiate the restrictions. Although portfolio risk measurement, especially estimating the probability of large losses, is difficult, banks are almost always in a better position, *vis à vis* supervisors, to estimate that risk. As a result, they

are positioned to exploit any inaccuracies in the regulatory capital requirements. Moreover, with the development of improved risk management tools
and more accurate internal models, banks are in a better position to decrease
over-weighted, and increase under-weighted risks; that is, to arbitrage or
"game" the capital requirements.[14]

If under current regulatory procedures the safety net is creating moral
hazard, and the relationship between bank risk and the triggers used to initiate
supervisory action is making the prompt corrective action procedures less
effective at resolving troubled institutions, then alternative means to reduce
these problems should be pursued. One potential method frequently recommended is to reduce the safety net by severely limiting deposit insurance
coverage.[15] The U.S. has attempted to move in this direction with passage of
prompt corrective action and the least-cost resolution provisions of FDICIA,
and the depositor preference provision as part of the Omnibus Budget
Reconciliation Act of 1993. In theory these provisions make all other liability
holders junior to domestic deposits and limit deposit insurance coverage to the
de jure coverage limit of $100,000. These provisions should provide uninsured
liability holders an incentive to discipline troubled banks and force the closure
of insolvent ones before they can generate large losses. As a result, this should
further reduce the insurance fund's expected losses. Additionally, the net effect
of substantially reducing the safety net should be to decrease banks' *ex ante*
risk exposure, and, hence, reduce their probability of failure.

Although curtailing deposit insurance may have substantial merits, it also
has some potentially significant drawbacks. Banks, especially banks that obtain
a large fraction of their funding from retail customers, may reduce the
effectiveness of ex ante discipline by reducing their reliance on uninsured funds
relative to insured funds, and by providing collateral to uninsured non-
depositor creditors. Moreover, while explicit insurance coverage may be
reduced, there are a number of reasons to expect that total coverage may remain
relatively high. The experience around the world in recent decades has been
that de facto deposit insurance exists regardless of the extent of *de jure*
coverage. For example, in the U.S. the least cost resolution provisions of
FDICIA provide for what is commonly called the systemic risk exception. The
FDIC may nevertheless cover losses to liability holders that are not covered by
de jure insurance in an attempt to preclude systemic problems. Such coverage
is possible if the Secretary of the Treasury, the FDIC Board and the Federal
Reserve Board concur that least cost resolution would "have serious adverse
effects on economic conditions or financial stability". Implicit coverage may
also be provided by Federal Reserve discount window loans that provide banks
with the funds needed to redeem uninsured liabilities prior to closure.[16]

Not only might implicit deposit insurance lead to more severe moral hazard problems, but it may also induce government actions that could further decrease market discipline beyond what an explicit deposit insurance system would. Milhaupt (1999) reviewed the experience of Japan in the 1990s; which had a very limited explicit deposit insurance system, but an implicit system essentially promising 100% coverage of deposits. He argues that the existence of the implicit system of deposit insurance likely resulted in substantially worse outcomes than would have an explicit system with more extensive coverage. The major argument is that implicit safety nets provide more scope for regulatory officials to make ad hoc decisions that appear optimal in the short-run (during their tenure in office) but led to sub-optimal long-run outcomes. In contrast, an explicit safety net can be accompanied with explicit closure and resolution rules that provide adequate weight to the long-run consequences of bank closure and resolution decisions.[17]

Although least cost resolution and depositor preference may reduce moral hazard, their potential weaknesses suggest that regulators could benefit from another source of market information and discipline. Ideally, this alternative source could not be repaid by insolvent banks, could not be collateralized, and would be highly unlikely to benefit from an *ex post* extension of the safety net. Liabilities that may meet these requirements are bond issues that explicitly state that their repayment is subordinated to the payment of all other creditors and the FDIC; that is, sub-debt.

From a regulatory standpoint, sub-debt has a number of attractive characteristics. One is that the debt-holders would take the entire portfolio risk into account when pricing a bank's risk exposure and not, as is common under current supervisory procedures, emphasize individual asset risks. Existing evidence, summarized in Section III, indicates that sub-debt yields are sensitive to the risk exposure of the issuing banking organization. Therefore, the regulator could structure the terms of qualifying sub-debt to make it homogeneous across firms so that the pricing of the debt could serve as a signal of the financial market's assessment of a bank's risk. Other market participants could also use the debt pricing to obtain a low cost signal of the bank's risk which they could then use to determine if, and on what terms, they would contract with the bank. Additionally, as detailed below in our proposed sub-debt plan, supervisors could use information from the sub-debt markets in the examination and supervisory process.

The existing capital requirements, however, hinder the use of sub-debt as an effective source of market discipline. Required characteristics for sub-debt to qualify as capital have been imposed which attempt to essentially transform it into a cheaper form of equity. For example, to qualify as capital under the existing guidelines, the debt must have an original maturity of at least five years and must be discounted on a straight-line bases when it has a maturity of less than five years. This effectively prevents distressed banks from having to redeem sub-debt that is being counted as regulatory capital, but it also hinders the direct disciplining role of debt since the bank does not have to approach the market very often. Additionally, the regulators' ability to use the pricing of bank's sub-debt to initiate prompt corrective action is inhibited by the lack of restrictions on who may own the debt. Currently it is common practice for banks to issue sub-debt to their parent holding company. Most large parent bank holding companies issue sub-debt to the financial markets, but nothing in the current regulations prevent the parents from issuing the debt in a private placement under which the current yield on the outstanding debt would not be publicly observable.

Although current restrictions on sub-debt limit its effectiveness as a capital source, on the surface there appears to be three potential means by which sub-debt could be used to achieve regulatory goals. It could provide: (1) a cushion to absorb losses and, thereby, reduce the expected cost of failure to the safety net, (2) a source of *direct discipline* on the bank in the form of higher funding costs, and (3) a source of *derived discipline* by providing risk signals to other market participants and to supervisors who can then discipline the bank. Whether sub-debt adequately serves as a *cushion* to absorb losses depends largely on the size of the debt issues, and, when appropriate, the type of funding source that sub-debt is substituting for. Whether it provides *direct discipline* depends on the extent to which the funding costs of banks are sufficiently affected by introducing sub-debt requirements and, therefore results in a change in their risk-taking behavior. This depends on the size of the debt requirement and the resulting degree to which the marketplace prices the risk and disciplines the bank. The extent to which sub-debt may be used to provide *derived discipline* depends largely on whether its yield accurately reflects changes in a bank's riskiness and the extent to which it is used by supervisors and other market participants.

For both direct and derived discipline the market must be capable of distinguishing risk differentials across banks and translating those into differential yields. Thus to be effective at achieving regulatory goals, the characteristics of a sub-debt program must be carefully determined to allow some combination of these three forces to operate. We will return to what we believe to be the preferred characteristics of a sub-debt program in a later section. Next we evaluate the evidence on whether the market is capable of differentiating riskiness across banks.

III. SUBORDINATED DEBT PRICING AND DIRECT DISCIPLINE IN BANKING: THE EMPIRICAL EVIDENCE

Above we argue that there are potential benefits of moving to a regulatory regime in which banks are required to issue sub-debt to have it comprise a significant portion of their capital. Many of these benefits occur because holders of sub-debt are likely to be at risk if a bank should fail, and they have an incentive to demand compensation for that risk. The demands for compensation for risk bearing should exert direct discipline on banks and provide a risk signal. These benefits, however, exist only to the extent that holders of sub-debt effectively price the riskiness of the bank in a manner suggested by economic theory. Therefore, before consideration can be given to introducing a new sub-debt proposal one must evaluate whether holders of sub-debt can be expected to demand a higher yield from riskier banks. Will investors gather information about a bank's activities and prospects, and the current condition of the bank, and effectively incorporate that information into the decision to buy and price that bank's debt? More generally, is market discipline effective in banking?

Here we summarize the empirical research on market pricing of risk and exerting of direct discipline in banking. We briefly touch on the pricing of risk in general, as revealed through analyses of bank liability prices and deposit flows, and we then give a more detailed coverage of the recent literature on sub-debt yields.[18] Most of the work on direct and derived discipline focuses on the pricing of sub-debt, however there is some analysis of the resulting behavioral changes of banks resulting from risk-related yield differentials. Finally we review the literature on whether there is additional information in debt prices beyond the information set of bank supervisors.

The most common empirical tests have analyzed the cross sectional relationship between interest rates paid on bank liabilities (typically large, uninsured certificates of deposit) and various measures of bank riskiness. Using supervisory information on the riskiness of the firm (e.g. CAMEL ratings), accounting measures or market measures of riskiness, most studies have found rates to be positively and significantly associated with the risk measures.[19] Additionally, the studies found that "bad" news was quickly incorporated into the cost of issuing large, uninsured certificate of deposits (CDs). In fact, even the largest banks, which many would argue were too-big-to-fail, and therefore had liabilities essentially guaranteed by an implicit safety net, were shown to have a risk premia embedded in the CD rates. Similarly, studies which have viewed the relationship between deposit growth and portfolio risk have generally found a relationship consistent with market discipline: uninsured depositors reduce their holdings at riskier institutions relative to those held at safer institutions.

More relevant for our purposes, however, is an assessment of the evidence of market pricing of risk and exerting of direct discipline in the market for sub-debt issued by banking organizations. We divide these studies into two groups. The early studies tested the relationship between the interest rate premium (defined as the rate on sub-debt minus the rate on long term U.S. Treasury securities) and various risk measures derived from balance sheets and income statements; e.g. leverage ratios, measures of profit variability, and loan loss ratios. These studies evaluated the pre-FDICIA period and did not find a significant statistical relationship between risk and the expected return demanded by investors.[20]

More recent research, however, analyzes data for a longer time period and generates results consistent with the earlier findings, and consistent with the market pricing of risk in the sub-debt market. Flannery and Sorescu (1996) argue that the apparent lack of relationship between risk and sub-debt yields in the earlier studies was most likely a result of conjectural government guarantees during the 1980s. This perceived guarantee was re-enforced by the regulatory treatment of holders of sub-debt during the rescue of Continental Illinois National Bank, and the formalization of the too-big-to-fail provision by the Comptroller of the Currency in Congressional testimony [see Carrington (1984)]. The market clearly believed that banking policy would at least partially protect the owners of banks during this period. Being senior to bank equity, sub-debt-holders could have rationally believed that they were protected as well. This implicit guarantee lasted until the late 1980s.

The implications of this perceived guarantee are that the degree of evidence concerning market pricing of risk in sub-debt markets should vary over the pre- and post-FDICIA period. Market pricing of risk should be more apparent in the latter portion of the period as Congress passed legislation (FIRREA and FDICIA) which was explicitly directed at curtailing these guarantees. Indeed, Flannery and Sorescu found bank-specific risk measures to be correlated with option-adjusted spreads in the 1983–91 period for a sample of 422 bonds issued by 83 different banking organizations. Further, this correlation appears to have increased as conjectural government guarantees weakened in the late 1980s and early 1990s. Despite this trend, however, option-adjusted spreads on sub-debt may also reflect the market's bank-specific estimate of a government bailout. The primary empirical model contains the log of bank assets as an explanatory variable and it is statistically significant in six of nine years in their sample, sometimes at the one percent level. This variable could indicate that the other balance sheet variables overstate the risk borne by sub-debt holders because these banks are safer (better diversified, or better managed) or because the conjectural guarantee is of greater value to large banks, or both. The study addresses the conjectural guarantee issue more directly by replacing the log of total assets, with a binary variable for inclusion on either the Comptroller's list or The Wall Street Journal's list of too-big-to-fail banks. The binary variable is negative and statistically significant at the 10% level in explaining option-adjusted spreads on their sub-debt in 1985–87 and in 1991. However, this binary variable does not exclude the possibility that balance sheet variables overstate the risks of banks on too-big-to-fail lists because these banks are more diversified or have better managers. Thus, based on these findings, it appears that bank sub-debt market participants are willing to invest in evaluating bank-specific risks when it is clearly in their interests to do so.

DeYoung, Flannery, Lang and Sorescu (1998) reaffirmed the results of the Flannery-Sorescu analysis over the 1989–95 period. This is valuable information because the earlier study had a relatively few number of years for inclusion in the post too-big-to-fail period. Over this longer period, without the presence of a conjectural government guarantee, spreads were found to be closely related to balance sheet and market measures of bank risk.[21]

Although the required sub-debt proposals have typically focused on individual banks, the studies discussed above have by necessity focused on sub-debt issues of bank holding companies. Until very recently almost all publicly traded debt was issued at the bank holding company level. Since problems at a bank holding company's bank affiliate can affect the profitability and value of the organization, there are incentives for investors to put pressure on the bank holding company to resolve these problems. These incentives, however, are less direct than are the incentives for investors that hold sub-debt that is issued directly by the bank; that is, the holder of bank holding company debt has a claim on additional assets controlled by the holding company and a lower priority claim on the bank's assets. Additionally, the strength of market discipline that is exerted by sub-debt-holders may also depend on who the owners are. In the case of independent banks, discussions with bank supervisors suggest that "insiders" hold most of their sub-debt. Although such debt does provide an additional cushion for the FDIC, it is not clear that these debt-holders would have risk-preferences that are closely aligned with the risk-preferences of the deposit insurer. Nor is it obvious that they would have the incentive to pressure regulators to intervene promptly with capital deficient banks. If sub-debt was issued by a bank that was part of a bank holding company, then it was typically held or guaranteed by the bank holding company itself. Such investors may not have the same incentives as would third-party investors when a bank was under financial stress.

One recent study evaluates publicly traded sub-debt issued both by bank holding companies and directly by banks. Analyzing sub-debt issues for 19 banks and 41 bank holding companies over the 1992–97 period, Jagtiani, Kaufman and Lemieux (1999) attempt to contrast the extent of market pricing of risk for two samples of debt issuers. They find that the market prices risk for both types of sub-debt about equally although bank holding company debt yields a higher risk premium. This reflects the lower priority on the bank's assets in case of insolvency or, as argued by others, is a result of the safety net being directed at the bank.[22] The important finding is that under a number of alternative specifications the market did appear to impose a risk premia on sub-debt issued at the *bank* level. They also find that the market tends to price risk more severely at poorly capitalized banks – that is, as predicted by theory, the spread-risk relationship is nonlinear based on the capitalization of the bank. This is important since most sub-debt proposals require that the bank issue the debt.

Finally, Morgan and Stiroh (2000) analyze whether or not the market is "tough enough" in pricing bank risk. Evaluating new bond issues between 1993–98 they test to see whether debt spreads reflect the risk of a bank's portfolio; thus they are evaluating whether the market prices *ex ante risk*. They do similar analysis for non-banks to evaluate whether the risk-spread relationship varies between the two sectors. Finally, they evaluate subsamples of the bank data to see if the "toughness" of the market differs across different sized banks. Their concern is that too-big-to-fail policies may still result in the market being "easier" on larger institutions.[23]

They find that the market does price risk exposure at banks. As the bank shifts its portfolio into riskier activities it is forced to pay greater spreads to investors. The risk-spread relationship is nearly identical across the bank and non-bank sectors. However they find that the risk-spread relationship is weaker for the larger banks. One interpretation of this result, the one they provide, is that larger banks are more likely to benefit from implicit guarantees. While there may be merit in this interpretation, balance sheet variables could be poorer proxies for several other (non-mutually exclusive) reasons including: (1) balance sheets may comprise a smaller fraction of the available information about larger banks because these banks appear more frequently in the news media and are covered by more analysts, (2) larger banks may have a larger fraction of their earnings determined by off-balance sheet items and non-traditional activities, such as securities underwriting, and (3) loans within a given category may be less homogenous for some large banks because of their greater involvement in foreign markets.

In summary, the majority of the literature suggests that the market accounts for risk when pricing sub-debt issued by banking organizations. During those periods when sub-debt premia was not found to be related to risk measures, there is significant evidence indicating that debt-holders were not at risk in spite of the riskiness of the debt-issuing bank and were relying on the government's conjectural guarantee. As the guarantee was decreased via policy and legislative changes in the late 1980s and early 1990s, debt-holders came to realize that they were no longer protected from losses and they rationally responded by more effectively taking market risks into account. Therefore, sub-debt-holders appear to be willing and able to invest in evaluation of the riskiness of bank assets, but only when they benefit from doing so.

While the above discussion indicates that the market incorporates risk differences into debt prices, a few related studies evaluate whether banks respond in an attempt to decrease the adverse (costly) impact of the higher yields. That is, do banks logically respond to market discipline in the expected manner, or do they essentially ignore the discipline and continue operating as usual. Is bank behavior affected by pricing of risk in credit markets?

Billett et al. (1998) evaluated the change in bank liability composition following a rating downgrade. Analyzing 109 downgrades by Moody's during the 1990–95 period they found that in the quarter of downgrades, bank's insured deposits significantly increased in both a relative and absolute sense. In contrast, the interest-sensitive uninsured liabilities (uninsured deposits and commercial paper) decreased significantly (by 6.6% and 28.0% respectively) over this same period. The authors found the shift toward insured deposits to continue into the following quarter. Similarly, evaluating the response to ratings upgrades they found that banks responded by significantly increasing their reliance on uninsured liabilities for two quarter following the ratings change. Both sets of findings are consistent with banks responding in the expected manner to market discipline.

Marino and Bennett (1999) found similar results when analyzing the shift in liabilities at large failing banks prior to their demise. Viewing portfolio trends for several years before failure they found that the liability structure of a troubled bank changed significantly in the period prior to failure, with uninsured and unsecured liabilities declining rapidly just before failure. "At failure, the amount of uninsured deposits and unsecured liabilities is much less than it was in the months or years before failure". They argue that the introduction of depositor preference legislation may lead to even stronger responses by liability holders in future bank failures as uninsured (and other lower priority depositors) seek means to protect themselves.

Instead of evaluating the relationship between risk and sub-debt yield spreads, Covitz et al. (2000) evaluated the decision of banking organizations to issue sub-debt. That is, was the riskiness of the institution associated with the decision to approach the market? The failure of riskier institutions to issue, other things constant, would be consistent with a rational response to market discipline; to avoid the associated high costs. Findings on the issuance decision also have implications for the yield spread analysis reviewed above. If the issuance decision is negatively associated with bank risk then spread analysis may actually *understate* the actual extent of market discipline.

Evaluating the issuance decision for the 50 largest banking organizations for each quarter over the 1987–1997 period, the findings of Covitz et al. were somewhat similar to those of Flannery and Sorescu (1996) in that there was little evidence of bank risk measures being associated with the probability of debt issuance in the earlier period. However, they had a significant negative effect on the decision during the 1988–92 period. Again, the changing relationship is typically associated with the regulator's decision to remove implicit coverage of all liabilities. These results are consistent with the firm avoiding new debt issues to circumvent the additional associated costs, and with the contention that the debt pricing literature may actually understate the full extent of market discipline by excluding banks which avoided issuing debt. The findings are not as strong after 1992, and the authors attribute this to the rather sanguine time period for banks and the resulting narrow spreads for all banks.

While most of the research reviewed here deals with banks in the U.S., Martinez Peria and Schmukler (1998) evaluate market discipline in banking in Argentina, Chile, and Mexico during the 1980s and 1990s. Using an unbalanced panel of banks in these countries, they test whether changes in bank fundamentals result in changes in deposits. They find evidence of market discipline. Accounting for macroeconomic influences, banking system factors, and bank-specific characteristics, they find that bank fundamentals are at least as important as other factors affecting changes in deposits.[24] Both insured and uninsured deposits respond to changes in bank fundamentals (risk measures), as do both large and small deposits. They attribute the market discipline imposed on insured deposits to a possible lack of credibility in the insurance scheme and the potential for delays in repayments. They conclude that their results are prima facie evidence in favor of recent regulatory efforts to increase the reliance on market discipline to control bank risk taking.

Finally, Bliss and Flannery (2000) stress that while previous studies found evidence of the ability of the market to *evaluate* the riskiness of banks (that is, to monitor firm behavior) they questioned whether the debt markets were able to *influence* the behavior of bank managers. Does management respond with portfolio shifts in an attempt to decrease the risk of the bank after debt holders inform them that they have become concerned with their risk profile (via larger debt spreads)? Evaluating large U.S. bank holding companies over the 1986–97 period the authors find no evidence that bank managers respond to changes in debt spreads by adjusting variables that they control in an attempt to realign the risk profile of the bank in a manner consistent with the wishes of debt holders. They conclude that there is no evidence of influence by debt holders and argue that regulators would be unwise to pursue a sub-debt program. Instead, efforts to influence the behavior of management must be retained by bank supervisors.

The Bliss and Flannery findings are significant outlyers in the literature. Unlike the findings of Billett et al., Covitz et al., Marino and Montgomery, and Martinez Peria and Schmukler, they do not find bank management responding to market signals in a way that elicits a positive response from the securities market. They conclude: "we find no prima facie support for the hypothesis that bond holders or stock holders consistently influence day-to-day managerial actions in a prominent manner consistent with their own interests".

Actually, they do not test this hypothesis. They attempt to capture one aspect of discipline imposed by the debt markets – *ex post* discipline. Do managers change their behavior following a change in yield spreads? However, this ignores the discipline most typically associated with sub-debt proposals – that is, the steady pressure or disciple that encourages management to behave in a conservative manner to avoid having the market impose direct costs through increased yield spreads. It is this *ex ante* disciple that encourages the firm to prudently manage risk, and is what most people think of when considering market discipline.[25] Their conclusions are analogous to saying that speed limit laws (or laws against robbing banks) are not effective in influencing behavior because speeders (bank robbers) are often repeat offenders. However, the argument entirely ignores the influence these laws have on the behavior of the vast majority of people. Similarly, viewing *ex post* responses to changing sub-debt yields totally ignores the influence on managers seeking to avoid "punishment" by the market.

Moreover, there are potential biases in the Bliss-Flannery methodology against finding evidence of debt holder influence. Security prices may change as a result of a bank announcing a new policy or as a result of new information reaching the market about existing policies. Consider first the case of a bank announcing a new policy. In the course of setting the policy, management should anticipate the impact on the wealth of the firm's shareholders.[26] If management anticipates that the action will reduce shareholder wealth then it should not undertake the policy. This is the *ex ante* discipline discussed above that will be unobservable because the managers do not announce and implement the policy change. Although corporate finance theory suggests that managers should not undertake actions that reduce shareholder wealth, the evidence suggests that they sometimes do. For example, a managerial action that often appears to reduce shareholder value is the acquisition of another firm.[27] However, in this case a manager with rational expectations would expect that announcing the new policy or action would be accompanied by a reduction in the per share value of the firm's common stock.[28] Given that the manager rationally anticipated the reduction in shareholder wealth, and nevertheless proceeded with the action, there is no reason to expect the firm to undertake some further action in response to the drop in share price (or increase in debt spreads). Thus, in those cases where market discipline is ineffective *ex ante*, we would ordinarily not expect to observe such discipline *ex post*.

Now consider the case of adverse new information arriving about past policies. Assume first that the signal to the market is fully revealing; that is, the market knows the exact extent of the loss to the bank. In this case, the bank managers must compare the costs and benefits of alternative means of responding to the new information. If the loss is small and the cost of all the responses is high then senior bank management may rationally do nothing. Alternatively, senior management may respond, but in ways that do not appear in the banks' financial statement, such as by firing the individuals responsible for the losses. Finally, Bliss and Flannery also evaluated whether the securities markets responded favorably to any response that does come from management. However, if management responds in an observable manner, we will not observe a subsequent positive market response unless market participants were sufficiently uncertain that management would take the appropriate action. If such action is assigned a high probability at the time the bad news is revealed then most of the positive effect of the subsequent action will be priced into the stock at the time the bad news is announced. Thus, unless we confine our observations to large stock price changes, we are unlikely to see them undertake costly responses, and even when the losses are large the response may take a form not readily observable in financial statements or may not be a surprise to the financial markets.

Next consider the case of adverse new information arriving about past policies, where the signal is only partially revealing to the market. In this case, management's response to the news may provide additional information to the market. If management does nothing then the market may assign a higher probability to the belief that the losses were small relative to their initial expectations. This could encourage fewer responses by managers. However, if management takes drastic action, such as cutting dividends or issuing new stock, then the market may infer that the losses were larger than they initially anticipated and further reduce the firm's share price. In this case, the Bliss and Flannery test would find that the market was effective in inducing managers to act but that the effect of their action was perverse which in their model raises doubts about market discipline.

Thus, the Bliss and Flannery methodology and tests are likely to reveal beneficial market discipline only if: (1) new information arises about past policies, (2) the signal to the market reveals almost all of the information, (3) market participants assign a significant probability that the manager will not take the appropriate action, (4) the gain from taking action exceeds the cost of the action, and (5) the optimal set of actions includes actions observable on the balance sheet. Such situations undoubtedly occur. However, Bliss and Flannery incorporate all stock price moves and, hence, their sample almost surely includes a large number of shocks to stock prices where we would not expect to identify a managerial response using their empirical technique. Thus, one should not be surprised if noise from all other possible situations where the firm's stock price declines obscures the market signal that the authors are looking for.

Nevertheless, based on their findings, Bliss and Flannery claim a rather strong policy position. They argue that "supervisors would be unwise to rely on investors – including subordinated debenture holders – to constrain BHC risk-taking. ... (S)upervisors must retain the responsibility for influencing managerial actions". The conclusions seem rather strong given the rather limited scope of their analysis and the associated biases against finding evidence of "influence".

In summary, the literature on the behavioral response of banks to market and supervisory discipline suggests that they respond in the expected manner: to decrease the costs of the discipline. Bliss and Flannery seem to be the only exception to this finding. The literature, however, is rather limited and there is a need for additional research.

A related topic concerns whether the information used by private markets to price bank risk is similar to that available to bank supervisors; either in content or the timing of its availability. It has been argued that via the on-sight examination process, bank supervisors have access to insider information, which the market generally does not have. Alternatively, the private market has the stronger incentive to obtain the necessary information to make informed investment decisions. Additionally, it may be that the information sought by the various "bank-watchers" differs since they each serve different roles. Equity-holders, for example, may be concerned with the potential for banks to generate efficiency gains instead of concentrating on the bank's probability of failure. In contrast, the objectives of sub-debt-holders and bank supervisors probably align quite well in that both are most interested in protecting against failure. Thus, it would be informative to contrast the availability of information available to the two potential disciplinarians.

Most of the recent research in this area suggests that supervisors may temporarily have inside information not immediately observable on bank financial statement and, hence, possibly not known by the market. Dahl, Hanweck and O'Keefe (1995) found that significant contributions to loan loss reserves typically occurred immediately following a bank examination, suggesting new information was uncovered during the exam and/or pressure exerted to have the bank report more accurately. Cole and Gunther (1998) attempted to predict bank failure with models using publicly available financial data, and then augmented their model with CAMEL ratings to test if the additional information improved the predictive power of the model. They found that the augmented model did more accurately predict bank failure, but only if the CAMEL rating was less than six months old. After that, the data appeared to be "stale" and to have already been incorporated into the market's information set. This staleness finding is rather typical in the literature suggesting that over time the additional information permeates to the broader market. Berger and Davies (1994), for example, found that CAMEL upgrades were quickly integrated into market prices (suggesting that the bank's may have been releasing the new examination information to the market) but downgrades were only incorporated with a lag (suggesting the bank was able to temporarily keep adverse information from the market, but not from examiners).

More directly related to sub-debt proposals, the study by DeYoung, Flannery, Lang and Sorescu (1998) considered the information content of bank examinations as it relates to secondary market sub-debt spreads. The study compared CAMEL ratings against various market assessments of bank condition and found that bank examination ratings contained private informa-tion about a bank's safety and soundness not available to the market. They tested whether the market incorporated new private supervisory information into the risk premium paid on holding company debentures, with a lag. They concluded that bank exams provided significant new information that was not internalized by financial markets for several months. The study did not consider the opposite effect: whether there was information in the private market beyond that which the examiners already had access to.

This last issue, however, was examined by Berger, Davies and Flannery (1998) when they analyzed the information sets of examiners[29] and the private market to see "who knows what, when?" They test to see whether private market assessments of the condition of bank holding companies change before or after supervisors change their assessments. Similarly, they evaluate whether information in private markets precedes changes in the assessments of supervisors?[30] Their general conclusion was that supervisory assessments and private market assessments complement each other in that pertinent information obtained by each group is only subsequently incorporated into the other group's assessments. Thus, each group appears to bring new and valuable information to the table, and that information is incorporated with a lag into the other group's information set.[31]

The bottom line appears to be that different market participants (supervisors, bond market participants, rating agencies, etc.) generate valuable complementary information which can be useful in the governance of banks, albeit more work in this area is warranted.

Therefore the evidence as a whole appears to be consistent with the presumption that sub-debt-holders effectively discipline banks in the expected manner. The effectiveness of a sub-debt requirement, however, would depend critically on the structure of the program. Below we briefly review previous sub-debt proposals and present a new one that we believe to have the most desirable characteristics.

IV. SUMMARY OF PAST PROPOSALS

Since the mid–1980s there have been a number of regulatory reform proposals aimed at capturing the benefits of sub-debt.[32] A detailed survey of past proposals is provided in Kwast et al. (1999) and is summarized in Table 1. Below we provide a partial review of these proposals stressing only those that emphasize the characteristics on which the proposal we develop in the next section is based. The typical benefits emphasized in the previous proposals result from the ability of sub-debt to provide a capital cushion, to impose both direct- and derived-discipline on banks, and from the tax benefits associated with debt.[33] Summarily, this results in the following benefits:

- a bank riskiness or asset quality signal for regulators and market participants,
- the potential for a more prompt failure resolution process resulting in fewer losses to the insurance fund,
- a more methodical failure resolution process resulting from the rather methodical pressure imposed by debt-holders as they, unlike depositors, are

Table 1. A Summary of Various Subordinated Debt Proposals.

Bibliographic Citation	Required Amount?	Debt Characteristics					Insolvency Procedures?	Participants? (All Banks?)
		Maturity?	Issuance?	Covenants?	Rate Cap?	Putable Debt		
Federal Deposit Insurance Corporation (1983).	Banks would be required to maintain a minimum protective cushion to support deposits (e.g. 10%) which would be met by use of a combination of equity and sub-debt.	Maturity selection should take into consideration the desirability of frequent exposure to market judgment. The total debt perhaps should mature serially (e.g. one-third every two years).	As banks grow they would be required to proportionately add to their "capitalization." Those heavily dependent on debt, primarily the larger banks, would have to go to the market frequently to expand their cushion and to refinance maturing issues.	Penalties would be imposed on banks that fell below minimum levels. Provisions where debt holders receive some equity interest and exercise some management control such as in the selection of members of the board of directors may be appropriate as may convertibility to common stock under certain provisions.	None.	Not discussed.	FDIC assistance might still be granted and serious disruption avoided in a manner which would not benefit stockholders and subordinate creditors. This could be accomplished by effecting a phantom merger transaction with a newly-chartered bank which has been capitalized with FDIC financial assistance. The new bank would assume the liabilities of the closed bank and purchase its high-quality assets.	Not discussed.

Table 1. Continued.

Bibliographic Citation	Required Amount?	Debt Characteristics					Insolvency Procedures?	Participants? (All Banks?)
		Maturity?	Issuance?	Covenants?	Rate Cap?	Putable Debt		
Benston, Eisenbeis, Horvitz, Kane and Kaufman (1986).	A significant level (e.g. 3 to 5% of deposits or a certain proportion of equity).	Short maturity, but long enough to prevent runs.	Frequent.	Yes, to restrict the ability of the banks to engage in risky activities.	None.	A small percentage of the issue should be redeemed at the option of the holder	Advised prompt closure when market value of equity is zero. Noted that in order to protect the FDIC, the notes would have to allow for wide discretion by the FDIC in arranging purchases and assumptions in cases of insolvency.	These authors indicated that they believed that large banks would be able to sell sub-debt notes through the national financial markets, small banks might be able to sell capital notes over the counter to customers locally (or locally by other means), but medium-sized banks would be too large to sell sufficient notes locally, but not large enough to have access to national markets

Table 1. Continued

| Bibliographic Citation | Required Amount? | Debt Characteristics | | | | | Insolvency Procedures? | Participants? (All Banks?) |
		Maturity?	Issuance?	Covenants?	Rate Cap?	Putable Debt		
Horvitz (1986)	A minimum of 4% of deposits.	Not discussed.	Not discussed.	Not discussed.	None.	Not discussed.	FDIC would choose when to close the bank. Sub-debt holders would provide a margin of error in the determination of when a bank should be closed and would reduce the loss to the FDIC.	Not discussed.
Litan and Rauch (1997).	A minimum of 1 to 2% of risk-weighted assets.	The subordinate bonds would have maturities of at least 1 year.	A fraction of the sub-debt outstanding would come due in each quarter.	Not discussed.	Not discussed.	Not discussed.	Not discussed.	Sub-debt would only be required of banks in organizations above a certain size (e.g. $10 billion in total assets.)

Table 1. Continued.

Bibliographic Citation	Required Amount?	Debt Characteristics						Insolvency Procedures?	Participants? (All Banks?)
		Maturity?	Issuance?	Covenants?	Rate Cap?	Putable Debt			
The Bankers Roundtable (1998).	A minimum of 2% of liabilities.	Not discussed.	Not discussed.	Not discussed.	Not discussed.	Not discussed.		Not discussed.	Banks would have the option of complying with either a Basle-type risk-based capital standard or on approaches that rely on more market-based elements. Those banks that (a) are "adequately capitalized" but not subject to the leverage requirements under prompt corrective action, or (b) determine appropriate capital levels using internal management procedures would be *required* to issue sub-debt.

Table 1. Continued.

Bibliographic Citation	Required Amount?	Debt Characteristics					Insolvency Procedures?	Participants? (All Banks?)
		Maturity?	Issuance?	Covenants?	Rate Cap?	Putable Debt		
Keehn (1989).	A minimum of 4% sub-debt to risk assets ratio along with a 4% equity requirement.	The subordinated bonds would have maturities of no less than five years.	Issues would be staggered to ensure that no more than 20%, and no less than 10%, mature within any one year.	Sanctions on bank dividend policy, payment of management fees, deposit growth, and deposit rates would be progressively increased as the bank's performance deteriorated.	None.	Not discussed.	Bank ownership would be converted to the sub-debt holders following a judicial or regulatory determination of insolvency. Creditors would be converted to common shareholders and would have a prescribed period to recapitalize the bank or find an acquirer; failing that, the bank would be liquidated.	Small banks could be allowed alternative means to meet the debt requirement.

Table 1. Continued.

| Bibliographic Citation | Required Amount? | Debt Characteristics | | | | | Insolvency Procedures? | Participants? (All Banks?) |
		Maturity?	Issuance?	Covenants?	Rate Cap?	Putable Debt		
Cooper and Fraser (1988).	A specified percentage of deposits (e.g. 3%).	The subordinate putable notes would not be long-term, but would be rolled over at frequent intervals. These notes would be variable rate instruments with rate adjustments and interest payments made frequently.	Frequent.	Convertible to equity.	Yes, bonds would be putable at 95% of par value.	The notes would carry a "put" feature. They could be redeemed at the option of the note holders at a fixed percent of par value (e.g. 95%). The notes would be redeemable not by the issuing bank but at the FDIC.	When a put occurred, the FDIC would be compensated for its payments on behalf of the issuing bank with non-voting equity shares of the bank. The bank would have a prescribed period in which it could repurchase these equity shares. If it did not do so by the end of the period, revocation of the bank's charter would occur and the FDIC would deal with the insolvent bank.	Authors believed that the put feature of the proposed sub-debt would create a viable market for the instrument, no matter how small the issuing bank. If not, they suggested that these banks could receive assistance from the FDIC or Federal Reserve in the placement of this debt with investors.

Table 1. Continued.

Bibliographic Citation	Required Amount?	Debt Characteristics					Insolvency Procedures?	Participants? (All Banks?)
		Maturity?	Issuance?	Covenants?	Rate Cap?	Putable Debt		
Wall (1989).	Par value of putable subdebt greater than 4 to 5% of risk-weighted assets.	Bondholders would be allowed to request redemption in cases where such redemption did not violate regulatory standards.	At the bank level, not the holding company level.	There would be restrictions on the percentage of putable debt that could be owned by insiders individually and in toto.	Not discussed.	Yes. Bondholders would be allowed to request redemption in cases where such redemption did not violate regulatory standards. With the exercise of a put, a bank would have 90 days to meet the requirements by issuing new debt or through reducing its sub-debt requirements, e.g. through the sale of assets.	Any bank that could not honor the redemption requests on its putable sub-debt at the end of 90 days without violating the regulatory requirements would be deemed insolvent and would be closed. If the proceeds of the sale or liquidation exceeded the total of deposits, that excess would first be returned to the sub-debt holders; the remainder, if any, would be paid to equity holders.	Small banks, defined as those with less than $2 billion in assets, would be exempted because of the limited market they might face for sub-debt instruments. Those banks would have the option of operating under the putable subordinated debt standard.

Table 1. Continued.

Bibliographic Citation	Required Amount?	Debt Characteristics					Insolvency Procedures?	Participants? (All Banks?)
		Maturity?	Issuance?	Covenants?	Rate Cap?	Putable Debt		
Evanoff (1993).	A significant proportion of total capital would be held in sub-debt. The 8% minimum capital requirement could be restructured to require a minimum of 4% equity and 4% subordinated debt.	Short enough so that the bank would have to go to the market on a regular basis, but long enough to tie debt holders to the bank and make the inability to run meaningful (e.g. 5 years).	Staggered so that banks would have to approach the market on a frequent basis (e.g. semi-annually).	Following the prompt corrective action (PCA) provisions of FDICIA, sanctions on bank dividend policy, payment of management fees, deposit growth, and deposit rates would be progressively increased as the bank's performance deteriorated. Implicit in the discussion seems to be the incorporation of the sub-debt requirements into PCA.	None.	A variant of the proposal would require the bank issue putable subordinated debt. The bank would have 90 days to issue replacement debt. If it could not do so, it would be taken over by the regulators.	Once a bank's debt capital fell below the required level, existing subordinated debt holders would be given an equity position and would have a prescribed period to recapitalize the bank or find an acquirer; failing that, the bank would be liquidated.	This author suggests that a few investment bankers had indicated some interest in establishing mutual funds for the sub-debt instruments issued by small banks. Also, his conversations with small bankers suggested that they could raise this type of debt relatively easily.

Table 1. Continued.

Bibliographic Citation	Required Amount?	Debt Characteristics					Insolvency Procedures?	Participants? (All Banks?)
		Maturity?	Issuance?	Covenants?	Rate Cap?	Putable Debt		
Calomiris (1997).	2% of total nonreserve assets or 2% of risk-weighted assets	Not discussed.	For rollovers, and to accommodate growth in the bank's balance sheet.	"Insiders" would not be permitted to hold subordinated debt. Further, holders of sub-debt would have no direct or indirect interest in the stock of the bank that issues the debt. Author suggested that the ideal sub-debt holders would be unrelated foreign financial institutions.	The subordinated debt would earn a yield no greater than 50 basis points above the riskless rate.	Not discussed.	Sub-debt holders must have their money at stake when a bank becomes insolvent.	Yes.

Table 1. Continued.

Bibliographic Citation	Required Amount?	Maturity?	Issuance?	Debt Characteristics			Insolvency Procedures?	Participants? (All Banks?)
				Covenants?	Rate Cap?	Putable Debt		
Calomiris (1999). NOTE: This plan is described as "a sub-debt plan for a developing country." While a plan targeted at the U.S. would differ in some important details (especially in terms of acceptable investors), such a plan would generally work along the lines of the developing country proposal.	Banks must "maintain" a minimum fraction (say 2%) of their risky (non-Treasury bill) assets in subordinated debt (sometimes called uninsured deposits).	Two years.	1/24 of the issue would mature each month.	Debt must be issued to large domestic banks or foreign financial institutions. See the "All Banks?" column for details.	Rates would be capped at the one-year Treasury bill rate plus a "maximum spread" (say, 3%).		Not discussed.	The plan would apply to all banks. Debt issued by small banks (those that may have difficulty accessing foreign banks and international finance markets) could be held by large domestic or foreign banks. Debt issued by large banks must be held by foreign financial institutions.
							Banks that could not issue would be required to shrink their assets by 1/24 (4.17%) during the next month. If additional contraction is required (because of prior growth) then the additional shrinkage could be achieved over three months. (He also discusses measuring assets and sub-debt using a three month moving average.) Presumably, this would result in the bank liquidating all of its assets over 24 to 27 months if it could no longer issue SND.	

Table 1. Continued.

Bibliographic Citation	Required Amount?	Debt Characteristics					Insolvency Procedures?	Participants? (All Banks?)
		Maturity?	Issuance?	Covenants?	Rate Cap?	Putable Debt		
The U.S. Shadow Regulatory Committee (2000).	2% of assets and off-balance sheet commitments	Must have a remaining maturity of at least one year to qualify.	If the debt traded frequently enough, secondary market prices would be adequate for signals to both the market and regulators. If the debt does not trade frequently in secondary markets, the bank would be required to make regular offerings in the primary market.	The debt should be of "minimum remaining maturity (say, one year), would be held at arm's length, and could not be repaid by the government or the FDIC. It could not be collateralized, and there would be a prohibition on its repayment in the event other uninsured debts were protected by the FDIC. The debt can be redeemed before maturity only when the proceeds from a new debt issue of at least equal size are realized.	Typically the market may "cap" yields on the debt through credit rationing. An imposed cap may also occasionally be necessary. If for three consecutive months the yield on the debt of a bank was above that on moderately risky corporate bonds with similar maturities, the bank would be in violation of its sub-debt requirement.	No.	Sub-debt holders must have their money at stake when a bank becomes insolvent.	Large banks. Initially this would be defined as banks with assets greater than $10 billion. Over time, the size threshold may be lowered.

Source: The bulk of the information and the format are from Table 1 of Kwast et al. (1999). Some marginal adjustments have been made and recent entries have been added.

forced to wait until the debt matures to "walk" away from the bank rather than run, and
- lower cost of capital because of the tax advantages of deducting interest payments on debt as an expense, enabling bank's cost of capital to decrease and/or supervisors to increase capital requirements.

Horvitz (1983, 1984, 1987) discussed each of these advantages in his initial sub-debt proposal and extended that discussion in Benston et al. (1986). He challenged the view that equity capital is necessarily preferred to debt. While equity is permanent and losses can indeed be charged against it, he questioned why one would want to keep a troubled bank in operation long enough to make this feature relevant. Similarly, while interest on debt does represent a fixed charge against bank earnings, whereas dividends on equity do not, a bank with problems significant enough to prevent these interest payments has most likely already incurred deposit withdrawals and has reached, or is approaching, insolvency. Arguing that higher capital levels were needed at the bank level, and were simply not feasible through equity alone, Horvitz stated that sub-debt requirements of "say, 4% of assets" were a means to increase total capital requirements to nine or 10%. Without providing specifics, it was argued that debt-holders would logically require debt covenants that would give them the right to close or take over the bank once net worth was exhausted. Thus, sub-debt was seen as an ideal cushion for the FDIC.

In a comprehensive bank regulatory reform proposal, Keehn (1989) incorporated sub-debt as a centerpiece of the "FRB-Chicago Proposal" for deregulation.[34] The plan called for a modification of the 8% capital requirement to require a minimum of 4% of risk-weighted assets be held as sub-debt. The bonds would have maturities of no less than five years, with the issues staggered to insure that between 10 and 20% of the debt would mature and be rolled over each year. The inability to do so would serve as a clear signal that the bank was in financial trouble triggering regulatory restrictions and debt covenants.[35] Debt covenants would enable the debt-holders to initiate closure procedures and would convert debt-holders to an equity position once equity was exhausted. They would have a limited time to recapitalize the bank, find a suitable acquirer, or liquidate the bank. It was argued that debt-holders could be expected to effectively discipline bank behavior, and provide for an orderly resolution process when failure did occur. The discipline imposed by sub-debt-holders could differ significantly from that imposed by depositors as outstanding sub-debt could not run from the bank. The potential for regulatory forbearance was also thought to be less as holders of sub-debt would be less concerned with giving the troubled bank additional time to correct its problems and would pressure regulators to act promptly when banks in which they were invested encountered difficulties.

To address concerns about the mispriced bank safety net and potential losses to the insurance fund, Wall (1989) introduced a sub-debt plan aimed at creating a banking environment that would function similar to one without deposit insurance; but the insurance would be maintained. The plan was to have banks issue and *maintain* 'puttable' sub-debt equal to 4 or 5% of risk-weighted assets. If the debt was put on the bank by debt-holders, the bank would have 90 days to make the necessary adjustments to insure the minimum regulatory requirements were satisfied. That is, it could either retire the debt and continue to meet the regulatory requirement because of excess debt holdings, issue new puttable debt, or shrink assets to satisfy the requirement. If after 90 days the bank could not satisfy the requirement, it would be resolved. The put option has advantages in that it would force the bank to continually satisfy the market of its soundness and not just when new debt issues come due. Additionally, while earlier plans discussed the need for bond covenants to protect debt-holders, *all* contingencies would be covered under this plan as the market could demand redemption of the bonds without cause. This would essentially eliminate the practice of regulatory forbearance, a significant concern during the late 1980s, and would subject the bank to increased market discipline. Wall also stressed the need for restrictions on debt-holders to limit insider holdings.

Calomiris (1997, 1998, 1999) augmented previous sub-debt proposals by imposing a minimum sub-debt requirement (say 2% of total assets) *and* imposing a yield ceiling (say 50 basis points above the riskless rate). The spread ceiling is seen as a simple means of implementing regulatory discipline for banks. If banks cannot roll over maturing debt at the mandated spread, they would be required to shrink their risk-weighted assets to maintain regulatory compliance. Debt would have two-year maturities with issues being staggered to have equal portions come due each month. This would limit the maximum required monthly asset reduction to approximately 4% of assets. To insure adequate discipline, Calomiris also incorporated restrictions on who would be eligible to hold the debt.[36]

The effectiveness of any sub-debt requirement depends critically on the structure and characteristics of the program. Most importantly, the character-istics should be consistent with the regulatory objectives such as increasing direct discipline to alter risk behavior, to increase derived discipline, or to limit or eliminate regulatory forbearance. The proposals discussed above each have some of these objectives in mind in determining their characteristics. Keehn, for example, was particularly interested in derived discipline. Wall's proposal is most effective at addressing regulatory forbearance. Calomiris' spread ceiling most directly uses derived discipline to force the bank into mandated behavioral changes when the spread begins to bind.

We believe that subordinated debt's greatest value in the near term is as a risk signal. However, the earliest proposals had limited discussion of the use of sub-debt for derived regulatory discipline. The next round of plans, such as those by Keehn and Wall, use derived discipline but the only signal that they obtain from the sub-debt market is the bank's ability to issue debt. We have considerable sympathy for this approach. These types of plans maximize the scope for the free market to allocate resources by imposing minimal restrictions while eliminating forbearance and protecting the deposit insurance fund. However, the cost of providing bank managers with this much freedom is to delay regulatory intervention until a bank is deemed by the markets to be "too risky to save". As Benston and Kaufman (1988a, 1988b) argue, proposals to delay regulatory intervention until closure may be time inconsistent in that such abrupt action may be perceived by regulators as suboptimal when the tripwire is finally triggered. Moreover, market discipline will be eroded to the extent that market participants do not believe the plan will be enforced. Benston and Kaufman argue that a plan of *gradually* stricter regulatory intervention as a bank's financial condition worsens may be more credible. A version of that proposal, commonly labeled "structured early intervention" or "prompt corrective action", was adopted as a part of the FDIC Improvement Act of 1991.

In theory, by imposing limits on sub-debt rates Calomiris provides a mechanism for this progressive discipline that could last for approximately two years. In practice, however, his plan would likely provide the same sort of abrupt discipline as would the prior proposals, with the primary difference being that Calomiris would likely trigger the discipline while the bank was in a stronger condition. By requiring banks to shrink if they cannot issue sub-debt at a sufficiently small premium, his plan would provide banks with a period of time during which they could respond by issuing new equity. If the bank could not issue equity then it would have to shrink and would most likely accomplish this by calling in maturing loans to good borrowers and selling its most liquid assets to minimize losses. However, the most liquid assets are also likely to be among the lowest risk assets implying that with each monthly decline in size, the bank would be left with a less liquid and more risky portfolio. This decrease in liquidity and increase in risk is likely to reduce most banks' viability significantly within, at most, a few months. Yet, the prior proposals that would rely on bank's ability to issue sub-debt at any price also gave managers some time to issue new equity either by automatically imposing a stay (Wall's proposal) or by requiring relatively infrequent rollovers (Keehn's proposal).

Thus, Calomiris' proposal is subject to the same sorts of concerns that arise with the earlier proposals.

Although Calomiris' proposal for relying on progressive discipline is more abrupt than it appears at first glance, his suggestion that regulators use the rates on sub-debt to trigger supervisory action provides a mechanism for phasing in stricter discipline. In the next section we provide a combination of Calomiris' idea of using market rates with Benston and Kaufman's proposal for progressively increasing discipline.[37]

V. A COMPREHENSIVE SUBORDINATED DEBT PROPOSAL

As discussed earlier, banking organizations' entry into new activities is raising additional questions about how to best regulate the risk behavior of financial firms. Ideally the new activities could avoid either greatly extending the safety net beyond its current reach or imposing costly supervision procedures to new activities. A plan incorporating sub-debt could help in meeting these challenges. Markets already provide most of the discipline on non-depository financial institutions, as well as virtually all non-financial firms. A carefully crafted plan may be able to tap similar market discipline to help limit the safety net without extending costly supervision.

Below we present and describe a detailed sub-debt proposal.[38] While the U.S. banking sector is the target, there are broader implications as international capital standards come into play. While others have argued that U.S. banking agencies could go forward without international cooperation, we think there are benefits from working with the international banking agencies, if possible. The explicit goals of our proposal are to: (1) limit the safety net exposure to loss, (2) establish risk measures that accurately assess the risks undertaken by banks, especially those that are part of large, complex financial organizations, and (3) provide supervisors with the ability to manage (but not prevent) the exit of failing organizations. The use of sub-debt can help achieve these goals by imposing some direct discipline on banks, providing more accurate risk measures, and providing the appropriate signals for derived discipline and, ultimately, failure resolution.

Setting the Ground Rules

As a starting point, a decision has to be made as to whether a new sub-debt program should be "fitted" within the existing regulatory framework, or whether adjustments to the framework are necessary to have the debt effectively fulfill its stated role. Obviously there are tradeoffs. In our view, however, the goals of the proposal cannot be effectively achieved in the current regulatory environment which *allows* banks to hold sub-debt, but does not require it. As a result, banks are most likely to opt-out of rolling over maturing debt or introducing new issues precisely in those situations when sub-debt would restrict their behavior and signal regulators that the bank is financially weak. Indeed, Covitz et al. (2000) found evidence of such behavior. Only a mandatory requirement would achieve the expected benefits. Thus, our proposal requires banks to hold minimum levels of sub-debt.

Similarly, other restrictions in the current regulatory environment limit the potential effectiveness of a sub-debt program. In our view, when developing a sub-debt policy, the form of the proposal should follow function. However, the role that sub-debt serves is significantly driven by its role in bank capital guidelines. In the current regulatory environment, that role is determined by the Basel Accord that counts sub-debt as an element of Tier 2 capital, with the associated restrictions, and limits the amount that may be counted as regulatory capital.

Maintaining the current restrictions has two bothersome implications. First, it dictates almost all of the terms of the sub-debt proposal. For example, U. S. banks operating under current Basel constraints have generally chosen to issue 10-year sub-debt. If there are perceived benefits from having a homogeneous debt instrument, in the current regulatory environment the optimal maturity would appear to be ten years. This is not to say that if left unconstrained financial firms would prefer 10-year maturities. Indeed bankers frequently criticize the restrictions imposed on sub-debt issues that, as discussed above, make it a less attractive form of capital. Ideally, without the restrictions imposed by Basel, the maturity would be much shorter to allow it to better match the duration of the bank balance sheet. However once the 10-year maturity is decided upon as a result of the restrictions, to avoid "chopping" the debt requirement too finely the frequency of issuance is operationally limited. For example, with a 2% sub-debt requirement, mandating issuance twice a year would require a $50 billion bank to regularly come to the market with $50 million issues – significantly smaller than the standard issue in today's markets. Thus adhering to the current Basel restrictions would determine one of the interdependent parameters, and thus drives them all. Adjusting the Basel restrictions would "free up" the parameters of any new sub-debt proposal.

The second implication of following the current Basel Accord is that sub-debt is not effectively designed to enhance market discipline. Given that sub-debt was considered an equity substitute in the capital structure, it was designed to function much like equity and to provide supervisory flexibility in dealing with distressed institutions. In particular, the value of the sub-debt is amortized over a five-year period to encourage banks to use longer-term debt. Further, the interest rate on the debt does not float; thus it is limited in its ability to impose direct discipline when there are changes in the banks risk exposure. Finally, because sub-debt is regarded as an inferior form of equity, the amount of sub-debt is limited in the Accord to 50% of the bank's Tier 1 capital.[39]

If indeed there are benefits to giving sub-debt a larger role in the bank capital structure, then consideration should be given to eliminating the current disadvantages to using it as capital. That is the approach taken in our proposal presented below.

The Proposal

Our sub-debt program would be implemented in stages as conditions permit.

Stage 1: Surveillance Stage
For immediate implementation:

- Sub-debt prices and other information should be used in monitoring the financial condition of the 25 largest banks and bank holding companies in the U.S.[40] Procedures should be implemented for acquiring the best possible pricing data on a frequent basis for these institutions, with supplementary data being collected for other issuing banks and bank holding companies. Supervisory staff could gain experience in evaluating how bank soundness relates to debt prices, spreads, etc., and how changes in these elements correlate with firm soundness.
- Simultaneously, in line with the mandate of the Gramm-Leach-Bliley Act, staffs of regulatory agencies should study the value of information derived from debt prices and quantities in determining bank soundness, and evaluate the usefulness of sub-debt in increasing market discipline in banking. Efforts should be made to obtain information on the depth and liquidity of debt issues, including the issues of smaller firms.
- If deemed necessary, the regulatory agencies should obtain the necessary authority (via congressional action or regulatory mandate) to allow the federal banking agencies to *require* banks and bank holding companies to issue a minimum amount of sub-debt with prescribed characteristics, and to use the debt levels and prices in implementing prompt corrective action as described in FDICIA. The legislation would explicitly prohibit the FDIC from absorbing losses for sub-debt-holders, thus excluding sub-debt from the systemic risk exception in FDICIA.

- The bank regulatory agencies should work to alter the Basel Accord to eliminate the unfavorable characteristics of sub-debt: the 50% of Tier 1 limitation and the required amortization.

Stage 2: Introductory Stage
To be implemented when authority to mandate sub-debt is obtained:

- The 25 largest banks would be required to issue a minimum of 2% of risk-weighted assets in sub-debt on an annual basis with qualifying issues at least 3 months apart to avoid long periods between issues or "bunching" of issues during particularly tranquil times.[41]
- The sub-debt must be issued to independent third parties and be tradable in the secondary market. The sub-debt's lead underwriter and market makers may not be institutions affiliated with the issuing bank, nor may the debt be held by affiliates. Additionally, no form of credit enhancement could support the debt.[42]
- The terms of the debt should explicitly state and emphasize its junior status, and the understanding that the holder would not have access to a "rescue" under the too-big-to-fail systemic risk clause. It is imperative that the debt-holders behave as unsecured, junior creditors.
- Failure to comply with the issuance requirement would trigger a presumption that the bank was critically undercapitalized. If the bank's outstanding sub-debt traded at yields comparable to those of firms with a below investment grade rating (Ba or lower – that is, junk bonds) for a period of two weeks or longer then the bank would be presumed to be severely undercapitalized.[43]
- Regulators would investigate whether the remaining capital triggers or tripwires associated with prompt corrective action could be augmented with sub-debt rate-based triggers. The analysis would consider both the form of the trigger mechanism (e.g. rate spreads over risk-free bonds, or relative to certain rating classes, etc.) and the exact rates/spreads which should serve as triggers.
- The sub-debt requirement would be phased in over a transition period.

Stage 3: The Mature Stage
To be implemented when adjustments to the Basel Accord allow for sufficient flexibility in setting the program parameters, or at such time as it becomes clear that adequate modifications in the international capital agreement are not possible:

- A minimum sub-debt requirement of at least 3% of risk-weighted-assets would apply to the largest 25 banks, with the expressed intent to extend the requirement to additional banks unless regulator's analysis of sub-debt markets finds evidence that the costs of issuance by additional banks would be prohibitive. The increased flexibility is expected to allow for an increase in the number of banks which can cost effectively be included in the program.

- The sub-debt must be 5-year, non-callable, fixed rate debt.
- There must be a minimum of two issues a year and the two qualifying issues must be at least two months apart.

Discussion of the Proposal

Stage 1

Stage 1 is essentially a surveillance and preparatory stage. It is necessary because more information about bank debt markets is needed, and the rest of our proposal requires that the regulators have the ability to require sub-debt issuance and access to data to implement the remaining aspects of the plan. This step is already being implemented in part. Information on bank debt markets is currently being developed. Staff at the Board of Governors of the Federal Reserve System are collecting and analyzing sub-debt price data, and research is underway at the Reserve Banks evaluating the relationship between bank risk and debt spreads.

Stage 2

Stage 2 is designed to introduce a sub-debt program and begin using sub-debt as a supplement to the current capital tripwires under prompt corrective action. The ultimate goal of Stage 2 is to use sub-debt-based risk measures to augment capital-based measures, assuming a satisfactory resolution of some practical problems discussed below. The requirement that the debt be sold to independent third parties, be tradable, that the market makers be unaffiliated with the bank, and that affiliates cannot hold the debt are all intended to prevent the bank or its affiliates from "jamming" the signal by buying the debt at above market prices.

The sub-debt tripwires initially set out in Stage 2 may reasonably be considered "loose". Banks that cannot issue sub-debt are probably at or near the brink of insolvency, especially given that they only need to find one issuance window during the course of a year. If a bank's sub-debt is trading at yields comparable to junk bonds then the bank is most likely having significant difficulties and supervisors should be actively involved. We would not ordinarily expect the supervisors to need assistance in identifying banks experiencing this degree of financial distress. However, the presence of such tripwires would reinforce the current mandate of prompt corrective action. Further, it would strengthen derived discipline by other market participants by setting lower bounds on acceptable sub-debt rates.

The use of sub-debt yields for all of the tripwires under prompt corrective action could offer significant advantages. As discussed earlier, market based tripwires are expected to be more closely associated with bank risk. It should be emphasized, however, that the sub-debt signal is intended to augment and not replace supervisory oversight. In theory, it is clear how combining market signals with supervisory decisions can lead to improved bank regulation. For example, the financial condition of banks may be such that some obviously need intensive oversight, and others obviously do not. However, there may be a third group where the need is less obvious. Combining market with supervisory information may increase the potential for correctly identifying the problem institutions in the third group. Additionally, if supervisors would, absent use of a market-based signal, exercise forbearance for banks that they know need intensive oversight, then supervisory effectiveness may be enhanced by also incorporating the market signal.

Two dimensions will need further work, however, before heavy reliance on sub-debt spreads for supervisory intervention is possible. First, regulators need to review the history of sub-debt rates to determine how best to extract the risk signals from sub-debt yields, and how best to deal with periods of illiquidity in the bond market.[44] Concerning the risk signal, should sub-debt spreads be measured relative to Treasury obligations? The yields on Aaa bonds? The yields on the lowest investment grade category (Baa) or some other instrument? Is it feasible to map sub-debt yields to implied ratings by comparing the yields on sub-debt with comparable maturity corporate bonds of similar maturity? What are the properties of sub-debt yields through time? In particular, are there times when the yields become unreliable, as claimed by some market participants in discussions with Kwast et al. (1999)? If so, how long are these periods and how can they best be identified?

A second dimension that needs further analysis deals with determining "acceptable" bank failure rates. The linking of sub-debt rates to prompt corrective action will imply a tighter link between the prompt corrective action categories and the risk of failure than is possible under the current Basel Accord risk measures. As emphasized by Mingo (1999), an increase in precision will force senior policymakers to be careful in deciding where to set the tripwires. This decision is less important under the current risk based capital framework because the risk measures used by the capital adequacy standards are so inaccurate that there is little point in trying to estimate the expected failure rate associated with any given capital adequacy standard. With credit spreads, decisions will need to be made concerning what risk of failure is acceptable for a bank to be identified as "well capitalized", "adequately capitalized", or "undercapitalized"? If regulators require failure rates that are too low then some intermediation activity will be inefficiently pushed out of the banking system. If acceptable failure rates are set too high then both the FDIC's insurance fund and the financial system may be subject to excessive risk. Thus far, neither supervisors nor the academic literature has seriously addressed this problem. However, Mingo's question cannot be avoided if supervisors start using more accurate risk measures. We address these issues by initially setting rather loose prompt corrective action triggers, and in so doing keep supervisory judgement as the primary risk measure and using sub-debt spreads as a failsafe mechanism. Thus, at this stage we recommend rather loose triggers and further study by regulators, academics and bankers to determine the proper course to take before proceeding to the next stage of the plan.

Stage 3
This is the mature stage. The increased amount of required sub-debt and the shorter maturity in Stage 3 should enhance the opportunity for sub-debt to exercise direct discipline on banks. Another advantage of this proposal is that banks would be somewhat compensated, via the increased attractiveness of sub-debt as regulatory capital, for any increased regulatory burden from holding the additional debt. The removal of these restrictions could be quite significant, as it would serve as a 'carrot' that will make the cost of holding the debt less burdensome than under current regulatory arrangements. While it is not obvious whether total regulatory burden will increase as a result of the proposal, it seems more likely that as a result of this carrot the net burden would be less. The 5-year maturities in this stage allow for more frequent issuance, which should increase direct market discipline and market information. At the same time, five years is thought to be sufficient to tie the debt to the bank and limit bank runs.

The principal difference in this stage is the recommendation to shorten the maturity of the sub-debt. The advantages of requiring a shorter maturity are that it will allow more frequent issuance and result in a larger fraction of the sub-debt being repriced every year. Banks should find this advantageous. A minor downside is that it may require regulators to recalibrate the sub-debt yield trigger points for prompt corrective action for the categories of well capitalized, adequately capitalized and undercapitalized. However, as indicated above, this recalibration will most likely be an ongoing process as additional market expertise is obtained.

One aspect of our proposal that may appear to be controversial is the movement toward eliminating restrictions on sub-debt imposed by the Basel Accord. However, once the decision is made to employ sub-debt for overseeing bank activities, the restrictions appear unnecessary and overly burdensome. They only serve to increase the cost to participating banks and to limit the flexibility of the program. Without the current restrictions banks would prefer to issue shorter-term debt and, in some situations, would be able to count more sub-debt as regulatory capital. Similarly, as discussed earlier, the parameters of any sub-debt policy will be driven in great part by current regulatory restrictions. Keeping those restrictions in place would therefore place an unnecessary burden on participating banks, and would limit regulators, without any obvious positive payoff. This is not to say that initiating changes to the Accord would be costless. Obviously negotiations would be required since other country members may want to continue to have sub-debt be an inferior form of capital. But from the participating U.S. banks' perspective, and the regulators' perspective concerning program flexibility, the elimination of these restrictions should result in net benefits. The effort to adjust Basel also does not slow the movement toward implementation of a sub-debt program since the program would be phased in through the three-stage process. However, laying out the broad parameters of the complete plan in advance would indicate a commitment by regulators and could increase the credibility of the program.[45] Once fully implemented, sub-debt would become an integral part of the bank regulatory structure.

VI. COMMON CONCERNS AND FREQUENTLY ASKED QUESTIONS ABOUT SUB-DEBT PROPOSALS

There are a number of common issues raised about the viability of sub-debt proposals. For completeness, below we address some of these issues and clarify exactly what sub-debt programs can be expected to accomplish. We also highlight where our proposed sub-debt program specifically addresses these issues. Indeed these issues were important in the development of that program and we believe the concerns to be significantly less important under our proposal.

❑ *Won't the regulatory agencies 'bail out' troubled institutions by making sub-debt holders at failed institutions whole if they would have suffered losses otherwise, thus eliminating the purported benefits of a sub-debt program?*

This is probably the most fundamental concern raised about the viability of sub-debt proposals. An implicit guarantee may at times be more distorting to market behavior than is an explicit guarantee. If debt-holders *believe* an implicit guarantee exists, that is, regulators will make them whole if the issuing bank encounters difficulties and cannot make payment on their debt, then they will behave accordingly. Acting as if they are not subject to losses, they will fail to impose the necessary discipline on which the benefits of sub-debt proposals rely. There was evidence of such indifference to bank risk levels in the 1980s when the handling of the Continental Illinois National Bank situation ingrained the too-big-to-fail doctrine into bank investor's decision making. In essence, if the market discipline is not allowed to work, it will not. This applies to sub-debt.

However, a bailout is unlikely under current arrangements and our proposal makes it even less likely. Sub-debt-holders are sophisticated investors. They understand their position of junior priority, and the resulting potential losses should the issuing firm encounter difficulties. There can be little merit in, nor sympathy to, arguments that the debt-holder was unsophisticated and unaware of their claimant status. Additionally, since banks are not subject to bankruptcy laws, the debt-holders could not argue for a preferred position by refusing to accept the bankruptcy reorganization plan. Thus they are unable to block the resolution. So pressures to rescue debt-holders should not result from their status as unsophisticated investors, nor their bargaining power in the failure resolution process.

The FDIC guaranteed the sub-debt of Continental Illinois National Bank in 1984, but it did so to avoid having to close the bank and not to protect the sub-debt-holders per se. The effect of FDICIA and its prompt corrective action, least cost resolution requirements, and too-big-to-fail policies, was to significantly curtail and limit the instances when uninsured liability holders would be protected from loses. Benston and Kaufman (1998) found that policy did change as a result of FDICIA, as significantly fewer uninsured depositors were protected from losses at both large and small banks after passage of the legislation. Similarly, Flannery and Sorescu (1996) found evidence that the markets viewed FDICIA as a credible change in policy and, as a result, sub-debt prices began reflecting differences in bank risk exposures. Thus, the market apparently already believes that sub-debt-holders are unlikely to be bailed out in the future.

Under our sub-debt proposal there would be still less potential for debt-holder rescues. Unlike deposits that are callable on demand, the intermediate term debt could only leave as it matured instead of initiating a bank run which has typically prompted the rescues we have seen in the past. Additionally sub-debt yield spreads are likely to provide more accurate risk measures for prompt corrective action rather than are book value capital ratios. Finally, under our proposal the sub-debt-holder would be explicitly excluded from the class of liabilities that could be covered under the systemic risk exception. This exclusion should be viewed favorably by banks since under the terms of the too-big-to-fail exception in FDICIA, losses from the rescue would have to be funded via a special assessment of banks. Therefore, they should encourage the FDIC to strictly limit the extent of the liabilities rescued.

❏ *Are there cost implications for banks?*

Interestingly, the costs associated with issuing sub-debt have been used as an argument both for *and* against sub-debt proposals. The standard argument is that there are relative cost advantages of issuing debt resulting from the tax treatment associated with it.[46] It is also argued that closely held banks may find debt to be a less expensive capital source as new equity injections would come from investors that realize they will have a minor ownership role.[47] Both influences would suggest increased reliance on sub-debt would be cost saving.

There are, however, some additional actual or potential costs to increased sub-debt issues. First, increased reliance on relatively frequent debt rollovers would generate transaction costs or issuance costs. There is disagreement as to just how expensive these costs would be. Some argue that the cost would be similar to that required for issuing bank CDs while others argue that the cost could be quite substantial. The issuance frequency discussed in most sub-debt proposals, however, is not very different from the current frequency of large banking organizations. Two issues per year, which is well within the recommendations in most sub-debt proposals, is relatively common in today's banking markets.[48]

A more significant concern seems to be where, within the overall banking organization, the debt would be issued. Most sub-debt proposals require the debt to be issued at the bank level whereas, until recently, most sub-debt was issued at the bank holding company level. This allowed the holding company the flexibility to distribute the proceeds throughout the affiliated firms in the organization. This occurred in spite of the fact that rating agencies typically rated bank debt higher than the debt of the holding company and, similarly, holding company debt typically traded at a premium to comparable bank debt.[49] This would suggest that the additional flexibility from issuing at the holding company level has value for the banking organization, and elimination of this flexibility, which most of the proposals would do, would impose costs. The recent trend toward issuing more debt at the bank level, however, would suggest the value of this flexibility has become less important than in the past.

A more important cost implication is imbedded in our sub-debt proposal. In the past, regulators have restricted the use of sub-debt by limiting the amount that could count as capital and by requiring that the value of the sub-debt be amortized over the last five years before maturity. These restrictions are imposed because, unlike equity, the firm will still need to make periodic payments on the debt, regardless of its financial condition. However, this does not decrease the effectiveness of sub-debt in serving the capital role as a cushion against losses. It still buffers the insurance fund. By eliminating these restrictions in our sub-debt proposal we enhance the value of the debt as capital and decrease the net cost of introducing the proposal.

❏ *Isn't there a problem in that sub-debt proposals are procyclical?*

A possible concern with sub-debt requirements is that they may encourage procyclical behavior by banks, increased lending during economic expansions and exacerbating the decline in lending during recessions. However, this is not unique to sub-debt programs; any regulatory requirement that does not adjust over the course of a business cycle has the potential to be procyclical if banks seek to only satisfy the minimum requirements. For example, Appendix D of Kwast et al. (1999), points out that bank capital adequacy ratios are likely to decline during recessions as banks experience higher loan losses, implying that regulation based on capital adequacy ratios has the potential to be procyclical.[50]

The procyclicality of a regulatory requirement may be at least partially offset if banks seek to maintain some cushion above minimum regulatory requirements that they may draw on during economic downturns. In the case of the regulatory capital adequacy requirements, both casual observation of recent bank behavior and formal empirical analysis from the 1980s and early 1990s suggest that banks do indeed seek to maintain such a cushion for contingencies.[51]

Moreover, a regulatory program that uses sub-debt yields as triggers for regulatory action can be designed to induce less procyclical behavior than would other types of regulatory requirements. Consider two ways to design the sub-debt triggers as discussed in Kwast et al. (1999). One design is to base regulatory action on a constant basis point spread over bonds with little or no credit risk, such as Treasury securities. Such a standard is more likely to become binding during recessions when banks are experiencing loan losses and investors demand higher risk premiums to continue holding bank bonds. Thus, a policy that sets triggers at a constant premium over Treasury may result in procyclical regulation in a manner similar to that of standard capital requirements.

Another way of designing the triggers, however, is to base them on a measure that has yields which vary countercyclically over the business cycle.

One such measure is the yields on corporate bonds of a given rating. There is evidence that bond-rating agencies seek to smooth ratings through business cycles. For example, Theodore (1999, p. 10) describes Moody's ratings policies as follows:

> Moody's bank ratings . . . aim at looking to the medium- to long-term, through cyclical trends. For example, a drop in quarterly, semi-annual or even annual earnings is not necessarily a reason to downgrade a bank's ratings. However, if the earnings drop is the result of a structural degradation of a bank's fundamentals, credit ratings need to reflect the new developing condition of the bank.

If the rating agencies are trying to "look through the business cycle," then the spreads on corporate bonds over default risk-free securities should be small during expansions because investors, but not the rating agencies, recognize a lower probability of default during expansions. Similarly, the spreads on corporate bonds over default risk-free bonds should rise during recessions as the market, but not the rating agencies, recognize the increased probability of default. Thus, prompt corrective action triggers based on sub-debt yields relative to corporate yields introduce an element of smoothing into the triggers. The triggers may be relatively tight during expansions when banks should be building financial strength and relatively loose during downturns as they draw down part of their reserves.

One case where the use of sub-debt yields may tend to reinforce the business cycle is when liquidity drops in all corporate bond markets and risk premiums (including liquidity risk premiums) temporarily soar.[52] However, our proposal recognizes this potential problem and provides for temporary relief until liquidity improves.

❏ *Aren't supervisors better gauges of the riskiness of a bank because they know more about each bank's exposure than does the market? If so, then why not rely exclusively on the supervisors instead of holders of sub-debt?*

In some cases the market's knowledge of a bank's exposure may indeed be a subset of the examiner's knowledge. However, we rely on markets to discipline firm risk taking in virtually every other sector of our economy, so markets must have some offsetting advantages. One such advantage is that the financial markets are likely to be better able to price the risks they observe because market prices reflect the consensus of many observers investing their own funds. Another advantage of markets is that they can avoid limitations inherent in any type of government supervision. Supervisors are rightfully reluctant to be making fundamental business decisions for banks unless or until results confirm the bank is becoming unsafe or unsound. Further, even when supervisors recognize a serious potential problem, they have the burden of being able to prove to a court that a bank is engaged in unsafe activities. In contrast, in financial markets the burden of proof is on the bank to show it is being safely managed. A further weakness of relying solely on bank supervisors is that they are ultimately accountable to the political system which suggests that noneconomic factors may enter into major decisions no matter how hard supervisors try to focus solely on the economics of a bank's position.[53] Sub-debt investors have no such accountability; they may be expected to focus solely on the economic condition of individual banks.

A typical concern surrounding sub-debt proposals is that the perceived intent is to supplant supervisors and rely solely on the forces of the marketplace to oversee bank behavior. In our proposal, the intent is to augment, not reduce supervisory oversight. If supervisors have additional information about the condition of a bank, there is nothing in the sub-debt proposals limiting their ability to impose sanctions on the activities of the bank. In addition to sub-debt serving the standard role as a loss absorbing capital cushion, it serves as an additional tool for use by both the private markets *and* the regulators to objectively discipline banks. In fact, one of the major components of our proposal was to have the supervisors incorporate the yield spreads for use in prompt corrective action. With private markets providing information, supervisors can focus their efforts on exceptional circumstances, leaving the well-understood risks for assessment by the marketplace.

❏ *Can't the case be made that sub-debt is inferior to equity?*

An alternative argument against greater reliance on sub-debt is that the same benefits, plus additional ones could be obtained by relying exclusively on equity. For example, Levonian (1999) argues that: (1) each dollar of increased equity will generate the same discipline as an additional dollar of sub-debt, (2) sub-debt is not a superior source of information about bank condition because market participants and regulators may use equity prices to infer the same information (thus, there is not difference in the extent of derived discipline), and (3) equity is more desirable because it can absorb losses without forcing the closure of the bank. These arguments have some theoretical merit, but are not nearly as strong in practice.

Levonian's argument that additional equity can generate as much direct discipline as a comparable amount of sub-debt is correct under certain circumstances. In some cases equity-holders benefit from increased risk exposure because they receive all of the benefits, but bear only part of the losses if the bank should become insolvent. Sub-debt generates direct discipline by adjusting the bank's cost of funds to offset changes in the risk borne by sub-debt-holders and, thereby making equity-holders bear more of the expected losses resulting from failure. Indeed, *if* the closure rule is independent of a bank's equity level then equal increases in outstanding equity and sub-debt will have the same effect on the proportion of losses in failure borne by equity-holders. The key to this result is that sub-debt-holders as well as equity-holders face limited liability. Thus, just as equity-holders do not demand compensation for risks they do not bear, sub-debt-holders similarly do not demand compensation for risks they do not bear.

One weaknesses of Levonian's arguments on direct discipline is the assumption of a fixed closure rule; that is, the value of assets is assumed to be random and the bank will be kept open, regardless of its condition, until time T at which time it can be closed. As such, his analysis is incapable of fully analyzing the merits of many sub-debt proposals, *including ours*, that are partially or wholly justified on the grounds that regulators have an incentive to engage in forbearance towards financially weak banks. These proposals advocate the use of sub-debt with mandatory triggers for regulatory action to limit bank regulators' ability to engage in forbearance. Moreover, if sub-debt is used to trigger regulatory action and this leads to reduced forbearance then that would have the desirable side effect of increasing the effectiveness of the direct discipline from both equity and sub-debt-holders. Equity-holders' incentive to take additional risk arises in large part because the bank's owners retain virtually all of the gains from successful, high risk ventures, but the safety net absorbs a large fraction of the losses. If the probability of forbearance is reduced then so is the probability that equity-holders may gain at the expense of the safety net.

An additional weakness of Levonian's argument on direct discipline is that it ignores the tax benefit of debt. One of Horvitz's arguments in favor of increased sub-debt requirements is that regulators could impose higher sub-debt requirements than they would impose on equity because of the cost advantages of sub-debt. Thus, Levonian's comparison of a bank issuing equal amounts of equity or sub-debt may understate the amount of discipline that would be generated by a plan that increases the role of sub-debt.[54] Furthermore, even if regulators do not impose higher capital requirements, banks' expected after tax earnings will be higher if they are allowed to issue debt rather than equity.

Levonian's finding that debt and equity provide equally good signals of a bank's risk exposure also collapses when we recognize some real world features that are not in his model. He builds his case by modeling subordinated debt as a contingent claim on the bank's assets and showing that, like equity-holders, debt-holders may also benefit from increased risk taking. He acknowledges that one important assumption of his analysis is that in constructing the model, one must know what investors assume about the rules used by regulators to determine when a bank will be closed. Without this knowledge, the size of the safety net subsidy impounded in equity prices cannot be inferred and, thus, neither can the value of the bank absent the safety net. The result could be that regulators could infer that a bank was solvent when it is actually insolvent, and vice versa.

A second, unacknowledged assumption is that in constructing the model one must also know the statistical process generating bank returns and the model parameters must be accurately estimated using historical data. Losses sufficiently large to generate bank failure are relatively rare events or, in the terms used in Value at Risk (VaR) analyses, are tail events. VaR analysis is used to estimate the largest loss on bank market risk portfolios that could occur with a given probability. However, the results from analyzing different VaR models suggest that their results are sensitive to the statistical distribution of the returns and the method used to estimate the parameters from historical data.[55] Both the statistical process generating bank portfolio returns and the parameters of that distribution must be estimated from stock return data in order to obtain information about a bank's probability of failure. Significant errors in estimating either may translate into large errors in estimating a bank's risk of failure.[56]

The problems with model error are especially severe in interpreting equity returns and prices because the relationship between risk and equity prices is likely to be non-monotonic. That is, over some ranges equity prices may decline in response to an increase in risk, especially if the risk is not adequately compensated for by higher expected returns. However, over other, higher risk ranges, a similar uncompensated increase in risk may lead to higher stock prices. Why is the relationship not monotonic? At lower levels of risk, any increase in risk will be borne almost entirely by equity-holders and they may respond to the higher risk by bidding down the firm's stock price. However, at higher levels of risk, most of the increase in risk of losses will be borne by creditors, whereas equity-holders will obtain most of the gains and, therefore, will bid up the firms' stock price.[57] Thus, merely observing an increase in equity returns is not sufficient to determine whether a bank has become more or less risky. In order to interpret the returns, one must have an accurate model of bank portfolio returns.

In contrast, over the normal range of bank operations, an increase in risk will unambiguously lead to lower sub-debt prices.[58] Supervisors would need the correct model of bank portfolio returns to obtain *all* of the information embedded in sub-debt prices. However, the monotonicity of the relationship implies that an increase in sub-debt risk premiums is almost certainly associated with an increase in a bank's risk.[59] Moreover, if the yield on sub-debt is at rates comparable to other credits rated "A" then all of the other bank's liabilities must similarly be no more risky than "A" because sub-debt is junior to all other debt.

A further practical problem with using equity prices arises if supervisors seek to focus on the riskiness of the bank, since that is the entity covered by the safety net. In the U.S., all large banks are virtually 100% owned by holding companies and do not have publicly traded stock. One possible reason for this is that the existence of minority shareholders at the bank level would inhibit managers' ability to operate the bank and its affiliates as a single entity. Thus, the regulators may be imposing substantial costs on holding companies if they require the subsidiary banks to issue publicly traded stock. In contrast, while most of the publicly traded sub-debt that is issued by banking organizations is issued by the holding company, a significant amount of traded sub-debt is also issued by the bank subsidiaries; and as noted above, this amount has increased in recent years. That some banks issue publicly traded sub-debt suggests that while the costs of issuing debt at the bank level may be greater than issuing at the holding company level, the cost difference may not be very large.

Finally, Levonian's analysis of the relative merits of increased equity and sub-debt in reducing the risk of failure relies on the argument that sub-debt will not generate additional direct discipline or provide superior risk signals. If sub-debt provides superior risk signals that may be used for derived supervisory discipline then a system relying on regulatory sub-debt requirements may be more effective at reducing the probability of failure than a system relying on equity. As argued in our proposal, the regulators may be able to use sub-debt yields in combination with prompt corrective action to encourage banks to reduce their risk of failure by setting the prompt corrective action triggers at yields comparable to highly rated firms. Thus, if further reducing the probability of failure is an important regulatory goal then the use of sub-debt yields as prompt corrective action triggers is more likely to be effective.

Thus, the argument that sub-debt is merely an inferior form of equity does not hold under closer analysis. Sub-debt does not have magical powers and higher equity levels do provide some discipline. However, the tax benefits of sub-debt reduce the cost of the debt relative to equity and imply that the regulators may impose higher total capital requirements if sub-debt is an important part of the mix. Furthermore, sub-debt may provide a useful signal about the riskiness of a bank's other liabilities even in the absence of a formal model of bank portfolio returns. In contrast, equity prices may be interpreted only in the context of a specific model, a model that will almost surely be wrong. Thus, sub-debt is superior both in providing information to regulators and as a trigger that limits regulatory forbearance.

❏ *Won't banks attempt to circumvent sub-debt discipline?*

Banks may be reasonably expected to minimize their costs of production, including the costs of complying with supervisory requirements. If the sub-debt is used to help enforce discipline, banks will seek to minimize those costs just as they currently seek to minimize the costs associated with meeting the capital requirements. This involves efforts to reduce both direct and derived discipline. Banks may reduce the burden of direct discipline by minimizing the amount of debt they are required to issue. They can reduce the effectiveness of both direct and derived discipline by minimizing the rate they pay on the debt.

Banks will attempt to minimize the amount of required sub-debt in the same way they currently reduce their capital requirements; by exploiting inaccuracies in the measurement of their risk exposure. Indeed, the problems with setting appropriate sub-debt requirements are identical to the problems with setting appropriate Tier 1 and total capital requirements under existing capital regulations. Consequently, the gains in direct discipline from sub-debt may be limited and may yield little more direct discipline than would result from an increase in the current capital requirements. Although efforts are ongoing to improve the regulatory risk measures used in the capital standards, we are not particularly sanguine about the near term prospects for the development of reliable, accurate measures of risk from direct analysis of bank portfolios. The problems of accurately measuring risk are likely to be especially severe for the banks the regulators are most concerned about, financially weak ones. Thus, while our proposal seeks to enhance direct discipline, it does not rely exclusively on this to discipline banks' risk exposure. As additional expertise is developed, it may be possible to place greater reliance on direct discipline in the future.

Banks may try to avoid derived discipline based on sub-debt yields by minimizing the rate they pay on sub-debt by misleading investors about the condition of the bank. However, again, this is not new. Banks currently have incentives to mislead investors (for example, to boost their stock price, or pay lower interest on current sub-debt or certificate of deposits). In fact, a variety of regulatory measures have been taken to reduce banks' ability to mislead; perhaps the most important of these being the disclosure and audit requirements imposed by the Securities and Exchange Commission on issuers of publicly traded securities. Bank regulators also require banking organizations to file financial statements and have on-site examinations during which the accuracy of the statements can be evaluated.

The ability of market participants to evaluate bank risk exposures given existing disclosure requirements may be seen from the performance of bank securities around the time of disclosures related to Latin American loan problems in the 1980s. Banks were not required to disclose lending by country at the start of these problems and refused to recognize the extent of the losses on their financial statements for several years. Nevertheless, several studies, most recently Musumeci and Sinkey (1990a, 1990b) find evidence that investors were able to determine which banks were most at risk early in the crisis. Moreover, when banks finally recognized the loan losses in their financial statements the markets interpreted this as good news, suggesting that bank stock prices had already discounted the losses associated with the loans.

Derived discipline depends on the ability of bank regulators and other market participants to observe market prices that accurately reflect the riskiness of issuing banks. Financially troubled banks may try to reduce the sensitivity of market prices by encouraging related parties to buy the debt at artificially high prices. While this course may be tempting to banks facing significant regulatory sanctions, successful deception is likely to be limited. The investors, the rating agencies and the regulators are all likely to notice big discrepancies between observed sub-debt prices and prices that fairly reflect the riskiness of the bank.

❏ *Do we currently know enough about the sub-debt market to proceed?*

Although we would like to know more about the sub-debt market, we think considerable information is already available. The studies surveyed and the new evidence presented in Kwast et al. provide considerable insight into the sub-debt market. These studies suggest that investors in sub-debt do discriminate on the basis of the riskiness of their portfolios.

Moreover, a review of the regulatory alternatives suggests that any durable solution to achieving an objective measure of banks' risk exposure will look something like our proposal. The problems that plague the existing risk-based capital guidelines are inherent in any attempt by the supervisors to measure the riskiness of a bank's portfolio based on a pre-specified set of criteria. Overtime, banks will find or will manufacture claims whose intrinsic contribution to the riskiness of the bank's portfolio is underestimated by the supervisory criteria.[60] That is, banks will attempt to arbitrage the capital requirements.

An alternative to supervisory determined criteria is to use market evaluations. The Basel Committee on Banking Supervision correctly moved in this direction with its proposed new capital adequacy framework. However, it chose to ask opinions of market participants rather than observing market prices and quantities. The Committee then compounded this by proposing to ask the opinions of the two parties, the banks and their rating agencies, with incentives to underestimate the true risk exposure.

A superior system for obtaining a market based risk measure will use observed data from financial markets on price or quantity, or both. That is, it will use a market test. The relevant question to be addressed is which instruments should be observed, how should these instruments be structured, and how can supervisors best extract the risk signal from the noise generated by other factors that may influence observed prices and quantities. In principle, any uninsured bank obligation can provide the necessary information. We favor sub-debt because we think it will provide the cleanest signal.

There are alternatives to sub-debt. Common equity may currently have the advantages of being issued by all large banks and of trading in more liquid markets. However, investors in bank common equity will sometimes bid up stock prices in response to *greater* risk taking so their signal can only be interpreted in the context of a model that backs the option value of putting the bank back to the firm's creditors (including the deposit insurer). In contrast, valuable information can be extracted from sub-debt without a complicated model. If a bank's debt trades at prices equivalent to Baa corporate bonds then its other liabilities are at least Baa quality.

Banks also issue a variety of other debt obligations that could be used to measure their risk exposure.[61] The use of any debt obligation that was explicitly excluded from the systemic risk exception in FDICIA could provide a superior risk measure to those proposed by the Basel Committee. We think that sub-debt is the best choice because it is the least senior of all debt obligations if a bank should fail and, therefore, its yields provide the clearest signal about the potential risk that the bank will fail. We think sufficient information exists to adopt a sub-debt proposal with the understanding that the plan will be refined and made more effective as additional information and analyses becomes available.

SUMMARY AND CONCLUSIONS

The goal of this article has been to provide a comprehensive review and evaluation of bank capital reform proposals that incorporate a mandatory sub-debt component. Toward that goal, we provided the arguments behind capital proposals incorporating sub-debt, and emphasized that the stated objective of the capital program should dictate which of the characteristics are included. We then reviewed the evidence on the extent of market pricing of risk and the direct discipline imposed by holders of bank liabilities and briefly summarized some of the existing sub-debt proposals emphasizing their differences and the reasoning for those differences. Next, we presented a new sub-debt proposal which incorporates many of the characteristics, and resulting advantages, described in the early sections of this article, as well as some new characteristics. Finally we responded to some of the common issues raised about the potential viability of sub-debt proposals.

We conclude that although legislative and regulatory reform during the 1990s attempted to properly align the incentives of both banks and bank supervisors, ongoing market developments are undercutting the effectiveness of both market and supervisory discipline. Arguably, the potential for systemic risk has increased in recent years as banks have grown larger and more complex. Unquestionably, banks' ability to game the regulatory risk measures has grown significantly over the same period.

We argue that a well structured sub-debt program provides a viable mechanism for providing increased market *and* supervisory discipline in banking. While markets do not have perfect foresight, they are both flexible enough to accept promising innovations and willing to acknowledge their mistakes, even if such recognition is politically inconvenient. Sub-debt is already proving to provide workable signals in today's financial markets. We propose to combine these signals with the gradual discipline provided under prompt corrective action with a goal of augmenting supervisory oversight with market-based discipline.

Our sub-debt proposal is couched within the existing evidence on market discipline in banking and draws on the insights of previous proposals and policy changes. It provides for phased implementation and leaves room for future modifications as additional details concerning the market for sub-debt are determined. The plan calls for specific changes in those areas were we feel confident the evidence is relatively clear, such as the fact that large solvent banks should be able to issue sub-debt at least once a year. In those areas where the evidence is weak to non-existent, we defer decisions until additional study has taken place. This should enhance the credibility of the plan. Although the details of the plan can evolve over time, once the basics are implemented the industry and the public would have the benefit of having bank behavior be significantly influenced by both market and supervisory oversight. The effective combination should make for a more efficient, safe and sound industry.

NOTES

1. See Title 1, Section 108 of the Gramm-Leach-Bliley Act.
2. For a relatively recent discussion of this issue see Feldman and Rolnick (1997).

3. Alternatives include eliminating or lowering deposit insurance coverage [Volcker (1985)], privatizing deposit insurance [England (1985), Ely (1985)], introducing co-insurance programs in which publicly provided deposit insurance would be heavily augmented with private insurance coverage [Baer (1985), Stern (1988,1997)], as well as returning deposit insurance to the *de jure* levels and encouraging regulatory discipline to mimic market discipline through some form of structured early intervention by supervisors [Benston and Kaufman (1988a, 1988b, 1994)].

4. Kane's (1977) analysis suggests that any binding regulation will elicit avoidance behavior by firms. Numerous empirical studies of banking support his contention; e.g. Pyle (1974), Startz (1979), Brewer (1988), Evanoff (1988).

5. For example, see Carey and Hrycay (2000).

6. Some would argue it was an explicit guarantee as a result of Comptroller of the Currency Conover's comments surrounding the Continental of Illinois reorganization in the 1980s; see Carrington (1984) and O'Hare and Shaw (1990).

7. For example, see Caprio, et al. (1998).

8. A key assumption in the argument that shareholders prefer more risk is that they may diversify across many companies so that their losses from the failure of any given firm is a small proportion of their total wealth. A firm's managers are likely to have a substantially larger part of their wealth invested in the firm, especially when the manager's human capital is included in wealth. Thus, managers may be more risk averse than are shareholders and may have an incentive to take less than the optimal amount of risk. However, equity-holders are likely to recognize the manager's incentives and to encourage managers (through additional compensation) to take more risk when the increased risk maximizes the value of the firm's equity. Noe, Rebello and Wall (1996) provide an example of how such compensation would work for banks.

9. See Buser, Chen and Kane (1981).

10. In contrast, if a firm issues long term debt and the debt matures after the investment is completed, then the firm may take on relatively high-risk projects before debt-holders can respond. Firms with long-lived, illiquid assets tend to rely more on long-term debt in part because they have a greater potential to experience an involuntary increase in their riskiness (such as during a recession) and want to avoid the additional funding cost short-term debt would impose during these periods.

11. See section 4 of Berger, Herring and Szego (1995) for a discussion of "systemic risk". In the literature there is disagreement on precisely what constitutes systemic risk and the extent to which it exists; see Bartholomew and Caprio (1998), Kaufman (1996) and Basing (1993).

12. It should be emphasized that introduction of the safety net did not result in all banks immediately taking excessive risks. In most cases the expected gains from excessive risk taking were less than the expected gains from operating prudently – those being the value of the government charter and the value of existing intangible assets that would be lost if the bank failed. Furthermore, both suppliers of funds and customers may be less likely to commit to long-term relationships with a bank that has a substantial probability of failing. However, the distorting impact of the safety net should not be understated. As the riskier banks took on additional risk, they funded those activities by paying more for deposits. To remain competitive, the banks choosing not to take on risky projects still had to respond by paying more for funding. The higher funding cost might then make riskier investments look more attractive for all banks.

13. For example, dividend payments may become restricted if the bank's total capital ratio falls below 8%. Interest rates paid on new deposits may be restricted when it falls to 6%.

14. See Jones 2000. While the development of more accurate risk models opens up the possibility for basing regulatory capital requirements on a bank's internal model, there are problems with confirming the accuracy of these models. Measuring the probability of large losses is extremely difficult, especially for those parts of the bank portfolio that are not traded in liquid financial markets. Moreover, the problems are exacerbated in that the very banks that are most likely to produce models that underestimate their true risk (i.e. financially weak banks) are precisely the ones that are likely to be of greatest supervisory concern.

15. Somewhat surprisingly, however, there have recently been statements by U.S. financial regulators about increasing deposit insurance to $200,000 per account [see Tanoue (2000)].

16. FDICIA discourages such loans. However, the Federal Reserve is only penalized and not prohibited from making extended discount window loans to undercapitalized banks. Additionally, the FDICIA penalties arise only if the bank is undercapitalized under the regulatory capital measures. A bank with market-value capital that is clearly inadequate for its actual risk exposure may have *book value* capital that is easily sufficient to cover its risks as measured by existing regulatory capital measures. For a discussion of potential problems induced by inappropriate discount window administration see Broaddus (2000).

17. Calomiris (1998) also strongly advocates the advantages of an explicit safety net over an implicit one. While regulators cannot prevent market participants from assigning positive probability to the existence of an implicit safety net, the approach currently being taken in the U.S. towards least cost resolution is likely contributing to the belief that the future use of implicit guarantees will be uncommon. Statements by regulatory authorities projecting the end of too-big-to-fail policies may also contribute to this belief [see Greenspan (2000)]. However, the closure of a large, complex bank raises a number of difficult questions about the treatment of some of its more complex activities, such as its derivatives activities. The market may reasonably conjecture that a high probability exists that the systemic risk exception will be invoked in the absence of a credible, previously announced plan for closing such a bank. Thus, if least cost resolution is to help generate additional market discipline at the largest and most complex banks, the regulatory agencies should develop and announce how these banks would be closed without invoking the system risk exception.

18. With few exceptions we only survey the literature on market discipline in the U.S. A review of the literature for developing countries is provided in Martinez Peria and Schmukler (1998). A more comprehensive literature survey of U.S. banking is provided in Kwast, et al. (1999).

19. A risk premia was found in Baer and Brewer (1986), Cargill (1989), Ellis and Flannery (1992), Hannan and Hanweck (1988), James (1988, 1990), and Keeley (1990). Earlier studies by Crane (1976), and Herzig-Marx and Weaver (1979) did not find evidence of market discipline. These earlier studies are reviewed in Gilbert (1990); particularly pp. 13–15. A more recent study of CD rates is Hall, et al. (1999).

20. These early studies include Beighley (1977), Fraser and McCormack (1978), Herzig-Marx (1979), Pettway (1976), Avery, Belton and Goldberg (1988), and Gorton and Santomero (1990).

21. Although an analysis of the spread-to-bank-risk relationship was not the expressed purpose of this study, it was a byproduct. Rather the purpose was to determine the extent to which bank examiners could ascertain information about banks beyond that obtained by private market agents. Nevertheless, part of the analysis included changes in bank spreads regressed on an array of balance sheet and market risk measures.

22. For a discussion of the latter argument see Kwast and Passmore (1997).

23. Kane (2000) and Penas and Unal (2000) also question whether too-big-to-fail, and the resulting implicit guarantees, is exclusively a policy of the past.

24. The authors compute the proportion of the variance explained by the bank risk measures and find that these variables explain a significant portion of the variance of deposits; a larger portion in more recent years.

25. The authors acknowledge that they ignore this aspect of potential influence by debt holders. Nevertheless, they still draw rather strong policy conclusions.

26. The bank should, of course, consider the impact of the action on its creditors. However, the impact on the creditors is important through its affect on the expected profitability of the action to the firm's shareholder.

27. See Pilloff (1996) and Pilloff and Santomerro (1997) for a review of the literature on merger effects.

28. While acquiring another firm may reduce shareholder wealth, such actions are unlikely to materially increase a bank's risk of failure given that bank supervisors must have approved all acquisitions during the Bliss and Flannery sample period. Indeed, we have difficulty imagining a situation where a manager would undertake action that would materially increase a bank's risk of failure and simultaneously reduce shareholder wealth. If the bank fails then the manager lose not only their investment in the bank's stock but also any firm specific human capital they may have developed and they may damage their reputation in the managerial labor market.

29. In this study, and others, the information available to examiners is assumed to be embedded in the official bank or holding company ratings; i.e. CAMEL or BOPEC ratings.

30. Formally the authors test to see if lagged supervisory variables help predict current market variables and if lagged market variables help predict current supervisory variables. They use Granger causality tests to determine whether information from one group helped 'predict' the assessment of the other group. The private market assessment used was ratings by Bond Market Rating agencies.

31. They also found that after taking into account the market assessment of bank condition, additional supervisory information (BOPEC data) did not contribute significantly to predicting future bank holding company performance.

32. More generally, in recent years there have been growing concern about the need to increase the role of market discipline in banking. See, for example, Ferguson (1999), Meyer (1999), Stern (1998), Boyd and Rolnick (1988), Broaddus (1999), and Moskow (1998).

33. This benefit is not relevant for all countries. Our emphasis is on U.S. banks.

34. Additional discussion of the role of sub-debt in this plan can be found in Evanoff (1993, 1994).

35. Regulatory restrictions would be prompt-corrective-action-type constraints such as limits to dividend payments, or restrictions on deposit and asset growth rates once core equity fell below 2% of risk weighted assets.

36. The sub-debt requirement is only one component of Calomiris' regulatory reform proposal aimed at modifying industry structure and the operating procedures of the International Monetary Fund. It would also include a mandatory minimum reserve requirement (20% of bank debt in Calomiris (1998)), minimum securities requirement, and explicit deposit insurance. Although some details of his proposal, such as requiring the debt be issued to foreign banks, may not be feasible for U.S. banks, the general approach provides interesting insights into the issues in designing a sub-debt plan for the U.S.

37. This is not the first time proposals have suggested sub-debt be linked with prompt corrective action, see Evanoff (1993, 1994) and Litan (2000).

38. The proposal is also discussed in Evanoff and Wall (2000a) and a more detailed description of the potential use of debt spreads for prompt corrective action is discussed in Evanoff and Wall (2000b).

39. As discussed earlier, the current bank capital requirement framework is being reevaluated [see Bank for International Settlement (1999)]. As part of the debate, some have recommended total elimination of the Tier 1 vs. Tier 2 distinction [e.g. Litan (2000)]. If this approach is taken we would recommend that minimum leverage requirements be maintained to insure sufficient levels of equity (although it would be in sub-debt holders self interest to insure this occurs) and to provide supervisors with an official tool for intervening when equity levels fall to unacceptable levels.

40. When fully implemented, the policy would apply to 'banks' instead of the bank holding company. During this surveillance stage, however, information could be gained at both levels.

41. The only exception would occur if general market conditions precluded debt issuance by the corporate sector (both financial and nonfinancial firms). This exception requires more specific details, but it would be an industry-wide exception instead of bank-specific.

42. The objective is to limit "regulatory gaming"; see Jones (2000). Additional minimum denomination constraints could be imposed to further insure that debt holders are sophisticated investors [e.g. see U.S. Shadow Regulatory Committee, 2000)].

43. Depending on the depth of the secondary market, this time period may need to be extended to a couple of weeks. Again, the timeframe could be modified as more market information is obtained. Additionally, to allow for flexibility under extreme conditions, procedures could be introduced by which the presumption could be overturned given the approval of the FDIC upon request by the bank's primary federal supervisor. The procedures for this exception, however, would be quite stringent. It would be somewhat similar to the procedures currently in place for too-big-to-fail exceptions; e.g. submission of a public document to Congress, etc.

44. For example, should risk be measured as the spread between the yield on a sub-debt issue and a comparable maturity U.S. Treasury security? The yield on a bank's sub-debt vs. the yield on comparable maturity corporate bonds in different ratings classes? Or the spread over Libor after the bond is swapped into floating rate funds?

45. This is not to say that the detailed parameters should be introduced at this time. As argued above, additional analysis is required before these could be decided upon.

46. Jones (1998) suggests the cost of equity could be twice that of debt once the tax differences are accounted for. Benston (1992) discusses the cost differences and other advantages of sub-debt over equity capital.

47. Alternatively, the current owners could inject equity but that may be costly in that it places them in a situation where they are relatively undiversified.

48. See Kwast et al. (1999) for a discussion of current market practices.

49. This holding company premium is typically associated with the bank having access to the safety net and the associated lower risk of default during times of financial stress. Alternatively, it has been argued the differential results from the different standing of the two debt-holders. Holders of bank debt have a higher priority claim on the assets during liquidation of the bank than do the holders of holding company debt, which essentially have an equity claim on the bank.

50. The appendix was prepared by Thomas Brady and William English of the Board of Governors of the Federal Reserve System. Most of the comments in this section attributed to Kwast et al. come from this appendix.

51. Arguably, to the extent the capital requirements caused a reduction in bank lending during the early 1990s, it was because banks were trying to increase their capital ratios due to new requirements at the same time they were experiencing higher loan losses. A discussion of this "capital crunch" literature is provided in Hancock and Wilcox (1997, 1998). After banks have time to rebalance their portfolios in response to new capital requirements they are likely to have a cushion to absorb the higher loan losses incurred during recessions. Wall and Peterson (1987, 1995) find evidence that banks seek to maintain capital ratios in excess of regulatory requirements and speculate that part of the reason for the higher ratios is to absorb unexpected losses.

52. The liquidity crunch in the Fall of 1998, or the Long Term Capital episode, is a possible example of such a problem period.

53. For example, the *American Banker* reports that the OCC is threatening to downgrade bank's safety and soundness rating if they fail to supply accurate CRA data; see Seiberg (1999).

54. To be fair to Levonian's analysis, he also assumes that the sub-debt may be continuously repriced to reflect changes in the bank's riskiness whereas existing regulatory standards prohibit any risk-based repricing. Thus, his analysis also overstates the amount of direct discipline arising from sub-debt designed to qualify as capital under existing capital standards.

55. See for example Kupiec (1995). The difficulty of identifying the probability of extreme events with small samples is also highlighted by Christoffersen, Diebold and Schuermann (1998) who argue that "for performing statistical inference on objects such as a 'once every hundred years' quantile, the relevant measure of sample size is likely better approximated by the number of nonoverlapping hundred-year intervals in the data set than by the actual number of data points."

56. One way of addressing the problem of determining the regulatory closure rule would be to use risk measures derived from equity returns to trigger a regulatory response. However, the use of such a rule would create a circular feedback from equity prices to regulatory action to equity prices that would need to be disentangled to properly interpret equity returns. We conjecture that if the return generating process and its parameters are known then it may be possible to disentangle the circular feedback to provide accurate risk measurements. However, if return generating process, its parameters, or both, are unknown then using equity prices as a trigger for regulatory action would likely compound the errors in estimating the bank's financial condition.

57. This analysis assumes that debt-holders cannot obtain adequate compensation for the increase in risk, as is likely to be the case with the existing safety net.

58. The exception arises when a bank suffers sufficient losses in excess of its equity. However, these exceptions should be relatively easy to identify from very high observed sub-debt yields since investors will likely not be expecting to be repaid in full.

59. The exception to this occurs when the risk-free interest rate increases or when the liquidity risk premium substantially increases. The risk-free rate is readily observable and easy to account for. We consider the issues associated with increasing liquidity premiums in the discussion of our sub-debt proposal.

60. Supervisor agencies could short-circuit this avoidance by having their examiners conduct subjective evaluations but that could easily result in examiners serving as shadow managers of banks.

61. Preferred stock is a form of equity but it would yield a clean signal unlike common equity. We do not propose the use of preferred stock for two reasons. First, dividend payments on preferred stock are not a deductible expense to the bank. Thus, forcing them to issue preferred stock would increase their costs. Second, discussions with market participants, as reported in Kwast et al. (1999, page 45), indicated that the preferred stock market is more heavily influenced by "relatively uninformed retail investors."

ACKNOWLEDGMENTS

The authors are economists at the Federal Reserve Bank of Chicago and the Federal Reserve Bank of Atlanta, respectively. They acknowledge constructive conversations about the topic with Herb Baer, Rob Bliss, Charles Calomiris, Bob DeYoung, Mark Flannery, George Kaufman, David Marshall, Jim Moser, and members of the Federal Reserve System's Task Force on Subordinated Debt and Debentures; particularly Dan Covitz, Diana Hancock, and Myron Kwast. The views expressed, however, are those of the authors and do not necessarily reflect the views of our colleagues mentioned above, the Federal Reserve Banks of Atlanta or Chicago, or the Federal Reserve System.

REFERENCES

Avery, R. B., Belton, T. M., & Goldberg, M. A. (1988). Market discipline in regulating bank risk: New evidence from the capital markets. *Journal of Money, Credit, and Banking*, 20.

Baer, H. (1985). Private prices, public insurance: The pricing of federal deposit insurance. *Economic Perspectives*, Federal Reserve Bank of Chicago.

Baer, H., & Brewer, E. (1986). Uninsured deposits as a source of market discipline: Some new evidence. *Economic Perspectives*, Federal Reserve Bank of Chicago (September).

Bank for International Settlement (1999). *A new capital adequacy framework*. Consultative Paper Issued by the Basel Committee on Banking Supervision, June.

The Bankers Roundtable (1998). *Market-Based Incentive Regulation and Supervision: A Paradigm for the Future*, Washington, D.C.

Bartholomew, P. F., & Caprio, G. (1998). Systemic risk, contagion, and the Southeast Asian financial crisis. Paper presented at a conference on *Restructuring Regulation & Financial Institutions*, Milken Institute (September), Santa Monica.

Basing, M. P. (1993). Comments on systemic risk. In: *Proceedings of a Conference on Bank Structure and Competition*. Chicago: Federal Reserve Bank of Chicago.

Beighley, H. P. (1977). The Risk Perceptions of Bank Holding Company Debtholders. *Journal of Bank Research* (Summer).

Benink, H. A., & Schmidt, R. H. (2000). Agenda for banking in Europe. In: G. G. Kaufman (Ed.), *Bank Fragility and Regulation: Evidence From Different Countries and Different Times*. Greenwich: JAI Press.

Benston, G. J. (1992). The purpose of capital for institutions with government-insured deposits. *Journal of Financial Services Research*, 5.

Benston, G. J., Eisenbeis, R. A., Horvitz, P. M., Kane, E. J., & Kaufman, G. G. (1986). *Perspectives on Safe and Sound Banking*. Cambridge: MIT Press.

Benston, G. J., & Kaufman, G. G. (1988a). *Risk and Solvency Regulation of Depository Institutions: Past Policies and Current Options*. Salomon Brothers Monograph Series in Finance and Economics #1988–1: Graduate School of Business Administration, New York University: New York.

Benston, G. J., & Kaufman, G. G. (1988b). Regulating bank safety and performance. In: W. S. Haraf & R.M.Kushmeider (Eds), *Restructuring Banking and Financial services in America*. Washington, D.C.: American Enterprise Institute for Public Policy Research.

Benston, G. J., & Kaufman, G. G. (1994). Improving the FDIC Improvement Act: What was done and what still needs to be done to fix the deposit insurance problem. In: G. G. Kaufman (Ed.), *Reforming Financial Institutions and Markets in the United States*. Boston: Kluwer Academic Publishers.

Benston, G. J., & Kaufman, G. G. (1998). Deposit insurance reform in the FDIC Improvement Act: The experience to date. *Economic Perspectives*. Federal Reserve Bank of Chicago. Second Quarter.

Berger, A. N., & Davies, S. M. (1994). The information content of bank examinations, in *Proceedings of a Conference on Bank Structure and Competition*. Chicago: Federal Reserve Bank of Chicago.

Berger, A. N., Davies, S. M., & Flannery, M. J. (1998). Comparing market and regulatory assessments of bank performance: Who knows what, when? *Working Paper Series*, Board of Governors of the Federal Reserve System, March.

Berger, A. N., Herring, R. J., & Szego, G. P. (1995). The role of capital in financial institutions. *Journal of Banking and Finance*, 19.

Billett, M. T., Garfinkel, J. A., & O'Neal, E. S. (1998), The cost of market vs. regulatory discipline in banking. *Journal of Financial Economics*, 48.

Bliss, R. R., & Flannery, M. J. (2000) Market discipline in the governance of U.S. bank holding companies: Monitoring vs. influencing. *Federal Reserve Bank of Chicago Working Paper*, WP–2000–3.

Boyd, J. H., & Rolnick, A. J. (1988) A case for reforming federal deposit insurance. *Annual Report*, Federal Reserve Bank of Minneapolis.

Brewer III, E. (1988). The impact of deregulation on the true cost of savings deposits. *Journal of Economics and Business*, 40.

Broaddus, J. A. Jr. (1999). Incentives and banking, Speech presented to the National Conference for Teachers of Advanced Placement Economics: Richmond, September 26.

Broaddus, J. A. Jr. (2000). Chicago: Market discipline and Fed lending. In: *Proceedings of a Conference on Bank Structure and Competition*. Federal Reserve Bank of Chicago, Chicago.

Buser, S. A., Chen, A. H., & Kane, E. J. (1981). Federal deposit insurance, regulatory policy, and optimal bank capital. *Journal of Finance*, 36.

Calomiris, C. W. (1997). *The Postmodern Bank Safety Net: Lessons from Developed and Developing Countries*. American Enterprise Institute for Public Policy Research, Washington.

Calomiris, C. W. (1998). *Blueprints for a New Global Financial Architecture*, September 23, American Enterprise Institute, Washington.

Calomiris, C. W. (1999). Building an incentive-compatible safety net. *Journal of Banking and Finance*, 23.

Calomiris, C. W., & Kahn, C. M. (1991). The role of demandable debt in structuring optimal banking arrangements. *American Economic Review*, 81.

Calomiris, C. W., & Powell, A. (2000). Can emerging market bank regulators establish credible discipline? The case of Argentina, 1992–1999. National Bureau of Economic Research Working Papers Series, #W7715, May.

Cargill, T. F. (1989). CAMEL ratings and the CD market. *Journal of Financial Services Research*, 3.

Caprio, G., Hunter, W. C., Kaufman, G. G., & Leipziger, D. M. (1998), *Preventing Bank Crises: Lessons from Recent Global Bank Failures*. Washington, D.C.: World Bank.

Carey, M., & Hrycay, M. (2000), Parameterizing credit risk models with rating data. *Proceedings of a Conference on Bank Structure and Competition*. Chicago: Federal Reserve Bank of Chicago.

Carrington, T. (1984). U.S. won't let 11 biggest banks in nation fail. *Wall Street Journal*, September 20.

Christoffersen, P. F., Diebold, F. X., & Schuermann, T. (1998). Horizon problems and extreme events in financial risk management. *Economic Policy Review*, Federal Reserve Bank of New York, 4.

Cole, R. A., & Gunther, J. W. (1998). Predicting bank failures: A comparison of on- and off-site monitoring systems. *Journal of Financial Services Research*, 13.

Cooper, K., & Fraser, D. R. (1988). The rising cost of bank failures: A proposed solution. *Journal of Retail Banking*, 10.

Covitz, D. M., Hancock, D., & Kwast, M. L. (2000). Market discipline, banking organizations and subordinated debt. Paper presented at the 2000 Global Finance Association Meetings, April 21, Chicago.

Crane, D. B. (1976). A study of interest rate spreads in the !974 CD market. *Journal of Bank Research*, 7.

Dahl, D., Hanweck, G., & O'Keefe, J. (1995). The influence of auditors and examiners on accounting discretion in the banking industry. *FDIC Working Paper*, October.

DeYoung, R., Flannery, M. J., Lang, W. W., & Sorescu, S. (1998). *The informational advantage of specialized monitors: The case of bank examiners*. Federal Reserve Bank of Chicago Working Paper Series, # 98–4, August.

Ellis, D. M., & Flannery, M. J. (1992). Does the debt market assess large banks' risk. *Journal of Monetary Economics*, 30.

Ely, B. (1985). Yes—Private sector depositor protection is a viable alternative to federal deposit insurance. In: *Proceedings of a Conference on Bank Structure and Competition*. Chicago: Federal Reserve Bank of Chicago.

England, C. (1985). A proposal for introducing private deposit insurance. In: *Proceedings of a Conference on Bank Structure and Competition*. Chicago: Federal Reserve Bank of Chicago.

Evanoff, D. D. (1988). Branch banking and service accessibility. *Journal of Money, Credit, and Banking*, 20.

Evanoff, D. D. (1993). Preferred sources of market discipline. *Yale Journal on Regulation*, 10.

Evanoff, D. D. (1994). Capital requirements and bank regulatory reform. In: C. A. Stone & A. Zissu (Eds), *Global Risk Based Capital Regulations: Capital Adequacy*. New York: Irwin.

Evanoff, D. D., & Wall, L. D. (2000a). Subordinated debt as bank capital: A proposal for regulatory reform. *Economic Perspectives*. Federal Reserve Bank of Chicago, Second Quarter.

Evanoff, D. D., & Wall, L. D. (2000b). The role of subordinated debt in bank safety and soundness regulations, In: *Proceedings of a Conference on Bank Structure and Competition*. Chicago: Federal Reserve Bank of Chicago.

Federal Deposit Insurance Corporation (1983). *Deposit Insurance in a Changing Environment: A study of the Current System of Deposit Insurance Pursuant to Section 712 of the Garn-St. Germain Depository Institution Act of 1982*. A Report to Congress on Deposit Insurance. Washington, D.C.: U.S. Government Printing Office.

Feldman, R. J., & Rolnick, A. J. (1997). Fixing FDICIA: A plan to address the too-big-to-fail problem. *Annual Report*. Federal Reserve Bank of Minneapolis.

Ferguson, R. W. Jr. (1999). Evolution of financial institutions and markets: Private and policy implications. Speech presented at New York University: New York, February 25.

Flannery, M. J. (1994). Debt maturity and the deadweight cost of leverage: Optimally financing banking firms. *The American Economic Review*, 84.

Flannery, M. J., & Sorescu, S. M. (1996). Evidence of bank market discipline in subordinated debenture yields: 1983–1991. *The Journal of Finance*, 51.

Fraser D. R., & McCormack, J. P. (1978). Large bank failures and investor risk perceptions: Evidence from the debt market. *Journal of Financial and Quantitative Analysis*, 13.

Gilbert, R. A. (1990). Market discipline of bank risk: Theory and evidence. *Economic Review*, Federal Reserve Bank of St. Louis (January/February).

Gorton, G., & Santomero, A. M. (1990). Market discipline and bank subordinated debt. *Journal of Money, Credit, and Banking*, 22.

Greenspan, A. (2000). Banking evolution. In: *Proceedings of a Conference on Bank Structure and Competition*. Chicago: Federal Reserve Bank of Chicago.

Hall, J. R., King, T. B., Meyer, A. P., & Vaughan, M. D. (1999). Do uninsured depositors and bank supervisors view bank risk similarly? A comparison of the factors affecting jumbo-CD yields and CAMEL scores. Presented at the Financial Management Association Meetings, Orlando Florida, November.

Hancock, D., & Wilcox, J. A. (1997). Bank capital, nonbank finance, and real estate activity. *Journal of Housing Research*, 8.

Hancock, D., & Wilcox, J. A. (1998). The 'credit crunch' and the availability of credit to small business. *Journal of Banking and Finance*, 22.

Hannan, T. H., & Hanweck, G. A. (1988) Bank insolvency risk and the market for large certificates of deposit. *Journal of Money, Credit, and Banking*, 20.

Herzig-Marx, C., & Weaver, A. (1979). Bank soundness and the market for large negotiable certificates of deposit. *Federal Reserve Bank of Chicago Staff Memoranda*, 79(1).

Horvitz, P. M. (1983). Market discipline is best provided by subordinated creditors. *American Banker*, July 15, p. 3.

Horvitz, P. M. (1984). Subordinated debt is key to new bank capital requirements. *American Banker*, December 31, p. 5.

Horvitz, P. M. (1987). A free-market approach to saving troubled banks. *American Banker*, December 10, p. 4.

Jagtiani, J., Kaufman, G. G., & Lemieux, C. (1999). Do markets discipline banks and bank holding companies? Evidence from debt pricing. presented at the American Economic Association meetings, January 3.

James, C. M. (1988). The use of loan sales and standby letters of credit by commercial banks. *Journal of Monetary Economics*, 22.

James, C. M. (1990). Heterogeneous creditors and the market value of bank LDC loan portfolios. *Journal of Monetary Economics*, 25.

Jones, D. S. (1998). Emerging problems with the Basle Accord: Regulatory capital arbitrage and related issues. Paper presented at a conference on *Credit Risk Modeling and the Regulatory Implications*, Bank of England (September).

Jones, D. S. (2000). Emerging problems with the Basel Capital Accord: Regulatory capital arbitrage and related issues. *Journal of Banking and Finance*, 24.

Kaufman, G. G. (1996). Bank failures, system risk, and bank regulation. *Cato Journal*, Spring.

Kane, E. J. (1977). Good intentions and unintended evil: The case against selective credit allocation. *Journal of Money, Credit, and Banking*, 9.

Kane, E. J. (2000). Incentives for banking megamergers: What motives might regulators infer from event-study evidence? In: *Proceedings of a Conference on Bank Structure and Competition*. Chicago: Federal Reserve Bank of Chicago.

Kane, E. J. (1989). *The S&L insurance mess: How did it happen?* Washington, D.C.: Urban Institute Press.

Keehn, S. (1989). *Banking on the Balance; Powers and the Safety Net*. Chicago: Federal Reserve Bank of Chicago.

Keeley, M. C. (1990). Deposit insurance, risk, and market power in banking. *American Economic Review*, 80.

Kupiec, P. H. (1995). Techniques for verifying the accuracy of risk measurement models. Board of Governors of the Federal Reserve System. *Finance and Economics Discussion Series*, 95(24).

Kwast, M. L., & Passmore, S. W. (1997). The subsidy provided by the federal safety net: Theory measurement and containment. Board of Governors of the Federal Reserve System. *Finance and Economics Discussion Series*, 97(58).

Kwast, M. L., Covitz, D. M., Hancock, D., Houpt, J. V., Adkins, D. P., Barger, N., Bouchard, B., Connolly, J. F., Brady, T. F., English, W. B., Evanoff, D. D., & Wall, L. D. (1999). Using subordinated debt as an instrument of market discipline. Report of a study group on subordinated notes and debentures, Board of Governors of the Federal Reserve System, M. Kwast (chair). *Staff Study*, No. 172, December.

Levonian, M. (1999). Using subordinated debt to enhance market discipline in banking. Memo, Federal Reserve Bank of San Francisco.

Litan, R. E. (2000) International Bank Capital Standards: Next Steps. In: J. R. Bisignano, W. C. Hunter & G. G. Kaufman (Eds), *Global Financial Crises: Lessons From Recent Events*. Boston: Kluwer Academic.

Litan, R. E., & Rauch, J. (1997). *American Finance for the 21st Century*. Washington, D.C.: U.S. Government Printing Office.

Marino, J. A., & Bennett, R. L. (1999). The consequences of national depositor preference. *Banking Review*. Federal Deposit Insurance Corporation, 12.

Martinez Peria, M. S., & Schmukler, S. L. (1998). Do depositors punish banks for 'bad' behavior? Examining market discipline in Argentina, Chile, and Mexico. *World Bank Working Paper Series, 2058* (December).

Meyer, L. H. (1999). Market discipline as a complement to bank supervision and regulation. Speech before the Conference on Reforming Bank Capital Standards, Council on Foreign Relations, New York, June 14.

Milhaupt, C. J. (1999). Japan's experience with deposit insurance and failing banks: Implications for financial regulatory design? *Monetary and Economic Studies, 17*.

Mingo, J. J. (1999). Policy implications of the Federal Reserve study of credit risk models at major US banking organizations. *Journal of Banking and Finance, 24*.

Morgan, D. P., & Stiroh, K. J. (2000). Bond market discipline of banks: Is the market tough enough? In: *Proceedings of a Conference on Bank Structure and Competition*. Chicago: Federal Reserve Bank of Chicago.

Moskow, M. H. (1998). Regulatory efforts to prevent banking crises. In: G. Caprio, W. C. Hunter, G. G. Kaufman & D. M. Leipziger (Eds), *Preventing Bank Crises: Lessons from Recent Global Bank Failures*. Washington, D.C.: World Bank.

Musumeci, J. J., & Sinkey, J. F. Jr. (1990a). The international debt crisis, investor contagion, and bank security returns in 1987: The Brazilian Experience. *Journal of Money, Credit and Banking, 22*.

Musumeci, J. J., & Sinkey, J. F. Jr. (1990b). The international debt crisis and bank loan-loss-reserve decisions: The signaling content of partially anticipated events. *Journal of Money, Credit, and Banking, 22*.

Noe, T. H., Rebello, M. J., & Wall, L. D. (1996). Managerial rents and regulatory intervention in troubled banks. *Journal of Banking and Finance, 20*.

O'Hara M., & Shaw, W. (1990). Deposit insurance and wealth effects: The Value of Being 'Too Big to Fail'. *The Journal of Finance, 45*.

Penas, M., & Unal, H. (2000). Bank mergers and subordinated debt yields. In: *Proceedings of a Conference on Bank Structure and Competition*. Chicago: Federal Reserve Bank of Chicago.

Pettway, R. H. (1976). The effects of large bank failures upon investor's risk cognizance in the commercial banking industry. *Journal of Financial and Quantitative Analysis, 11*.

Pilloff, S. J. (1996). Performance changes and shareholder wealth creation associated with mergers of publicly traded banking institution. *Journal of Money, Credit, and Banking, 28*.

Pilloff, S. J., & Santomero, A. M. (1997). The value effects of bank mergers and acquisitions. Working paper 9707, Wharton Financial Institutions Center, Philadelphia.

Pyle, D. H. (1974). The losses on savings deposits from interest rate regulation. *Bell Journal of Economics and Management, 5*.

Seiberg, J. (1999). CAMELs penalty threatened if flaws found in CRA data. *American Banker*, April 27, p.2.

Startz, R. (1979). Implicit interest on demand deposits. *Journal of Monetary Economics, 5*.

Stern, G. H. (1992). Banking's middle ground: Balancing excessive regulation and taxpayer risk. *Annual Report*. Federal Reserve Bank of Minneapolis.

Stern, G. H. (1998). Market discipline as bank regulator. *The Region*. Federal Reserve Bank of Minneapolis (June).

Tanoue, D. (2000). Statement Before the Annual Convention Of the Independent Community Bankers of America, San Antonio, March 7.

Theodore, S. S. (1999). *Rating Methodology: Bank Credit Risk*. New York: Moody's Investor Services, Global Credit Research.

U.S. Shadow Regulatory Committee (2000). *Reforming Bank Capital Regulation*. Washington, D.C.: The AEI Press.

Volcker, P. (1985). Statement before the Committee on Banking, Housing and Urban Affairs. U.S. Senate, 99th Congress, 1st session.

Wall, L. D.(1989). A plan for reducing future deposit insurance losses: Puttable subordinated debt. *Economic Review*. Federal Reserve Bank of Atlanta.

Wall, L. D.and David R. Peterson (1987). The effect of capital adequacy guidelines on large bank holding companies. *Journal of Banking and Finance*, 11.

Wall, L. D., & Peterson, D. R. (1995). Bank holding company capital targets in the early 1990s: The regulators versus the markets. *Journal of Banking and Finance*, 19.

CHALLENGES TO THE STRUCTURE OF FINANCIAL SUPERVISION IN THE EU

Karel Lannoo

INTRODUCTION

A debate on the most appropriate structure for financial supervision has started in Europe. The reasons are manifold and arise primarily out of market developments. In several member states, financial conglomerates have become the dominant players, posing challenges to supervisors of all disciplines in the exercise of effective control. At the same time, financial products have become increasingly complex, combining features of different disciplines, whose supervision requires new and enhanced skills. Against this background, the traditional functional division of financial sector supervision looks increasingly outdated.

Other problems are emerging as a result of increased market integration, which has been stimulated by EMU and the establishment of the single market. European financial market liberalisation is based on the principle of home country prudential control. The increasing size and scope of large cross-border financial groups should make formally no difference to this, but it has been debated how far this principle will continue to be applicable. The demand will also grow for further rationalisation and standardisation of the methods of supervision, to simplify pan-European operations and reduce their cost. European groups active in different member states are currently faced with multiple reporting requirements, supervisory techniques and hence costs. If cross-border financial sector consolidation is to be encouraged in Europe for

Bank Fragility and Regulation: Evidence from Different Countries, Volume 12,
pages 121–161.
2000 by Elsevier Science Inc.
ISBN: 0-7623-0698-X

reasons of benefit to users and for reasons of efficiency, this issue will need to be tackled as well.

Efforts to introduce reforms at national level have, to varying extents, led to more horizontal or cross-sectoral approaches in financial supervision. At the extreme end, some states have merged their financial sector supervision in a single authority, introduced a radical supervisory redesign based on the objectives of supervision, while others have provided for structures of cross-sectoral supervisory co-operation of varying degrees of formality.

The purpose of this chapter is to extend this discussion to the European level and examine what changes are required for an integrated financial market. There is clearly an awareness that things need to be adapted at European level, as reflected in the European Commission's Financial Services Action Plan as well as in statements by various regulators and by members of the ECB. But the debate has only started.

We start with an analysis of the changes that have taken place in the European financial system. The next part examines the institutional structure of financial supervision at the national level. A final part discusses the European angle of this design, the current provisions, the role of the ECB, and the required changes in the institutional structure to accommodate growing market integration.

II. THE EUROPEAN FINANCIAL SYSTEM IN EVOLUTION

Europe's financial system remains strongly bank-based. Compared to the U.S., banks play a much more dominant role in Europe, whereas bond and equity markets are more developed in the U.S. (Fig. 1). The asymmetry between the two systems results largely from different regulatory preferences: Europe has the universal banking model, whereas the U.S. financial system was segmented in the 1933 Glass-Steagall Act, which separated commercial from investment banking. The U.S. regime stimulated tough competition between intermediaries and provided the environment in which capital market financing, specialisation and innovation flourished. Under the EU's single market rules, banks are allowed to combine their commercial and investment banking activities under a single roof, which further stimulated bank-financing.

European financial market liberalisation and the creation of the Single Market stirred a process of restructuring and scale enlargement in European banking, a trend that is being further advanced by EMU. The number of banks is falling and concentration increasing. Total assets of EU-based banks continued to grow. They went up from 177% of GDP in 1985 to reach 215%

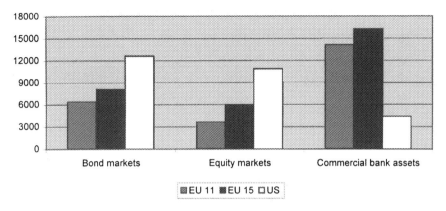

Fig. 1. A Comparison of Equity, Bond and Bank Markets in the U.S. and EU. Total assets in euro bn (1998, except for bank assets 1997).

of GDP in 1997 (OECD, 1999). Total assets of U.S. commercial banks remained stable and stood at 57% of GDP in 1997. During the same period, securitisation increased dramatically in the U.S., but only very moderately in Europe (BIS Review, June 1999).

At the same time, a tendency towards conglomeration started in European finance. Unlike the U.S., where the Bank Holding Company Act (1956) restricted links between banks and non-bank financial corporations, such limitations are not in place in Europe. Although bank and insurance companies need to be separately incorporated, nothing prohibits both from falling under the control of a single holding company. Data on mergers and acquisitions in financial services in the U.S. and Europe document this process. In Europe, close to one-third of all deals (29.7%, and 7% bank-insurance, see Table 1) in the financial services sector in the period 1985–1998 were across sector, whereas this was 17% in the U.S. (and 7% for bank-insurance). The U.S. figure is heavily influenced by the Citicorp-Travellers merger, since a cross section was 15.4% for the period 1985–1997 (and only 0.2% for bank-insurance). Mergers and acquisitions among banks in the same period represent close to half of all financial sector deals in the U.S., compared to 36.2% in Europe (Table 1). There are, however, important cross-country variations. In smaller European countries, such as the Benelux, conglomerates have become the dominant financial services providers, whereas in France and Germany, specialisation has prevailed. The latter was probably as well due to limited foreign entry in both countries' market.

Table 1. Mergers and Acquisitions in the financial services sector, 1985–1999 (total value, billions of $).

Domestic M&A deals 1985–1999 (bn of U.S.D)

	U.S.				Europe			
	Bank	Securities	Insurance	total	Bank	Securities	Insurance	total
Bank	475	24	0.3	499.3	229	15	22	266
Securities firm	6	111	32	149	55	40	41	136
Insurance comp.	73	16	153	242	14	10	74	98
Total	554	151	185.3	**890.3**	298	65	137	**500**
cross-sector as % of total				*17.0*				*31.4*
bank-insurance as % of total				*8.2*				*7.2*

Cross-border M&A deals

	U.S.- non U.S.				Intra-Europe				Europe-non Europe			
	Bank	Securities	Insurance	total	Bank	Securities	Insurance	total	Bank	Securities	Insurance	total
Bank	32.1	7.4	0.2	39.7	37.6	6.7	0.4	44.7	39	6.8	1	46.8
Securities firm	5.7	25.2	6	36.9	8.8	17	1.9	27.7	19.6	19.6	22.2	61.4
Insurance comp.	0.6	4.1	62.6	67.3	20.2	1.5	79.4	101.1	1.1	3.8	57.9	62.8
Total	38.4	36.7	68.8	**143.9**	66.6	25.2	81.7	**173.5**	59.7	30.2	81.1	**171**
cross-sector as % of total				*16.7*				*22.8*				*31.9*
bank-insurance as % of total				*0.6*				*11.9*				*1.2*

Table 1. Continued.

Total M&A in financial services (1985–99)

Bank	Total U.S. acquitors			Total Europe acquitors				
	Securities	Insurance	total	Bank	Securities	Insurance	total	
Bank	507.1	31.4	0.5	539	305.6	28.5	23.4	357.5
Securities firm	11.7	136.2	38	185.9	83.4	76.6	65.1	225.1
Insurance comp.	73.6	20.1	215.6	309.3	35.3	15.3	211.3	261.9
Total	592.4	187.7	254.1	**1034.2**	424.3	120.4	299.8	**844.5**
Cross-sector as % of total				*17.0*				*29.7*
bank-insurance as % of total				*7.2*				*7.0*
bank-bank as % of total				*49.0*				*36.2*
Insurance-insurance as % of total				*20.8*				*25.0*

The figures reported are the sum of equity values of the target institutions
Source: Data kindly provided by Ingo Walter, NYU, based upon Thomson Financial Securities data.

The strong contrast between the EU and the U.S. financial system may reduce in the years ahead. In the EU, the start of EMU signalled a shift towards more direct capital market financing, with a strong growth of the corporate and other non-government bond markets. The corporate bond market has grown with a factor of 2.5 in the first year of EMU. Several countries enacted legislation to allow a mortgage bond market to emerge. In the U.S., the segmentation of the financial sector looks to become definitively repealed. The Gramm-Leach-Bliley Act (1999) lifts restrictions on U.S.-based financial institutions, when licensed as a Financial Holding Company (FHC), to work as financial conglomerates. Some 117 institutions have applied for FHC status in the U.S. so far.

At product level, financial institutions have responded to growing competition through the introduction of new products and services and diversification of the product range. Combined bank-securities, bank-insurance, insurance-securities and even bank-securities-insurance are offered on the market by a single firm. The sector-specific characteristics of such products are irrelevant for consumers, they only wish that the same level of consumer protection and conduct of business rules are applied for each product. This development has rendered the job of financial supervisors more difficult.

Although there was initially no support in the economies of scope and scale literature for this process of financial sector consolidation, recent research has found a higher degree of cost efficiency in universal banks and conglomerates as compared to more specialised banks. De-specialisation may lead to more efficient financial systems (Vander Vennet, 1998). Also technological progress has affected efficient bank size, by allowing management to keep growing business under control. Recent research also showed that the overall cost saving of IT investments increased with the size of the bank (Molyneux, 1997). Others have demonstrated that the overall profitability of large banks is higher than small banks, with about twice as many small banks (weighted average) being non-profit bearing as compared to large banks. This difference is even larger in the U.S. (Inzerillo et al., 1999). Financial sector consolidation can thus be expected to continue.

Financial market liberalisation has hardened competitive conditions for European banking. On an aggregate basis, performance of European banking has not changed, and it is low as compared to the U.S. commercial banks. In certain countries, probably those with the most protected markets before, it has led to declining performance levels. Return on assets of all European banks, measured as profit before tax as a percentage of total assets, stands at about 0.50% for the period 1995–1997, as compared to 1.83% for the U.S. commercial banks (OECD, 1999). Some countries are consistently doing much better than the EU average, such as the UK-based banks, but in others, such as France and Italy, the situation is well below average, with a return on assets of 0.31% in 1997.

EMU should lead to a greater degree of financial market interpenetration, which has been limited so far. The disappearance of the constraints of currency-matching rules and the dominance of European-wide bond and equity indexes should stimulate European banks and institutional investors to start to spread assets at euro-wide level. Also cross-border banking penetration should grow. In 1997, the market share of foreign branches and subsidiaries exceeded 10% in only five EU countries (1997): in declining order of proportion, Luxembourg, Ireland, the UK, Belgium and Greece (ECB, 1999).

In sum, monetary union involves the continuation of a process of financial market liberalisation in Europe, which is starting to acquire more European-wide dimensions. Three issues are important for supervisors in re-designing of the supervisory framework at European level: (1) The Europeanisation of financial markets and the emergence of Europe as a whole as the home market; (2) The changes which EMU is bringing about in the largely bank-based European financial system; (3) The trend towards conglomeration.

Europeanisation of financial markets may potentially reduce the grip which supervisors had in a national context on institutions under their supervision and may increase the possibility for regulatory arbitrage. While regulatory competition is in itself not a problem, as long as the minimum standards are sufficiently high, the question emerges whether the structure of supervisory co-operation is sufficiently developed to cope with stronger market integration cross border, or whether supervisors will continue to seek to favour the national public interest.

The trend towards more market-based finance may alleviate the job of supervisors, since it should strengthen market discipline in European finance. However, other elements of the regulatory set-up and in the attitude of market actors will need to move in parallel to increase the transparency of the financial system. This relates to accounting standards, reporting systems and corporate governance mechanisms. One of the reasons for relatively tight supervision in the banking sector is the agency problem and the transformation of short-term liabilities (deposits) into illiquid long-term assets (commercial loans). A bank can afford this asymmetry of maturity as long as withdrawals by depositors take place randomly over time and assets are held to term. A depositor may, however, not realise when the quality of the assets of a bank deteriorate, and also the market will not act as disciplining factor, since most loans remain on the books of banks, and not marketed on a daily basis. It follows that problems in a bank-based system can accumulate and become apparent when it is already too late.

The trend towards conglomeration is an additional challenge for supervisors. While conglomeration may increase cost efficiency and diversifies risk for financial groups, the task of supervision does not become easier. With entities separately authorised and controlled, supervisory authorities risk being unaware of the overall risk profile of the group. The risks at group level do not necessarily equal the sum of the risks of the different entities of the group: the group might have large exposures that are not readily apparent at the single entity level. Risks in the different parts of the business are aggregated and less transparent, which may also reduce market discipline. The danger of double-gearing of capital or uncontrolled intra-group transactions to cover losses in one entity with gains from another, also arises. Finally, a loss of confidence in one part of the group can affect the whole business, and thus increase volatility (Danthine et al., 1999). In the following section, we discuss how some countries have tackled this problem by adapting the institutional structure of financial supervision. We first look at the changes taking place at national level, and then move to the European dimension.

II. THE STRUCTURE OF FINANCIAL SUPERVISION

The single financial market programme was a process of financial re-regulation in the EU. National regulation was re-drafted on the basis of European benchmarks, set forward in directives. This did not, at least directly, affect the structure of financial supervision at local level. Nothing in EU financial services law currently prescribes how financial supervision should be organised. Member states are simply required to ensure that the sectors covered are adequately supervised and basic minimum requirements (own funds, large exposures) are observed.

Traditionally, the structure of financial supervision was based on the functional divisions in the financial services sector and the perceived differences in risk profiles. Supervision in banking has typically had a higher profile than in insurance, because of the systemic element and hence the close involvement of the central bank. Securities market supervision was until recently largely based on sectoral self-regulation, but internationalisation of markets and European harmonisation of securities regulation has forced many member states to create securities supervisory bodies.

The move of monetary policy powers to the ECB has stimulated a debate in some countries whether banking supervision needs to remain under the same roof as the central bank, at least in the countries where this is still the case. The tendency towards conglomeration in the financial services industry is an argument in favour of a single supervisory authority, although conglomeration may also strengthen the arguments for more supervision by the objectives of regulation. The pros and cons of these different constellations are analysed below.

Central Bank Versus Separate Banking Supervision

Monetary policy and banking supervisory functions are separated in one-half of the Community countries and combined in the other half (See Table 2). Generally speaking, the arguments in favour of combining both functions revolve around the fact that it is the central bank's role to ensure the stability of the financial system and prevent contagious systemic crises (Goodhart et al., 1997). The performance of bank supervisory and regulatory functions contribute to better control of overall financial stability whoever undertakes them. The issue is whether they can be done better in a central bank. Through its role as lender-of-last-resort (LOLR), the central bank should, it is argued, be involved in supervision as well. At the same time, however, the possibility that a conflict of interest arises argues against combining both functions. The central bank's participation in bank rescues may endanger price stability and increase moral hazard. It may create competitive distortions if central bank money is allocated at preferential rates to a bank in trouble as compared to other banks. Finally, it may raise the expectation in the private sector that a central bank supervisor would be unduly influenced because of the reputational risk by considerations of financial system stability when determining monetary policy. This could seriously undermine the central bank's credibility.

The fact that both regimes are equally represented in the EU shows that there are no conclusive arguments for or against either model. According to Goodhart and Schoenmaker (1995), the question of the appropriate design has to be approached in the context of the particular financial or banking structure of each country rather than as an abstract problem to be solved. Their analysis of bank failures over the last two decades shows there to be a much higher frequency of failures in countries with a separated regime than in those with a combined one. This does not, however, lead immediately to the conclusion that the latter regime is better. Many other factors come into play, such as the degree of financial deregulation, the quality of regulation, the willingness of the government to let a bank fail, or the existence of oligopolies in banking. Goodhart and Schoenmaker also found a stronger likelihood of commercial banks being involved in rescues in a combined regime, through the authority of the central bank, but they see this as a receding possibility.

In recent years, the trend towards more integrated supervision has led to moving bank supervisory functions away from the central bank. The arguments for keeping banking supervision under the roof of the central bank have become less authoritative as compared to the need to respond effectively to the increasing complexity of finance (see Briault, 1999). This was most clearly exemplified by the announcement in May 1997 of the proposed establishment in the UK of the Financial Services Authority (FSA), an integrated financial supervisor, involving the transfer of the banking supervisory function from the

Table 2. Supervisors of Banking, Securities and Insurance in Europe, Japan and the U.S.

	Banking	Securities	Insurance
B	BS	BS	I
DK	M	M	M
DE	B	S	I
EL	CB	S	I
E	CB	S	I
F	B/CB	S	I
I	CB	S	I
IRL	CB	CB	G
L	BS	BS	I
NL	CB	S	I
AU	G	G	G
P	CB	S	I
SF	BS	BS	I
SW	M	M	M
UK	M	M	M
CH	BS	BS	I
CZ	CB	SI	SI
H	B	S	I
N	M	M	M
PL	CB	S	I
SLOE	CB	S	G
USA	B/CB	S	I
J	M	M	M

Note: CB = Central Bank, BS = banking and securities supervisor, M = single financial supervisory authority, B = specialised banking supervisor, S = specialised securities supervisor, I = specialised insurance supervisor, SI = specialised securities and insurance supervisor, G = government department.

Bank of England.[1] An additional reason for this development is the acceptance that only the government, and not the central bank, can take responsibility for ultimate financial support of banks in trouble. The ability of central banks to organise and co-ordinate bank rescues has been slipping, and bank rescues have become more expensive, going beyond the sums which the central bank can provide from its own resources. This was demonstrated earlier this decade in Finland, Norway and Sweden, but also more recently in Italy and France. There has consequently been no alternative but to rely on taxpayer funding, leading to more demand for political control of supervisory functions. Close co-operation between the supervisory and the monetary policy authorities remains crucial, however. Only the monetary policy authorities can provide immediate liquidity to the market in case of trouble. But price stability cannot be achieved if financial stability is not in place. This is distinction is operational in the eurozone, where, under the Maastricht Treaty, the ESCB is responsible for monetary policy, and the national authorities for financial stability.

Integrated Financial Supervisor vs. Specialist Supervisors

A second issue to be addressed is whether financial supervision should be assigned to one entity or whether it should be determined by the function of business of the institutions under supervision or by the type of supervision (prudential or conduct of business). The conglomeration trend in the financial sector and the creation of the FSA in the UK has stimulated a discussion elsewhere in Europe on integrated financial supervisory authorities. An integrated authority is seen to generate economies of scale (and probably economies of scope) in supervision, as well as some practical and political advantages (Table 3). It offers one-stop shopping for authorisations of conglomerate financial groups, and eliminates any confusion over who exercises lead supervision and final control. Expertise is pooled and co-operation between the different functional supervisors is guaranteed. Unnecessary overlaps are avoided and support services such as personnel, administration and documentation can be merged. An integrated authority should thus over time lead to lower supervisory fees, at least in these countries where the financial sector contributes directly to the cost of supervision, and to a lower cost of supervision in general.

The benefits of an integrated supervisory authority in the supervision of conglomerates are very material, as well for supervisors as for the supervised. In the FSA, for example, the larger and more complex conglomerates are supervised by a separate division, the Complex Groups Division. It defines complex groups as having a minimum of three authorisable financial services

Table 3. Comparative Advantages of the Dominant Models in Financial Supervision

Integrated Financial Supervisor	Specialist Supervisor
• One-stop shopping for authorisations • Pooling of expertise and economies of scale (certain units could be merged, e.g. authorisations, support services) • Lower supervisory fees • Adapted to evolution in financial sector towards more complex financial products and financial conglomerates • Co-operation between type of financial business guaranteed; one lead supervisor or a single supervisory team for conglomerates • No regulatory arbitrage, regulatory neutrality • More transparent to consumers • Single rulebook (a possibility)	Lower profile • Clearly defined mandate • Easier to manage • More adapted to the differences in risk profiles and nature of the respective financial business (e.g. retail versus wholesale), clear focus on objectives and rationale of regulation • Closer to the business (but not necessarily) • Better knowledge of the business, more specialisation • Stimulates inter-agency competition

activities, of a significant scale, with a complex structure, an international presence and involved in complex products. The FSA had at the time of writing some 57 complex groups under supervision, with many more authorised activities, comprising a total of some 200 individual supervised firms. Most of FSA's supervision is still happening on a sectoral basis, coordinated for each group by a lead supervisor within the FSA, the FSA plans a limited experiment with an alternative approach whereby all or most of its supervisory activities for a single group are co-ordinated in a single supervisory team. Moreover, the FSA is integrating 14 different rulebooks of the different sectoral supervisors into a single Handbook of Rules and Guidance. The benefits for complex groups are thus not only single stop shopping and a single rulebook, but also a single supervisory team.

An integrated supervisor will however only be effective if it is more than a combination of divisions, and if synergies can be exploited. It has been argued that the crucial thing is not whether all the functional supervisors are only a single roof or not, but whether they communicate. If an integrated supervisor is no more than a combination of banking, insurance and investment business divisions, the full benefits of a single regulatory authority will not be achieved.

A possible argument against an integrated supervisor is its potentially higher profile. It might be argued that the perception could somehow be created that the whole financial sector is secure, which may reduce the incentives for providers to prudently manage their business, and for users to carefully choose their financial services' provider. It could also be argued that the failure of one institution could have more widespread effects in a combined regime because the supervisor was active in a number of different sectors. This risk has to be offset by educating users of financial services in the risks as well as the benefits of financial products.

The advantages of a specialist supervisor are a lower profile and a clearer focus on the sector under supervision. It could allow for a greater proximity to smaller firms on which a single regulator may be less inclined to focus, more specialisation and better awareness of the problems of the sector. Two arguments stand out: a growing need for specialisation in supervision and inter-agency competition. Very distinct skills are required from supervisors, ranging from monitoring potentially dangerous exposures in increasingly globalised financial markets and validating statistical models in a bank's value-at-risk models to supervising complex financial groups or tracking market behaviour of investment funds, as well as a large degree of financial specialisation. It is an open question whether a single regulator can find it easier to recruit and retain specialists. It could be easier where there are specialisms such as market risk, credit risk and most forms of legal and operational risk, which apply across a range of different firms, and not just firms in a particular sector (Briault, 1999).

The second argument, the advantage of inter-agency competition, is relevant, although perhaps difficult to advance in this context. Where several agencies work side by side, institutional competition can work and create incentives for each agency to work efficiently, while reducing capture (Fender & von Hagen, 1998). An example is the U.S. structure of banking supervision, where banks can be chartered at either the state or national level. In the EU, regulatory competition between states forms an integral part of the single market programme. Many will argue, however, that inter-agency competition does not make sense. Competition between regulatory regimes runs the risk of reducing rather than improving quality, and it may better serve the interests of the supervised than of the public.

An overview of financial sector supervision in the EU and the rest of Europe demonstrates that three EU countries (Denmark, Sweden and the UK) as well as Norway have a integrated financial services authority. In some of these countries (as also recently in Japan and South-Korea), the integration of supervision resulted from serious trouble in their financial sector or grave oversights in surveillance. In Austria, Belgium, Germany and Ireland, the creation an integrated authority has been raised or is on the political agenda. In the other countries, a broad mixture of systems exists, ranging from separate supervisors, sometimes split between two agencies in the same supervisory discipline, to combined banking-and-securities or combined securities-and-insurance supervisors (see Table 2).

Supervision by Objective

Another outcome of the conglomeration trend is that supervision will become more objective-driven, since the functional divisions of the business will be increasingly blurred. One possible model is that surveillance could be carried out separately by one agency for systemic stability reasons, a second for prudential supervision, and a third for conduct-of-business considerations. Conduct-of-business supervision looks after transparency, disclosure, fair and honest practices, and equality of market participants. The "stability" agency should concentrate on macro-prudential problems, which affect the conduct of monetary policy or overall financial stability, while the prudential agency controls the solvency and soundness of individual financial institutions and enforces depositor and investor protection.

Such a horizontal supervisory structure was instituted in Australia, further to the Wallis Committee of Inquiry in 1997. The Australian Prudential Regulatory Authority (APRA) supervises financial institutions on prudential grounds; the Reserve Bank of Australia looks after systemic stability and provides liquidity assistance; and the Australian Securities and Investment Commission (ASIC) controls market integrity and conduct-of-business rules. APRA and ASIC report to the Treasury. Several EU countries have elements of an objective-driven system of supervision, mainly as far as the relationship between the banking and the securities supervisor is concerned. In Italy, for example, banks and securities houses are controlled by the Banca d'Italia on financial stability and prudential grounds and by the CONSOB for conduct-of-business rules for the banking and securities industry. The UK had a broadly similar structure before all supervisory functions were merged in the FSA. However, one of the reasons for bringing together prudential and conduct of business supervision in the UK was the increasing overlap in their activities with the increasing tendency of both types of supervisor to pay heightened attention to senior management capabilities, high level systems and controls and other common issues (Briault, 1999).

An advantage of supervision by objective is said to be that it is well adapted to conglomeration in the financial sector while remaining sufficiently focused, though the overlap in activities just referred to are to be weighed against this. Another argument is that the result of a integrated supervisory authority could be that the different objectives of supervision are merged and later disappear, which could ultimately lead to more regulation, also for the wholesale business. This fear was raised in discussions on the new Financial Services and Markets Bill in the UK (Clifford Chance, 1998). At the same time, it can be countered that well drafted statutory objectives, statutory specification of the range of different considerations the regulator should bear in mind and extensive accountability should satisfactorily handle these issues for a single regulator.

An in-between solution was recently adopted by the Netherlands, probably the EU country with the highest market share for financial conglomerates. To avoid institutional reorganisation and all the related political problems, but to allow for adaptation to market developments and a clear focus on the objectives of supervision, a Council of Financial Supervisors was established in August 1999. The Council is not a separate institution, but is an organ for regular consultation between the three sectoral supervisors (the banking supervisor (in the central bank), the insurance and securities supervisors) for cross-sectoral problems in prudential and non-securities related conduct-of-business control. The Dutch central bank remains solely in charge of systemic control, and the securities supervisor becomes responsible for all securities-related conduct-of-business control. According to the Dutch Ministry of Finance (1999), the Council would force supervisors to agree on effective control of cross-sectoral issues, but the final responsibility would remain with the individual supervisors. It remains to be seen how effectively these arrangements work.

The Dutch experiment points to interesting routes for other countries and for the European structure. It may only be a half-way solution towards a more streamlined structure of financial supervision in the longer run, but it could also indicate that the optimal solution needs to combine sectoral and cross-sectoral supervision. Three relevant implications for the European debate are the need for regular cross-sectoral consultation, the decision to leave the central bank in charge of systemic issues, while keeping securities market supervision separate.

IV. THE EUROPEAN ANGLE

European financial market regulations allowed markets to integrate under the control of the home country. Home country supervisors are in charge of licensing branches across the EU and exercising consolidated supervision. To that end, a framework for regular exchange of information and co-operation at bilateral and European level is in place. A variety of committees have been established to deal with a range of issues, including advising the Commission on improvements to the legal and regulatory framework at European level, to exchange views about supervisory policy and practice, and, in some cases, to discuss specific cases. The host country remains in charge to deal with problems related to the stability of the financial system. With the start of EMU, macro-prudential oversight is coordinated by the ECB.

The developments outlined in Part II raise the question whether this framework is still appropriate. While it is not the role of the EC institutions to prescribe the supervisory structure at national level, adaptations may be required to face growing market interpenetration, conglomeration and Europeanisation of financial institutions.

On the Home Country Principle

The home country control principle was successful in opening-up markets in the EU, at least in banking. The harmonisation of the essential elements of authorisation and supervision of banks in the second banking co-ordination directive (2BCD) allowed the single licence for cross-border provision of services and branching to work. Host country controls for prudential purposes were virtually abolished, administrative burdens reduced and capital requirements for branches (where applied) eliminated. Moreover, the introduction of European legislation provided a major incentive for national legislators to streamline their applicable laws. Some problems remained, relating to the application of the notification procedure for host country operations and the application of the general good clause, but they were tentatively clarified in an interpretative Communication of the European Commission (1996), which was not, however, wholeheartedly supported. Another issue, the liquidity control of branches by host country authorities for monetary policy reasons (Art. 14, 2BCD), has become irrelevant in EMU. The article is under review by the authorities.

The home country is in charge of exercising consolidated supervision of a bank throughout the EU. To avoid opaque structures, it is required that the home country is the place of the head office of the bank in the EU (in the so-called "BCCI directive"). In international perspective, home country control is also the basic method for the supervision of cross-border banking in the Core Principles on Banking Supervision of the Basel Committee. The general intention is that the home supervisor has to act as the lead supervisor for branches, joint ventures and subsidiaries all over the world and needs to exercise consolidated supervision. Host country supervisors are expected to communicate all necessary information to the home country authorities.

In the area of investment services and retail insurance, the home country control principle has only been partially put into effect. The harmonisation in the for investment services providers in the investment services directive (ISD) has gone less far than in banking, and more powers reside with the host country for the control of the respect of local conduct of business rules, which have not been harmonised, although they work on the basis of harmonised principles. The European Commission is committed to further harmonisation, as was indicated in the Financial Services Action Plan. In insurance, differences in contract law and taxation have limited the reach of the single licence for small risks, and thus of home country control principle. For large risks, however, markets have become integrated.

Harmonisation of conduct of business rules in financial services has proven more challenging, because it revolves round differing views on what constitutes appropriate protection for consumers in historically very different market places. It also tends to require more on-site examination, which is more demanding on a cross-border basis. It is notable that new EU legislation involving conduct of business regulation goes for maximum harmonisation, as for example most recently in the draft distance selling of financial services directive.

Two fundamental questions can be raised with regard to the working of the home country control principle: (1) the functioning of the principle in an EU context so far, and (2) its relevance in a more integrated European financial market. The home country control principle is part of the limited harmonisation approach of the single market as set out in the Cassis de Dijon ruling (1978) of the European Court of Justice. Only essential requirements are harmonised to allow markets to integrate. Additional rules should adjust in a competitive process between jurisdictions. This raises the issue of regulatory competition, and the degree of competition that is permissible in an EU context.

The home country control principle was probably well adapted to an environment of limited competition. As long as cross-border business is limited, as was generally the case until the start of EMU (see Part II), regulatory competition probably had some effect in aligning the most striking differences between regimes, while the overall impact remains limited, because markets have not been very integrated. In a more integrated market, a process of further harmonisation can be expected as a result of pressures from the market and the authorities, at national and European level. This will be required to reduce remaining powers of the host country in each of the disciplines (for e.g. the notification procedure and the general good principle) or expand harmonisation where it was too limited (eg in banking, the deposit guarantee directive, which prohibited the "export" of higher levels of depositor protection in the EU).

The second question is whether the home country *per se* will continue to be relevant in an EU context. The big players in the European market will increasingly have a range of home markets, so could the EU as a whole become the home market? It has been suggested in the past (Gros, quoted in Schoenmaker, 1995) that the single financial market could follow the two tier U.S. system of state- and federally-chartered banks. Large European banks could than choose to be federally chartered and be allowed to regard Europe as a whole as their "home" country. This does, however, raise several fundamental problems: (i) financial services legislation is not sufficiently harmonised today to allow this to happen; (ii) it would require an EU Treaty change to create such a body (as would be required for a European SEC, or FSA;[2] (iii) financial supervision implies accountability and tax powers for eventual bail-outs. While the former could perhaps be created to exist at European level, the latter would be much more difficult, and would entail implicit agreement between member states for burden-sharing of bail-outs; (iv) there is no appropriate European framework of courts to impose sanctions for violations of law or to challenge the use of powers made; (v) a dual framework may be seen by smaller banks (and member states) as a competitive distortion; and (vi) there would be major company law ramifications to be considered.

European Supervisory Co-operation

Growing cross-border banking, home country control and the operation of host state regulation all raise the issue of bilateral and European co-operation between supervisory authorities. Memoranda of Understanding provide the underpinning for co-operation at the bilateral level. At European level, several committees are in place to ensure collaboration between supervisors.

Co-operation at Bilateral Level
Memoranda of Understanding (MoUs) are a form of agreements between supervisors, which have no legal force, but set the respective tasks and obligations of both parties. In principle, the EU directives make formal agreements between supervisory authorities of the member states superfluous, since they make co-operation a legal obligation. In practice, supervisors have continued to conclude MoUs to clarify what is involved in the supervision of financial institutions and markets, such as information exchange and mutual assistance, establishment procedures and on-site examinations. In banking, some 78 bilateral MoUs had been signed between EEA banking supervisors by the end of 1997 (Padoa-Schioppa, 1999), while there is a multilateral Protocol to the Insurance Directives which serves as an MoU.

Little more is available in the public domain about the scope of MoUs that have been negotiated on the supervision of banks. Perhaps this can be justified from a moral hazard and liability point of view, but it does raise the question whether the authorities should consider a higher degree of transparency. This could signal to the markets that supervisors have kept pace with growing market integration. More information is available on MoUs between securities commissions and regulated markets. In the latter case, the arguments against transparency do not apply, and regulatory tasks are often shared, and on a different basis across countries, between the securities commission and the stock exchange.

Co-operation through MoUs raises the question of effective co-ordination of supervision. Although not formalised, the supervisor who exercises consolidated supervision is seen as the co-ordinator. This does however raise a problem for the insurance sector, where consolidation is not commonly accepted as a principle. According to a recent report by the Economic and Financial Committee (European Commission, 2000b), there is a lack of clarity on the co-ordinated supervision of insurance groups. This applies even more for conglomerates with a predominantly insurance focus. It has been reported that some conglomerates recently restructured as principally insurance groups to escape consolidated supervision.

MoUs raise the question of supervisory methods and the content of information exchange. According to Mayes (1999), MoUs do not provide for routine transfer of routine information among supervisors, but only in the case where possible supervisory problems arise, including suspected misconduct. This is perhaps natural, but when information is transferred, the question arises what precise information is transferred and whether supervisory methods have been sufficiently harmonised for information transfer to be effective. Limited evidence suggests that much may remain to be done in this domain. According to Prati and Schinasi (1997), supervisory practices differ considerably in the EU. The Vice-Governor of Austrian national bank was recently quoted saying that the differences in banking and supervisory systems in the EU are so big that they will only be overcome in the very long term, if at all.[3]

As a way around this problem, it has been proposed that enhanced market disclosure about the bank's capital structure and its risk profile would help in providing the necessary information to supervisors (Mayes, 1999). Since information exchange between supervisors may not be sufficiently developed in certain areas, strengthening market discipline would probably be a more efficient and faster way to facilitate the work of supervisors in a European context. This point is also stressed in the proposed "pillar three" of the Basel Capital Accord Review.

Co-operation at European Level
At European level, several Committees exist to promote co-operation between
supervisory authorities. Among the tasks are:

(1) to provide a forum for the exchange of views and to act as sounding board
    for the Commission on any proposals for supplements or amendments to
    legislation;
(2) to discuss and adopt technical adaptations to the directives within the
    perimeters foreseen in the directives (the "comitology" procedure);
(3) to discuss and compare issues of supervisory technique and to facilitate the
    exchange of information and co-operation with respect to problems with
    individual institutions.

This is however a general characterisation, which varies between the sectors of
financial services. The Committees are most developed in banking. The highest
number of committees exist for securities markets, but with the least powers.
An umbrella, cross-discipline EU committee of financial supervisors does not
exist.

In banking, three committees are in place (see appendix). The Banking
Advisory Committee (BAC) principally advises the European Commission
with regard to policy issues in the formulation and implementation of EC
legislation for the banking sector. It can also, if foreseen by the directives, agree
on technical adaptations to the directives (the "comitology" procedure). In
order to do this, it brings together senior supervisory and finance ministry
officials. The "Groupe de Contact", which consists only of banking supervisors
of the European Economic Area (EEA), has dealt for nearly 30 years with
practical banking supervision issues, including undertaking comparative
studies, discusses arrangements for exchange of information and handles co-
operation with respect to issues arising from individual institutions. The
Banking Supervisory Committee of the ECB brings together the authorities
responsible for monetary policy and payment systems oversight in the
European System of Central Banks with EU banking supervisors to discuss
macro-prudential matters and financial stability issues. It also assists the ECB
in the preparation of the ECB's advice on draft EU and national banking
legislation (in respect of euro area countries) as laid down in Article 105(4) of
the EU Treaty and Article 25(1) of the ESCB/ECB statute. Each of these three
committees co-operates closely with the others, making papers available as
appropriate.

In insurance, the BAC is broadly paralleled by the Insurance Committee and
the Groupe de Contact by the Conference of Insurance Supervisors.

In the securities field, strictly speaking, no parallel to the legislative committees existing in the banking and insurance field is in place. This means that any technical adaptation of the core directives (the investment services directive and the capital adequacy directive) needs to take the form of a formal amendment, with the problems and delays this can imply. This situation should now be remedied, following the agreement in the European Parliament on the way legislative committees should be structured. However, a High Level Securities Supervisors Committee, bringing together representatives of member states' securities supervisory authorities and finance ministries, has been in place since 1992. It assists the Commission on policy issues relating to securities markets and the development of the relevant European legislation. Two "Contact Committees", one for the listing and prospectus rules and one for unit trusts (UCITS), exist to facilitate harmonised implementation of directives through regular consultations between the member states and to advise the Commission on any supplements or amendments. These committees have no "comitology" powers, which explains why they never acquired particular influence.

The conflict between European Commission, Council and Parliament on the implementing powers of a formal securities committee led in December 1997 to the creation of the Forum of European Securities Commissions (FESCO). FESCO brings together the statutory securities commissions of the European Economic Area (EEA).[4] FESCO's work concentrates on developing common regulatory standards and enhancing co-operation between members on enforcement and market surveillance issues.

The Role of the ECB

According to the EU Treaty, the ECB is in charge of monetary policy and the smooth operation of payment systems, whereas financial supervision and stability remain the competence of the member states. This division of roles has been the subject of wide debate over the last months, and focused principally on the unrestrained lender-of-last-resort (LOLR) facilities of the separate national central banks in EMU, which may potentially conflict with the monetary policy role of the ECB. It has therefore been argued to give the ECB an explicit LOLR function.

In essence, the reason for giving the ECB an explicit lender-of-last resort role is the possible conflict between the ECB's responsibility for determining liquidity in the Eurosystem and the financial stability competences at local level. Local responsibility for LOLR operations can conflict with euro monetary policy and possibly stimulate excessive risk-taking. This was related to the fear, which has faded away, that the national central banks would dominate the eurosystem, and that the ECB would not be sufficiently powerful to impose common rules. It has now been agreed that the ECB's Governing Council should be consulted on LOLR operations that have EMU-wide implications.[5] This also implies, however, that the ECB will co-ordinate LOLR operations of banks with widespread operations across Europe. As soon as a bank operates in more than two EU countries on a major scale, and is of systemic importance at European level, it is more likely that the ECB will take a leading role in rescue operations as *primus inter pares* and as a neutral body. The ECB's Banking Supervisory Committee should be instrumental in ensuring regular consultation on these matters between national central bank officials and supervisors, and ensuring that the ECB is sufficiently informed.

Unlike the national central banks, however, the ECB has limited financial means and is not backed by a ministry of finance for an eventual bank rescue involving injections of capital. The ECB can only lend against good collateral. Even if the ECB assumes the coordinating role for the monetary policy aspects of LOLR operations relating to European financial groups, a solution will need to be found for this issue as well. A bail-out of such groups will only be possible under a burden-sharing arrangement between the different home countries. However, the risk is not imaginary that national ministries of finance and parliaments will be unwilling to pick up problems which have, in their eyes, originated in other parts of the EU (Goodhart, 1999).[6] This discussion also raises problems related to European competition policy, as approaches to banks in trouble differ across countries and affect the level playing field. The latter issue is discussed in more detail below.

The recent debate on the LOLR role of the ECB also revealed that the issue had been confused with a generalised liquidity problem in the Eurosystem. This is closely related to the monetary policy function of the central bank, on which there is no formal disagreement on the responsibility of the ECB to act. The ECB should be well informed about one of the reasons of such liquidity shortages, a gridlock in the payment system, through its task in promoting the smooth operation of payment systems. The ESCB's large value payment system, TARGET, had a market share of 70% in large value payments in the first year of EMU.

Another element of the consensus is the agreement that the procedure to confer specific tasks concerning policies relating to prudential supervision of banks and other financial institutions to the ECB, as foreseen under Article 105.6 of the EU Treaty, should not be activitated. It could give rise to conflicts of interest with the ECB's monetary policy functions, which can at this stage best be avoided. It would also require a complete redesign of the structure of financial supervision in the EU, which is based on the principle of member state home country control. The provision is currently seen as an ultimate fall-back option, if the relationship between the ECB and the national supervisory authorities would not work, in case irresponsible behaviour by authorities at national level would have spill-over effects in the whole euro-zone.

How to Respond to Growing Market Integration

The deeper challenges in financial supervision are related to the characteristics of the European financial system and the increased competition and market integration, which is stimulated by EMU. It will require agreement on the part of policy-makers and supervisors to act rapidly on the completion of the regulatory framework and the adaptation of the structure of financial supervision to market developments. Elements of the provisions worked out in the Netherlands provide some indication of the issues to be addressed at a European level, though because the tasks are different at a national and a European level – it is unlikely that any national structure will offer a model suitable at the European level. It comprises three elements: the surveillance of systemic issues, involving regulators, central banks and finance ministries; the need for closer co-operation between supervisors in a European board of financial supervisors to discuss cross-sectoral matters and to handle issues related to conglomerate groups; and the option to handle market supervision separately. If supervision is to remain at a national level, then a further levelling of the playing field for financial institutions in the EU also needs to be considered urgently.

Systemic Issues

National central banks and supervisory authorities should step up their efforts to monitor market developments at European level and alert national and European authorities to exposures with a potentially systemic impact. Monetary union has connected 11 previously separate markets into a single currency zone. That this has effectively happened is clear from the interbank market, which has become a deep euro money market. Banks have integrated their euro treasury operations and manage collateral on a euro-wide basis. The parallel to this development is that also systemic effects will immediately have much wider dimensions, whereas previously they were probably limited to the national boundaries. Interbank deposits represent about 19% of bank assets in euroland.

It is therefore essential that the euro-zone is watched as one market. The ECB has its Banking Supervisory Committee, but the question has been raised whether this group will be sufficiently comprehensive in its approach to European financial markets, and whether the ECB will have sufficient access to research to effectively monitor markets. A case has therefore been made for a European Observatory of Systemic Risk (Aglietta and de Boissieu, 1998). The aim would be to have one body in place to monitor market developments across Europe and alert national and European authorities to exposures with a potentially systemic impact. In practice, such an entity could most efficiently operate in a co-operative structure within the ESCB.[7] Such work is already undertaken within the existing structure of the ECB's Banking Supervision Committee. However, it may be useful to create a clearly distinct structure for this, and to signal this to the markets to provide reassurance that adequate account is being taken of the new environment created by the euro. Secondly, it will be important to take account of securities markets developments and of non-bank intermediaries.

A Future Structure for European Regulatory and Supervisory Co-operation
Three layers can be distinguished in the European structure of regulatory and supervisory co-operation, for each of which one coordinating body should be appointed:

(1) *Co-ordination in regulatory policy.* The Financial Services Policy Group (FSPG), instituted in 1999, should be continued to discuss priorities in financial regulation at European level. After the adoption of the financial services action plan, it was announced that the FSPG would continue "to provide strategic advice, to discuss cross-sectoral developments and to monitor progress under the Action Plan" (Ecofin Council, 25 May 1999). A higher profile may, however, be needed, and a clear hierarchy in the decision process. These specialised matters are difficult to be dealt with directly by the Ecofin Council.

(2) *Co-ordination in supervisory matters.* No structure is in place to deal with cross-sectoral supervisory issues at the moment. A European Forum of Financial Supervisors should therefore be urgently considered. This Forum should have 2 major tasks:
   • Ensure effective supervisory co-ordination for large European financial conglomerates. The Forum will have to monitor whether the different bilateral Memoranda of Understanding (MoU), on a sectoral and cross-sectoral basis, provide a sufficient overall picture of the exposures of a group. A multi-sectoral MoU or protocol could be worked out for the exchange of information between supervisors on a cross-sector and cross-border basis to ensure that financial groups with operations in a

range of different countries are properly supervised, with clear arrangements for the appointment of a lead supervisor.

- Co-ordination of supervisory practices: The Forum should have set an objective ultimately to harmonise supervisory practices in the EU whether through legislative or non-legislative means. The exchange of information on supervisory techniques should allow the Forum to make arrangements for the establishment of standards of best practice in financial supervision, which should over time lead to more convergence in supervisory practices in the EU and hence to a more efficient and integrated single market.

The Forum should be composed of the chairman of the different sectoral supervisory committees, with the European Commission acting as secretariat. Other supervisors would be invited on an ad-hoc basis.

(3) *Co-ordination in financial stability matters*: Monitoring of financial stability should happen through the mechanism of something like the Observatory for Systemic Risk, discussed above. Effective emergency intervention should be coordinated by the Economic and Financial Committee (EFC), the body for regular consultation between the finance ministries, the ECB and the European Commission. Such ad-hoc committee should be composed of the competent representatives of the member states finance ministries and supervisory authorities, with the chairman of the European Forum of Financial Supervisors, a representative of the European Central Bank and the European Commission.

Expressed schematically, the structure looks as given in Table 4. Committees in between square brackets do not yet exist, committees in bold are related to proposals made in this chapter.

The creation of a European Forum of Financial Supervisors could also be a useful way to stimulate where necessary co-operation between sectoral supervisors at the national level. Banking and insurance supervisors have gone their own ways in, for example, negotiating directives, and it is only with the growth of conglomerates that the resulting inconsistencies are beginning to be recognised and require resolution. Such a Forum would encourage them to agree on joint approaches to integrated groups or common views on cross-sectoral matters.

Supervision of Securities Markets
Securities market supervision involves both the supervision of markets and exchanges, narrowly defined, and of the firms that trade on them. It is essentially focused on devising, implementing and enforcing conduct-of-

Table 4.   The Structure of European Supervisory and Regulatory Cooperation

	Banking	Insurance	Securities Markets	Cross-sector and horizontal matters
Regulatory	Banking Advisory Committee (BAC)	Insurance Committee (IAC)	[Securities Committee]	FSPG Mixed Technical Group on Financial Conglomerates
Supervisory	Groupe de Contact	Conference of Insurance Supervisors	FESCO	*[Forum of Financial Supervisors]*
Financial stability	Banking Supervision Committee (ESCB plus EU non-central bank supervisors)			EFC *[Observatory for Systemic Risk]*

business rules: the control of integrity and transparency of markets, the behaviour of individual participants and the protection of investors. It is a different task from supervising the financial soundness of institutions, and it can be argued to keep both separate.

The development of a harmonised regulatory framework for EU securities markets and for investment business generally is less advanced than in the area of banking. Harmonisation has not gone as far and more reliance is placed on mutual recognition, as for example in conduct-of-business rules, which has hampered market integration. At member state level, the creation of separate supervisory authorities is of recent, and in some cases, very recent origin. Far-reaching differences remain in the institutional structure of supervision, the division between regulation and self-regulation, or between the powers of the national securities market regulator and the various market authorities.

The rapid integration of capital markets in EMU and the lack of a regulatory framework for the integration of stock markets in the EU have led some to argue for a European SEC to help overcome these barriers. Although it is not always clear just what proponents mean, and whether they are focussed simply on markets and exchanges or also on firms, we believe that it would be a step too far. Not only is there a prior need for more regulatory harmonisation, which the European Commission is committed to achieving, but also the arguments for a more integrated supervisory authority are less compelling for securities markets than for financial institutions. Risks related to inadequate respect of conduct of business rules are overall less disturbing than those related to insufficient institutional supervision. It follows that some degree of competition between systems may do no harm and could indeed be desirable. This is implicit in the principles governing the single market, as long as it does not hamper market integration. It also fits with the current structure of supervision of EU securities markets, where the dividing line between regulation and self-regulation differs importantly from country to country (Lannoo, 1999).

In order to achieve further harmonisation of securities market regulation, the next step should be an acceleration of the decision procedure towards the creation of an EU Securities Committee, to parallel the other two EC regulatory committees and for it to review not only to the ISD and CAD, but also the other securities directives. Moreover, clarity should be achieved to establish its relationship with the other existing securities committees which are in place, and a division of labour agreed with FESCO, the Forum of European Securities Commissions.

FESCO was created in December 1997 to enhance the exchange of information between the national securities commissions, to provide the broadest possible mutual assistance to strengthen market surveillance and effective enforcement against abuse, to ensure uniform implementation of EU directives and to develop common regulatory standards in areas that are not harmonised by European directives. Each FESCO member is committed to implementing these standards in its home jurisdiction.

In a recent agreement, FESCO has come forward with a categorisation of investors for the purpose of conduct of business rules.[8] For large and institutional investors, some protections afforded by conduct of business rules may be waived. The paper does, however, not address the crucial issue of home vs. host state rules, and implies that a total harmonisation of conduct of business rules is feasible, which seems fairly illusory. It does not solve the problem which exists today of the possible application of overlapping or conflicting rules of conduct in cross-border trading. Even if certain rules may be waived under the FESCO agreement, it does not guarantee that the conduct of business rules will be the same for cross-border trades. A communication is therefore urgently needed from the European Commission on the interpretation of article 11 of the investment services directive (ISD), which allows for a distinction between wholesale and retail investors, allowing the former to be subject to home country conduct of business rules only, whereas retail investors would be given more protection. This should, at a later stage, lead to a limited amendment of the directive.

A Further Levelling of the Playing Field at EU Level

A more integrated financial market will highlight the shortcomings in the EU regulatory framework. Three areas are at the core of the policy debate, and are closely related to the level playing field: (1) common approaches to banks in trouble; (2) the strict application of EU competition policy rules to state aids in banking; (3) greater transparency in the rules applicable to banking mergers.

Several European banks have been bailed out over the last decade at high public expense. The governments in question were motivated by a variety of fears, including the belief that the bank was "too big to fail" and cause too much economic damage to both depositors and borrowers, that a failure might be contagious and spread through interbank settlement systems (as in so-called Herstatt risk), or lead to a general loss of confidence in the banking system and trigger damaging bank runs. As a result, a moral hazard problem remains.

Designing a safety net in the banking sector is a difficult exercise. On the extreme end are economists who argue that there is little proof of systemic risk in banking, but that bank failures happen in isolation. However, these bank failures may be induced by bad government policies. Excessively explicit safety nets in banking lead to imprudent risk-taking and induce moral hazard. Bank managers may be aware in some countries that the government will not let a bank fail and do not make sound risk assessments. On the basis of a large data set, Kaufman (1996) showed that there was little proof of systemic risk in banking. There were less bank failures in the U.S. before 1930, when deposit guarantee systems were introduced in the U.S., than after. Kaufman argues that bank failures result from bad management and economic downturns, but do not fall like dominos, eliminating the capital of each bank in a chain. As a result, government should focus on the macroeconomy, and let badly-managed banks fail.

Notwithstanding these objections, it is still commonly accepted that there is some kind of systemic risk in banking. The U.S. research may not be applicable in the context of the very differently structured European banking system. Interbank loans form a much more important part of European banking, and may be an important transmitter of systemic shocks.[9] The problem is how to respond to the phenomenon without creating adverse incentives for bank managers. So far, governments have kept LOLR procedures deliberately vague. To reduce moral hazard, procedural and practical details of emergency actions are secret. The design of LOLR support in EMU is also seen as part of this "constructive ambiguity" (Schinasi, 1998). Others have argued that this approach should no longer be applicable. Maintaining a high degree of ambiguity may itself have led to excessive risk-taking by financial institutions and too much forbearance by authorities in the face of banking problems. Such a policy can only be modified in a climate of greater transparency concerning the support which will be offered to banks in trouble, and under what circumstances (Enoch et al., 1997).

Within a European context, the choice of responses is limited, since several policies have been applied in the member states. Some states have selectively let certain banks fail, whereas others have used large amounts of taxpayers' money to rescue a bank and/or gone to considerable efforts to arrange rescues through mergers. Such policies may have reduced market discipline in European banking and stimulated over-capacity. A more common policy for bank exit policies can thus only be implemented with clear indications from governments.

A combination of preventive (ex ante) and remedial (ex post) measures is needed. As part of the ex-ante policies, prompt corrective action (PCA) should be implemented across the EU. With PCA, supervisors undertake a gradualist response to banks in trouble. They typically set pre-specified minimum capital ratios which initiate a progressive series of restrictions on the problem bank's activities. This reduces the potential for regulators to apply forbearance and allow problems to become magnified, and reduces the danger that responses will be inconsistent with competitive neutrality (ESFRC, 1998). The need for prompt corrective action is now formally proposed by the Basel Committee in its capital review, as part of the so-called "pillar two", the supervisory review process. It sets out that early intervention by the authorities may be needed where a bank's capital is falling relative to its risk. The focus of Basel is primarily on moral suasion to improve risk management and internal controls, whereas higher minimum capital ratios for supervisory intervention, so-called "trigger ratios" are the exception: "In a few regimes, capital ratios represent triggers for supervisory action" (Basel paper, p. 58). This position was supported in the recent Commission paper on the review of the regulatory capital requirements (European Commission, 1999). However, the Basel Review is used by the European Commission as a justification for the differences in national supervisory practices, which seems in contradiction with the need for more convergence of supervisory practices in the context of strong market integration.[10]

As regards pillar three of the supervisory review, disclosure, it is unclear at this stage how far it should go. The Basel Committee came out in favour of extensive disclosure of actual regulatory capital ratios, the capital structure and risk exposure, without clarifying whether the capital requirement imposed by supervisors should be disclosed. The Commission, however, while generally being supportive of disclosure, affirmed that the capital requirement imposed by supervisors upon a bank (as distinct from its holding of regulatory capital) should not be made public. Publication of supervisors assessments could blunt the incentive for depositors and investors to make their own credit assessment, according to the European Commission, and changes in ratios could be incorrectly interpreted by analysts and lead to overreaction such as deposit runs. The latter could in its turn constrain action by supervisors (European Commission, 1999b, p. 79). It could on the other hand also be argued that this may maintain the old thinking on constructive ambiguity, and perhaps not provide the right incentives to supervisors on how to deal with institutions in trouble.

Harmonised remedial policies are probably less of a policy priority at the moment. With PCA procedures in place, the likelihood of the supervisors actually needing to liquidate banks should be reduced. However, harmonised bank and insurance winding-up procedures have become more urgent given the increasing scale of cross-border business. Proposals were blocked for many years because of differences in views on the feasibility of a European approach to bankruptcy procedures. The Commission's Financial Services Action Plan reiterated the need for urgent adoption of these measures, which seems now finally to have got effect. Both measures were recently adopted by the EU Council.[11]

In the event that a bank is bailed out, the process is in principle subject to the EU rules on state aid, as set out in Article 92 of the EU Treaty. These rules have been detailed, as far as their application to the banking sector is concerned, in the Crédit Lyonnais case.[12] While acknowledging the special nature of the banking sector, the Commission says that Community law, especially the solvency ratio directive, has clearly set a criterion of "equal competitive conditions". Thus, if state financial support is provided to banks, the Commission must establish whether the Treaty rules are being respected. Exceptions can be made, however, if a serious disturbance threatens the economy (Art. 92.3.b).

It has been argued that the banking sector should be exempted from the application of Art. 92 of the Treaty because of its special character and its role in financial stability (Grande, 1999). Banking supervisors should have independence in their assessment of the means of dealing with problem banks. Since banking supervision is kept at the local level in the EU, state aid should also be taken out of EU hands and decentralised. This would, however, open the door to dangerous precedents, and clear the way for all other forms of hidden state aids, such as state-guaranteed loans. It would also be inconsistent with giving the ECB some a-priori involvement in LOLR procedures at local level, as discussed above. What could be argued for is some form of accelerated procedure for handling state aid issues in relation to state support for banks.

If state aid control were somehow to be decentralised, there would also be no way to equalise competition in Community-wide bank take-overs. As indicated earlier, restructuring of financial markets in the EU has hitherto mainly taken place at national level, which has led to high levels of concentration in certain national markets. More European cross-border consolidation will increase competition and reduce the danger of oligopolies at national level. Emphasising the arguments of the special character of the banking sector would make it easier for local authorities to intervene in foreign hostile bank take-overs and further stimulate purely national consolidation. It should be clear that cross-border transactions involving the control of banks, or indeed other financial institutions, should not be prevented or burdened for reasons other than anti-trust or safety and soundness concerns.

Take-over legislation, however, is not harmonised at EU level. Securities laws differ importantly from one country to another in the Community, with large differences in the rights attached to shares, in the powers of boards of directors and shareholders and in company law generally. Also the role of the supervisory authorities for take-overs differs importantly, or in some countries rules do not even yet exist (Lannoo, 1999). In the domain of banking, the national central bank, banking supervisor or ministry of finance are, to different degrees across countries, entitled to scrutinise bank take-overs, on the grounds that they are responsible for financial stability and prudential supervision. These authorities often have extensive discretionary powers, as was exemplified recently in France, Italy and Portugal. EU authorities should make sure that the general EU Treaty rules are respected, and the supervisory aspects of bank take-overs are based on the prudential rules of the EU's 2nd banking and solvency ratio directives, so as to ensure that eventual refusals have a clear basis. In the case of the Portuguese objections to the BSCH/Champalimaud merger, the European Commission referred the case to the European Court for non-compliance with the merger control regulation. This case was withdrawn in March 2000 after Portugal blocked its opposition to the concentration.

The securities law aspects of take-overs are dealt with in the draft EU take-over bids directive, on which a political agreement was reached in June 1999. This directive may, however, not change much, since many matters are left to the national implementing law. Moreover, the directive has 2004 as implementation deadline.

In the insurance sector, bail-outs or insolvencies have been very rare. Liabilities of insurance companies are backed mostly by readily marketable assets, established to cover future claims from the policies underwritten. Rules on the prudential asset spread are defined in the EU's third insurance directives. In addition, insurance companies are required to hold a certain amount of additional resources for unexpected losses, the solvency margin, and they usually reinsure part of their risks with reinsurance companies. According to a Commission report, this system has worked well: over the last 20 years, only a few cases of deficiencies of insurance companies were observed in the European Economic Area (EEA). A significant proportion of these could be remedied through a capital increase or by a take-over by other insurance undertakings, thus avoiding final insolvency and winding-up.[13]

The potential for systemic risk in the insurance sector is not currently regarded as particularly significant. However three factors could render insurance companies more prone to systemic risk: (i) elements of consumer protection law which allow consumers to withdraw policies easily (and before maturity), or regulation which requires a guaranteed nominal rate of return on life insurance policies, as is set by legislation in most EU member states; (ii) macro-economic instability, deflation and fall in asset values, as was the case in Japan; (iii) the emergence of *bancassurance* firms or integrated financial conglomerates. In case of the first two factors, systemic risk would be provoked by imprudent government policies, the last is, within a European perspective, the most critical for regulators at present. The current lack of cross-border co-ordination in dealing with insurance groups and predominantly insurance-led conglomerates should begin to be addressed following the implementation of the Insurance Groups Directive.

A summary of the required changes in light of EMU and growing market integration is given in Table 5.

V. CONCLUSIONS

Financial supervision in a European context needs to evolve progressively with growing market integration, but a more centralised approach in financial supervision can only be justified where national or local approaches are no longer adequate for performing the task. A co-ordinated approach is now necessary to handle systemic issues that will no longer be limited to national borders, but also, and increasingly, for monitoring financial institutions with operations in a range of European countries. There is a vital need to identify a lead supervisor for each financial group and to reach agreement on precisely what the responsibilities of a lead supervisor would be. On the other hand, it is less compelling for the control of conduct-of-business rules in retail financial services or in dealing in securities markets.

In addressing the structure of financial supervision at European level, a more horizontal approach, based on the objectives of supervision, is required. It is adapted to the conglomeration trend in the financial sector and makes it easier to detect and handle lacunae in the present supervisory structure. For systemic issues, there is no discussion of leaving the central banks in charge of these matters, but the role of the ESCB could still benefit from more public clarification, and some joint body created to monitor aggregate exposures. In addition, central banks, supervisors and finance ministries will need to co-operate to draft principles governing bail-outs of European-wide groups, which currently implicitly fall to the country of control and consolidated supervision. Since the LOLR role presumes the back-up of a finance ministry, who may not

Table 5.   Objectives of financial supervision and changes in the perspective of growing European market integration

Objective of supervision	Current structure	Required changes
Systemic risk (financial stability)	• National supervisory authorities and/or NCBs	• Role for ESCB/ECB and national supervisors in monitoring systemic exposures in European financial markets • Create European Observatory of Systemic Risk • Give role to Economic and Financial Committee (EFC) to coordinate emergency intervention
Prudential control (solvency control/protection of depositors/investors/ policyholders)	• National supervisory authorities (home country) • Bilateral Memoranda of Understanding • Different attitudes to banks in trouble • Excessive forbearance	• Strengthen supervisory co-ordination through creation of Forum of Financial Supervisors • Prompt corrective action policies EU-wide • Harmonise supervisory practices • Harmonise winding up arrangements • Align bank exit policies
Conduct of business (protection of consumers and investors)	• Host country (country where service is provided) for retail and wholesale business • No level playing field for bank take-overs	• Home country rules for wholesale business • Common interpretation of rules (FESCO) • Application of EU Treaty rules for bank take-overs

be prepared to bail out creditors in other member states, burden-sharing between European countries is for the time being the only way forward.

On the supervisory side, more co-ordination is needed between the different sectoral committees. This is not in place for the time being, but is probably what is most needed in view of the continuing restructuring in European finance. A kind of European Forum of Financial Supervisors should therefore be urgently created. This forum should primarily discuss problems in the adequate supervision of large European financial groups, and if necessary, draft a multi-lateral and -sectoral MoU. Such a body should also set a work programme to align supervisory practices in the EU to ease pan-European operations.

How the institutional framework for financial supervision will look like in a decade is still an open question at this point. From what is already happening in the markets, a more uniform system of supervision will at some stage be required, and the strict sectoral division of financial supervision will be increasingly out of date. A reconfiguration of the structures of financial supervision, based on a clear setting out of the objectives of financial supervision, would be useful.

A further institutionalisation of supervisory functions at European level is, as circumstances currently stand, legally and practically impossible and in any case unlikely to be politically acceptable. Whether in due course there will be unified European institutions rather than networks of national authorities will depend a lot both on the ways in which markets develop and authorities react. Efficiency of operation will be a major issue, as will consistency with underlying national differences, not least in many detailed aspects of market structure. Whether EU and national authorities will see merit in transcending their individual perspectives when reacting to developments set into motion by EMU and the internal market, and contemplate the establishment of transnational supervisors remains a very open question.

ACKNOWLEDGMENT

This chapter was written in the context of a Centre for European Policy Studies (CEPS) working party on the subject. Valuable ideas were contributed by the Working Party Chairman, David Green, the Working Party members, and those who made presentations to the Working Party, but the chapter is not – and could not purport to be – agreed by each member of the Working Party. For more information about CEPS, see www.ceps.be

NOTES

1. The FSA has rule-making powers and is accountable to the government and Parliament. Its statutory objectives are: (a) to maintain confidence in the financial system, (b) to promote public understanding of the financial system, (c) to secure the appropriate degree of consumer protection, (d) to reduce financial crime. The Bank of England remains responsible for ensuring the overall stability of the financial system. The Bank would be the vehicle for lender of last resort operations, if any, and with the prior agreement of the Treasury. A Memorandum of Understanding between the Treasury, the Bank of England and the FSA sets out the respective responsibilities of the different bodies.

2. It has been suggested that the ECB might assume such a role but it should be noted that Treaty Article 105.6 "The Council may (. . .) confer upon the ECB specific tasks concerning policies relating to the prudential supervision of credit institutions and other financial institutions with the exception of insurance undertakings", only refers to "specific tasks concerning policies", not day-to-day supervision, in which case a Treaty change would also be required.

3. "Die Unterschiedde in den Banken- und Aufsichtssytemen sind so gross, dass sie sich, wenn uberhaupt, nur auf sehr lange Sicht überwinden lassen", Gertrude Tumpel-Gugerell, Vice-Governor of the Bank of Austria at the Alpbach Forum, quoted in Handelsblatt, 3.9.1999.

4. Switzerland is not part of FESCO, as it is not a member of the EEA.

5. As stated by Tommaso Padoa Schioppa, member of the ECB executive board, at the CFS Conference "Systemic risk and lender of last resort facilities", Frankfurt, 11 June 1999. An agreement on this subject is said to have been reached in the ECB's Governing Council at the end of July.

6. Some ministries of finance are currently thought to be pushing for a debate on this subject, but others potentially involved are said to be unwilling to address such issues in the abstract.

7. One of the issues which could be monitored by the Observatory is a European risk centre (see Meister, 2000).

8. FESCO, Categorisation of investors for the purpose of the application of the conduct of business rules, 15 March 2000.

9. Interbank assets form 17% of the balance sheet of EU banks, as compared to 3% in the US. Some 28% of these loans are collateralised in the EU. See Lannoo (2000).

10. "Beyond basic enabling powers, each competent authority operates in a different legal, accounting and cultural context, and it is appropriate that supervisory approaches differ. The Instruments chosen to implement the new principles should allow supervisors to adopt different supervisory approaches," European Commission, 1999b, p. 70.

11. The EU Council reached a political agreement on the winding-up procedures for banks on May 8, 2000 and on those for insurance companies on May 25.

12. Commission Decision of 26 July 1995 giving conditional approval to the aid granted by France to Crédit Lyonnais, OJ L 308 of 21.12.1995.

13. European Commission, Report to the Insurance Committee on the Need for Further Harmonisation of the Solvency Margin, COM (97) 398, 24.07.97.

14. This survey is largely based upon the Banking Advisory Committee's most recent report of the chairman (1994–1997)

REFERENCES

Aglietta, M., & de Boissieu, C. (1998), Problèmes prudentiels. In: *Co-ordination européenne des politiques economiques*. Paris: Conseil d'analyse économique.

Basel Committee on Banking Supervision (1999). *A New Capital Adequacy Framework*, Consultative Paper, June.

BIS Quarterly Review (????). *International banking and financial market developments*, various issues.

Briault, C. (1999). *The rationale for a single national financial services regulator*, FSA Occasional Paper.

Clifford C. (1998). *The draft financial services and markets bill, A framework for the future*, September.

Dale, R., & Wolfe, S. (1998). The structure of financial regulation. *Journal of financial regulation and compliance*, 6(4), 326–350.

Davies, H. (1999). *Euro-Regulation, Lecture for the European Financial Forum*, Brussels, 8 April.

Danthine, J-P., Giavazzi, F., Vives, X., & von Thadden, E-L. (1999), *The Future of European Banking*, Monitoring European Integration, CEPR.

Deutsche Bank Research (1999). *M&A rules in Europe's banking industry: a need for reform?* August 20.

Dewatripont, M., & Tirole, J. (1994). *The prudential regulation of banks*. MIT-Press.

Fender, I., & von Hagen, J. (1998). *Central bank policy in a more perfect financial system*, ZEI policy paper B98–03.

Enoch, C., Stella, P., & Khamis, M. (1997). *Transparency and Ambiguity in Central Bank Safety Net Operations*, IMF Working Paper 97/138, October.

European Central Bank (1999). *Effects of EMU on the EU banking system in the medium to long term*, February.

European Commission. *Banking Advisory Committee*, Report of the Chairman, Various issues.

European Commission (2000b). *Report on Financial Stability*, Prepared by the ad-hoc working group of the Economic and Financial Committee, Economic Papers, Number 143, May.

European Commission (2000a). *Institutional Arrangements for the Regulation and Supervision of the Financial Sector*, January.

European Commission (1999b). *A review of regulatory capital requirements for EU credit institutions and investment firms*, Consultation document, November.

European Commission (1999a). *Financial Services Action Plan*.

European Commission (1998). *Financial services: Building a framework for action*. Communication to the Council and the European Parliament, 28 October.

European Investment Bank (1999). European banking after EMU. *EIB Papers*, 4(1).

European Shadow Financial Regulatory Committee (ESFRC) (1998). *Dealing with problem banks in Europe*, Statement No.1, 22 June.

European Shadow Financial Regulatory Committee (1998). *EMU, the ECB and financial supervision*, Statement No. 2, 19 October.

Favero, C., Freixas, X., Persson, T., & Wyplosz, C. (2000). *One Money, Many Countries, Monitoring the European Central Bank 2*, CEPR.

Goodhart, C. (1999). *Myths about the Lender of Last Resort*, mimeo.

Goodhart, C., Hartmann, P., Llewellyn, D. T., Rojas-Suarez, L., & Weisbrod, S. R. (1997), *Financial regulation: Why, how and where now?* Routledge.

Goodhart, C., & Schoenmaker, D. (1995). Should the functions of monetary policy and banking supervision be separated? In: *Oxford Economic Papers* (Vol. 47, pp. 539–560).

Grande, M. (1999). *Possible decentralisation of state aid control in the banking sector*, Paper presented at the EU Competition Workshops on State Aid, EUI, June.

Green, David (2000). Enhanced co-operation among regulators and the role of national regulators in a global market. In: *Journal of International Financial Markets* (Vol 2, Issue 1, pp. 7–12).

Gros, D. (1998). *European Financial Markets and Global Financial Turmoil: Any Danger of a Credit Crunch?* CEPS Working Document No. 127.

Inzerillo U., Morelli, P., & Pittaluga, G. (2000), Deregulation and changes in the European Banking Industry. In: Galli, Giampaolo & Jacques Pelkmans (Eds), *Regulatory Reform and Competitiveness in Europe* (2000).

Kaufman, G. G. (1995), Comment on systemic risk. *Research in Financial Services Private and Public Policy*, 7, p. 47–52.

Kaufman, G. G. (1996), Bank failures, systemic risk and regulation, *Cato Journal*, *16*(1), 17–45.

Lannoo, K., & Stadler, V. (2000), *The EU Repo Markets*, Study for the European Commission.

Lannoo, K. (1999). *Does Europe Need an SEC?*, European Capital Markets Institute (ECMI), Occasional Paper No. 1, November.

Lannoo, K., & Gros, D. (1998), *Capital markets and EMU*, Report of a CEPS Working Party, CEPS, July.

Lannoo, K. (1995), The Single Market in Banking – A First Assessment, *Butterworths Journal of Banking and Financial Law*, November, London.

Mayes, D. (1999). *On the problems of the home country*, mimeo.

Meister, E. (2000), *Die Hüter eines stabilen Finanzsystems*, Frankfurter Allgemeine, 8 April.

Ministry of Finance, The Netherlands (1999). *Institutionele vormgeving van het toezicht op de financiële marktsector*, April.

OECD (1999). *Bank Profitability Statistics*.

Molyneux, P. (1997). *Internet and the Global Challenges for Financial Services in Europe*, Paper presented at a CEPS seminar, October.

Padoa-Schioppa, T. (1999). EMU and Banking Supervision. *International Finance*, 2(2), 295–308.

Prati, A., & Schinasi, G. (1998). *Will the ECB be the lender of last resort in EMU?* Paper presented at the SUERF Conference, Frankfurt, October 1998.

Schoenmaker, D. (1995). *Banking Supervision in Stage Three of EMU, in CEPS*.

Shadow Financial Regulatory Committees of Europe, Japan, and the U.S. (1999). *Improving the Basle Committee's New Capital Adequacy Framework*, Joint Statement of a Sub-group, June.

Vander Vennet R. (1998). *Cost and profit dynamics in financial conglomerates and universal banks*. Paper presented at the Suerf Conference, October.

White, W. R. (1998). *The Coming Transformation of Continental European Banking*, BIS Working Papers No. 54, June.

APPENDIX

EU AND EEA FORA FOR CO-OPERATION IN FINANCIAL SUPERVISION

Banking
 (1) Banking Advisory Committee (BAC)[14]
    • established in 1977 by the First Banking Co-ordination Directive
    • threefold role: (1) assists the European Commission in drawing up new proposals for banking legislation, (2) helps to ensure adequate implementation, (3) serves as the "regulatory committee" under the so-called "comitology" procedures for technical amendments to EC banking legislation, these are changes which can be made outside the normal legislative procedure
    • consists of high-level officials from finance ministries, central banks and supervisory authorities of the member states and from the Commission, with a maximum of three representatives per national delegation; officials from other EEA countries and the ECB participate as observers; the chairman of the Groupe de Contact also attends
    • chairman is chosen for a three year period from representatives of member states, secretarial services are provided by the European Commission
    • meets three to four times a year
    • discussions are confidential, but a tri-annual report is published by the chairman
    • when committee acts as "regulatory committee", it is chaired by the European Commission
    • does not consider specific problems related to individual credit institutions
 (2) Groupe de Contact (established 1972)
    • set up by banking supervisors of EEA member states on a co-operative basis
    • deals with micro-prudential co-operation, including on information sharing both in general and in particular cases, and carries out comparative studies on techniques of supervision. It also assembles, as required under the banking directives, various EEA-wide statistical services including on solvency, profitability and liquidity
    • consists of one official from each banking supervisory authority in the EEA; an official from the Commission also attends as adviser on legal

issues but does not attend discussions dealing either with individual firms or sensitive supervisory assessments.

(3) Banking Supervision Committee of the ECB (established 1998)
- succeeded Sub-committee on Banking Supervision of the European Monetary Institute, which had originally been created in 1990 as the Banking Supervisory Sub-committee of the Committee of Governors of the EC Central Banks
- assists the ESCB with regard to policy issues in the area of macro-prudential supervision, this is the stability of financial institutions and markets, and in preparing ECB opinions on legislation as provided for under the Treaty
- consists of high-level officials from all central banks and non-central bank supervisory authorities in member states plus ECB officials; Commission officials participate as observers
- duplication of work is avoided through regular informal co-ordination meetings between chairmen of each of the three committees dealing with banking supervisory matters

Securities Markets
(4) Contact Committee (established 1979)
- advisory committee, without comitology role (except for one issue, which was never touched)
- facilitates harmonised implementation and advise the Commission on any supplements or amendments to the 1979 stock exchange admission, 1980 listing particulars, 1989 prospectus, 1989 insider dealing, 1988 major holdings and forthcoming take-over bids directives
- allows regular consultation between the member states on these matters
(5) UCITS Contact Committee (established 1985)
- advisory committee, without comitology role
- facilitates harmonised implementation and advises the Commission on any amendments to the 1985 UCITS directive (unit trusts directive)
(6) High-Level Committee of Securities Market Supervisors (established 1985)
- strategic committee, meets 2 to 3 times a year at the initiative of the European Commission
- no formal legal basis, functions as Commission working group until Securities Committee is formally established by an EU directive
- advises the European Commission on regulatory and supervisory matters

(7) FESCO (Forum of European Securities Commissions, established December 1997)
   • originates from Informal Group of Chairmen of EU Securities Commissions
   • brings together securities commissions of the European Economic Area (the EU, Iceland and Norway)
   • aims to enhance the exchange of information between national securities commissions, to provide the broadest possible mutual assistance to enhance market surveillance and effective enforcement, to enhance uniform implementation of EU directives and to develop common regulatory standards in areas that are not harmonised by European directives
(8) Securities Committee (proposed)
   • high-level committee with implementing powers for the investment services and capital adequacy directives
   • rejected twice because of procedural problems and sensitivity of European Parliament to "comitology"
   • relaunched in the Commission's financial services action plan (May 1999), to be proposed end–2000

Insurance
(9) Insurance Committee (established 1992)
   • assists the European Commission with regard to policy issues in the formulation and implementation of EC legislation for the insurance sector, consultative role for new Commission proposals
   • consists of high-level officials from finance ministries and supervisory authorities of the member states plus Commission officials; officials from other EEA countries participate as observers
   • serves as "regulatory committee" under the so-called "comitology" procedures for technical amendments to EC insurance legislation (life and non-life insurance)
   • does not consider specific problems related to individual insurance undertakings
(10) Conference of Insurance Supervisory Authorities of the EU (established 1958)
   • forum for debate among EU supervisors on micro-prudential issues relating to individual insurance undertakings
   • agreed on 'protocols', a form of multilateral memorandum of understanding between insurance supervisors, to deal with supervisory problems

- composed of 15 EU states and 3 EEA countries, with European Commission as observer (no formal link with EU)
- meets twice a year

Cross-Sector Fora

(11) Commission Mixed Technical Group on Financial Conglomerates
- Established in 1999, involving representatives of the sectoral regulatory committees
- Considers information sharing between supervisors and co-ordination of prudential supervision on a cross-sectoral and cross-border basis, capital adequacy at group level and intra-group transactions,

COMMENT

Robert DeYoung

The organizing principle for today's sessions is extremely broad, and includes four concepts – bank fragility, bank regulation, different geographic locations, and different temporal locations. Individually, the chapters in this first session have in common only one of these four concepts – bank regulation – but as a group these chapters link together all four of the principle organizing concepts. Together, they analyze the impact of past, present, and potential regulations on banking crises in the United States, the European Union, and worldwide.

To consider this many ideas at once, it helps to start out with a simple, overarching framework like the one shown in Fig. 1. The figure, titled "Cycle of Regulatory Causes and Consequences", depicts the straightforward notion that a good many of the bank regulatory problems faced by governments around the world themselves stem from earlier regulatory efforts to prevent contagious bank runs (1), by providing deposit insurance (2). But like most interventions into markets, deposit insurance produces ancillary consequences – namely, if failing banks can 'put' their deposit liabilities to the government, then financially troubled banks with insured deposits face a moral hazard incentive to make risky investments (3). Thus, in a world where banks can issue insured deposits, an additional layer of regulation becomes necessary to counter-act moral hazard risk-taking. Minimum equity capital requirements (4) are designed to reduce these risk-taking incentives by maintaining large amounts of investor capital at risk.

But the cycle doesn't stop there. Banks can satisfy the letter of risk-based capital rules but circumvent their meaning, for example, by holding more equity capital but taking increased credit risk (5). So a third round of

Bank Fragility and Regulation: Evidence from Different Countries, Volume 12,
pages 163–173.
Copyright © 2000 by Elsevier Science Inc.
All rights of reproduction in any form reserved.
ISBN: 0-7623-0698-X

regulations becomes necessary to shore-up the capital rules (6). This is where regulators find themselves today, considering new regulations that would allow banks to use their own internal risk models to decide how much risk capital is necessary. But this is no end game, either, because like the regulatory fixes from earlier in the cycle, internal models approaches have incentive incompatibility problems, too. If not carefully constructed, capital regulation using internal models is somewhat akin to letting the fox guard the hen house.

Although this iterative process of regulation, followed by circumvention, followed by re-regulation may gradually dampen the cycle of regulatory cause and consequence – especially if it is accompanied by common sense acts like geographic and product deregulation which can allow banks to reduce risk by diversifying – multiple layers of increasingly complex regulations may just as

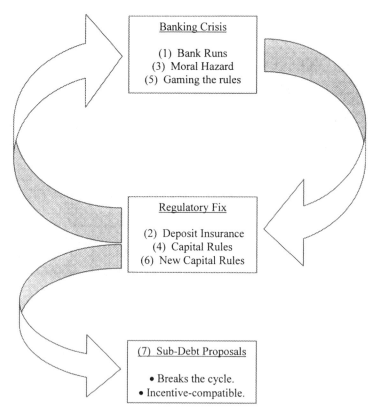

Fig. 1. Cycle of Regulatory Causes-and-Consequences.

likely spawn unexpected reactions by banks that amplify the cycle. In contrast to this approach, two of the chapters in this session argue that the cycle could be short-circuited if banks were required to issue traded subordinated debt (7). Proponents argue that regulation that makes sub-debt mandatory – unlike deposit insurance, risk-based capital, or internal models approaches – is incentive-compatible. Market participants with pure upside benefits (i.e. the sub-debt holders) have incentives to keep bank risk-taking in check, or at a minimum will sell their investment if bank risk-taking increases, which sends an important signal to supervisors.

I. A SUBORDINATED DEBT PROPOSAL FOR U.S. BANKS

The chapter by Evanoff and Wall ("Subordinated Debt and Bank Capital Reform") outlines an explicit subordinated debt proposal for U.S. banks. Although the details of this proposal differ somewhat from the details of other sub-debt proposals, the general thrust of all these proposals is similar. Of course, the devil is always in the details, and Evanoff and Wall sort out and catalog the detailed differences between their proposal and previous proposals. The authors also provide help for the less-than-fully-initiated reader with an excellent question-and-answer section about subordinated debt proposals in general.

Most proponents of mandatory subordinated debt stress its potential to control bank risk-taking in three ways: it will increase direct market discipline of banks that take excessive risks; it will provide supervisors with more timely information about changes in bank riskiness; and it will improve the effectiveness of prompt corrective action tripwires by providing market signals as triggers. We should keep in mind that however logical these claims seem, at this point they are just claims, and that there are other points of view about just how effectively subordinated debt could be used to help control risk-taking at banks.

For example, proponents point out that an increase in bank riskiness will be reflected in a lower price (higher yield) for subordinated debt, and this will increase the bank's cost of funding the next time it is required to sell subordinated debt to the market. But the bank can avoid this direct market discipline by taking some risk-reducing action (e.g. reducing the riskiness of its assets, slowing its rate of growth, raising additional equity capital). However, there is no guarantee that the bank will take these actions, or take them in measures large enough to offset fully the initial increase in risk. Bliss and Flannery (2000) argue that changes in a bank's securities prices will certainly help stakeholders monitor the bank, but will not necessarily influence bank management to make changes absent supervisory coercion. Lang and Robertson (2000) argue that direct market discipline effects from subordinated debt are likely to be weak, because the overall costs in higher interest expenses will in many cases be small compared to the expected benefit to bank owners and/or managers from taking increased risk.

Another important claim is that mandatory sub-debt will provide more timely information (in between scheduled exams) or higher quality information (because traders' money is at risk) than what examiners can learn themselves about a bank's safety and soundness. Whether or not the bond market gathers information ahead of the supervisor is an empirically testable question, and has been examined to a limited extent for banking companies that already issue subordinated debt. Evanoff and Wall review this small but growing literature, and I agree with their assessments that: (a) information generated by various market participants (bond markets, equity markets, rating agencies, etc.) appears to be complementary to supervisors' information set, but that (b) more work in this area is warranted.

Certainly, more intense study of how subordinated debt prices react to changes in bank risk-taking would help regulators accurately parameterize any market-based tripwires for prompt corrective action. However, the Lucas critique applies here. In response to changes in bank riskiness, bank subordinated debt yields currently move up and down unfettered by any possibility that these movements will trigger a regulatory intervention – but when market-based trip wires are put in place, will these yields react the same way? Will investors place a ceiling on sub-debt yields once market-based tripwires guarantee regulatory intervention for banks with high or increasing yields? DeYoung, Flannery, Lang and Sorescu (2001) find evidence consistent with this notion: they find that movements in sub-debt yields reflect the likelihood of *regulatory* discipline. Thus, the past behavior of subordinated debt prices may not be an accurate indicator of the future behavior of subordinated debt prices under a different regulatory regime.

On balance, what should we conclude about subordinated debt proposals? Upon close inspection, advocates of these policies are proceeding based on economic logic and their faith in the efficiency of bond markets; there is relatively little information about how well mandatory sub-debt will work in practice. However, logic is always a good place to start. And since the costs of running the experiment to reveal how well mandatory sub-debt will work are relatively low, and the benefits are potentially large, it seems like an experiment worth running.

II. REGULATORY PROPOSALS IN THE EUROPEAN UNION

The chapter by Benink and Schmidt ("A Regulatory Agenda for Banking in Europe") also discusses a proposal for mandatory subordinated debt, presented alongside seven other regulatory proposals made by the European Shadow Financial Regulatory Committee (ESFRC) during its first two years of existence. In my opinion, this chapter could have been titled "The ESFRC: Get to know us!" It is an excellent introduction for those (like me) who knew little of this group beforehand; having read the paper, the Euro Shadow group now seems like an old friend.

Not surprisingly, the Euro Shadow group is in many ways similar to the pre-existing U.S. Shadow Financial Regulatory Committee. This is not by accident, as some of the organizing members of the U.S. Shadow group (notably, George Kaufman) encouraged the formation of the ESFRC. The organizing framework is similar, albeit with international representation; the group's main objective to issue periodic statements on financial regulatory policies is the same; and many of the statements issued so far by the Euro Shadow group address issues debated in recent years by the U.S. Shadow group.

But the differences between the U.S. and European groups are more interesting. The authors describe a "european sensibility" concerning the appropriate role for government in financial markets. For example, the typical European policymaker would be more likely than the typical U.S. policymaker to advocate the use of regulation to channel credit to certain sectors, to raise cheap funds for the government, or to protect domestic banks from entry and competition. Historically there has been less interaction between academics and government practitioners in Europe than in the U.S., so building a bridge over which new academic ideas can be presented to practitioners is a more primary role for the Euro Shadow group. And perhaps most importantly, statements issued by the Euro Shadow group must take into account numerous differences in culture, history, and economic conditions across the EU member nations. Hence, making statements acceptable to members for all countries can require quite a bit of compromise, which in the end runs the danger of watering down the content of the statements.

In chronological order of issue, the eight proposals made so far by the Euro Shadow group have addressed: early regulatory intervention for troubled banks; information exchanges among the monetary and supervisory authorities; capital requirements for banks investing in over-the-counter derivatives;

reforming the Basel capital framework; reforming deposit insurance; coordinating bank merger policy across member nations; the inter-relationships between internal ratings models and subordinated debt requirements; and the rationalization of securities exchanges across national borders. The "common thread" winding through these eight statements – and one that is quite consistent with the basic message of Fig. 1 – is that regulation must be done in an incentive-compatible manner. In other words, regulations should not create incentives for banks to act contrary to the goal of the regulations (e.g. moral hazard, loan concentrations designed to circumvent risk-based capital), nor should they create incentives for regulators to delay taking actions (e.g. time-inconsistent policies, regulatory forbearance).

The sixth of the eight ESFRC statements proposes that member nations be allowed to stand in the way of cross-border mergers only if: (a) the merger in question is anticompetitive, or (b) it poses safety and soundness problems. At first blush, the need for such a statement is not obvious – why else would a government agency deny a merger? *A brief excursion through some EU merger data suggests why concern may be necessary.* All else equal, one would expect banking industry consolidation in the EU to follow a similar pattern as in the U.S., which has experienced a massive consolidation during the past decade. The Single Europe Act and the Second Banking Directive were implemented in 1992 and 1993, respectively, freeing the way for a similar pan-European consolidation of financial institutions. But the data in Figs 2 and 3 (from the Securities Data Company) show a surprising sluggishness.

Figure 2 shows that the annual number of financial institution M&As (between publicly traded banks, insurance companies, or securities firms with equity worth over $1 million) in the EU has increased since the 1980s, but the balance between domestic and cross-border M&As has remained roughly constant. As the continent transforms into a "single EU", wouldn't one expect cross-border mergers to dominate domestic mergers, as firms move across borders? Figure 3 shows that the total annual value of financial institution M&As has skyrocketed in the U.S., but not in the EU, even though the U.S. and the EU have roughly the same size economies and deregulated financial institution structures at roughly the same time.

This sluggishness is consistent with recent research suggesting that foreign banks must overcome numerous cultural, linguistic, regulatory, and nationalistic barriers when they cross borders (e.g. Parkhe & Miller, 1999, Berger & DeYoung, 2000). These barriers, which do not exist for geographically expanding banks in the U.S., may be slowing the pace of geographic consolidation in the EU. The Euro Shadow group's concerns about preventing legal and regulatory barriers to cross-border EU mergers seem well placed.

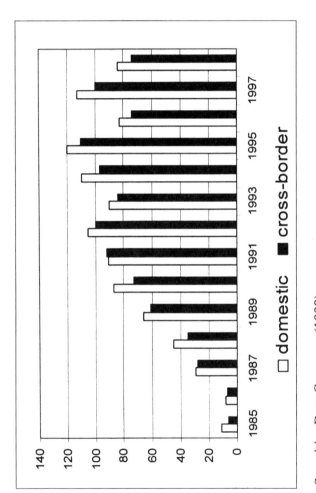

Securities Data Company (1998)

Fig. 2. Annual number of large financial institutions M&As in the EU.

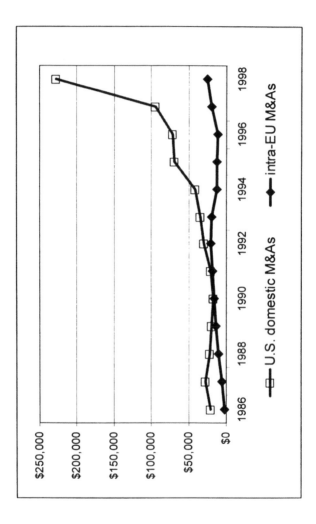

Securities Data Company (1998)

Fig. 3. Annual value of large financial institutions M&As. 2-year moving averages in millions of 1998 dollars.

III. BANKING CRISES AND REGULATIONS AROUND THE GLOBE

While the previous chapter illustrates that financial regulators in the EU face challenges very different from those facing U.S. regulators, the chapter by Barth, Caudill, Hall, and Yago ("Cross-Country Evidence on Banking Crises, Financial Structure and Bank Regulation") explores an even broader range of regulatory differences. These authors test empirically whether differences in regulations and financial systems across 64 different countries are related to the banking crises that occurred in those countries over the past two decades. The value of such an inquiry is obvious – if systematic causes of banking crises can be identified, then this information can be used to beneficially change financial regulation to help avoid such crises in the future.

The authors construct a panel of data from 64 countries during the 1980s and early 1990s. Within this window, the authors identify 32 separate banking crises. They construct a binomial logit model that can be used to estimate the probability of, and the determinants of, a banking crisis occurring. The model is much like those estimated in the previous literature, but it includes two sets of new explanatory variables: the degree of regulatory restrictions in each of the countries, and the market vs. banking orientation of the financial systems in each of the countries. (In addition, the authors estimate an OLS model in which they attempt to identify what determines the costs of these banking crises. This is a more difficult task, chiefly because it is nearly impossible to measure the costs of such events, and also because the authors have only a small number of observations with which to estimate the cost model. I will limit the remainder of my remarks to the logit model.)

The results of the logit model suggest that the probability of a banking crisis increases as regulatory restrictions tighten. The results also suggest that there is no systematic relationship between the orientation of a country's financial system and the probability that it will experience a banking crisis. These are intriguing results, but in some cases the statistical precision of the results is low, which weakens the punch of the study. I have three suggestions which may help increase the sharpness of the test results.

First, crises may be precipitated by cross-country contagion effects. The likelihood of a banking crisis may be higher if a neighboring country or major trading partner is experiencing a banking crisis of its own. However, the model fails to control for this potentially important phenomenon. The authors could easily create a new right-hand-side variable to control for this by summing the value of the dependent variable for all the countries in the same geographic region in each year. I would expect a positive coefficient on this variable.

Second, one of the chapter's main results is based on the estimated coefficient on the variable *RESTRICT*, which is an average of five different indices of regulatory restrictiveness in each country. This averaging across regulatory dimensions destroys information, and it may cause the estimated test coefficient to attenuate toward zero (for example, perhaps two of the five individual restrictions are positively related to banking crises, while the other three individual restrictions are negatively related to banking crises). By disaggregating this variable and running additional tests, the authors may be able to reveal stronger relationships between regulations and banking crises. The authors may find that some restrictions are more de-stabilizing than others, and that some restrictions may actually have a stabilizing influence. (The same suggestion holds for the right-hand-side variable *MKTvsBANK*, which is also constructed as an average of multiple indicators.)

Third, following standard practice, the authors specify all of the right-hand-side variables linearly. However, they also cite a statement by White (2000) that ". . . financial systems having both strong markets and strong intermediaries are likely to be more stable . . ." This statement suggests a U-shape for *MKTvsBANK* in which banking crises are less likely for intermediate values of *MKTvsBANK*, but more likely at either the extreme high and low values of this variable. Thus, the authors may get a more precise coefficient estimate for this variable if they include it using a quadratic specification.

Coming full circle, what does this chapter teach us about the "Cycle of Regulatory Causes and Consequences"? Empirical studies like this one may help us learn which types of regulatory fixes either exacerbate or dampen the cycle depicted in Fig. 1.

ACKNOWLEDGMENT

DeYoung's views are his own and do not necessarily reflect those of the Federal Reserve Bank of Chicago or the Federal Reserve Board.

REFERENCES

Barth, J. R., Caudill, S. B., Hall, T., & Yago, G. (2000). *Cross-Country Evidence on Banking Crises, Financial Structure and Bank Regulation*. This volume.

Benink, H. A., & Schmidt, R. H. (2000). *A Regulatory Agenda for Banking in Europe*. This volume.

Berger, A. N., & DeYoung, R. (2000). *The Effects of Geographic Expansion on Bank Efficiency*. Federal Reserve Bank of Chicago. Unpublished manuscript.

Bliss, R., & Flannery, M. J. (2000). *Market Discipline in the Governance of U. S. Bank Holding Companies: Monitroing vs. Influencing.* Federal Reserve Bank of Chicago. Working Paper 2000–3.

DeYoung, R., Flannery, M. J., Lang, W. W., & Sorescu, S. (2001). The Information Content of Bank Exam Ratings and Subordinated Dept Prices. *Journal of Money, Credit, and Banking* (forthcoming).

Evanoff, D. D., & Wall, L. D. (2000). *Subordinated Debt and Bank Capital Reform.* This volume.

Lang, W. W., & Robertson, D. (2000). *Analysis of Proposals for a Minimum Subordinated Debt Requirement.* Office of the Comptroller of the Currency. Working Paper 2000–4.

Parkhe, A., & Miller, S. R. (1999). *Is There a Liability of Foreignness in Global Banking?* Michigan State University. Unpublished manuscript.

White, W. R. (2000). *What Have We Learned From Recent Financial Crises and Policy Responses?* Bank of International Settlements, Working Paper No. 84.

PART II

DEPOSIT RATE PREMIUMS AND THE DEMAND FOR FUNDS BY THRIFTS

David Aadland, Drew Dahl and Alan Stephens

ABSTRACT

We empirically examine interest rates established on the national market for insured thrift deposits during a period spanning passage of the Financial Institutions Reform, Recovery and Enforcement Act of 1989. Our analysis indicates that changes in the demand for funds by thrifts in periods of financial stress exerted a pronounced influence on the deposit rate premiums paid by thrifts over comparable Treasuries. This contrasts with the conventional wisdom that default risk is the primary systematic determinant of rate premiums.

I. INTRODUCTION

Interest rate premiums on insured deposits over Treasury bills have been analyzed extensively in attempts to infer the capacity of creditors to impose "market discipline" on managers and owners of financial institutions. Recent studies by Cook and Spellman (1991, 1994), among others, focus on the thrift industry, and, more particularly, on the pricing of risk associated with possible default by the deposit guarantor. We extend these studies by considering an

Bank Fragility and Regulation: Evidence from Different Countries, Volume 12, pages 177–189.

Copyright © 2000 by Elsevier Science Inc.
All rights of reproduction in any form reserved.

ISBN: 0-7623-0698-X

alternative rationale for deposit rate premiums that is not based on the riskiness of deposit insurance but rather on the role of institutional demand for funds.

Our analysis empirically examines industry-wide interest rate premiums on insured thrift deposits. Deposit rates are obtained on a monthly basis, 1986 to 1995, from a published list of financial institutions which offered the highest interest rates available nationwide. We isolate thrifts from among these listed institutions and average their offered rates. From this industry-aggregated average we subtract the interest rate on equivalent maturity and date-matched Treasury securities. The resulting succession of monthly interest rate premiums is used in a regression model to identify how the premiums change over time and how they change in response to changes in financial conditions within the thrift industry.

An empirical advantage of our study, relative to prior research, is that the sample spans legislation enacted in 1989 which effectively eliminated investor perceptions concerning the default risk of deposit insurance. Before 1989, both the riskiness of deposit insurance *and* institutional demand for funds may have exerted significant influence on premiums. After 1989, the risk effect is effectively eliminated. Thus, it is possible for us to observe the behavior of deposit rate premiums in the presence of perceived guarantor default risk (before 1989) as well as in the absence of perceived guarantor default risk (after 1989). Studies by Cook and Spellman (1991, 1994) and Strahan (1995) were limited to pre-1989 sample periods when it was more difficult to disentangle the effect of default risk from the effect of the demand for funds by thrifts.

Our results indicate that declines in the financial condition of the thrift industry were associated with increases in rate premiums on insured deposits in the late 1980s. This is consistent with Cook and Spellman (1994), who also empirically associated weak thrift financial condition with higher premiums on insured deposits. They assume that weak financial condition is a proxy strictly for risk, and does not proxy in any way for institutional funds demand.

We further find that the inverse relationship between financial condition and rate premiums persisted in the 1990s. This appears to be inexplicable on the basis of risk and directs attention, alternatively, to the role of funds demand. It underscores concerns expressed by Ellis and Flannery (1992) with presumptions that "risk is the primary systematic determinant" of deposit rate spreads over Treasuries.

The chapter is organized as follows. Section II illustrates patterns in deposit rate spreads over Treasuries, focusing on how, and why, changes occurred over the sample period. Section III develops the model. Section IV presents the results of our regression model, with particular attention devoted to effects of changes in deposit insurance guarantees in 1989. Section V concludes.

II. RATE PREMIUMS AND DEPOSIT VOLUMES

To create premiums, we begin with deposit rates obtained from weekly surveys conducted by Banxquote and published periodically in various outlets. Banxquote has been used recently as a source of rate data by, among others, Gilkeson and Porter (1998). The survey approach also was used by Cook and Spellman (1991), who acquired rate information on one-year deposits in telephone surveys of large thrifts.

One part of the Banxquote survey lists the five financial institutions (banks, thrifts, mutual savings banks) with the highest reported yields in various maturity categories. We focus specifically on rates with six-month maturity and with denominations of $95,000 to $100,000. After elimination of banks and mutual savings banks, we average the rates observed for the thrifts which remain on the list.

We selected the Banxquote publication date which falls nearest to the end of a given month. The six-month Treasury rate for that same day is subtracted from the deposit rate to create date-matched spreads at monthly intervals.[1] Our resulting rate premiums are defined to be the average interest rate on insured deposits, with six-month maturities, offered by the subset of thrifts that were among the handful of financial institutions competing most aggressively for funds on the national market. The premiums are calculated monthly from February, 1986 to December, 1995.

A disadvantage of our sample is that the average premium reflects a relatively small number of thrifts. We note, however, that the time-series pattern of our rates is generally similar to the time-series patterns for related deposit rates. For instance, the correlation is 96% between the rates used in this study and the month-end bank average deposit rate on six-month maturities.[2]

In the 1980s, the rates we use are dominated by undercapitalized and rapidly growing thrifts. This reflects the widely acknowledged propensity for thrifts to gamble on growth under "moral hazard" incentives in which the penalty for risk-taking is borne disproportionately by the deposit insurer (see Strahan, 1995; Park & Peristiani, 1998). During this period, owners and managers of troubled thrifts were observed to offer higher and higher interest rates in an attempt to attract new funds (Shoven et al., 1995).

In the 1990s, our rates also are dominated by undercapitalized and rapidly growing thrifts. To further investigate this point, we identified 19 thrifts in our sample for which we were able to obtain institution-specific financial data in 1993, 1994, and 1995.[3] In Table 1, we present mean values for these institutions. Insured deposits at the 19 thrifts grew, depending on the year, from 6.5% to nearly 12% annually, while insured deposits for the entire industry

Table 1. Mean Financial Data for 19 High-Rate Offering Thrift Institutions (1993–1995).

Variables	High Rate-Paying Thrifts				All Thrifts			
	1993	1994	1995	1993–5	1993	1994	1995	1993–5
Total Insured Deposits (TID)	$345,878	$358,217	$375,239	$352,795	$326,125	$327,004	$346,321	$333,181
TID Growth	0.076***	0.119***	0.065***	0.0919***	−0.068	−0.046	−0.001	−0.0385
Noncurrent Assets to TA Ratio	0.04293**	0.04122*	0.03926	0.04212***	0.02100	0.01380	0.01200	0.01560
Equity to Capital Ratio	0.06992*	0.06333**	0.07407*	0.06844***	0.07840	0.07930	0.08390	0.08053
Return on Assets	0.00047*	−0.00251*	0.00675	0.00192***	0.00710	0.00660	0.00770	0.00713
Loan Loss Allowance to Loans Ratio	0.01591	0.01884*	0.02042	0.01684	0.01360	0.01200	0.01120	0.01227

Notes: Mean growth rates are an equally weighted average of growth rates across thrifts. Dollar amounts are in thousands. *, **, and *** indicate means for high rate-paying thrifts differ significantly from all thrifts at the 10%, 5% and 1% level, respectively.

declined in two years and remained steady in the third year. Note also that these thrifts, relative to the industry, are unprofitable (lower returns on assets), undercapitalized (equity capital ratio) and characterized by high loan loss allowances and noncurrent loans. We conclude that moral hazard incentives are not unique to the 1980s.

Our sample spans enactment of the Financial Institutions Reform, Recovery, and Enforcement Act of 1989 (FIRREA). FIRREA is important to our analysis insofar as it effectively eliminated perceived risks of Federal deposit insurance guarantees which some studies claim to have existed prior to its enactment. Cook and Spellman (1994), for instance, conclude that the market priced guarantor risk in the 1980s and that "guarantor-risk pricing was responsive to the insolvency of the guarantor, the attempts to recapitalize the guarantor and the efforts to resolve insolvent thrifts."

FIRREA contained several provisions that may have contributed to the effective elimination of risk pricing in Federal deposit insurance. The provisions: (1) explicitly directed thrifts to display a logo proclaiming that "insured deposits are backed by the full faith and credit of the U.S. Government;" (2) abolished the discredited Federal Savings and Loan Insurance Corporation (FSLIC) and replaced it with the Savings Association Insurance Fund; (3) created, and funded, the Resolution Trust Corporation to administer insolvent institutions; and (4) imposed stricter accounting and other standards on thrifts. White (1991) concludes that, after FIRREA, insured depositors "should never again have to worry if their deposits are safe" and that thrifts "should not have to pay an interest premium to depositors because of the latter's worries about the strength of the fund."

Figure 1 depicts the spreads over the period February, 1986 to December, 1995. Prior to FIRREA, spreads vary significantly, ranging from a minimum of 75 basis points to a maximum of 330 basis points. The average spread is 172 basis points, with a standard deviation of 59 basis points and a coefficient of variation equal to 33.7.

An influence of FSLIC risk on deposit premiums is suggested by the observed changes in interest rate spreads. The spreads increase in early 1987, which is consistent with Cook and Spellman's (1994) contention that investor perceptions of FSLIC default risk increased following the January, 1987 announcement by the U.S. General Accounting Office that the FSLIC was insolvent. The spreads decrease in late 1989, which is consistent with Strahan's (1995) conclusion that investor confidence was restored by enactment of FIRREA.

The foregoing interpretation of observed changes in spreads reflects an impact on deposit premiums associated with the willingness of investors to supply funds to the deposit market. Such an impact, however, is contradicted by observed variation in spreads after passage of FIRREA. As illustrated in Fig. 1, the spreads after FIRREA average 61 basis points, have a standard deviation of 35 basis points and coefficient of variation equal to 57.6.[4] This appears to be inexplicable based on perceived changes in default risk given the strength and stability of the governmental guarantee over this period.

III. THE MODEL

Our empirical approach follows Cook and Spellman (1994), who regress premiums on insured thrift deposits over Treasuries against cross-sectional measures of firm risk and other variables. We estimate a reduced-form regression model, which expresses the dependent variable, industry-wide deposit rate premiums (as previously defined), as a function of independent variables hypothesized to influence either the supply or demand for insured

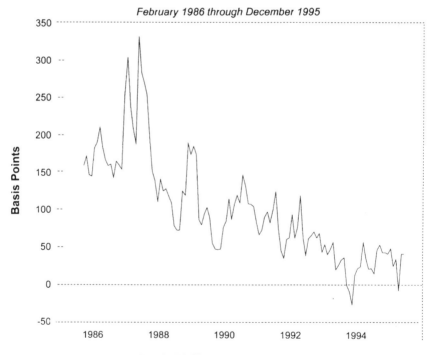

Fig. 1. Thrift–Treasury Spreads.

thrift deposits. The premiums, denoted as SPREAD, are measured monthly, 1986 to 1995. There are 119 observations.

A key factor in our model is a dummy variable, FIRREA, which identifies observations that occur after passage of the act in 1989 (FIRREA is unitary after August, 1989 and zero otherwise). This variable controls for influences of the act on both risk perceptions of guarantor default and on the demand for funds by thrifts. Reduced demand would have occurred to the extent that weak thrifts were removed from the market, either directly, because of a limitation on issuance of brokered deposits by thrifts, or indirectly, because of the accelerated resolutions of insolvent savings associations made possible by additional Federal funding. Increased supply may have reflected renewed investor confidence in deposit insurance. The hypothesized sign on the coefficient of this variable is negative.

An important aspect of our tests concerns the propensity for interest rates on deposits to increase in response to poor financial health as struggling thrifts attempt to replace a runoff of uninsured deposits or to undertake additional investments in risky attempts at recovery (the moral hazard story). To capture the potential effect of thrift industry health, we include a variable, TOBINQ, which is the ratio of thrift market value to thrift book value. The numerator of TOBINQ represents, at the end of each month, the aggregated market value of publicly traded thrifts. The denominator, the aggregated book value of thrifts, is measured quarterly.[5]

To account for a structural change in the relationship between financial condition and rate premiums which may have occurred at the time of FIRREA, we include interactions of TOBINQ with two dummy variables. One of these variables, PREFIRREA*TOBINQ, isolates how financial condition influenced rate premiums prior to FIRREA. It interacts a dummy variable indicating time (PREFIRREA is unitary before August, 1989 and 0 after) with TOBINQ. If deterioration in thrift industry condition is associated with higher interest rates in the period prior to FIRREA, the coefficient on this variable should be negative. This influence could reflect either guarantor default risk or thrift demand for funds.

The second variable interacts FIRREA, as previously defined, and TOBINQ. This interaction variable, FIRREA*TOBINQ, isolates how financial condition influenced rate premiums after FIRREA. The hypothesized sign on the coefficient for this variable is negative. Since default risk was essentially eliminated by FIRREA, a negative coefficient should attributable mainly to an increase in the demand for insured deposits by thrifts.[6]

Collectively, therefore, the coefficients on PREFIRREA*TOBINQ and FIRREA*TOBINQ can be used to compare the level of deposit premiums during the late 1980s, when financial condition proxies for default risk and funds demand, to the level of deposit premiums during the 1990s, when financial condition proxies only for funds demand. The statistical significance, as well as the magnitude, of the coefficients on these variables provide insight into the interpretation of prior studies which were limited to sample periods prior to FIRREA.

Several other control variables are included in the model. A dummy variable, D1988, is used to account for two regulatory events (D1988 is unitary after January, 1988 and 0 otherwise). One event was the Competitive Equality Banking Act, enacted in October, 1987, which recapitalized the FSLIC. Another event was the consolidation of 205 insolvent thrifts in Texas under the Southwest Plan in February, 1988. Since either event may have reduced the perceived default risk of deposit insurance or reduced the demand for funds by thrifts, the hypothesized sign on the coefficient for the variable is negative. Interpretation of this variable, however, is complicated by investor reaction and/or anticipation, which makes it difficult to attribute the timing of changes in spreads to specific dates. These complexities are illustrated by the subjective explanations of changes in spreads provided by prior research (see Strahan, 1995, and Cook & Spellman, 1994).[7]

Other variables are the dollar value of real estate loans at commercial banks, RELOAN, which accounts for the movements in the national housing market. It is measured monthly. Disposable personal income, ECON, is intended to capture the variability in overall macroeconomic activity not directly associated with the housing market. It also is measured monthly.[8] The real volume of investment in money market mutual funds, MMMF, accounts for the extent of competition in the deposit market exerted by non-depository intermediaries. It is measured monthly. TAX, which measures the average state income tax rates, controls for the tax disadvantage of interest on deposits relative to interest on Treasury Bills (Treasury interest is not taxed at the state level). It is measured annually.[9]

Our regression model is:

$$\text{SPREAD}_t = \alpha_0 + \alpha_1 \text{ECON}_t + \alpha_2 \text{RELOAN}_t + \alpha_3 \text{TAX}_t$$

$$+ \alpha_4 \text{MMMF}_t + \alpha_5 \text{PREFIRREA*TOBINQ}_t$$

$$+ \alpha_6 \text{FIRREA*TOBINQ}_t$$

$$+ \alpha_7 \text{FIRREA}_t + \alpha_8 \text{D1988}_t + E_t$$

Table 2. Descriptive Statistics of Key Variables (1986: 2–1995: 12)

Variable	Descriptive Statistics			
	Mean	Std Dev	Min	Max
Nominal 6 Month CD Rate	6.940	2.079	3.580	10.900
Nominal 6 Month T-Bill Rate	5.933	1.733	2.830	9.600
6 Month CD/T-Bill Spread (SPREAD)	1.007	0.697	–0.260	3.320
Market-to-Book Value (TOBINQ)	0.915	0.178	0.493	1.386
Real Disposable Personal Income (ECON)*	4497.03	247.559	3988.60	4971.70
Real Estate Loans by Commercial Banks (RELOAN)	5.939	0.772	4.082	7.015
Money Market Mutual Funds (MMMF)*	2922.76	572.401	1964.14	4086.50
Median State and Local Tax Liability (TAX)	9.469	0.544	8.300	10.000

* Billions of 1992 dollars

Because (1) is a reduced-form of the underlying supply and demand equations, it can be estimated consistently using ordinary least squares (OLS) techniques.

IV. RESULTS

Table 2 provides descriptive statistics for the dependent and independent variables in the model. Information is also provided on six-month deposit and Treasury rates separately. Note that the rate premiums, which are the differences in deposit and Treasury rates, average about 100 basis points. The market-to-book ratio ranges from 0.493 to 1.386, with a mean of 0.915.

The first column of Table 3 reports the estimation results for equation (1) defined in the preceding section. The model explains 82% of the variation in deposit rate premiums over our sample period.

The coefficient on PREFIRREA*TOBINQ is negative and significant, as hypothesized, which indicates that deterioration in the condition of the thrift industry exerted upward pressure on spreads in the late 1980s. This finding is consistent with prior research by Cook and Spellman (1991, 1994) and by Park and Peristiani (1998). It supports, but fails to distinguish between, a rationale based on the supply of funds (default risk associated with incomplete deposit insurance guarantees) and a rationale based on the demand for funds (growth incentives for thrifts in periods of financial stress). The magnitude of the coefficient indicates that (at the means) a one percent decline in thrift industry condition is associated with a 1.80% increase in deposit premiums.

The coefficient on FIRREA*TOBINQ is negative and significant, indicating that thrift industry health played a role in changing levels of deposit rate premiums after passage of FIRREA. The economic impact of changes in industry condition is lower in the period after FIRREA, insofar as a one percent increase in industry condition after FIRREA is associated with a 0.79% decrease in spreads. The lesser effect presumably reflects the elimination of the

Table 3. Ordinary Least Squares Estimates of Thrift CD-Treasury Spreads (1986: 2–1995: 12).

Variables	Model 1 (6 month)	Model 2 (3 month)	Model 3 (6 month)	Model 4 (6 month)
Constant	10.0386***	9.5658***	7.9983***	3.8727
	(1.7631)	(1.8321)	(1.9156)	(2.4878)
ECON	−0.0020***	−0.0018***	−0.0023***	−0.0018***
	(0.0004)	(0.0004)	(0.0004)	(0.0005)
RELOAN	−0.0557	0.0024	0.6659**	0.1867
	(0.3208)	(0.3334)	(0.2887)	(0.3456)
TAX	0.0786	0.1066	0.0887	0.3113*
	(0.1359)	(0.1412)	(0.1626)	(0.1771)
MMMF	0.0008***	0.0008***	0.0005**	0.0007***
	(0.0002)	(0.0002)	(0.0002)	(0.0003)
PREFIRREA* TOBINQ	−1.9789***	−2.5956***		
	(0.3969)	(0.4125)		
FIRREA* TOBINQ	−0.8661***	00.8548***		
	(0.3120)	(0.3243)		
PREFIRREA* SLINDEX			−0.0258***	
			(0.0084)	
FIRREA* SLINDEZ			−0.0095*	
			(0.0057)	
PREFIRREA* EQAS				−4.2515***
				(1.1545
FIRREA* EQAS				−3.1014
				(2.1639)
FIRREA	−1.7076***	−2.2323***	−1.8267***	−0.4025
	(0.3719)	(0.3865)	(0.5465)	(0.2643)
D1988	−1.0538***	−1.3936***	−1.0528***	−1.1142***
	(0.1630)	(0.1694)	(0.1781)	(0.1812)
R^2	0.8230	0.8204	0.7986	0.8011

Note: The dependent variable, unless otherwise stated, is the six-month spread on the highest yielding nationally traded CDs over Treasuries. Standard errors are in parentheses. Model 2 uses the three-month spread on the highest yielding nationally traded CDs over Treasuries.
* 10% significance level
** 5% significance level
*** 1% significance level

supply side impact, but may also reflect a reduction in demand influences, since problem thrifts were scrutinized more carefully in the 1990s.

The finding of a negative relationship between interest rate premiums and financial condition after FIRREA cannot be explained on the basis of significant and varying levels of investor confidence in deposit insurance (as was possible in the late 1980s). This offers insight into the contention of Cook and Spellman (1994) that funds demand did not contribute to deposit premiums in the late 1980s that they estimated to vary by as much as 200 basis points.

The relationship between premiums and financial condition, more generally, underscores the role of funds demand. We base this statement directly on our results for the post-FIRREA period and indirectly, by implication, to the pre-FIRREA period i.e. if demand influenced premiums after enactment of FIRREA, it seems likely that demand also influenced premiums prior to FIRREA. To the extent that thrifts under financial stress have incentives to increase insured deposits on national markets, our results link the demand for funds by thrifts with interest rate premiums on insured deposits.

With respect to other variables in the model, the coefficient on ECON was negative and significant. This indicates that interest rate spreads are negatively correlated with real economic activity, a result closely related to Friedman and Kuttner (1992), who find that interest rate spreads contain significant information about future movements in real income. MMMF was positive and significant, indicating that money market mutual funds acted as an alternative investment opportunity for households (see Gilkenson & Porter, 1997). The coefficients on the dummy variables FIRREA and D1988 were statistically significant and exerted substantial downward pressure on spreads of 170 and 105 basis points, respectively.

The remaining two variables do not appear to play an important role in the determination of spreads. The coefficient on RELOAN is statistically insignificant, which does not support the notion that increased activity in the real estate market tends to raise the relative demand for deposits by thrifts and increase spreads. The effect of TAX was positive, as expected, but statistically insignificant.

To check for the robustness of our results, we also report results for alternate specifications and data definitions.[10] In column 2, we replace the dependent variable with the spread on three-month, rather than six month maturities. In column 3, we measure the condition of the thrift industry with SLINDEX, which is a monthly stock market index of nationally traded thrifts. Likewise, in column 4, we use EQAS, which is a twelve-month moving average of the equity-to-asset ratio of thrifts one month prior to failure.[11] The results for columns 2, 3 and 4 are generally similar to those reported in column 1.

V. CONCLUSION

In an analysis of the national market for insured thrift deposits, we find that, in the 1990s, volatility in interest rate premiums was significant and that premiums increased with declines in the financial condition of the thrift industry. These findings are inconsistent with a dominant role for default risk in the determination of spreads insofar as enactment of FIRREA in 1989 greatly solidified investor perceptions of the strength of deposit insurance.

We conclude that changes in the demand for funds by thrifts in periods of financial stress exert a pronounced influence on interest rate premiums. This conclusion is important to the extent that it highlights the necessity to control for demand when attempting to isolate the influence of supply on deposit spreads over Treasuries. It contrasts with the presumption of some prior studies that default risk is the primary systematic determinant of spreads, thereby supporting an alternative description of a national market for deposits in which premiums are attributed to factors other than investor concerns about credit risk (Crane, 1976; Gilkeson & Porter, 1998).

NOTES

1. The Treasury rates are obtained from the FRED database of the Federal Reserve Bank of St. Louis.
2. The bank average deposit rates are obtained from the FRED database.
3. The financial information was obtained through the Federal Deposit Insurance Corporation.
4. The negative spreads in 1994 are consistent with Gilkeson and Porter (1998).
5. Data on market and book values is obtained from Compustat. Book value data was unavailable on a monthly basis.
6. Following Cook and Spellman (1994), we assume that liquidity, transactions costs and related factors that may influence investor selection of Treasury securities versus insured deposits are unchanging over time.
7. Strahan (1995), for instance, finds that investors perceived FSLIC default risk to be high in June, 1987, while Cook and Spellman (1994), in that same month, reach the opposite conclusion. Similarly, Strahan (1995), in late 1987, documents a reduction in perceived FSLIC default risk, while Cook and Spellman (1994), during that same period, find dramatic increases.
8. RELOAN and ECON were obtained from the FRED database of the Federal Reserve Bank of St. Louis. Both are both seasonally adjusted and measured in constant 1992 dollars using the Consumer Price Index and a chain-weighted deflator, respectively.
9. This variable is the median (state and local) income tax as a percentage of gross income in 51 cities throughout the U. S. It is obtained from "Tax Rates and Tax Burdens in the District of Columbia: A Nationwide Comparison, Annual."

10. We also ran alternative models which adjusted for potential impacts of autocorrelation and heteroskedasticity. The results were qualitatively identical.

11. SLINDEX was created using data obtained from Standard and Poor's (S&P) Compustat PC Plus. EQAS was created using data on failed thrifts obtained from the Office of Thrift Supervision. We thank John O'Keefe of the FDIC for providing us with this data.

REFERENCES

Cook, D., & Spellman, L. (1994). Repudiation Risk and Restitution Costs: Toward Understanding Premiums on Insured Deposits. *Journal of Money, Credit and Banking, 26*, 439–459.

Cook, D., & Spellman, L. (1991). Federal Financial Guarantees and the Occasional Market Pricing of Default Risk: Evidence from Insured Deposits. *Journal of Banking and Finance, 15*, 1113–1130.

Crane, D. (1976). A Study of Interest Rate Spreads in the 1974 CD Market. *Journal of Bank Research*, 213–224.

Ellis, D., & Flannery, M. (1992). Does the Debt Market Assess Large Banks' Risk? Time Series Evidence from Money Center CD's. *Journal of Monetary Economics, 30*, 481–502.

Gilkeson, J., & Porter, G. (1998). Large Retail Time Deposits and U.S. Treasury Securities (1986–95): Evidence of a Segmenting Market. *Managerial Finance, 24*, 26–47.

Friedman, B., & Kuttner, K. (1992). Money, Income, Prices and Interest Rates. *American Economic Review, 82*, 472–492.

Park, S., & Peristiani, S. (1998). Market Discipline by Thrift Depositors. *Journal of Money,Credit and Banking, 30*, 347–364.

Shoven, J., Smart, S., & Waldfogel, J. (1992). Real Interest Rates and the Savings and Loan Crisis: The Moral Hazard Problem. *Journal of Economic Perspectives, 6*, 155–167.

Strahan, P. (1995). Asset Returns and Economic Disasters: Evidence from the S&L Crisis. *Journal of Monetary Economics, 36*, 189–217.

White, L. J. (1991). *The S&L Debacle: Public Policy Lessons for Bank and Thrift Regulation*. New York, N.Y.: Oxford University Press.

A REGULATORY REGIME FOR FINANCIAL STABILITY

David T. Llewellyn

ABSTRACT

As bank failures clearly involve avoidable costs, there is a welfare benefit to be derived from lowering their probability and reducing the cost of those that do occur. This study suggests a paradigm for ensuring financial stability. A central theme is that, what are often viewed as alternatives, are in fact complements within an overall regulatory strategy. The discussion is set within the context of what is termed a regulatory regime which is wider than the rules and monitoring conducted by regulatory agencies. Just as the causes of banking crises are multi-dimensional, so the principles of an effective regulatory regime also need to incorporate a wider range of issues than externally imposed rules on bank behaviour. The key components of the regime are: (1) the rules established by regulatory agencies; (2) monitoring and supervision by official agencies; (3) the incentive structures faced by regulatory agencies, consumers and banks; (4) the role of market discipline and monitoring; (5) intervention arrangements in the event of bank failures; (6) the role of internal corporate governance arrangements within banks, and (7) the disciplining and accountability arrangements applied to regulatory agencies. The central theme is that the components of the regulatory regime need to be combined in an overall regulatory strategy, and that while all are necessary, none are sufficient. The objective is to optimise a regulatory strategy by combining the components of the regime, bearing in mind the

Bank Fragility and Regulation: Evidence from Different Countries, Volume 12,
pages 191–237.
Copyright © 2000 by Elsevier Science Inc.
All rights of reproduction in any form reserved.
ISBN: 0-7623-0698-X

negative trade-offs that may be encountered. Thus, if regulation is badly constructed or taken too far, there may be negative impacts on other components to the extent that the overall effect is diluted. This work also argues that the optimum mix of the components of the regime will vary between countries, over time for all countries, and between banks.

I. INTRODUCTION AND ISSUES

The objective of this chapter is to draw lessons from recent banking sector crises most especially with respect to the design of an optimum "regulatory regime." Just as the causes of banking crises are multi-dimensional, so the principles of an effective *regulatory regime* also need to incorporate a wider range of issues than externally imposed rules on bank behaviour. This suggests that strategies to avoid future crises also need to be multi-dimensional involving macro policy, the conduct of regulation and supervision, the creation of appropriate incentive structures, the development of market discipline, and the internal governance and management of financial institutions.

In this context, the study considers alternative approaches to achieving the objective of financial stability. A maintained theme is that what are often defined as alternatives are in fact complements within an overall regulatory strategy. The discussion is set within the context of what will be termed a *regulatory regime* which is wider than the rules and monitoring conducted by regulatory agencies. In essence, the focus is on how the components of a *regulatory regime* are to be combined to produce an optimum regulatory strategy. This follows on the tradition of Lindgren et al. (1996) who emphasise the three key strands of governance: internal to the firm; the discipline of the market, and regulation and supervision by official agencies. However, the study takes their paradigm further and discusses alternative approaches to regulation and supervision.

When a particular regulatory problem emerges, the instinct of a regulator is often to respond by creating new rules. This implies an *incremental approach* to regulation by focusing upon the rules component of the *regulatory regime*. The work argues that there are potentially serious problems with such an incremental rules-approach in that it may blunt the power of the other mechanisms in the regime and may, in the process, reduce the overall effectiveness of the regime.

Although there is considerable academic debate about whether or not banks should be regulated at all, this issue is not addressed here. Some studies (notably those of Benston & Kaufman, 1995) argue that the economic rationale for bank regulation has not been robustly established and that, in some cases, banking problems have their origin in regulatory rather than market failure. In particular, they give emphasis to the moral hazard effects of safety-net arrangements. A similar argument is put forward in Schwartz (1995).

Our starting point is two-fold: (i) by the nature of their structure banks are potentially vulnerable, and (ii) bank failures involve avoidable costs. With respect to the former, Kaufman (2000) stresses the traditional features of low ratios of cash and capital to assets, and a high ratio of demand to total deposits. Under some circumstances, these features may induce bank runs, spillover effects to innocent banks, reduced availability of credit (a credit crunch), reduced money supply, impairment of the efficiency of the payments system, and greater and costly uncertainty.

With respect to the costs of bank failures, in the case of Indonesia, Malaysia, South Korea and Thailand, non-performing loans of banks recently amounted to around 30% of total assets. Banking crises have involved substantial costs. In around 25% of cases the cost has exceeded 10% of GNP (e.g. in Spain, Venezuela, Bulgaria, Mexico, Argentina, Hungary). Evans (2000) suggests that the costs of crises amounted to 45% of GDP in the case of Indonesia, 15% in the case of Korea and 40% in the case of Thailand. These figures include the costs of meeting obligations to depositors under the blanket guarantees that the authorities introduced to handle systemic crises, and public sector payments to financing the recapitalisation of insolvent banks. Barth et al. (2000) also note that the costs of recent bank crises in Chile, Argentina, Korea and Indonesia are estimated at 41%, 55%, 60%, and 80% of GDP respectively.

As bank failures clearly involve avoidable costs that may be significant, there is a welfare benefit to be derived from lowering the probability of bank failures, and reducing the cost of bank failures that do occur. In what follows these are the twin objectives of the *regulatory regime*. The objective of this chapter is to suggest a wider paradigm for ensuring financial stability, i.e. reducing the probability of bank failures and the costs of those that do occur.

The general economic rationale for financial regulation (in terms of externalities, market imperfections, economies of scale in monitoring, grid-lock problems, and moral hazard associated with safety nets) has been outlined elsewhere (Llewellyn, 1999). For purposes of this study, the economic rationale for regulation is taken as given.

While this ground will not be repeated, two observations are made at the outset. Firstly, the presence of an economic rationale for regulation, and a consumer demand for it, does not justify everything that a regulator does. Secondly, the case for regulation does not exclude a powerful role for other mechanisms to achieve the objectives of systemic stability and legitimate (but limited) consumer protection. On the contrary, the central theme is to emphasis that the various components of the *regulatory regime* need to be combined in an overall *regulatory strategy*, and that while all are necessary, none are sufficient. There is always a potential danger that the regulation component, if pressed too far, will blunt other mechanisms and in the process compromise the impact of the overall impact.

The structure of the work is as follows. The main themes are summarised in the remainder of this section. Section II offers a brief overview of recent banking crises as a context for the main themes of this chapter. Section III establishes the concept of the *regulatory regime* and the trade-offs that can exist between its components. This is followed by a more detailed discussion of each of the seven components of the regime. Section V discuses the concept of what is termed *contract regulation* whereby regulated firms are able to self-select regulatory contracts. Section VI reviews how the optimum structure of a regulatory regime will vary for different countries and will change over time. Section VII suggests a series of desirable shifts within the *regulatory regime* and offers a brief assessment of the recently-issued Basel Committee consultative paper on capital adequacy. A brief overall assessment is offered in Section VIII.

After a brief overview of the experience of recent banking crises, the main themes of the study may be summarised as follows:

(1) Debate about regulation is often excessively polarised with too many dichotomies. What are often posed as alternative approaches are in truth complementary mechanisms. It is emphasised that the skill in formulating regulatory strategy is not so much in choosing between the various options, but in the way the seven components of the *regulatory regime* are combined.

(2) Regulation needs to be viewed and analysed not solely in the narrow terms of the rules and edicts of regulatory agencies, but in the wider context of a *regulatory regime* which has seven core components:
   - the rules established by regulatory agencies (the regulation component);
   - monitoring and supervision by official agencies;
   - the incentive structures faced by regulatory agencies, consumers and, most especially, banks;
   - the role of market discipline and monitoring;
   - intervention arrangements in the event of compliance failures of one sort or another;
   - the role of internal corporate governance arrangements within financial firms, and

- the disciplining and accountability arrangements applied to regulatory agencies.

(3) *Regulatory strategy* is not to be viewed solely in terms of the rules and supervision of regulatory agencies. The debate about regulation is often too narrow because it focuses almost exclusively on the first component of the regime, namely rules imposed by the regulator. The debate should rather be about how to optimise the combination of the seven components of the regime. Strategy should focus on optimising the overall *regulatory regime* rather than any one component. This is a difficult and demanding mandate, and to the regulator the more effective approach in the short-run might appear to be imposing more rules. The danger is of thinking in terms of incremental change to regulation, rather than strategically with respect to the overall regime. The objective is to move towards an optimum mix of the components, combined with careful choice of the various regulatory instruments within each. Thus, it is not a question of choosing between *either* regulation *or* market disciplines.

(4) Several reservations are entered about the conventional approach to regulation for financial stability:
- it tends to be excessively 'rules based',
- excessive reliance is placed on the first component of the *regulatory regime*,
- insufficient emphasis is given to incentive structures, the role of market discipline, and corporate governance arrangements within banks,
- insufficient attention is given to potential trade-offs within the *regulatory regime* and the negative externalities of rules,
- regulation tends to be insufficiently differentiated between banks whose risk profiles are not homogeneous.

(5) A key issue for the regulator is how its actions can not only contribute directly to the objectives of regulation, but how they impact on the other components of the regime. Most important is the issue of how regulation affects incentive structures within firms, and the role played by market discipline and monitoring.

(6) The optimising strategy needs to be set in the context of trade-offs between the various components of the regime. In some circumstances the more emphasis that is given to one of the components (e.g. regulation) the less powerful becomes one or more of the others (e.g. market discipline on financial firms) and to an extent that may reduce the overall effectiveness and efficiency of the regime.

(7) The optimum mix of the components of the *regulatory regime* will vary between countries, over time for all countries, and between banks.

(8) The optimum mix of the components of the regime changes over time as market conditions and compliance culture change. It is argued that, in current conditions, there needs to be a shift within the regime in five dimensions: less reliance placed on detailed and prescriptive rules; more emphasis given to official supervision; a greater focus on incentive structures; an enhanced and strengthened role for market discipline and monitoring, and a more central role for corporate governance arrangements within banks.

(9) As financial firms and different types of financial business are not homogeneous, the optimum regulatory approach will be different for different banks and businesses. This has been recognised by the regulatory authorities in the UK with more emphasis being given to a risk-based approach. However, there should be yet more differentiation. The skill lies in making sufficient differentiations to reflect the heterogeneous nature of regulated firms, while not unduly complicating the regulatory process to an extent that can cause unwarranted inequality of treatment.

(10) One particular approach to regulation is what will be termed *contract regulation*. In this model, once the regulator has established objectives and a set of general principles, individual banks are able to choose their own regulation. Once the choice has been agreed with the regulator, a contract is established between them. If the bank fails to deliver on the contract, sanctions are applied in the normal way, and the regulator has the option of withdrawing the choice from the regulated firm and imposing its own contract.

This all amounts to emphasising an overall "regulatory strategy" rather than focusing on regulation per se. A central theme is that regulation is an important, but only one, component of a regulatory regime designed to achieve the objectives of systemic stability and consumer protection. Giving too much emphasis to regulation per se has the danger that the importance of the other components are down-played, or even marginalised.

Regulation is about changing the behaviour of regulated institutions on the grounds that unconstrained market behaviour tends to produce socially sub-optimum outcomes. A key question is the extent to which behaviour is to be altered by way of externally imposed *rules*, or through creating *incentives* for firms to behave in a particular way.

II. THE EXPERIENCE OF BANKING CRISES

Almost always and everywhere banking crises are a complex and interactive mix of economic, financial and structural weaknesses. For an excellent survey of the two-way link between banking systems and macro policy, see Lindgren et al. (1996). The trigger for many crises has been macro-economic in origin and often associated with a sudden withdrawal of liquid external capital from a country. As noted by Brownbridge and Kirkpatrick (2000), financial crises have often involved triple crises of currencies, financial sectors, and corporate sectors. Similarly, it has been argued that East Asian countries were vulnerable to a financial crisis because of "reinforcing dynamics between capital flows, macro-policies, and weak financial and corporate sector institutions" (Alba et al., 1998). The link between balance of payments and banking crises is certainly not a recent phenomenon and has been extensively studied (e.g. Kaminsky & Reinhart, 1998; Godlayn & Valdes, 1997; Sachs et al., 1996). The close parallels between banking and currency crises is emphasised by Kaufman (2000).

In most (but not all) cases, systemic crises (as opposed to the failure of individual banks within a stable system) are preceded by major macroeconomic adjustment, which often leads to the economy moving into recession after a previous strong cyclical upswing (Llewellyn, 2000). While financial crises have often been preceded by sharp fluctuations in the macro economy and asset prices, it would be a mistake to seek the origin of such crises and financial instability exclusively in macroeconomic instability. While macro instability may often be the proximate cause, banking crises usually emerge because instability in the macro economy reveals existing weaknesses within the banking system. It is usually the case that the seeds of a problem (e.g. over-lending, weak risk analysis and control, etc.) are sown in the earlier upswing of the cycle. The downswing phase reveals previous errors and over-optimism. Mistakes made in the upswing emerge in the downswing. In South East Asia, for instance, a decade of substantial economic growth up to 1997 concealed the effects of questionable bank lending policies.

This is not exclusively a feature of less developed and emerging economies. Koskenkyla (2000) notes that a rapid pace of bank lending was a contributory factor in the Scandinavian banking crises in the early 1990s which also had the effect of raising asset prices to unsustainable levels, raising the optimism of bankers, and impacting on the real economy through a wealth effect as well as directly on aggregate demand. In particular, the case is made that trends (real and nominal) in the economy and bank behaviour are not independent but tend to be reinforcing. Berg (1993) and Benink and Llewellyn (1994) also argue that demand and price trends in an economy are not totally exogenous to the banking system.

Analyses of recent financial crises, in both developed and less-developed countries (see, for instance, Brealey, 1999, Corsetti et al., 1998, Lindgren et al.,

1996, and Llewellyn, 2000) indicate that "regulatory failures" are not exclusively (or even mainly) a problem that the rules were wrong. Five common characteristics have been weak internal risk analysis, management and control systems within banks; inadequate official supervision; weak (or even perverse) incentives within the financial system generally and financial institutions in particular; inadequate information disclosure, and inadequate corporate governance arrangements both within banks and their large corporate customers.

While, as already noted, banking crises can be triggered by developments in the macro economy, an unstable or unpredictable macro-economic environment is neither a necessary nor sufficient condition for banking crises to emerge. The fault also lies internally within banks, and with failures of regulation, supervision, and market discipline on banks. This reinforces the concept of a *regulatory regime* and the potential trade-offs between its components.

Banks can fail, and bank insolvencies can be concealed, within a reasonably stable macro economic environment if, for instance, internal risk analysis and management systems are weak, incentive structures are perverse, regulation and supervision are inadequate, market discipline is weak, and corporate governance arrangements are not well developed. Equally, if these are in place, banks can avoid insolvency even within a volatile economic environment.

III. THE REGULATORY REGIME

The concept of a *regulatory regime* is wider than the prevailing set of prudential and conduct of business rules established by regulatory agencies. External regulation has a positive role in fostering a safe and sound financial system and consumer protection. However, this role, while important, is limited, and insufficient in itself. Equally, and increasingly important, are the other components of the regime and most especially the incentive structures faced by financial firms, and the efficiency of the necessary monitoring and supervision by official agencies and the market.

There are several reasons why emphasis is given to the overall *regulatory regime* rather than myopically to regulation:

- prescriptive regulation is not invariably effective in achieving the twin components of financial stability: reducing the probability of bank failures and the costs of those that do occur;
- regulation may not be the most effective way of securing these objectives;

- regulation is itself costly both in terms of its direct costs and unwarranted distortions that may arise (e.g. via inaccurate risk weights applied in capital adequacy arrangements) when regulation is inefficiently constructed;
- regulation may not be the most efficient mechanism for achieving financial stability objectives as alternative routes may achieve the same degree of effectiveness at lower cost;
- regulation tends to be inflexible and insufficiently differentiated;
- there are always potential dangers arising from a monopolist regulator;
- regulation may impair the effectiveness and efficiency of other mechanisms for achieving the objective of financial stability.

A maintained theme is that a *regulatory regime* needs to be viewed more widely than externally-imposed regulation on financial institutions. In current conditions it would be a mistake to rely wholly, or even predominantly, on external regulation, monitoring and supervision by the "official sector." The world of banking and finance is too complex and volatile to warrant dependence on a simple set of prescriptive rules for prudent behaviour. The central role of incentive structures is constantly emphasised. There are many reasons (market imperfections and failures, externalities, "grid lock" problems, and moral hazards associated with safety-net arrangements) why incentive structures within financial firms may not be aligned with regulatory objectives (Llewellyn, 1999).

This means that a central consideration for the regulator is the impact its own rules have on regulated firms' incentive structures, whether they might have perverse effects, and what regulation can do to improve incentives. Incentive structures need to be at the centre of all aspects of regulation because if these are wrong it is unlikely that the other mechanisms in the regime will achieve the regulatory objectives. It is necessary to consider not only how the various components of the regime impact directly on regulatory objectives, but also how they operate indirectly through their impact on the incentives of regulated firms and others. Incentive structures are at the heart of the regulatory process.

Trade-offs Within the Regime

Within the *regulatory regime* trade-offs emerge at two levels. In terms of regulatory strategy, a choice has to be made about the balance of the various components and the relative weight to be assigned to each. For instance, a powerful role for official regulation with little weight assigned to market discipline might be chosen, or alternatively a relatively light touch of regulation but with heavy reliance on the other components. A given degree of effectiveness can be provided by different combinations of rules, supervision, market discipline etc. and with various degrees of discretion applied by the regulator.

The second form of trade-off relates to how the components of the regime may be causally related. In some circumstances the more emphasis that is given to one of the components (e.g. regulation) the less powerful becomes one or more of the others (e.g. market discipline on banks) and to an extent that may reduce the overall impact. Thus, while regulation may be viewed as a response to market failures, weak market discipline, and inadequate corporate govern-ance arrangements, causation may also operate in the other direction with regulation weakening these other mechanisms. For instance, the more emphasis that is given to detailed, extensive and prescriptive rules, the weaker might be the role of incentive structures, market discipline and corporate governance arrangements within financial firms. This has been put by Simpson (2000) as follows: "In a market which is heavily regulated for internal standards of integrity, the incentives to fair dealing diminish. Within the company culture, such norms of fair dealing as 'the way we do things around here' would eventually be replaced by 'It's OK if we can get away with it'." In other words, an excessive reliance on detailed and prescriptive rules may weaken incentive structures and market discipline.

Similarly, an excessive focus on detailed and prescriptive rules may weaken corporate governance mechanisms within financial firms, and may blunt the incentive of others to monitor and control the behaviour of banks. Weakness in corporate governance mechanisms may also be a reflection of banks being monitored, regulated and supervised by official agencies. The way intervention is conducted in the event of bank distress (e.g. whether forbearance is practised) may also have adverse incentive effects on the behaviour of banks and the willingness of markets to monitor and control banks' risk-taking.

An empirical study of regulation in the United States by Billett et al. (1998) suggests that some types of regulation may undermine market discipline. They examine the costs of market discipline and regulation and show that, as a bank's risk increases, the cost of uninsured deposits rises and the bank switches to insured deposits. This is because changes in regulatory costs are less sensitive to changes in risk than are market costs. They also show that when rating agencies down-grade a bank, the bank tends to increase its use of insured deposits. The authors conclude: "The disparate costs of insured deposits and uninsured liabilities, combined with the ability and willingness of banks to alter their exposure to each, challenge the notion that market discipline can be an effective deterrent against excessive risk taking."

The public policy objective is to optimise the outcome of a regulatory strategy in terms of mixing the components of the regime, bearing in mind the possibility of negative trade-offs. The key to optimising overall effectiveness is the mix of the seven core components. All are necessary but none alone are sufficient. The skill of the regulator in devising a regulatory strategy lies in how the various components in the regime are combined.

IV. COMPONENTS OF A *REGULATORY REGIME*

Having established the overall framework and the nature of the *regulatory regime* this section considers some of the key issues related to each of the seven components with particular reference to regulatory strategy designed to optimise the overall effect of the regime as a whole rather than any of the components.

Regulation

Five particular issues arise with respect to the regulation part of the regime: the type of rules established; the weight to be given to formal and prescriptive rules of behaviour, the form of the rules that are established, the impact that rules may have on the other components of the *regulatory regime*, and the extent to which regulation and supervision differentiate between different banks.

Type of Rules
Four types of rules can be identified: (1) with respect to the prudential management of banks and other financial firms (e.g. capital adequacy rules, large exposure limitations, rules on inter-connected lending, etc.), (2) with respect to conduct of business (e.g. how financial firms conduct business with their customers, disclosure requirements, etc.); (3) rules with respect to allowable business (e.g. the extent to which banks are allowed to conduct securities and insurance business); and (4) rules with respect to ownership, i.e. who is allowed to own banks. A detailed consideration of these different types of rules goes beyond the scope of this paper. Nevertheless, Barth et al. (2000), in an extension of the model of Demirguc-Kunt and Detragiache (1998), find some evidence that regulatory restrictions on activities and ownership increase the probability of bank crises.

Prescriptive Rules
A former U.S. regulator has noted that: "Financial services regulation has traditionally tended towards a style that is command-and-control, dictating

precisely what a regulated entity can do and how it should do it . . . generally, they focus on the specific steps needed to accomplish a certain regulatory task and specify with detail the actions to be taken by the regulated firm" (Wallman, 1999). This experience of the U.S. also suggests that the interaction of the interests of the regulator and the regulated may tend towards a high degree of prescription in the regulatory process. Regulators tend to look for standards they can easily monitor and enforce, while the regulated seek standards they can comply with. The result is that regulators seek precision and detail in their requirements, while the regulated look for certainty and firm guidance on what they are to do. Wallman suggests that: "The result is specific and detailed guidance, not the kind of pronouncements that reflect fundamental concepts and allow the market to develop on its own."

Although precise rules have their attractions for both regulators and regulated firms, several problems emerge with a highly prescriptive approach to regulation:

- An excessive degree of prescription may bring regulation into disrepute if it is perceived by the industry as being excessive, with many redundant rules.
- Risks are often too complex to be covered by simple rules.
- Balance sheet rules reflect the position of an institution only at a particular point in time, and its position can change substantially within a short period.
- An inflexible approach based on a detailed rule book has the effect of impeding firms from choosing their own least-cost way of meeting regulatory objectives.
- Detailed and extensive rules may stifle innovation.
- A prescriptive regime tends to focus upon firms' processes rather than outcomes and the ultimate objectives of regulation. The rules may become the focus of compliance rather than the objectives they are designed to achieve. In this regard, it can give rise to a perverse culture of "box ticking" by regulated firms. The letter of the regulation may be obeyed but not the spirit or intention.
- A prescriptive approach is inclined towards "rules escalation" whereby rules are added over time, but few are withdrawn.
- A highly prescriptive approach may create a confrontational relationship between the regulator and regulated firms, or alternatively cause firms to overreact and engage in excessive efforts at internal compliance out of fear of being challenged by the regulator. In this sense, regulation may become more prescriptive and detailed than is intended by the regulator because of the culture that a rules-based approach generates.

- In the interests of "competitive neutrality," rules may be applied equally to all firms, although firms may be sufficiently heterogeneous to warrant different approaches. A highly prescriptive approach to regulation reduces the scope for legitimate differentiations. Treating as equal firms that in practice are not equal is not competitive neutrality.
- A prescriptive rules approach may in practice prove to be inflexible and not sufficiently responsive to market conditions.
- A potential moral hazard arises in that firms may assume that, if something is not explicitly covered in regulations, there is no regulatory dimension to the issue.
- Detailed rules may also have perverse effects if they are regarded as actual standards to be adopted rather than minimum standards with the result that, in some cases, actual behaviour of regulated firms may be of a lower standard than without rules. This is most especially the case if each firm assumes its competitors will adopt the minimum regulatory standard.

Form of Rules
A second issue relates to the type of rules chosen by the regulator. Black (1994) distinguishes different types of rules along three dimensions: precision (how much is prescribed and covered in the rule), simplicity (the degree to which the rule may be easily applied to concrete situations), and clarity. The more precise is the rule, the easier it is to enforce. On the other hand, precise rules are less flexible within the overall regime.

Impact of Rules
A third issue is whether the degree of precision in rules has a positive or negative impact on compliance, and the other components of the regime. For reasons already suggested, precision and detail may have a negative effect on compliance and compliance culture: if something is not explicitly disallowed it is presumed to be allowed. Conversely, a regime based more on broad principles than detailed and extensive rules has certain advantages: principles are easily understood and remembered, they apply to all behaviour, and they are more likely to have a positive impact on overall compliance culture. It might also be the case (as suggested by Black, 1994) that principles are more likely to become board issues with the board of financial firms adopting compliance with principles as a high level policy issue, rather than a culture of "leaving it to the compliance department." As put by Black, "it helps chief executives to see the moral wood for the technical trees."

Differentiation

A central issue in regulation for financial stability is the extent to which it differentiates between different banks according to their risk characteristics and their risk analysis, management and control systems. Most especially when supervisory resources are scarce, but also in the interests of efficiency in the banking system, supervision needs to be more detailed and extensive with banks deemed to be riskier than others. The objective of "competitive neutrality" in regulation does not mean that all banks are to be treated in the same way if their risk characteristics are different. Reflecting the practice in the UK, Richardson and Stephenson (2000) argue that the Financial Services Authority (and formerly the Bank of England) treats the requirements of the Basel Accord as minima and requires individual banks to hold more capital than the minima dependent upon their risk exposure. Capital requirements are set individually for each bank. The authors list the major factors that are taken into account when setting individual bank's capital requirements: experience and quality of the bank's management; the bank's risk appetite; the quality of risk analysis, management and control systems; the nature of the markets in which it operates; the quality, reliability and volatility of earnings; the quality of the bank's capital and access to new capital; the degree of diversification; exposure concentrations; the complexity of a bank's legal and organisational structure; the support and control provided by shareholders, and the degree to which a bank is supervised by other jurisdictions. As the authors note: "these considerations imply that the appropriate margin above the minimum regulatory capital requirements will differ across banks."

Monitoring and Supervision

Because of the nature of financial contracts between financial firms and their customers, continuous monitoring of the behaviour of financial firms is needed. The question is who is to undertake the necessary monitoring: customers, shareholders, rating agencies, etc. In practice, there can be only a limited monitoring role for retail depositors due to major information asymmetries which cannot easily be rectified, and because depositors face the less costly option of withdrawal of deposits. Saunders and Wilson (1996) review the empirical evidence on the role of informed depositors. The funding structure of a bank may also militate against effective monitoring in that, unlike with non-financial companies, creditors tend to be numerous with a small stake for each.

As most (especially retail) customers cannot in practice undertake monitoring, and in the presence of deposit insurance they may have no incentive to do so, an important role of regulatory agencies is to monitor the behaviour of banks on behalf of consumers. In effect, consumers delegate the task of monitoring to a regulatory agency. There are strong efficiency reasons for consumers to delegate monitoring and supervision to a specialist agency to act on their behalf as the transactions costs for the consumer are lowered by such delegation (Llewellyn, 1999). However, this is not to argue that a regulatory agency should become a monopolist monitor and supervisor of financial firms.

In practice, in countries that have recently experienced banking crises "some form of supervisory failure was a factor in almost all the sample countries" (Lindgren et al., 1996). In many countries supervisory agencies did not enforce compliance with regulations (Reisen, 1998). In Korea and Indonesia in particular, banks did not comply with regulatory capital adequacy requirements or other regulations (UNCTAD, 1998). In particular, connected lending restrictions were not adequately supervised partly because of political pressure and the lack of transparency in the accounts of banks and their corporate customers.

In many crisis countries there was often a lack of political will on the part of supervisory agencies to exercise strong supervision. This may be associated with adverse incentive structures faced by politicians and others who may gain from imprudent banking, (Fink & Haiss, 2000). While prudent banking is a public good, hazardous behaviour can be beneficial to some stake-holders. Others have noted the lack of political will to exercise strong supervision in the transitional economies of Eastern Europe (Baer & Gray, 1996).

A further dimension to supervisory failure in crisis countries was that supervisory intensity was often not adjusted in line with liberalisation in financial systems and the new business operations and risk characteristics of banks that emerged in a more de-regulated market environment. This is discussed in more detail in the next section. This was also the case with Scandinavian countries when, in the second half the 1980s, banks responded aggressively to de-regulation. The nature and intensity of official supervision needs to reflect the nature of the regulatory environment. In practice, while the latter changed this was often not accompanied by sufficiently intensified supervision.

Incentive Structures

The maintained theme is that the incentive structures and moral hazards faced by decision-makers (bank owners and managers, lenders to banks, borrowers and regulators) are major parts of the *regulatory regime*. The overall issue is two-fold: there need to be appropriate internal incentives for management to behave in appropriate ways, and the regulator has a role in ensuring that internal incentives are compatible with regulatory objectives. Overall, we need to know more about incentive structures within financial firms and whether, for instance, incentive structures align with compliance. Research is also needed into how regulation impacts positively and negatively on incentives within regulated firms. We have already alluded to the possibility that detailed rules may have the negative effect of blunting compliance incentives.

Within the *regulatory regime* paradigm, a central role for regulation is to create appropriate incentives within regulated firms so that the incentives faced by decision-makers are consistent with financial stability. At the same time, regulation needs to avoid the danger of blunting the incentives of other agents (e.g. rating agencies, depositors, shareholders, debt-holders) that have a disciplining role with banks. The position has been put well by Schinasi et al. (1999): "Policy makers are therefore faced with the difficult challenge of balancing efforts to manage systemic risk against efforts to ensure that market participants bear the costs of imprudent risk taking and have incentives to behave prudently." They argue that banks have complex incentive structures. There are internal incentives that motivate key decision-makers involved with risk, corporate governance mechanisms (such as accountability to share-holders), an external market in corporate control, market disciplines which may affect the cost of capital and deposits, and accountability to bank supervisors. The presence of regulation and official supervision overlays the structure of incentives faced by bank decision-makers.

The key is to align incentives of the various stake-holders in the decision-making process. The alignment of incentive structures has three dimensions: between the objectives set by regulators and supervisors and those of the bank; between the overall business objectives of the bank and those of actual decision-makers in the management structure, and between managers and owners of banks. Conflicts can arise at each level, making incentive structures within banks particularly complex.

If incentive structures are hazardous, regulation will always face formidable obstacles. There are several dimensions to this in the case of banks: the extent to which reward structures are based on the volume of business undertaken; the extent to which the risk characteristics of decisions are incorporated into reward structures; the nature of internal control systems within banks; internal monitoring of the decision-making of loan officers; the nature of profit-sharing schemes and the extent to which decision-makers also share in losses, etc. Reward systems based on short-term profits can also be hazardous as they may induce managers to pay less attention to the longer-term risk characteristics of their decisions. High staff turnover, and the speed with which officers are moved within the bank, may also create incentives for excessive risk-taking. A similar effect can arise through the herd-behaviour that is common in banking. In the case of the Barings collapse, managers who were supposedly monitoring the trading activity of Leeson also benefited through bonuses derived from the profits he was making for the bank.

It is clear that some incentive structures may lead to dysfunctional behaviour (Pendergast, 1993). This may often emerge when incentives within regulated firms relate to volume that create a clear bias towards writing business. Bank managers may be rewarded by the volume of loans, not by their risk-adjusted profitability. Many cases of bank distress have been associated with inappropriate incentive structures creating a bias in favour of balance sheet growth, and with moral hazard created by anticipated lender-of-last-resort actions (Llewellyn, 2000). Dale (1996) suggests that profit-related bonuses were an important feature in the Barings collapse.

Laws, regulations, and supervisory actions provide incentives for regulated firms to adjust their actions and behaviour, and to control their own risks internally. In this regard, they can be viewed as *incentive contracts*. Within this general framework, regulation involves a process of creating incentive compatible contracts so that regulated firms have an incentive to act consistently with the objectives of financial stability. Well designed incentive contracts induce appropriate behaviour by regulated firms. Conversely, if they are badly constructed and improperly designed, they might fail to reduce systemic risk (and other hazards regulation is designed to avoid) or have undesirable side-effects on the process of financial intermediation (e.g. impose high costs). At centre stage is the issue of whether all parties have the right incentives to act in a way that satisfies the objectives of regulation.

Given that incentives for individuals can never be fully aligned with the objectives of the bank, there need to be external pressures on managers to encourage adequate internal control systems to be established. Several procedures, processes and structures can, for instance, reinforce internal risk control mechanisms. These include internal auditors, internal audit committees, procedures for reporting to senior management (and perhaps to the super-visors), and making a named board member of financial firms responsible for compliance and risk analysis and management systems. In some countries (e.g. New Zealand) the incentive on bank managers has been strengthened by a policy of increased personal liability for bank directors, and bank directors are personally liable in cases involving disclosure of incomplete or erroneous information. The Financial Services Authority in the UK has also proposed that individual directors and senior managers of financial firms should, under some circumstances, be made personally liable for compliance failures.

The form and intensity of supervision can differentiate between regulated institutions according to their relative risk and the efficiency of their internal control mechanisms (Goodhart et al., 1998). Supervisors can strengthen incentives by, for instance, relating the frequency and intensity of their supervision and inspection visits (and possibly rules) to the perceived adequacy of the internal risk control procedures, and compliance arrangements. In addition, regulators can create appropriate incentives by calibrating the external burden of regulation (e.g. number of inspection visits, allowable business etc.) to the quality of management and the efficiency of internal incentives. Evans (1999) suggests several routes through which incentive structures can be improved: greater disclosure by financial institutions; subjecting local banks to more foreign competition; ensuring a closer alignment of regulatory and economic capital; greater use of risk-based incentives by supervisors, and lower capital adequacy requirements for banks headquartered in jurisdictions which comply with the BIS's core principles of supervision.

With respect to prudential issues, capital requirements should be structured so as to create incentives for the correct pricing of absolute and relative risk. In this area in particular, the potential for regulation to create perverse incentives and moral hazard is well established. The basic problem is that if regulatory capital requirements do not accurately map risk then banks are encouraged to engage in regulatory arbitrage. For instance, if differential capital requirements are set against different types of assets (e.g. through applying differential risk weights) the rules should be based on calculations of relative risk. If risk weights are incorrectly specified, perverse incentives may be created for banks because the implied capital requirements are either more or less than justified by true relative risk calculations. One critique of the current Basel capital arrangements is that risk weights bear little relation to the relative risk characteristics of different assets, and the loan book largely carries a uniform risk weight even though the risk characteristics of different loans within a bank's portfolio vary considerably. The current BIS consultation paper seeks to address this issue.

The moral hazard associated with perceived safety-net arrangements have been extensively analysed in the literature. Garcia (1996) in particular analyses the trade-off between systemic stability and moral hazard. Three possible hazards are associated with deposit insurance: banks may be induced to take excessive risk as they are not required to pay the risk premium on insured deposits; there are particular incentives for excessive risk-taking when a bank's capital ratio falls to a low level; and depositors may also be induced to seek high-risk banks due to the one-way-option bet.

Deposit insurance has two opposing impacts on systemic risk. By reducing the rationality of bank runs (though this is dependent on the extent and coverage of the deposit insurance scheme and the extent of any co-insurance) it has the effect of lowering the potential for financial instability. On the other hand, for reasons outlined above, the moral hazard effects of deposit insurance may increase risk in the system. Given that there is little firm empirical evidence for bank runs in systems without deposit insurance (including in the U.S. prior to deposit insurance), the second factor probably outweighs the first. There is something of a trade-off in this: the stronger is the deposit protection scheme, the smaller is the probability of bank runs and systemic instability, but the greater is the moral hazard. This reinforces the case for deposit insurance to be accompanied by regulation to contain risk-taking by banks subject to deposit insurance. Reviewing the experience of bank crises in various countries, Demirguc-Kunt and Datragiache (1998) argue on the basis of their sample of countries: "Our evidence suggests that, in the period under consideration, moral hazard played a significant role in bringing about systemic banking problems, perhaps because countries with deposit insurance schemes were not generally successful at implementing appropriate prudential regulation and supervision, or because the deposit insurance schemes were not properly designed." However, this conclusion cannot be generalised to all countries given that the U.S. and the countries of the European Union have deposit protection schemes.

Bhattacharya et al. (1998) consider various schemes to attenuate moral hazards associated with deposit-insurance. These include cash-reserve requirements, risk-sensitive capital requirements and deposit insurance premia, partial deposit insurance, bank closure policy, and bank charter value.

There is a particular issue with respect to the incentive structure of state-owned, or state-controlled, banks as their incentives may be ill-defined, if not hazardous. Such banks are not subject to the normal disciplining pressures of the market, their "owners" do not monitor their behaviour, and there is no disciplining effect from the market in corporate control. Managers of such banks may face incentives and pressure to make loans for public policy reasons. Political interference in such banks, and the unwitting encouragement of bad banking practices, can itself become a powerful ingredient in bank distress. Lindgren et al. (1996) found, for instance, that banks that were, or had recently been, state-owned or controlled were a factor in most of the instances of unsoundness in their sample of banking crises.

Several adverse incentive structures can be identified in many of the countries that have recently experienced distressed banking systems:

- The expectation that government commitment to the exchange rate was absolute induced imprudent and unhedged foreign currency borrowing both by banks and companies.
- Expectations of bail-outs or support for industrial companies (which had at various times been in receipt of government support) meant that the bankruptcy threat was weak. This may also have affected foreign creditors.
- A belief in the role of the lender-of-last-resort and expectations that banks would not be allowed to fail. The IMF notes that the perception of implicit guarantees was probably strengthened by the bailouts in the resolution of earlier banking crises in Thailand (1983–87), Malaysia (1985–88) and Indonesia (1994).
- The effect of close relationships between banks, the government, other official agencies and industrial corporations which often meant that lending relationships that would normally be conducted at arms-length became intertwined in a complex structure of economic and financial linkages within sometimes opaque corporate structures. This also meant that corporate governance arrangements, both within banks and their borrowing customers, were often weak and ill-defined.

Market Discipline

The fourth component of the *regulatory regime* relates to the arrangements for market discipline on banks. The central theme is that regulation can never be an alternative to market discipline. On the contrary, market discipline needs to be reinforced within the regime. In fact, market discipline is one of the three pillars in the proposed new Basel capital adequacy regime. A starting point is that, as noted by Lang and Robertson (2000), the existence of deposit insurance creates a large class of debt-holders who have no incentive to engage in costly monitoring of banks.

Monitoring is not only conducted by official agencies whose specialist task it is. In well-developed regimes, the market has incentives to monitor the behaviour of financial firms. The disciplines imposed by the market can be as powerful as any sanctions imposed by official agencies. The disciplining role of the markets (including the inter-bank market) was weak in the crisis countries of South East Asia in the 1990s. This was due predominantly to the lack of disclosure and transparency of banks, and to the fact that little reliance could be placed on the quality of accountancy data provided in bank accounts. In many cases standard accountancy and auditing procedures were not applied rigorously, and in some cases there was wilful mis-representation of the financial position of banks and non-financial companies. This is not an issue for less developed countries alone. For instance, Nakaso et al. (2000) argue that market discipline did not operate efficiently in Japan due largely to insufficient financial infrastructure (weak accountancy rules, inadequate disclosure, etc.).

Market discipline works effectively only on the basis of full and accurate information disclosure and transparency. Good quality, timely and relevant information needs to be available to all market participants and regulators so that asset quality, creditworthiness and the condition of financial institutions can be adequately assessed.

A potentially powerful disciplining power of markets derives from the market in corporate control which, through the threat of removing control from incumbent management, is a discipline on managers to be efficient and not endanger the solvency of their banks. As put in a recent IMF study: "An open and competitive banking market exerts its own form of discipline against weak banks while encouraging well-managed banks" (Lindgren et al., 1996).

Several parties are potentially able to monitor the management of banks and other financial firms: owners, bank depositors and customers, rating agencies, official agencies (e.g. the central bank or other regulatory body), and other banks in the market. In practice, excessive emphasis has been given to official agencies. The danger in this is that a monopoly monitor is established with many of the standard problems associated with monopoly power. There may even be adverse incentive effects in that, given that regulatory agencies conduct monitoring and supervision on a delegated basis, the incentive for others to conduct monitoring may be weakened.

In the interests of an effective and efficient regulatory regime, the role of all potential monitors (and notably the market) needs to be strengthened, with greater incentives for other parties to monitor financial firms in parallel with official agencies. An advantage of having agents other than official supervisory bodies monitor banks is that it removes the inherent danger of having monitoring and supervision conducted by a monopolist with less than perfect and complete information with the result that inevitably mistakes will be made. A monopolist supervisor may also have a different agenda than purely the maintenance of financial stability. It has been noted that "Broader approaches to bank supervision reach beyond the issues of defining capital and accounting standards, and envisage co-opting other market participants by giving them a greater stake in bank survival. This approach increases the likelihood that problems will be detected earlier . . . [it involves] broadening the number of those who are directly concerned about keeping the banks safe and sound," (Caprio & Honahan, 1998).

Given how the business of banking has evolved, and the nature of the market environment in which banks now operate, market discipline needs to be strengthened. The issue is not about market vs. agency discipline, but the mix of all aspects of monitoring, supervision and discipline. In its recent consultation document on capital adequacy the Basel Committee recognised that supervisors have a strong interest in facilitating effective market discipline as a lever to strengthen the safety and soundness of the banking system. It argues: "market discipline has the potential to reinforce capital regulation and other supervisory efforts to promote safety and soundness in banks and financial systems. Market discipline imposes strong incentives on banks to conduct their business in a safe, sound and efficient manner."

Some analysts (e.g. Calomiris, 1997) are sceptical about the power of official supervisory agencies to identify the risk characteristics of banks compared with the power and incentives of markets. Along with others, (including Evanoff and Wall (2000) who present a detailed set of proposals for the implementation of a subordinated debt rule), he has advocated banks being required to issue a minimum amount of subordinated and uninsured debt as part of the capital base. Holders of subordinated debt have an incentive to monitor the risk-taking of banks. As noted by Lang and Robertson (2000), discipline can be imposed through three routes: the cost of raising funds, market signals as expressed in risk premia implicit in the price of subordinated debt, and through supervisors themselves responding to market signals. Discipline would be applied by the market as its assessment of risk would be reflected in the risk premium in the price of traded debt. In particular, because of the nature of the debt contract, holders of a bank's subordinated debt do not share in the potential upside gain through the bank's risk-taking, but stand to lose if the bank fails. They therefore have a particular incentive to monitor the bank's risk profile compared with shareholders who, under some circumstances, have an incentive to support a high-risk profile. This is particularly the case when a "gamble for resurrection" strategy becomes optimal for shareholders. In this respect, there is a degree of symmetry between the reward structures faced by equity and subordinated debt holders in that equity-holders have the prospect of unlimited upside gain while losses are restricted to the value of their holding, while debt-holders do not share in any excess rewards (in the absence of default their rewards are fixed) but face the prospect of total loss in the event of default. For such a scheme to work, however, it must be well-established that holders of such subordinated debt will never be rescued in the event of the bank failing.

The impact of an increase in the debt-equity ratio (arising through substituting subordinated debt for equity) on the incentives for risk-taking by banks is ambiguous. On the one hand, a rise in the ratio raises the proportion of liability holders who have an incentive to monitor risk. This might be expected to lower the risk-appetite of banks. On the other hand, a decline in the equity ratio may raise the risk-appetite of equity holders as they have less to lose and may face a rational gamble-for-resurrection option. A decline in the equity ratio also has the disadvantage of increasing the probability of insolvency. It is also the case that the market disciplining role of subordinated debt may be limited because in practice such debt will always be a small proportion of a bank's total liabilities. The most powerful route is likely to be through market signals and how these induce supervisors to respond.

A scheme along these lines has been introduced in Argentina whereby holders of subordinated debt must be entities of substance which are independent of a bank's shareholders, and it requires issue of the debt in relatively lumpy amounts on a regular basis (Calomiris, 1997). However, while there is a potentially powerful role for market discipline to operate through the pricing of subordinated debt, the interests of holders of such debt do not necessarily precisely coincide with those of depositors or the public interest more generally (Dewatripont & Tirole, 1994). It is not, therefore, a substitute for official monitoring. It is intended as an extension of the role of market monitoring.

A further example of market discipline could be to link deposit insurance premia paid by banks to the implied risk of the bank as incorporated in subordinated debt yields or classifications of rating agencies.

The merit of increasing the role of market discipline is that large, well-informed creditors (including other banks) have the resources, expertise, market knowledge, and incentives to conduct monitoring and to impose market discipline. For instance, the hazardous state of BCCI was reflected in market prices and inter-bank interest rates before the Bank of England closed the bank. Market reports also indicate that some money brokers in London had ceased to deal with BCCI in advance of it being closed.

Leaving aside the merits and drawbacks of particular mechanisms that might be proposed (and one such mechanism has been suggested above as an example), the overall assessment is that regulation needs to reinforce, not replace, market discipline. The *regulatory regime* needs to be structured so as to provide greater incentives than exist at present for markets to monitor banks and other financial firms.

In addition, there is considerable advantage in regulators utilising market data in their supervisory procedures whenever possible. Evidence indicates that markets give signals about the credit-standing of financial firms which, when combined with inside information gained by supervisory procedures, can increase the efficiency of the overall supervisory process. Flannery (1998) suggests that market information may improve two features of the overall process: (1) regulators can identify developing problems more promptly, and (2) regulators have the incentive and justification to take action more quickly once problems have been identified. He concludes that market information should be incorporated into the process of identifying and correcting problems.

If financial markets are able to assess a bank's market value as reflected in the market price, an asset-pricing model can in principle be used to infer the risk of insolvency that the market has assigned to each bank. Such a model has been applied to UK banks by Hall and Miles (1990). Similar analysis for countries which had recently liberalised their financial systems has been applied by Fischer and Gueyie (1995). On the other hand, there are clear limitations to such an approach (see Simons & Cross, 1991) and hence it would be hazardous to rely exclusively on it. For instance, it assumes that markets have sufficient data upon which to make accurate assessments of banks, and it equally assumes that the market is able to efficiently assess the available information and incorporate it into an efficient pricing of bank securities.

An additional route is to develop the role of rating agencies in the oversight role. Rating agencies have considerable resources and expertise in monitoring banks and making assessments of risk. It could be made a requirement, as in Argentina, for all banks to have a rating which would be made public.

While market discipline is potentially powerful, it has its limitations and Bliss and Flannery (2000) argue that there is no strong evidence that equity and debt-holders do in fact affect managerial decisions. This means that, in practice, it is unlikely to be an effective complete alternative to the role of official regulatory and supervisory agencies:

- Markets are concerned with the private costs of a bank failure and reflect the risk of this in market prices. The social cost of bank failures, on the other hand, may exceed the private cost (Llewellyn, 1999) and hence the total cost of a bank failure may not be fully reflected in market prices.
- The cost of private monitoring and information collection may exceed the benefits.
- Market disciplines are not effective in monitoring and disciplining public sector banks.
- 'Free-rider' problems may emerge.
- In many countries, there are limits imposed on the extent to which the market in corporate control (the take-over market) is allowed to operate. In particular, there are often limits, if not bars, on the extent to which foreign

institutions are able to take control of banks, even though they may offer a solution to under-capitalised institutions.

• The market is able to efficiently price bank securities and inter-bank loans only to the extent that relevant information is available, and in many cases the necessary information is not available. Disclosure requirements are, therefore, an integral part of the market disciplining process.

• It is not self-evident that market participants always have the necessary expertise to make risk assessment of complex, and sometimes opaque, banks. In addition, there are some areas within a bank (e.g. its risk analysis and control systems) where disclosure is not feasible.

• In some countries, the market in debt of all kinds (including securities and debt issued by banks) is limited, inefficient and cartelised although market discipline can also operate through inter-bank and swaps markets.

• When debt issues are very small it is not always economic for rating agencies to conduct a full credit rating on a bank.

While there are clear limitations to the role of market discipline (discussed further in Lane, 1993) the global trend is in the direction of placing more emphasis on market data in the supervisory process. The theme being developed is not that market monitoring and discipline can effectively replace official supervision, but that it has a powerful role which should be strengthened within the overall *regulatory regime*. In addition, Caprio (1997) argues that broadening the number of those who are directly concerned about the safety and soundness of banks reduces the extent to which insider political pressure can be brought to bear on bank regulation and supervision. In fact, the recent consultative document issued by the Basel Committee on Banking Supervision (Basel Committee, 1999a) incorporates the role of market discipline as one of the three pillars of a proposed new approach to banking supervision. The Committee emphasises that its approach "will encourage high disclosure standards and enhance the role of market participants in encouraging banks to hold adequate capital."

As neither the market nor regulatory agencies are perfect, the obvious solution is to utilise both with neither having a monopoly of wisdom and judgement. The conclusion is that more systematic research is needed into the predictive power of market data, and how market information can usefully be incorporated into the supervisory process both by regulators and the markets.

This section should not conclude without reference to competition. However well-intentioned, regulation has the potential to compromise competition and to condone, if not in some cases endorse, unwarranted entry barriers, restrictive practices, and other anti-competitive mechanisms. Historically regulation in finance has often been anti-competitive in nature. But this is not an inherent property of regulation. The purpose of regulation is not to displace competitive pressures or market mechanisms, but to correct for market imperfections and failures. As there are clear consumer benefits and efficiency gains to be secured through competition, regulation should not be constructed in a way that impairs it. Regulation and competition need not be in conflict: on the contrary, properly constructed they are complementary. Regulation can also make competition more effective in the market place by, for instance, requiring the disclosure of relevant information that can aid market participants to make informed choices.

Discipline can also be exerted by competition. Opening domestic financial markets to external competition can contribute to the promotion of market discipline. There are many benefits to be derived from foreign institutions entering a country. They bring expertise and experience and, because they themselves are diversified throughout the world, what is a macro shock to a particular country becomes a regional shock, and hence they are more able to sustain purely national shocks which domestic institutions are less able to do. It is generally the case that competition that develops from outside a system tends to have a greater impact on competition and efficiency than internal competition. Foreign institutions tend to be less subject to domestic political pressures in the conduct of their business, and are also less susceptible to local euphoria which, at times, leads to excessive lending and over-optimistic expectations.

Intervention

A key component of the *regulatory regime* is the nature, timing and form of intervention by regulatory agencies in the event of either some form of compliance failure within a regulated firm, or when financial distress occurs with banks. While not downgrading the significance of the former, in the interest of brevity we reserve discussion of this issue to the question of intervention in the event of bank distress.

The closure of an insolvent or, under a SEIR regime, a near-insolvent bank, can impose a powerful discipline on the future behaviour of banks. Such 'creative destruction' has a positive dimension. It is also necessary to define the nature of 'closure'. It does not necessarily mean that, even in the absence of deposit insurance, depositors lose. Nor do bank-customer relationships and information sharing need to be destroyed. As with the bankruptcy of any company, there is always some residual value within an insolvent bank. Bank closure may simply mean a change in ownership of a bank and the imposition of losses on equity holders. In most countries, 'bank closure' has not meant the destruction of the bank. Thus, Barings was purchased by ING Bank. In many instances, regulatory authorities have brokered a change in ownership of insolvent banks while imposing losses on shareholders. The skill in intervention that leads to the 'closure' of an institution lies in ensuring that what remains of value is maintained.

Intervention arrangements are important not the least because they have incentive and moral hazard effects which potentially influence future behaviour by banks and their customers. These arrangements may also have important implications for the total cost of intervention (e.g. initial forbearance often has the effect of raising the eventual cost of subsequent intervention), and the distribution of those costs between tax-payers and other agents. Different intervention arrangements also have implications for the future efficiency of the financial system in that, for instance, forbearance may have the effect of sustaining inefficient banks and excess capacity in the banking sector.

The issue focuses on when intervention is to be made. The experience of banking crises in both developed and developing countries indicates that a well-defined strategy for responding to the possible insolvency of financial institutions is needed. A response strategy in the event of bank distress has three key components:

- taking prompt corrective action to address financial problems before they reach critical proportions;
- being prepared to close insolvent financial institutions while nevertheless not destroying what value remains;
- closing of unviable institutions, and vigorously monitoring of weak and/or restructured institutions.

A key issue relates to rules vs. discretion in the event of bank distress: the extent to which intervention should be circumscribed by clearly-defined rules (so that intervention agencies have no discretion about whether, how and when to act), or whether there should always be discretion simply because relevant circumstances cannot be set out in advance. The obvious prima facie advantage to allowing discretion is that it is impossible to foresee all future circumstances and conditions for when a bank might become distressed and close to (or actually) insolvent. It might be judged that it is not always the right policy to close a bank in such circumstances.

However, there are strong arguments against allowing such discretion and in favour of a rules approach to intervention. Firstly, it enhances the credibility of the intervention agency in that market participants, including banks, have a high degree of certainty that action will be taken. Secondly, allowing discretion may increase the probability of forbearance which usually eventually leads to higher costs when intervention is finally made. Kane (2000), for instance, argues that officials may forbear because they face different incentives from those of the market: their own welfare, the interests of the agency they represent, political interests, reputation, future employment prospects, etc. Perhaps less plausibly, he also argues that, under some circumstances, the present generation of tax-payers may believe they can shift the cost of resolution to future generations. Thirdly, and this was relevant in some countries which recently experienced banking distress, it removes the danger of undue political interference in the disciplining of banks and regulated firms. Experience in many countries indicates that supervisory authorities face substantial pressure to delay action and intervention. Fourthly, and related to the first, a rules approach to intervention is likely to have a beneficial impact on ex ante behaviour of financial firms.

A rules-based approach, by removing any prospect that a hazardous bank might be treated leniently, has the advantage of enhancing the incentives for bank managers to manage their banks prudently so as to reduce the probability of insolvency, (Glaessner & Mas, 1995). It also enhances the credibility of the regulator's threat to close institutions. Finally, it guards against hazards associated with risk-averse regulators who themselves might be dis-inclined to take action for fear that it will be interpreted as a regulatory failure, and the temptation to allow a firm to trade-out of its difficulty. This amounts to the regulator also "gambling for resurrection." In this sense, a rules approach may be of assistance to the intervention agency as its hands are tied, and it is forced to do what it believes to be the right thing.

Put another way, time-inconsistency and credibility problems should be addressed through pre-commitments and graduated responses with the possibility of over-rides. Many analysts have advocated various forms of pre-determined intervention through a general policy of "Structured Early Intervention and Resolution" (SEIR). There is a case for a graduated-response approach since, for example, there is no magical capital ratio below which an institution is in danger and above which it is safe. Other things equal, potential danger gradually increases as the capital ratio declines. This in itself suggests that there should be a graduated series of responses from the regulator as capital diminishes. No single dividing line should trigger action but there should be a series of such trigger points with the effect of going through any one of them being relatively minor, but the cumulative effect being large. Goldstein and Turner (1996) argue that SEIR is designed to imitate the remedial action which private bond holders would impose on banks in the absence of government insurance or guarantees. In this sense it is a mimic of market solutions to troubled banks. An example of the rules-based approach is to be found in the Prompt Corrective Action (PCA) rules in the U.S. These specify graduated intervention by the regulators with pre-determined responses triggered by capital thresholds. In fact, several countries have such rules of intervention (Basel Committee, 1999a). SEIR strategies can, therefore, act as a powerful incentive for prudent behaviour.

The need to maintain the credibility of supervisory agencies creates a strong case against forbearance. The overall conclusion is that there should be a clear bias (though not a bar) against forbearance when a bank is in difficulty. While there should be a strong presumption against forbearance, and that this is best secured through having clearly-defined rules, there will always be exceptional circumstances when it might be warranted in the interests of systemic stability. However, when forbearance is exercised the regulatory agency should, in some way or another, be made accountable for its actions.

A useful case study is to be found in the example of Finland where strict conditions were imposed in the support programme. These are summarised by Konskenkyla (2000) as:

- support was to be transparent and public;
- the attractiveness of public funding of the programme was to be minimised;
- the owners of supported banks were, where possible, to be held financially responsible;
- the terms of the programme were to support the efficiency of the banking system and the promotion of necessary structural adjustments within the system;
- the potential impact on competitive distortions were to be minimised;
- banks receiving support were to be publicly monitored;
- the employment terms of bank directors were to be reasonable and possible inequities removed.

It is also the case that some bank directors and managers in Finland have been held financially liable for hazardous behaviour (see Halme, 2000).

Corporate Governance

The focus of corporate governance is the principal-agent relationship that exists between managers and shareholders (owners) of companies. The owners (principals) delegate the task of management to professional managers (agents) who, in theory, act in the interests of the shareholders. In practice, managers have information advantages over shareholders and also have their own interests which may not coincide with those of the owners. Differences may emerge between the owners and managers with respect to their appetite for risk. For instance, managers may at times have a greater appetite for risk than do shareholders because they do not stand to lose if the risk fails. On the other hand, at other times (e.g. when capital in the bank is low) shareholders may have a strong appetite for risk in a gamble for resurrection strategy.

In the final analysis, all aspects of the management of financial firms (including compliance) are ultimately corporate governance issues. This means that, while shareholders may at times have an incentive to take high risks, if a financial firm behaves hazardously it is, to some extent, a symptom of weak corporate governance. This may include, for instance, a hazardous corporate structure for the financial firm; inter-connected lending within a closely-related group of companies; lack of internal control systems; weak surveillance by (especially non-executive) directors, and ineffective internal audit arrangements which often includes serious under-reporting of problem loans. Corporate governance arrangements were evidently weak and under-developed in banks in many of the countries that have recently experienced bank distress.

A particular feature of corporate governance relates to cross-share-holdings and inter-connected lending within a group, (Falkena & Llewellyn, 2000). With respect to Japan, Nabaso et al. (2000) note that such cross-share-holdings, which have long been a feature of Japanese corporate structures, increased during the 'bubble era' that preceded the banking crisis. In some cases, banks sold capital to companies (in order to raise their capital-asset ratios) and at the same time purchased stock in the companies. Several problems arise in cross-share-holding arrangements: credit assessment may be weak; the mix of debt and equity contracts held by banks may create conflicts of interest; when equity prices fall banks simultaneously face credit and market risk; and banks often count unrealised gains as capital even when in practice they cannot be realised.

There are several reasons why corporate governance arrangements operate differently with banks than with other types of firms. Firstly, banks are subject to regulation which adds an additional dimension to corporate governance arrangements. Secondly, banks are also subject to continuous supervision and monitoring by official agencies. This has two immediate implications for private corporate governance: shareholders and official agencies are to some extent duplicating monitoring activity, and the actions of official agencies may have an impact on the incentives faced by other monitors, such as shareholders and even depositors. However, official and market monitoring are not perfectly substitutable. Thirdly, banks have a fiduciary relationship with their customers (e.g. they are holding the wealth of depositors) which is rare with other types of firm. This creates additional principal-agent relationships (and potentially agency costs) with banks that generally do not exist with non-financial firms.

A fourth reason why corporate governance mechanisms are different in banks is that there is a systemic dimension. Because in some circumstances (e.g. presence of externalities) the social cost of a bank failure may exceed the private costs, there is a systemic concern with the behaviour of banks that does not exist with other companies. Fifthly, banks are subject to safety-net arrangements that are not available to other companies. This has implications for incentive structures faced by owners, managers, depositors and the market with respect to monitoring and control.

All these considerations have an impact on the two mechanisms for exercising discipline on the management of firms: internal corporate governance and the market in corporate control. While there are significant differences between banks and other firms, corporate governance issues in banks have received remarkably little attention. A key issue noted by Flannery (1998) is that little is known about how the two governance systems (regulation and private) interact with each other and, in particular, the extent to which they are complementary or offsetting.

A key issue in the management of banks is the extent to which corporate governance arrangements are suitable and efficient for the management and control of risks. In the UK, the FSA has argued as follows: "Senior management set the business strategy, regulatory climate, and ethical standards of the firm. . . . Effective management of these activities will benefit firms and contribute to the delivery of the FSA's statutory objectives." Corporate governance arrangements include issues of corporate structure, the power of shareholders to exercise accountability of managers, the transparency of corporate structures, the authority and power of directors, internal audit arrangements, and lines of accountability of managers. In the final analysis, shareholders are the ultimate risk-takers and agency problems may induce managers to take more risks with the bank than the owners would wish. This in turn raises issues about what information shareholders have about the actions of the managers to which they delegate decision-making powers, the extent to which shareholders are represented on the board of directors of the bank, and the extent to which shareholders have power to discipline managers.

Corporate governance arrangements need to provide for effective monitoring and supervision of the risk-taking profile of banks. These arrangements need to provide for, inter alia, a management structure with clear lines of accountability; independent non-executive directors on the board; an independent audit committee; the four-eyes principle for important decisions involving the risk profile of the bank; a transparent ownership structure; internal structures that enable the risk profile of the firm to be clear, transparent and managed; and the creation and monitoring of risk analysis and management systems. There would also be advantage in having a board director being responsible for the bank's risk analysis, management and control systems. Some bank ownership structures also produce ineffective corporate governance. Particular corporate structures (e.g. when banks are part of larger conglomerates) may encourage connected lending and weak risk analysis of borrowers. This was the case in a significant number of bank failures in the countries of South East Asia and Latin America. Some corporate structures also make it comparatively easy for banks to conceal their losses and unsound financial position.

The Basel Committee has appropriately argued that effective oversight by a bank's board of directors and senior management is critical. It suggests that the board should approve overall policies of the bank and its internal systems. It argues in particular that: "lack of adequate corporate governance in the banks seems to have been an important contributory factor in the Asian crisis. The boards of directors and management committees of the banks did not play the role they were expected to play" (Basel Committee, 1999b). According to the Committee, good corporate governance includes:

- establishing strategic objectives and a set of corporate values that are communicated throughout the banking organisation;
- setting and enforcing clear lines of responsibility and accountability throughout the organisation;
- ensuring that board members are qualified for their positions, have a clear understanding of their role in corporate governance and are not subject to undue influence from management or outside concerns;
- ensuring there is appropriate oversight by senior management;
- effectively utilising the work conducted by internal and external auditors;
- ensuring that compensation approaches are consistent with the bank's ethical values, objectives, strategy and control environment;
- conducting corporate governance in a transparent manner.

Some useful insights have been provided by Sinha (1999) who concludes, for instance, that while the regulatory authorities may approve the appointment of non-executive directors of banks, such directors often monitor top management less effectively than is the case in manufacturing firms. Sinha compares corporate governance arrangements in banks and manufacturing firms in the UK and finds that top management turnover in banks is less than in other firms, and that turnover seems not to be related to share price performance. Prowse (1997) also shows that accountability to shareholders, and the effectiveness of board monitoring, is lower in banks than in non-financial firms.

An interesting possibility is the extent to which all this results from moral hazard associated with official regulation and supervision: a further negative trade-off within the *regulatory regime*. It could be that the assumption that regulatory authorities impose regulation and monitor banks reduces the incentive for non-executive directors and shareholders to do so. The presumption may be that regulators have more information than do non-executive directors and shareholders, and that their own monitoring would only be wastefully duplicating that being conducted by official supervisors. Further research is needed into the role of non-executive directors and institutional investors in the effectiveness of corporate governance mechanisms in banks.

There is a further dimension to this issue. A major market discipline on any firm comes from the market in corporate control where, in principle, alternative managements seek control of companies. It is reasonably well established that there is something of a trade-off between internal corporate governance mechanisms and the power of the market in corporate control (the take-over market). In general, corporate governance arrangements tend to be stronger when the market in corporate control operates weakly. Sinha (1998) argues that this trade-off does not apply to banks as corporate governance arrangements are weak and so is the discipline of the market in corporate control. It is possible that restrictions imposed on the ownership of banks may reduce the disciplining power of markets.

Disciplines on the Regulator

Four perspectives reinforce the case for regulatory authorities being subject to strong disciplining and accountability measures: (1) there is an ever-present potential for over-regulation as it may be both over-demanded and over-supplied (Goodhart et al., 1998); (2) regulatory agencies have considerable power on both consumers and regulated firms; (3) the regulator is often supplying regulatory services as a monopolist although, in the U.S., there is scope for banks to switch regulators, and (4) the regulator is not subject to the normal disciplines of the market in the supply of its services.

These issues can be illustrated by the recent experience of the UK which has created a single regulatory authorities for all financial institutions and markets. As well as conferring substantial powers, the Financial Services Authority has substantial discretion in the use of its powers. In some respects, the way this discretion will be used will prove to be more significant than the powers it has. This in turn emphasises the importance of the disciplining and accountability mechanisms of the FSA, and of the FSA being open in the way it plans to develop its approach to regulation The agency has been open in describing its intended approach to regulation (see, for instance, its document *Meeting Our Responsibilities*).

Several accountability mechanisms have been put in place with respect to the FSA. Its objectives have been clearly defined in the Bill, and the FSA reports directly to Parliament. In addition, there is a formal legislative requirement for the FSA to use its resources in the most efficient way, and to make any regulatory burden proportionate to its benefits. The last-mentioned includes a requirement on the FSA to conduct cost-benefit analyses on its regulation. The Bill also outlines a strong set of accountability mechanisms including the scope for judicial review, public reporting mechanisms to the Treasury, requirements for consultation, the creation of Consumer and Practitioner Panels, independent review of its rules and decisions including by the Office of Fair Trading, independent investigation of complaints against the FSA, and an independent appeals and enforcement procedure. A further disciplining mechanisms is the requirement to conduct a cost-benefit study on major regulatory changes.

V. CONTRACT REGULATION

We return to the question of differentiation between banks. A given degree of *regulatory intensity* does not in itself imply anything about the degree of prescription or detail. Even within the regulation component of the regime a wide range of options is available, and in particular with respect to the degree of discretion exercised by the regulator. At the risk of over-simplification, two alternative approaches may be identified. At one end of the spectrum, the regulator lays down precise regulatory requirements that are applied to all banks. While there may be limited differentiations within the rules, the presumption is for a high degree of uniformity. At the other end of the spectrum (in what might be termed *Contract Regulation*) the regulator establishes objectives and general principles. It is then for each regulated firm to demonstrate to the regulator how these objectives and principles are to be satisfied by its own chosen procedures.

A detailed and prescriptive rule book approach may add to compliance costs without commensurate benefit in terms of meeting the objectives of regulation. If the objectives can be achieved by an alternative regime that is less costly for banks to operate with lower compliance costs, there would be advantage in reducing the dead-weight costs. It may, for instance, be possible to achieve the same objectives in a way that allows firms more scope to choose the manner in which they satisfy the regulator's requirements, and at the same time minimise their own compliance costs.

Under this regime, the regulator sets a clear set of objectives and general principles. It is then for each bank to demonstrate how these objectives and principles are to be satisfied by its own chosen procedures. In effect, the bank chooses its own regulation but within the strict constraints set by the objectives and principles set by the regulator. Put another way, the firm is able to choose its preferred route to achieving the objectives of regulation. Presumably, each bank would choose its own least-cost way of satisfying the regulator. Once the regulator has agreed with a bank how the objectives and principles are to be satisfied, a contract is established between the regulator and the bank. The contract requires the bank to deliver on its agreed standards and procedures, and sanctions apply in the case of non-performance on the contract. If the bank does not deliver on the contract, sanctions apply in the normal way and the regulator has the option of withdrawing the choice from the bank which would then be required to accept a standard contract devised by the regulator.

The advantage of this general approach is that individual banks are able to minimise their own costs of regulation by submitting to the regulator a plan that, while fully satisfying the requirements of the regulator, most suits their own particular circumstances and structure. As part of this paradigm, and in order to save costs in devising their own regime, banks would also have the option of adopting an approach established by the regulator. In effect, what is involved is a regime of "self-selecting regulatory contracts." *Contract regulation* necessarily implies increased differentiation in the regulatory arrangements between banks.

An analogy can be drawn with regulation in other areas. For instance, pollution regulation (say with respect to factories not contaminating local rivers) is framed in terms of the ultimate objective related to the measurable quality of water. Regulation does not prescribe how the factory is to undertake its production processes in order to meet the objective. It is for each firm to choose its own least-cost way of satisfying water quality standards. Providing the standards are met, the regulator is indifferent about how the standards are achieved, or what the production processes are. This is in sharp contrast to most aspects of financial regulation.

Under a regime of *contract regulation* the role of the regulator is five-fold: defining the degree of regulatory intensity, establishing regulatory objectives, approving self-selected contracts, monitoring standards and the performance on agreed contracts, and disciplining infringements of contracts. A by-product advantage is that the regulator would learn more about optimum regulatory arrangements through the experience of the variety of contracts.

While there are clear limits to how far this regime could be taken in practice, in some areas the regulator could offer a menu of contracts to regulated firms requiring them to self-select. Many countries are moving toward a pre-commitment approach to regulation (Kupiec & O'Brien, 1997). In this approach, each bank agrees with the supervisory agency the models and procedures it will use to evaluate their risks but are subject to penalties if they violate these procedures. The main feature is that each bank indicates how much it is expected to lose from its trading operation over the next quarter and sets aside capital to cover it. It is penalised if losses exceed the stated level. There are several advantages to a pre-commitment strategy: it avoids the necessity of detailed and prescriptive regulation, it creates powerful incentives for bank decision-makers (the choice of an excessive amount of capital imposes costs on the bank while choosing too low a level of capital risks the imposition of penalties), and it is flexible to the extent that it offers scope for each bank to choose a level of capital which is appropriate to its own particular circumstances. On the other hand, Estrella (1998) argues that the precise design of the penalty structure is likely to be complex.

VI. DIFFERENTIATIONS IN THE REGIME

A central theme has been that the two components of the financial stability objective (reducing the probability of bank failures and minimising the costs of those that do occur) are most effectively and efficiently served by a regulatory strategy that optimises the *regulatory regime*. This is necessarily more complex than myopically focusing upon regulation per se. The skill lies in combining the seven key components incorporating various positive and negative trade-offs that may exist between them.

However, there is no presumption for a single optimum combination of the components of the regime. On the contrary, optima will vary between countries at any point in time, over time for all countries, and between different banks within a country at any particular time. The optimum mix of the components of a *regulatory regime* and of instruments will change over time as financial structures, market conditions and compliance cultures evolve. For instance, the combination of external regulation and market discipline that is most effective and efficient in one set of market circumstances, and one type of financial structure in a country, may become ill-suited if structures change. Also, if the norms and compliance culture of the industry change, it may be appropriate to rely less on detailed and prescriptive regulation, at least for some banks.

Neither does the same approach and mix of components in the *regulatory regime* need to apply to all regulated firms, or all types of business. On the contrary, given that none of these are homogeneous, it would be sub-optimal to apply the same approach. A key issue is the extent to which differentiations are to be made between different banks.

Financial systems are changing substantially and to an extent that may undermine traditional approaches to regulation and most especially the balance between regulation and official supervision, and the role of market discipline. In particular, globalisation, the pace of financial innovation and the creation of new financial instruments, the blurring of traditional distinctions between different types of financial firm, the speed with which portfolios can change through banks trading in derivatives etc., and the increased complexity of banking business, create a fundamentally new – in particular, more competitive – environment in which regulation and supervision are undertaken. They also change the viability of different approaches to regulation which, if it is to be effective, must constantly respond to changes in the market environment in which regulated firms operate.

This also means that the optimum mix of the components of the *resulting regime* will change over time in response to considerations such as:

- the expertise that exists within banks and the extent to which reliance can be placed on internal management;
- the incentive structures within banks and those faced by regulators, supervisors and intervention agencies;
- the quality of risk analysis, management and control systems within banks;
- the skills of regulatory and supervisory agencies;
- the nature and efficiency of the basic financial infrastructure of a country: quality and reliability of accounting and auditing; nature, definition and enforceability of property rights; enforceability of collateral contracts; information disclosure and transparency, etc.;
- the existence of financial markets;
- the efficiency of financial markets most especially with respect to issues such as the extent to which market prices accurately reflect all publicly available information about the true value and risk characteristics of banks;
- the existence of financial instruments to enable banks to mitigate risks;
- the strength of incentives for stake-holders to monitor the risk characteristics of banks;
- the extent of moral hazard created by public intervention (e.g. deposit insurance);
- whether rating agencies provide rating services to investors in banks;
- the complexity and opaqueness of bank structures;

- ownership structures of banks and the extent to which owners are able to effectively monitor banks and influence the behaviour of bank managers to whom they delegate the responsibility of managing the bank;
- the degree of complexity of the business operations of banks;
- the existence or otherwise of an effective market in corporate control in the banking sector;
- the degree of ownership independence of banks from their corporate customers;
- the extent to which decision-making in banks is independent of political influence;
- the capital structure of banks.

With respect to the differences in the optimum structure of the *regulatory regime* as between countries, it is likely that in developing countries a substantial reliance will be placed on the explicit regulation component. This will reflect, for instance, considerations such as limited banking expertise; relatively unsophisticated techniques of risk analysis and management; a shortage of high-quality supervisory personnel; rudimentary financial infrastructure, financial markets, and financial instruments; absence of rating agencies; limited corporate governance mechanisms, and sometimes close relationships between banks and their corporate customers.

These considerations will vary from country to country though, in general, they imply that for developing countries more reliance probably needs to be placed on formal, prescriptive rules with less reliance on discretionary supervision, incentive structures, market discipline and corporate governance arrangements.

A potential problem in allowing different mixes of the components of the regime between countries is that competitive neutrality issues may arise. Banks in countries that rely more on detailed and prescriptive regulation may be placed at a competitive disadvantage vis à vis other nationalities of banks competing on an international basis. Conversely, banks operating in a less prescriptive regime may gain competitive advantages. However, this only applies to the extent that the differences that exist do not reflect risk considerations. It cannot legitimately be claimed that a bank with inadequate risk analysis and management systems and which, as a result, is subject to more formal regulation than other banks, is inequitably being penalised or placed at an unwarranted competitive disadvantage.

Over time, and as the complexity of banks operations increases, it is likely that less reliance can be placed on detailed and prescriptive rules. Risk becomes too complex and volatile an issue to be adequately covered by a simple set of prescriptive rules. Also, as markets develop and become more efficient, a greater role can be envisaged for market discipline. Similarly, less reliance may be needed on regulation to the extent that the skills within banks raise the sophistication and accuracy of banks' risk analysis and management systems.

Equally banks within a country are not homogeneous with respect to their skills, risk analysis and management systems, corporate governance arrangements, their overall significance within the financial system, legal, organisational, and corporate structures, or access to markets for capital. These differences may also create differences between banks in the optimum mix of the components of the *regulatory regime*.

VII. SHIFTS WITHIN THE *REGULATORY REGIME*

Drawing together some of the earlier themes, several shifts within the *regulatory regime* are recommended in order to maximise its overall effectiveness and efficiency:

- Less emphasis to be given to formal and detailed prescriptive rules dictating the behaviour of regulated firms.
- A greater focus to be given to incentive structures within regulated firms, and how regulation might have a beneficial impact on such structures.
- Market discipline and market monitoring of financial firms need to be strengthened within the overall regime.
- Greater differentiation between banks and different types of financial business.
- Less emphasis to be placed on detailed and prescriptive rules and more on internal risk analysis, management and control systems. In some areas, externally imposed regulation in the form of prescriptive and detailed rules is becoming increasingly inappropriate and ineffective. More emphasis needs to be given to monitoring risk management and control systems, and to recasting the nature and functions of external regulation away from generalised rule-setting towards establishing incentives and sanctions to reinforce such internal control systems. The recently issued consultative document by the Basel Committee on Banking Supervision (Basel Committee, 1999a) explicitly recognises that a major role of the supervisory process is to monitor banks' own internal capital management processes and "the setting of targets for capital that are commensurate with the bank's particular risk profile and control environment. This process would be subject to supervisory review and intervention, where appropriate."
- Corporate governance mechanism for financial firms need to be strengthened so that, for instance, owners play a greater role in the monitoring and control

of banks, and compliance issues are identified as the ultimate responsibility of a nominated main board director.

This chapter has emphasised the central importance of incentive structures and the potential for regulation to affect them. The key is how to align incentive structures to reduce the conflict between the objectives of the firm and those of the regulator. It is not a question of replacing one mechanism by another. It amounts to a re-balancing within the regime. It is unfortunate that public discussion of regulation often poses false dichotomies rather than recognising that the key issue is how the various mechanisms are to be combined. To make the case for regulation is not to undermine the central importance of market disciplines. Equally, to emphasis the role of incentives and market monitoring is not to argue that there is no role for regulation or supervision by an official agency.

Recent Trends in Regulatory Practice

Space precludes a detailed review of how regulatory arrangements have been evolving in practice. However, in some areas substantial changes have been made and others are in the pipeline. This section briefly considers some of the trends that are emerging with respect to the international approach to the prudential regulation and supervision of banks. While the BIS would not necessarily adopt the paradigm of the *regulatory regime* outlined earlier, there are some shifts in approach along the lines outlined in this chapter.

When setting capital adequacy standards on banks, the regulator confronts a negative trade-off between the efficiency and costs of financial intermediation on the one hand, and financial stability on the other. Although it is a complex calculation [absent the Modigliani-Miller theorem (which does not, in any case, apply to banks with deposit insurance)] as the cost of equity exceeds the cost of debt (deposits) the total cost of financial intermediation rises as the equity-assets ratio rises. If the regulator imposes an unnecessarily high capital ratio (in the sense that it exceeds what is warranted by the risk profile of the bank) an avoidable cost is imposed on society through a high cost of financial intermediation. On the other hand, a high capital ratio reduces the probability of bank failure and hence the social costs of financial instability. It also means that a higher proportion of the costs of a bank failure are borne by specialist risk-takers rather than depositors.

When judging the efficiency and effectiveness of capital adequacy regulation, four basic criteria are to be applied: (1) does it bring regulatory capital into line with economic capital?; (2) does it create the correct risk-management incentives for owners and managers of banks?; (3) does it produce the correct internal allocation of capital as between alternative risk assets and therefore the correct pricing of risk?, and (4) to what extent does it create moral hazard?.

BIS Approach to Capital Adequacy

The problems with the current BIS capital adequacy regime (1988 Accord) are well established. In particular:

- The risk-weights applied to different assets and contingent liabilities are not based on precise measures of absolute and relative risk. This in turn creates incentives for banks to misallocate the internal distribution of capital, to choose an uneconomic structure of assets, and to arbitrage capital requirements. It is also liable to produce a mis-pricing of risks. There is, for instance, an incentive to choose assets whose *regulatory risk-weights* are low relative to the *economic (true) risk weights* even though, in absolute terms, the risk weights may be higher than on alternative assets. The distortion arises not because of the differences in risk weights but to the extent that differentials between regulatory and economic risk weights vary across different asset classes.
- The methodology involves the summing of risk assets and does not take into account the extent to which assets and risks are efficiently diversified.
- No allowance is made for risk-mitigating factors such as hedging strategies within the banking book though allowance is made for risk mitigation in the trading book.
- Almost all loans carry a risk-weight of unity whereas the major differences within a bank's overall portfolio exist within the loan book.
- Banks are able to arbitrage their regulatory capital requirements in a way that lowers capital costs without any corresponding reduction in risk.
- The current Basel Accord only applies to credit and market risk.

Although some national regulatory and supervisory authorities have discretion in how the Accord is applied (subject to certain minima), and therefore the distortions may not be as serious in practice as the Accord might suggest, the fact remains that the Accord is seriously flawed. However, there are many countries where no discretion is allowed and the Basel requirements are adopted precisely.

Partly because of these weaknesses, the Basel Committee on Banking Supervision has recently proposed a new framework for setting capital adequacy requirements (Basel Committee, 1999a). It has issued a substantial consultation document which, if adopted, would represent a significant shift in the approach to bank regulation. This is not discussed in detail here other than to note that it is based on three pillars: minimum capital requirements, the supervisory review process, and market discipline requirements. The proposed new approach can be viewed in terms of the *regulatory regime* paradigm:

- Substantial emphasis is given to the importance of banks developing their own risk analysis, management and control systems, and it is envisaged that incentives will be strengthened for this.
- The Committee's consultative paper stresses the important role of supervision in the overall regulatory process. This second pillar of the capital adequacy framework will: "seek to ensure that a bank's capital position is consistent with its overall risk profile and strategy and, as such, will encourage *early supervisory intervention*" (italics added).
- In an attempt to bring regulatory capital more into alignment with economic capital, it is proposed to widen the range of risk weights and to introduce weights greater than unity.
- More types of risks are to be covered including legal, reputational and operational risk.
- Capital requirements are to take into account the volatility of risks and the extent to which risks are diversified.
- Although a modified form of the current Accord will remain as the "standardised" approach, the Committee believes that for some sophisticated banks use of internal and external credit ratings should be incorporated, and also that portfolio models of risk could contribute towards aligning economic and regulatory capital requirements. However, the Committee does not believe that portfolio models of risk can be used in the foreseeable future. The Committee recognises that use of internal ratings is likely to incorporate information about customers that is not available either to regulators or external rating agencies. In effect, in some respects this would involve asking banks themselves what they believe their capital should be. This is a form of pre-commitment. In practice, while banks will slot loans into buckets according to the internal ratings, the capital requirements for each bucket will be set by Basel. The object is to bring the regulatory process more into line with the way banks undertake risk assessment.
- A major aspect of the proposed new approach is to ask banks what they judge their capital should be. Any use of internal ratings would be subject to supervisor approval: this is an element of what earlier was termed *contract regulation*.
- Allowance is to be made for risk-mitigating factors.

- Greater emphasis is to be given to the role of market discipline. The third pillar in the proposed new approach is market discipline. It will encourage high standards of transparency and disclosure standards and "enhance the role of market participants encouraging banks to hold adequate capital." It is envisaged that market discipline should play a greater role in the monitoring of banks and the creation of appropriate incentives. The Committee has recognised that supervisors have a strong interest in facilitating effective market discipline as a lever to strengthen the safety and soundness of the banking system. It argues: "market discipline has the potential to reinforce capital regulation and other supervisory efforts to promote safety and soundness in banks and financial systems. Market discipline imposes strong incentives on banks to conduct their business in a safe, sound and efficient manner."
- The proposals also include the possibility of external credit assessments in determining risk weights for some types of bank assets. This would enhance the role of external rating agencies in the regulatory process. The Committee also suggests there could usefully be greater use of the assessments by credit rating agencies with respect to asset securitisations made by banks.
- The consultation document gives some emphasis to the important role that shareholders have in monitoring and controlling banks.

Overall, the new approach being proposed envisages more differentiation between banks, a less formal reliance on prescriptive rules, elements of choice for regulated institutions, an enhanced role for market discipline, a greater focus on risk analysis and management systems, some degree of pre-commitment, and a recognition that incentives for prudential behaviour have an important role in the overall approach to regulation. The new approach would create incentives for banks to improve their risk management methods and to develop their own estimates of economic capital. Equally, there would be powerful incentives for supervisors to develop and enhance their monitoring skills (Stephen & Fischer, 2000).

VIII. ASSESSMENT

This study has introduced the concepts of *regulatory regime* and *regulatory strategy*. Seven components of the regime have been identified: each are important but none alone is sufficient for achieving the objectives of regulation. They are complementary and not alternatives. Regulatory strategy is ultimately about optimising the outcome of the overall regime rather than any one of the components. Regulators need to consider that, if regulation is badly constructed or taken too far, there may be negative impacts on other components to the extent that the overall effect is diluted. However, there may also be positive relationships between the components, and regulation can have a beneficial effect on incentive structures within financial firms.

Effective regulation and supervision of banks and financial institutions has the potential to make a significant contribution to the stability and robustness of a financial system. However, there are limits to what regulation and supervision can achieve in practice. Although regulation is an important part of the *regulatory regime*, it is only a part and the other components are equally important. In the final analysis, there is no viable alternative to placing the main responsibility for risk management and general compliance on the shoulders of the management of financial institutions. Management must not be able to hide behind the cloak of regulation or pretend that, if regulation and supervisory arrangements are in place, this absolves them from their own responsibility. Nothing should ever be seen as taking away the responsibility of supervision of financial firms by shareholders, managers and the markets.

The objective is to optimise the outcome of a regulatory strategy in terms of mixing the components of the regime, bearing in mind that negative trade-offs may be encountered. The emphasis is on the *combination* of mechanisms rather than alternative approaches to achieving the objectives. The skill of the regulator in devising a regulatory strategy lies in how the various components in the regime are combined, and how the various instruments available to the regulator (rules, principles, guidelines, mandatory disclosure requirements, authorisation, supervision, intervention, sanctions, redress, etc.) are to be used.

ACKNOWLEDGMENTS

The author wishes to acknowledge financial support from the British Academy in the preparation of this study, and is very grateful for valuable comments on an earlier draft from Marsha Courchane, Gillian Garcia, Glenn Hoggarth, Patricia Jackson, Klaas Knot, David Marston, Peter Sinclair, Larry Wall and participants at an International Monetary Fund central banking seminar held in Wahington, D.C. in June, 2000. The usual disclaimer applies.

REFERENCES

Alba, P., Bhattacharya, G., Claessens, S., Ghash, S., & Hernandez, L. (1998). The role of Macroeconomic and Financial Sector Linkages in East Asia's Financial Crisis, *mimeo*. World Bank.

Baer, H., & Gray, C. (1996). Debt as a Control Device in Transitional Economies: The Experiences of Hungary and Poland. In: R. Frydman, C. Gray & A. Rapaczynski (Eds), *Corporate*

Governance in Central Europe and Russia (Vol. 1). Budapest: Central European University Press.

Barth, J., Caudill, S., Hall, T., & Yago, G. (2000). *Cross-Country Evidence on Banking Crises, Financial Structure and Bank Regulation*, paper presented at Western Economic Association International conference, Vancouver, June.

Basel Committee (1999a). *A New Capital Adequacy Framework*. Consultative Paper, Basel Committee on Banking Supervision, BIS, Basel, June.

Basel Committee (1999b). *Enhancing Corporate Governance for Banking Organisations*. Basle Committee on Banking Supervision, BIS, Basel.

Benink, H., & Llewellyn, D. T. (1994). Fragile Banking in Norway, Sweden and Finland. *Journal of International Financial Markets, Institutions and Money, 14*(314), 5–20.

Benston, G., & Kaufman, G. (1995). Is the Banking and Payments System Fragile? *Journal of Financial Services Research*, September.

Berg, S. A. (1993). The Banking Crises in the Scandinavian Countries. In: *Bank Structure and Competition*. Federal Reserve Bank of Chicago.

Bhattacharya, S., Boot, A., & Thakor, A. V. (1998). The Economics of Bank Regulation. *Journal of Money, Credit and Banking*, November, pp. 745–770.

Billett, M., Garfinkel, J., & O'Neal, E. (1998). The Cost of Market versus Regulatory Discipline in Banking. *Journal of Financial Economics*, 333–358

Black, J. (1994). Which Arrow? Rule Type and Regulatory Policy. *Public Law*, June.

Bliss, R. & Flannery, M. (2000). Market Discipline in the Governance of U.S. Bank Holding Companies: Monitoring vs Influence. Working Paper Series Federal Reserve Bank of Chicago, WP–00–03, Chicago, March.

Brealey, R. (1999). The Asian Crisis: Lessons for Crisis Management and Prevention, Bank of England *Quarterly Bulletin*, August, pp. 285–296.

Briault, C. (1999). The rationale of a Single Regulator. *Occasional Paper*, No. 2, Financial Service Authority, London.

Brownbridge, M., & Kirkpatrick, C. (2000). Financial Sector Regulation: Lessons of the Asian Crisis. *Development Policy Review* (forthcoming).

Calomiris, C. (1997). *The Postmodern Safety Net*. Washington, D.C.: American Enterprise Institute.

Caprio, G. (1997). *Safe and Sound Banking in Developing Countries: We're not in Kansas Anymore*. Policy Research Paper, No. 1739, World Bank, Washington.

Corsetti, G., Pesenti, P., & Rabini, N. (1998). *What Caused the Asia Currency and Financial Crisis?* Banca D'Italia, Temi di Discussione, December

Dale, R. (1996). *Risk and Regulation in Global Securities Markets*. London: Wiley.

Demirguc-Kunt, K., & Detragiache, E, (1998). The Determinants of Bank Crisis in Developing and Developed Countries, IMF *Staff Papers*, March.

Dewatripont, M., & Tirole, J. (1994). *The Prudential Regulation of Banks*. Cambridge, MA: MIT Press.

Estrella, A. (1998). Formulas or Supervision? Remarks on the Future of Regulatory Capital, Federal Reserve Bank of New York. *Economic Policy Review*, October.

Evanoff, D., & Wall, L. (2000). Subordinated Debt and Bank Capital Reform, paper presented at Western Economic Association International Conference, Vancouver, June.

Evans, H, (2000). Plumbers and Architects: A Supervisory Perspective on International Financial Architecture, *Occasional Paper*, No. 4, Financial Services Authority, London, January.

Falkena, H., & Llewellyn, D. T. (2000). *The Economics of Banking*, SA Financial Sector Forum, Johannesburg.

Fink, G., & Haiss, P. (2000). *Lemming Banking: Conflict Avoidance by Herd Instint to Eliminate Excess Capacity*, paper presented at SUERF Colloquium, Vienna, May.

Fischer, K., & Gueyie, J. (1995). *Financial Liberalisation and Bank Solvency*, University of Laval, Quebec, August.

Flannery, M. (1998). Using Market Information in Prudential Bank Supervision: A Review of the U.S. Empirical Evidence. *Journal of Money, Credit and Banking*, August, pp. 273–305.

Garcia, G. G. (1999b). Deposit Insurance: Obtaining the Benefits and Avoiding the Pitfalls, IMF Working Paper, August.

Glaessner, T., & Mas, I. (1995). Incentives and the Resolution of Bank Distress. *World Bank Research Observer*, Vol. 10, No. 1, February, 53–73.

Godlayn, I., & Valdes, R. (1997). *Capital Flows and the Twin Crises: The Role of Liquidity*. IMF Working Paper, 97/87, July.

Goldstein, M., & Turner, P. (1996) Banking Crises in Emerging Economies, BIS *Economic Papers*, No. 46, BIS, Basle.

Goodhart, C. C., Hartmann, P., Llewellyn, D. T., Rojas-Suarez, L., & Weisbrod, S. (1998). *Financial Regulation: Why, How and Where Now?* London: Routledge.

Hall, S., & Miles, D. (1990). *Monitoring Bank Risk: A Market Based Approach*, Discussion Paper, Birkbeck College, London, April.

Halme, L. (2000). Bank Corporate Governance and Financial Stability. In: L. Halme, C. Hawkesby, J. Healey, I. Soapar & F. Soussa (Eds), *Selected Issues for Financial Safety Nets and Market Discipline*. London, Centre for Central Banking Studies.

Kaminsky, G. & Reinhart, C. (1998). The Twin Crises: The Causes of Banking and Balance of Payments Problems, Board of Governors, Federal Reserve System. *International Finance Discussion Papers*, No. 554.

Kane, E. (2000). Dynamic Inconsistency of Capital Forbearance: Long Run vs Short Run Effects of Too-Big-To-Fail Policymaking, paper presented to IMF Central Banking Conference, Washington, D.C., June.

Kaufman, G. (2000). Banking and Currency Crises and Systemic Risk: A Taxonomy and Review, New York University Salomon Centre Study on *Financial Markets, Institutions and Instruments*, Volume 9, No. 2, New York, May.

Konskenkyla, H. (2000). The Nordic Countries' Banking Crises and the Lessons Learned, paper presented at FDIC Conference, Washington, D.C., September.

Kupiec, H., & O'Brien, J. (1997). The Pre-Commitment Approach: Using Incentives to Set Market Risk Capital Requirements, *Finance and Economics Discussion Series*, no. 1997–14, Federal Reserve Board, Washington D. C., March.

Lane, T. (1993). Market Discipline, IMF *Staff Papers*, March, page 55.

Lang, W., & Robertson, D. (2000). Analysis of Proposals for a Minimum Subordinated Debt Requirement, paper presented at Western Economic Association International conference, Vancouver, June.

Lindgren, C. J., Garcia, G., & Saal, M. (1996), *Bank Soundness and Macroeconomic Policy*, Washington, International Monetary Fund.

Llewellyn, D. T. (1999). The Economic Rationale of Financial Regulation. *Occasional Paper*, No. 1, Financial Services Authority, London

Llewellyn, D. T. (2000). Regulatory Lessons from Recent Banking Crises. De Nederlandsche Bank Staff Paper, Amsterdam, May.

Nakaso, H., Hattori, M., Nagae, T., Hamada, H., Kanamori, T., Kamiguchi, H., Dezawa, T., Takahashi, K., Kamimura, A., Suzuki, T., & Sumida, K. (2000). Changes in Bank

Behaviour during the Financial Crisis: Experiences of the Financial Crisis in Japan, paper presented to IMF Central Banking Conference, Washington, D.C., June.

Prendergast, C. (1993). The Provision of Incentives in Firms. *Journal of Economic Literature*, March, pages 7–63.

Prowse, S. (1997). Corporate Control in Commercial Banks. *Journal of Financial Research, 20*, 509–527.

Reisen, H. (1998). *Domestic Causes of Currency Crises: Policy Lessons for Crisis Avoidance.* OECD Development Centre, Technical Paper 136, OECD, Paris.

Richardson, J., & Stephenson, M. (2000). Some Aspects of Regulatory Capital. *Occasional Paper*, No. 7, Financial Services Authority, London.

Sachs, J., Torrell, A., & Velesco, A. (1996). Financial Crises in Emerging Markets: The Lessons from 1995. *Brookings Papers* 1, Brookings Institution, Washington.

Saunders, A., & Wilson, B. (1996). Contagious Bank Runs: Evidence from the 1929–1933 Period. *Journal of Financial Intermediation, 5*, 409–423.

Schinasi, G., Drees, B., & Lee, W. (1999). Managing Global Finance and Risk. *Finance and Development*, December.

Schwartz, A. (1995). Coping with Financial Fragility: A Global Perspective. *Journal of Financial Services Research*, September.

Simons, K., & Cross, S. (1991). Do Capital Markets Predict Problems in Large Commercial Banks? *New England Economic Review*, May, 51–56.

Simpson, D. (2000). Cost Benefit Analysis and Competition. In: *Some Cost Benefit Issues in Financial Regulation*. Financial Services Authority, London.

Sinha, R. (1999). *Corporate Governance in Financial Services Firms*, Loughborough University Banking Centre Paper No 121/98, Loughborough University.

Stephen, D., & Fischer, M. (2000). *On internal ratings and the Basel Accord: Issues for Financial Institutions and Regulators in the Measurement and Management of Credit Risk*, paper presented at IMF Central Banking Conference, Washington, D.C., June.

UNCTAD (1998). *Trade and Development Report*, United Nations, Geneva.

Wallman, S. (1999). Information Technology Revolution and its Impact on Regulation and Regulatory Structure. In: R Littan & A Santomero (Eds), *Brookings-Wharton Papers on Financial Services*. Washington: Brookings Institution Press.

THE DEVELOPMENT OF INTERNAL MODELS APPROACHES TO BANK REGULATION AND SUPERVISION: LESSONS FROM THE MARKET RISK AMENDMENT

Jose A. Lopez and Marc R. Saidenberg

ABSTRACT

Over the past decade, banks have devoted many resources to developing internal risk models for the purpose of better quantifying the risks they face and allocating economic capital. These efforts have been recognized and encouraged by bank regulators. For example, the 1997 Market Risk Amendment (MRA) to the Basel Capital Accord formally incorporates banks' internal, market risk models into regulatory capital calculations. That is, the regulatory capital requirements for banks' market risk exposures are explicitly a function of the banks' own value-at-risk estimates. A key component in the design and implementation of the MRA was the development of qualitative and quantitative standards that must be satisfied in order for banks' models to be used for regulatory capital purposes. In this chapter, we examine the MRA and recent regulatory experience to draw out lessons for the design and implementation of internal models-based capital regimes for other types of risk.

Bank Fragility and Regulation: Evidence from Different Countries, Volume 12, pages 239–253.
2000 by Elsevier Science Inc.
ISBN: 0-7623-0698-X

I. INTRODUCTION

In June 1999, the Basel Committee on Banking Supervision issued a consultative paper, entitled "A New Capital Adequacy Framework", that outlines the three pillars to effective bank regulation: regulatory capital requirements, supervision, and market discipline. A key element of that document was the possible recognition of banks' internal risk ratings for the determination of capital requirements for credit risk. The new framework also raised the possibility of capital charges for interest rate and other risks being based on internal models. In short, the new framework clearly indicates that internal models currently play an important role in banks' own assessments of risks and, in the future, will do so in regulatory assessments of risk.

Over the last ten to fifteen years, financial institutions have significantly increased their use of econometric models to measure and manage their risk exposures. These developments have been both a product of and a driver of increased trading activities, increased emphasis on risk-adjusted returns on capital, and significant advances in finance and computer technology.

Given these developments, bank supervisors have also focused their attention on the use of such "internal models" for supervisory purposes such as the focus on banks' overall risk management systems. Supervisors have taken steps in using the "internal models" approach with the adoption of the Market Risk Amendment (MRA) to the 1988 Basel Capital Accord. The current regulatory framework (effective January 1998) applies to commercial banks whose trading activities account for more than 10% of total assets or are greater than $1 billion. The MRA capital requirements cover all assets in trading accounts (i.e. assets carried at current market value) and all foreign exchange and commodity positions, wherever located.

Regulatory concerns about market risk and how they have been addressed via the MRA should provide insight into the regulatory concerns about credit and other bank risks. A key component in the design and implementation of the MRA was the development of qualitative and quantitative standards that must be satisfied in order for banks' models to be used for regulatory capital purposes. These qualitative standards for bank risk management include independent risk control units and both internal and external audits. These standards also cover the integration of the models and quantitative methods into the management process as well as model reviews through "backtesting" and "stress-testing" exercises. The MRA also includes quantitative criteria such as capital requirements based on VaR estimates and explicit links to model performance via "backtesting".

We can draw lessons from the recent design and implementation of the MRA for the possible extension of an internal models approach to other risks. For example, the Basel committee recently issued a short note that found that models-based capital charges for market risk were sufficient to cover market losses, even in the stressed market conditions of the third and fourth quarters of 1998. Closer examination of this period (and the year earlier) as well as the reactions of banks and their regulators should give additional insight into the measures that must be set in place for possible extension of internal models approaches to other risk categories.

The development of the corresponding regulatory standards for credit and operational risk models will clearly be much more challenging than for market risk models. The design and implementation of the MRA, however, give us a framework to discuss the prudential, model, and validation standards that will need to be developed for other internal models-based capital regimes.

II. THE MARKET RISK AMENDMENT: THEORY AND IMPLEMENTATION

Why is a models-based approach to capital requirements reasonable?

The overarching rationale for an internal models approach to capital requirements is to tailor the required capital to the actual risks faced by specific institutions. By linking regulatory capital requirements to bank-specific measures of risk, we should be able to create capital requirements that conform more closely to banks' actual risk exposures. By using banks' internal risk measurements (instead of uniform regulatory measures of risk exposure), the subsequent capital charges should more accurately reflect individual banks' true risk exposures.

Note that this approach is quite distinct from previous regulatory practice, which either did not acknowledge differences in bank risk characteristics or applied a common regulatory standard to all banks (i.e. 8% of risk-adjusted assets). Such an important change in regulatory and supervisory practice has required and will require much effort to design and implement successfully.

The internal models approach is consistent with the shift in supervisory interest from a focus on risk measurement to a more comprehensive evaluation of banks' overall risk management. Over the past several years, supervisors have placed increasing emphasis on banks' internal processes for measuring risks and for ensuring that capital, liquidity and other financial resources are adequate in relation to the organizations' risk profiles. As noted in a recent Federal Reserve supervisory letter (SR 99–18), supervisors must evaluate whether a bank's internal capital adequacy analysis meaningfully ties the identification, measurement, monitoring and evaluation of risk to the institution's capital needs.

Since models are a natural way to examine these issues, banks and supervisors have moved in this direction. Since market risk is readily quantified and analyzed, this was the first area in which such modeling was put into place. Hence, market risk measures are currently more developed than those for other risks are, and prudential standards are more readily available, especially since the launch of Riskmetrics in the mid–1990's.

These risk measures, such as value-at-risk (VaR) estimates, should be useful for assessing the level of bank risk exposure at a point in time, but they will also be useful for monitoring risk exposures across time. The changes in these measures should provide supervisors with useful indicators. In addition, a capital charge based on internal models could provide supervisors with a consistent framework for making comparisons across institutions.

Details of the Market Risk Amendment

The current, U.S. capital rules for the market risk exposure of large, commercial banks, effective as of 1998, are explicitly based on VaR estimates. The rules cover a bank's total trading activity, which is all assets in a bank's trading account (i.e. assets carried at their current market value) as well as all foreign exchange and commodity positions wherever located in the bank. Any bank or bank holding company whose total trading activity accounts for more than 10% of its total assets or is more than $1 billion must hold regulatory capital against their market risk exposure. The capital charge is to be calculated using the so-called "internal models" approach.

Under this approach, capital charges are based on VaR estimates generated by banks' internal, risk management models using the standardizing parameters of a ten-day holding period and 99% coverage. In other words, a bank's market risk capital charge is based on its own estimate of the potential loss that would not be exceeded with 1% probability over the subsequent two-week period.

The actual market risk capital that a bank must hold at a point in time is the larger of the dollar value of its 10-day VaR estimate or a multiple of the average of the previous sixty days' estimates in dollar terms. Note that a charge for specific risk is also added. The regulatory multiplier is set to three, but it may increase as a function of the number of times that a bank's daily losses exceed its one-day VaR estimates. As described by Hendricks and Hirtle (1997), the regulatory multiplier adjusts the reported VaR estimates up to what regulators consider to be a minimum capital requirement reflecting their concerns regarding prudent capital standards and model accuracy. The regulatory multiplier explicitly links the accuracy of a bank's VaR model to its capital charge by varying over time.

The regulatory multiplier is a step function that depends on the number of exceptions observed over the last 250 trading days. Exceptions are defined as occasions when the one-day trading portfolio return is less than the corresponding one-day VaR estimate. The possible number of exceptions is divided into three zones. Within the green zone of four or fewer exceptions, a VaR model is deemed "acceptably accurate" to the regulators, and the multiplier remains at its minimum value of three. Within the yellow zone of five to nine exceptions, the multiplier increases incrementally with the number of exceptions. Within the red zone of ten or more exceptions, the VaR model is deemed to be "inaccurate" for regulatory purposes, and the multiplier increases to its maximum value of four. The institution must also explicitly take steps to improve its risk management system.

Lessons from the Design and Implementation of the MRA

The design and implementation of the MRA should provide valuable lessons for how to structure internal model approaches for other risk categories. Specifically, the minimum qualitative requirements for internal market risk management and the quantitative requirements for model construction and backtesting are instructive. The qualitative requirements are perceived to be principals of sound risk management that should be in place, regardless of the type of risk being modeled. This section provides greater detail on these issues and alludes to their use for credit risk modeling.

Lessons from the Design of the MRA
Although the quantitative criteria embodied in the MRA attracted much attention prior to its implementation, the qualitative criteria were potentially of greater importance from a regulatory standpoint. For example, the MRA requires that firms establish an independent risk control unit. That is, the unit in charge of gathering, processing and presenting internal risk measures must be independent of any single business unit and must report directly to senior management. Such an organizational structure would provide safeguards against inappropriate actions, such as violations of trading limits and use of inaccurate or inappropriate market data sources.

Another qualitative requirement based on sound risk management principles is that the firm conduct annual, independent surveys of the risk control unit. Such audits, whether internal or external, are useful for maintaining objectivity in the risk measurement and management processes and can serve as a starting point for dialogue with examiners. Such audits should focus on issues such as the adequacy of documentation for of risk management systems, the setting and enforcement of market risk limits, the organization of the risk control unit and a review of the pricing models that feed output into the VaR models.

Another key qualitative requirement of the MRA is that the firm must integrate the output from their market-risk models into its daily risk management. This effort requires both well-functioning management information systems as well as serious effort on the part of senior management. For example, the firm should have clearly documented procedures for report generation and risk decision criteria. The procedures, by which this information is used to set, monitor, and ensure compliance with risk limits should also be clearly documented. This requirement, as well as the other qualitative requirements, serves to insure that sound risk management principles are in place in an institution and to encourage the improvement of the firm's risk management procedures.

Given that financial risk management is a quantitative exercise, the MRA contains several quantitative criteria that should also be embodied in internal model approaches for other risk categories. For example, in order to construct a capital requirement that is applicable across firms, regulators will require a certain degree of standardization of model inputs. As described above, in the design of the MRA, regulators set standard parameters for the VaR percentile and the assumed portfolio holding period as well as certain others.

Beside parameter values for regulatory inputs, model assumptions are also of concern to regulators. With respect to VaR models, such issues as what risk factors are assumed to be independent and how options are incorporated into the model are very important to the accuracy of the reported VaR estimates. Within the MRA's supervisory framework, regulators require that such key modeling assumptions be clearly documented and justified. The sensitivity of the VaR estimates with respect to such assumptions should also be discussed and used to justify the firm's modeling decisions.

Analogous to examining a model's sensitivity to key assumptions, regulators insist that firms examine the model's performance under various scenarios. Examining model performance under standard conditions, which is known as "backtesting", is explicitly required, as described above. However, "stress-testing" exercises are crucial for gaining insight into the performance of a firm's risk management system in times of financial market crisis. For market risk, "stress" scenarios are readily generated and should be a standard part of a firm's analysis of its internal models. Such stress tests provide regulators with information that they are interested in because they focus more on downside risks. Stress testing will clearly be a key issue in implementing internal model approaches for other types of risks.

Lessons from the Implementation of the MRA
The MRA's regulatory capital requirements for market risk exposure have been in effect in the U.S. since the start of 1998. From the regulatory experience during this period, two general sets of lessons have arisen.

The first lesson is the overriding importance of a firm's management culture to a successful implementation and the ongoing performance of a financial risk management system. While managing risk on a daily basis is a challenge, the sternest tests of risk management systems are in terms of crisis; as noted by Scholes (2000), "[p]lanning for crises is more important than VaR analysis." Thus, firms with actively involved management should have better performing risk management systems. An important way to gauge active management is with the firm's stress-testing philosophy. Firms that actively engage in forward-looking stress-testing exercises generally should have management that is planning for more likely future crisis scenarios and thus may be better prepared. For further discussion of stress-testing methodologies, see the report prepared by the Basel Committee on the Global Financial System (2000).

The second set of lessons is actual experience with the challenges associated with the empirical validation of VaR models. Certainly there are challenges with accounting for actual observed profits and losses arising from firms' market risk positions. However, such concerns can be directly addressed.

The greater challenge lies in the statistical tests used to determine the performance of firms' VaR estimates. The MRA's backtesting framework is based on the binomial test, which determines whether the observed frequency of VaR exceptions matches the expected frequency. Although this test is a reasonable starting point, it is problematic because of its low power to detect inaccurate VaR estimates; that is, this test will indicate that a set of VaR estimates is accurate and acceptable too frequently. For further discussion of this point, see Kupiec (1995), Lopez (1999) and Berkowitz (2000). This flaw in the binomial test requires regulators to rely on other indicators of model performance to develop an informed opinion on the model's accuracy. For example, regulators can examine the magnitude of VaR exceptions to derive further information on model performance; see Lopez (1999), Berkowitz (1999), and Lopez and Walter (2000) for discussion of such alternative tests.

Regarding actual firm performance, the BIS published a report in the fall of 1999 analyzing the performance of 40 banks in nine countries that were subject to the MRA requirements during the latter half of 1999. The report found that there were no cases of surveyed institutions experiencing trading losses over any ten-day consecutive period that exceeded their capital requirements, even though this was a particular volatile period in many financial markets. As to one-day exceptions, over half of the institutions reported none over the period.

Clearly, these results are fine from a regulatory perspective; that is, regulatory capital requirements have been effective in protecting firms' capital against market risk losses. However, it raises an important issue regarding the tension between model accuracy and capital adequacy. If the goal is model accuracy, then VaR exceptions and losses should occur. In general, regulators would like capital requirements to be more risk-sensitive and hence more accurate, but they would also feel comfortable with a "buffer" to help ensure capital adequacy. This tension will play a key role in the solutions developed for future internal-models approaches to regulatory capital.

III. CHALLENGES FOR INTERNAL-MODEL APPROACHES FOR CREDIT AND OTHER RISKS

Just as with market risk, regulators should be able to create capital requirements that conform more closely to banks' actual risk exposures by linking capital requirements to bank-specific measures of risk. By using banks' internal measures of credit and other risks, regulatory capital charges should more accurately reflect individual banks' true risk exposures. The design and implementation of the MRA outlined above provides valuable lessons for how to structure internal model approaches for these other risk categories. The quantitative requirements for model construction and backtesting and the minimum qualitative requirements for internal market risk management can be instructive.

As noted above, a key component in the design and implementation of the MRA was the development of qualitative and quantitative standards that must be satisfied in order for banks' models to be used for regulatory capital purposes. These standards can be thought of as addressing three general sets of regulatory concerns regarding the details of a capital framework based on internal models and the integrity of the internal models that were now being permitted to set regulatory capital.

Similar to the MRA, quantitative and qualitative standards for credit and other risks would likely need to address three general components: prudential standards defining the model-based estimate of risk to be used in the capital charge; modeling standards describing the elements that an acceptable risk model would incorporate; and validation techniques to ensure that models estimates are reasonably accurate and comparable across institutions. Although much of the discussion that follows relates specifically to the development of an internal models-based capital requirement for credit risk, many if not all of these issues would also need to be addressed in order to develop an internal models approach for other risks.

Although banks' internal models have already been incorporated into the determination of capital requirements for market risk, credit and operational risk models are not a simple extension of their market risk counterparts for a few key reasons. Data for the calibration and validation of models and key inputs are much less available than for market risk since modeling horizons are much longer. Such models must also cover many more instrument types. Additionally, issues of data quality and price accuracy are much more prevalent for these modeling efforts since these data are much less standard across banks and across markets than for market risk.

Banks and researchers both often report that data limitations are one of the key impediments to the design and implementation of credit risk models. Most loans are not marked to market, as such the forecasts from a typical credit risk model are not derived from a projection of future prices based on a comprehensive record of historical prices.

The available data to estimate credit risk models is also severely limited because of the infrequent nature of default events and the longer-term time horizons used in measuring credit risk. Typically banks and model developers, in specifying model parameters, are required to use simplifying assumptions and proxy data.

Finally, the relative size of the banking book and the likelihood of bank solvency if modeled credit risk estimates are inaccurate underscore the need for a better understanding of a model's sensitivity to structural assumptions and parameter estimates.

The development of validation standards for credit and operational risk models is fundamentally more difficult than the development and implementation of the backtesting standards for market risk models. Where market risk models typically employ a horizon of a few days, credit risk models generally rely on a time frame of one year or more. These longer holding periods present problems to banks and supervisors in assessing the accuracy of these models. Additionally, a quantitative validation standard similar to that in the Market Risk Amendment would require an impractical number of years of data, spanning multiple credit cycles.

Recently, the Basel Supervisors Committee in a report specifically addressing credit risk modeling noted that risk modeling may indeed prove to result in better internal risk management, and may have the potential to be used in the supervisory oversight of banking organizations (Basel Committee on

Banking Supervision, 1999). The Committee concluded, however, that before an internal models approach could be used to determine regulatory capital requirements for credit risk, regulators would have to be confident that not only are these models being used to actively manage risk, but that they are also conceptually sound, empirically valid, and produce capital requirements that are comparable across institutions. This report concluded that at this time, significant issues with respect to data availability and model validation would need to be addressed before these objectives can be met.

Below we highlight some of the challenges that would need to be addressed in order to develop the quantitative qualitative standards that would accompany an internal models-based capital regime for credit or other risks.

Quantitative Standards for Credit and Other Risks

How to Determine Minimum Capital Requirements?

The first component of the MRA quantitative standards addresses how to determine the models-based minimum capital requirements. The basis for the MRA capital requirements is a risk measurement model that estimates the distribution of gains and losses on the bank's portfolio over some future time horizon. A regulatory capital requirement for credit or operational risk could be based on the output of banks' internal models in a similar fashion. As described above, the capital charge could be based on an estimate of a particular percentile of a credit or operational loss distribution over a given time horizon. Although these parameters would likely differ from those used in the market risk capital framework, the basic structure of the framework could be replicated.

These quantitative standards specified to establish the basic degree of stringency of the capital charge would need to be specified by regulators to ensure that the regulatory capital requirements provide a suitable degree of capital coverage and would be comparable across banks. Mirroring the some of the basic elements of the MRA outlined above, these quantitative standards would need to establish the appropriate definition of loss, planning horizon, and target loss percentile.

An obvious concern is how to measure losses? Two widely established practices have emerged in credit risk modeling, estimates of loss due solely to default, and estimates of loss from credit migrations. These differences have been captured by so-called default-mode and mark-to-market (or mark-to-model) modeling approaches. A quantitative standard for credit risk broadly would need to specify whether the capital requirement would be based on a default mode or multi-state loss concept and additionally the horizon over which these losses should be measured. Some of the issues that would need to be addressed include the adoption of an approach that is potentially inconsistency with many banks' modeling practices as well as the potential inconsistency with a mark-to-market definition of loss and historical cost accounting.

The quantitative standards accompanying a models-based capital regime for other risks would also need to establish a horizon or holding period over which losses are estimated. Although the required capital for market risk under the MRA is calculated to an assumed ten-day holding period, credit and operational risk models typically employ holding periods of one or more years. These longer holding periods are consistent with the time it takes to recognize such losses and typical planning period for capital budgeting.

The loss definition and holding period standards are linked, since supervisors may face a tradeoff between the length of the planning horizon and the definition of loss. There are several alternatives that could be used in conjunction with either a default or multi-state loss definition, including a fixed horizon of one year, a fixed horizon of more than one year, and a "lifetime" horizon that would cover the maturity of credits in a bank's portfolio.

Again mirroring the MRA, one of the key prudential parameters a quantitative standard for an internal models approach would need to address is the specified target loss percentile or confidence interval. As in the market risk setting, the capital charge could be calculated based on the level of losses at a specified percentile of the loss distribution (e.g. 99.9th or 99.97th). The specified percentile could be chosen so that, in conjunction with other parameters, the capital charge would provide the level of prudential coverage desired by the supervisory authorities.

Finally, standards for an internal models-based approach might also need to address the inclusion of a scaling factor. As noted earlier it has been asserted that the role of the scaling factor is to translate the model based estimates into a capital requirement that reflects both the accuracy of a bank's model and the desired capital coverage (Hendricks & Hirtle 1997). The inclusion of the regulatory scaling factor in the Market Risk Amendment has been often debated. At a minimum, the use of a scaling factor in a models-based capital regime for credit or other risks could again be a focal point.

What Features of Credit Risk Models Need to be Standardized?

The credit and operational risk models used to determine capital requirements would most likely also have to meet certain quantitative. Regulators face a trade off in establishing these standards. Given the current rapid state of evolution of these models, regulators need to recognize the risk of establishing standards that are highly restrictive. Although a certain degree of standardization is needed, there is great diversity of practice.

The quantitative standards could ensure greater consistency by requiring specific mathematical approaches or the use of certain approved models. At this time, however, there is little basis for concluding that one specific approach to credit risk modeling is uniformly better than all others in all situations. Such standards could either impede future modeling advances or require frequent revisions to encompass innovations and advances in modeling.

Responding to the report by the Basel Committee on credit risk modeling practices, bankers argued that no one model type was suitable across all portfolios. Respondents noted that techniques used to measure credit risk in corporate loan portfolios, in trading and derivatives portfolios and in retail portfolios logically might be different from each other.

Although not specifically addressed earlier, the MRA also establishes quantitative standards for the data used to calibrate market risk models. The data used to calibrate credit and operational risk models should provide adequate historical coverage. The data should also be applicable to the specific business mix of the bank. With regard to historical coverage, quantitative standards would likely require that the data be sufficient to reflect credit cycle effects. With regard to bank-specific applicability, standards would need to establish that the data used to estimate model parameters are appropriate for the current composition of its portfolio.The development of comparable standards for credit and operational risk face a trade off between establishing an appropriate historical window and firm applicability.

What are Appropriate Validation Procedures?
Unlike in the market risk setting, formal backtesting of credit risk model results may not feasible due to the length of a typical credit cycle and the resultant limited number of independent observations of actual outcomes. Lopez and Saidenberg (2000) discuss some of the challenges and limitations of backtesting credit risk models as well as the limited methods available. As a result, quantitative standards for credit and operational risk model validation will likely have to draw on a combination of tests, at least until more internal data become available and more robust statistical methodologies are developed.

At this time quantitative standards for a model-based credit or operational risk regime would likely need to incorporate a range of possible alternatives. These alternatives include stress testing, sensitivity analysis, and test-deck exercises. Robust validation standards will be needed to ensure the integrity of any future internal models-based capital requirement. Even if regulators could be somewhat open minded as to the form of validation, the development of acceptable alternative approaches for validation is almost certainly one of the key be that will need to addressed before the implementation of other models-based capital requirements.

Qualitative Standards for Credit and Other Risks

The lessons learned from design and implementation of the MRA discussed above as well as the challenges of establishing meaningful quantitative model and validation standards highlight the importance of the accompanying qualitative standards.

Within the supervisory process, there has been growing emphasis on qualitative reviews of banks' methods for measuring, managing, and controlling risk. Supervisors also have developed significant experience assessing the integrity of banks' market risk models against a range of qualitative sound practice standards. In order to develop a models-based capital requirement for other risk, supervisors will likely need to place even greater reliance on banks' adherence to qualitative standards. This alone will require a shift in supervisors' thinking and might delay the implementation of a models-based approach for credit and other risks.

Many of the issues addressed through MRA are even more relevant for the measurement and management of credit and operational risk especially the integration of these risk measurement procedures into management decision-making. Given that banks have long been in the credit business, many of these management procedures are in place and may only need to be updated. However, the move from traditional credit risk management to model-driven risk management could be difficult for management. For example, large institutions may have credit risk management procedures that are effective for traditional lending, but would need enhancement for credit trading and credit derivative activities.

Building on the qualitative standards outlined above for the MRA of the, banks' use of credit and operational risk models for regulatory capital purposes would also likely be contingent upon their meeting a set of standards aimed at ensuring that the models are sound and implemented with integrity. Such qualitative standards could include compliance with a documented set of internal policies, controls, and procedures concerning the operation of risk measurement systems. These standards would also likely address the need for an independent risk control unit responsible for the design and implementation of a bank's model and a regular independent review of the models. Finally, the qualitative standards would almost certainly include a "use test" to ensure that the models used for regulatory capital are closely integrated into the risk management process of the bank.

IV. CONCLUSION

The trend in regulatory approach is toward more risk-focused capital charges and the unbundling of regulatory capital requirements. Growing regulatory capital arbitrage by banks requires the replacement of the 1988 Accord because it is not sufficiently risk sensitive. The increased emphasis on risk-sensitive capital requirements will require greater reliance on banks' internal risk assessments. For credit risk, the use external ratings to determine required capital would likely be just a first step. The use of banks' internal risk ratings to establish minimum capital requirements would be a further step in this direction. Such an approach should lead to an improvement in terms of risk sensitivity. An approach that links capital requirements to banks' internal risk ratings as well as other transaction characteristics will not be able to capture other important risk concerns such as single borrower, industry and country concentrations.

A full internal models approach is still down the road, but the lessons learned from the Market Risk Amendment will lay the foundation for such a future approach. The design and implementation of the MRA highlight some of the challenges of establishing quantitative model and validation criteria. They also highlight the importance of the accompanying qualitative standards. Both the quantitative and qualitative criteria are necessary to ensure model consistency across institutions, across national borders and across time.

Supervisors have accepted risk management and capital regulations based on probabilistic measures for market risk. The lessons learned from the design and implementation of the MRA suggest that before the adoption of additional models-based capital regimes, banks and supervisors will need to continue to push their thinking even further along these lines, especially with respect to evaluation tools.

ACKNOWLEDGMENT

The views expressed in this chapter are those of the authors and not necessarily those of the Federal Reserve Bank of New York, the Federal Reserve Bank of San Francisco or the Federal Reserve System.

REFERENCES

Basel Committee on Banking Supervision (1999). Credit Risk Modeling: Current Practices and Applications. Manuscript.

Basel Committee on Banking Supervision (1999). Performance of Models-Based Capital Charges for Market Risk. Manuscript.

Basel Committee on Banking Supervision (2000). Summary of Responses Received on the Report 'Credit Risk Modeling: Current Practices and Applications'. Manuscript.

Basel Committee on the Global Financial System (2000). Stress Testing by Large Financial Institutions: Current Practice and Aggregation Issues. Manuscript.

Berkowitz, J. (1999). Evaluating the Forecasts of Risk Models. FEDS Discussion Paper No. 11, Federal Reserve Board of Governors.

Hendricks, D., & Hirtle, B. (1997). Bank Capital Requirements for Market Risk: The Internal Models Approach. *Federal Reserve Bank of New York Economic Policy Review*, December 1–12.

Jackson, P., & Perraudin, W. (2000). Regulatory Implications of Credit Risk Modeling. *Journal of Banking and Finance*, 24, 1–14.

Kupiec, P. (1995). Techniques for Verifying the Accuracy of Risk Measurement Models. *Journal of Derivatives*, 3, 73–84.

Lopez, J. A. (1999). Methods for Evaluating Value-at-Risk Estimates. Federal *Reserve Bank of San Francisco Economic Review*, 2, 3–15.

Lopez, J. A., & Saidenberg, M. R. (2000). Evaluating Credit Risk Models. *Journal of Banking and Finance*, 24, 151–167.

Lopez, J. A., & Walter, C. A. (2000). Evaluating Covariance Matrix Forecasts in a Value-at-Risk Framework. Manuscript, Economic Research Department, Federal Reserve Bank of San Francisco.

Scholes, M. S. (2000). Crisis and Risk Management. *American Economic Review Papers and Proceedings*, 90, 17–21.

COMMENT

Marsha J. Courchane

ABSTRACT

The three chapters in this session examining issues of bank fragility and regulation range from a comprehensive blueprint for 'ideal' regulation to an empirical example of 'band-aid' regulation – quickly implementing some rules post-failure. In the middle, we are served by a discussion of some lessons learned from the market risk amendment that could be applied to approaches taken for the regulation of other internal models, including those used for credit risk.

The three chapters vary not only in their depth and coverage of regulation issues, but in the complexity and sophistication of their arguments. David Llewellyn's study, "Alternative Approaches to Regulation and Corporate Governance in Financial Firms" takes an approach that I refer to as *consolidated risk management* and that the author prefers to call a *regulatory regime*. He explores thoroughly all aspects of this regime, offering several suggestions for improvements in bank regulation approaches. The second chapter in the spectrum, by Jose Lopez and Marc Saidenberg, "The Development of Internal Models Approaches to Bank Regulation and Supervision: Lessons from the Market Risk Amendment" has made some strides toward interpretation of the "Performance of Models-Based Capital Charges for Market Risk" document released by the Basel Committee on Banking Supervision in 1999, but other than detailing some components of what has worked with respect to market risk, they have not yet provided a framework (in theory or practice) for what might be feasible in modeling credit

Bank Fragility and Regulation: Evidence from Different Countries, Volume 12, pages 255–262.
Copyright © 2000 by Elsevier Science Inc.
All rights of reproduction in any form reserved.
ISBN: 0-7623-0698-X

risk. Finally, David Aadland, Drew Dahl, and Alan Stephens, in "Deposit Rate Premiums and the Demand for Funds by Thrifts" take as given the regulatory response through the Financial Institutions, Reform, Recovery and Enforcement Act of 1989 (FIRREA), and use that to define before and after periods for measuring demand and supply for funds at thrift institutions.

My comments will follow the construct above, from the most general chapter by Llewellyn to the most topic-specific paper by Dahl, et al., concluding with a discussion of the policy implications of the issues raised for bank regulation by all three chapters.

The Llewellyn work introduces the design of an optimum "regulatory regime", and details the necessary components of such a regime including: rules, monitoring and supervision, incentive structures, market discipline and monitoring, intervention arrangements, corporate governance and disciplining and accountability. This study might be considered utopian in its reach, but a chapter such as this should be required reading for decision makers at all banking regulatory agencies. Too often in the pace of rapid regulatory change, the focus becomes solely on incremental or marginal changes to a proposal already on the table, and neglect of basic principles for regulation persists. While this chapter takes as given the economic rationale for regulation (be it externalities, market imperfections, economies of scale in monitoring, moral hazard or other reasons), it does not take as given or sufficient any one element of the regulatory strategy.

The development of the consolidated risk management approach detailed in this paper, follows from its finding that recent financial crises share five common characteristics:

• Weak internal risk analysis, management & control systems in banks
• Inadequate official supervision
• Weak (or perverse) incentives within the financial system
• Inadequate information disclosure
• Inadequate corporate governance

The cause of the crises might differ, although the claim is made that often systemic crises are preceded by major macroeconomic adjustments, often associated with withdrawal of liquid external capital from a country.

The hypothesis follows that consolidated risk management, and the adoption of a regulatory regime, requires tradeoffs within the regime, specifically:

• balancing of the components and assignment of the weights
• establishment of causal relationships among the components.

Somewhat simply put then, the true public policy objective should be to 'optimise the outcome' of the regulatory strategy in terms of the regime component mix, and recognize the possibility of negative tradeoffs. The skill is in using the tools.

The problem, of course, is that what reads well in theory, may be very difficult to effect in practice. That does not mean that this effort is without merit, as being too idealistic. Rather, it is very useful in detailing the components, in presenting possible mixed strategies, and in forcing regulators to think back outside a 'marginalized' box.

The arguments are thoughtful, very well written and logically organized. I think it offers some important insights, imparting a unified plan to regulation of financial institutions. There is not a single one of the components that is not important. Problems in implementation, however, can occur with any of the components. Changes over time will occur and fluidity of response is crucial. Taking a much broader approach to the issue of how to regulate and supervise will be of value to central bankers, regulatory authorities and even to those in the 'quasi public' sector. Effecting change, even recognizing the need for a broader approach, may still be difficult to manage, given the myriad of regulators and coordination difficulties of within-country banking agency regulation. Across country difficulties, which will grow in importance with the development of the European Union, may prove even less easy to resolve.

Evaluation of the regulatory regime provided by David Llewellyn, brings sharply into focus the problems with the paper by Jose Lopez and Marc Saidenberg, "The Development of Internal Models Approaches to Bank Regulation and Supervision: Lessons from the Market Risk Amendment". This chapter takes as given the operating structure implemented with the market risk amendment and attempts to use lessons drawn from that regulatory experience in the application of regulatory design for models-based approaches to other types of risk (but specifically credit risk). Clearly the Basle Accord, which set the current regulatory capital standard for banks, will be rationalized. The two leading proposals for effecting that change are a "modified-Basle" or ratings-based approach, and a "full-models" approach. It is the internal models approach that was incorporated in the Market Risk Amendment. It is this approach that the authors state as "consistent with the shift in supervisory interest from a focus on risk measurement to a more comprehensive evaluation of banks' overall risk management". The authors also note as key to the MRA "the development of qualitative and quantitative standards that must be satisfied". In essence, they point out that the system is rules based. They point out that data needs to be available, and models must be validated. They then list some features of credit risk models in need of standardization for regulatory purposes.

This chapter falls short on several dimensions. First, it is unclear what purpose the authors have in mind. The only point clearly made is that regulating financial institutions with respect to credit risk, using bank specific internal models will pose challenges for regulators, even in excess of those posed by supervision of market risk. Other than that, it offers little. It inadequately presents and interprets results from the Basle Committee reports. It includes no discussion of many of the problems inherent in credit risk management, nor does it take an unbiased view of potential approaches. The authors cite their paper and one other (Jackson & Perraudin, 2000) in the special issue of the *Journal of Banking and Finance* on credit risk issues (Volume 24, January 2000). If the topic of interest is whether internal models work for credit risk in the same degree to which they have been used for market risk, then the paper already published by the authors in this special issue addresses this much better than does the current work. If the intent was to provide a more broad approach to what might be difficulties in moving toward institutionally specific measurements of credit risk, necessitated by prudential regulation, then this chapter fails in that objective. It is not broad, but very narrow in its focus. In fact, a paper which does a nice job of looking at 'consolidated risk management' was presented at this same conference (Cumming & Hirtle, 2000). If a possible objective was to highlight the debate over approaches taken to banking regulation, neither is that objective reached. Here, the authors assume that the models approach is the right one, ignoring much of the debate on the issue by other researchers.

Certainly, there is heightened current interest in credit risk modeling. The special issue of the *Journal of Banking and Finance* (January 2000) covers nearly every aspect of the credit risk measurement and regulatory environment. Banks have become increasingly quantitative, and that is seen across the risk spectrum, not only in the measurement of market risk. Regulators are concerned with improving bank capital regulation, and ensuring that banks adequately capitalize against all risks, including credit risk. Hence, the topic is of considerable interest. This study, however, adds little to the literature or the discussion.

In the context of the 'regulatory regime' presented earlier in these comments, a more interesting approach might have the authors moving back a step to restate the problem before offering a solution. Rather than asking what standards should be set for application of credit VaR techniques, they might want to ask whether the more fundamental issue with credit risk can be addressed with credit VaR models. In this chapter (as in others) there seems to be widespread acceptance of the tool, and how it could be used for regulatory purposes, even though other authors detail specific problems inherent in its use.

Some urge caution in adopting standards, some question model use entirely, some suggest that this particular type of model is inadequate as either a measure of credit risk or as a method for allocating credit risk capital (see Kupiec, 2000).

The authors here are guilty of looking at the margin without questioning the structure and in so doing, add little. They provide a brief overview of the regulatory capital requirements for market risk exposure that have been in place since 1998. They cite the BIS report on performance of models-based capital charges for market risk (1999) and provide some summary of responses (from BIS again) on credit risk modeling: current practices and applications. They state the basic point that market risk modeling is easier, credit risk modeling is harder and they assume that the models based approaches are better than previous supervisory practices. They suggest a need for credit model consistency and calibration to a common supervisory standard. Other than that, not much else is provided here, and what is provided is derivative of the two BIS reports.

They would benefit from reading the Llewellyn chapter and from advice offered by John Mingo in the special issue – "problems associated with any reform of Basle are so complex that only one conclusion seems clearly supportable – do not rush to judgment" (see Mingo, 2000, p. 31).

The third chapter does not focus on the regulatory process, but on what the impact of that process might be on the demand for funds by thrifts. They argue that passage of the Financial Institutions Reform, Recovery and Enforcement Act of 1989 (FIRREA) and, in particular, display of the logo mandated by FIRREA stating that "insured deposits are backed by the full faith and credit of the U.S. Government" restored investor confidence in thrift institutions by providing an "explicit and credible third party guarantee". They hypothesize influences on both default risk perceptions and demand for funds by thrifts resulting from the Act's passage. They show that changes in the demand for funds by thrifts in this period of financial stress exerted a *profound* influence on deposit rate premiums paid by thrifts over comparable Treasuries. They contrast this with the conventional view that it was default risk that serves as the primary systematic determinant of rate premiums.

They have three primary findings:

• volatility in rate premiums over Treasuries was significant post-FIRREA;
• declines in the financial condition of thrifts were associated with associated increases in rate premiums; and
• those thrifts that aggressively bid for deposits in the mid–90s had fast deposit growth but weak financial condition.

The primary problem with the work is that it oversimplifies effects and neglects the complementary impacts of several of the rapidly passed legislative efforts during the thrift crisis. Because of this oversimplification, the authors draw conclusions that are much stronger than justified given the omitted factors in their analysis. While I doubt that anyone would quibble with the idea that demand side effects must also be controlled for – to conclude that default risk is not an important determinant of spreads would be too strong a statement. The argument presented that states that the weak financial condition and fast deposit growth are in some sense causally linked is not adequately explored. For example, it might be because of the weak condition that the thrifts are trying to grow deposit growth, but the beneficial results appear with a lag not captured with this data.

The study raises as many questions as it answers. For example, given significant and variable pricing effects driven by perceptions of FSLIC guarantor risk, what is the difference between pre-and post-FIRREA volatility? While the assumption of an upward sloping (at least in the short run) supply curve in the market for deposits, might be perfectly plausible, it is also true that if they had assumed a perfectly elastic supply of funds, they could not generate the desired result. Hence, while reasonable, this is also a necessary assumption and the authors might want to note the extent to which results are driven by the assumption.

A major shortcoming is the single effect dummy introduced for FIRREA. While the analysis is fairly straightforward, what about other shifts during the period? In fact, the regulatory changes were introduced at a fast and furious pace during the late eighties. Other than the FIRREA dummy (obviously) and SWPLAN, the authors examine no other key shift parameters during this period of time. There were clearly major regulatory initiatives that might have directly affected the arguments they make. For example, investor confidence might have been affected by passage of the Competitive Equality in Banking Act of 1987, which sought to recapitalize the Federal Savings and Loan Insurance Corporation (FSLIC). Another important factor would come from the prompt corrective action and least cost resolutions in the Federal Deposit Insurance Corporation Improvement Act (1991). Others have argued that PCA and LCR represent the most important tool the federal government has to minimize deposit insurance losses from insolvent thrifts (see Ely, 1999). If so, that surely affected investor confidence and the supply of deposit funds to thrifts. Rather than formulating a Chow test just for FIRREA, they might want to consider other regulatory impacts. In putting their findings into context, some mention needs to be made of the magnitude of the changes in structure in the thrift industry.

In terms of variables included, rather than omitted, I find the insignificance of RELOANS intriguing. While the authors speculate that increased activity in the real estate market does not raise the relative demand of deposits by thrifts an alternative hypothesis would be that liquidity is being supplied to the real estate markets through increased activity of the secondary mortgage markets through the government sponsored enterprises Fannie Mae and Freddie Mac.

Some mention needs to be made of the magnitude of the changes in structure in the thrift industry. From 2,600 S&Ls in 1989 with assets of $1.2 trillion, by 1994 there were only 1,543 thrifts with assets of around $775 billion (30–40% changes). The customers inconvenienced by these significant structural changes, regardless of whether any deposit funds were insured or uninsured might move out of the thrift industry entirely and care not at all about incremental changes in interest rate premiums.

To conclude, the article has not sufficiently explored the complexities of the thrift crisis to be able to conclude that the conventional wisdom of the "rate spread to Treasuries as a default premium," or "risk as the primary systematic determinant of deposit spreads" is erroneous.

In the broader context of these comments, the regulatory regime was thoroughly tested during the thrift crisis and much of the legislation flowing immediately and causally from that crisis came from staunching the flow of investor confidence by applying a quick regulatory remedy to the immediate pain. It worked, but may have had lasting consequences that would not have been considered 'optimal' if there had been time for more reflection and discussion along the lines suggested by the Llewellyn paper. Now, a decade after passage of FIRREA and FIDICIA, and during Basle Accord deliberations, the recognition of the principle that one should not rush into any regulatory change without due and proper consideration of all the consequences and tradeoffs should be apparent to all regulators and politicians. Restating a conclusion from Llewellyn, "Effective regulation and supervision of banks and financial institutions has the potential to make a significant contribution to the stability and robustness of a financial system. . . . {however} Nothing should ever be seen as taking away the responsibility for supervision of financial firms by shareholders, managers and the markets."

REFERENCES

Cumming, C., & Hirtle, B. (2000). *The Challenges of Risk Management in Diversified Financial Companies.* Presented at Western Economic Association meetings, Vancouver, B. C., Canada.

Ely, B. (1999). *Banks do Not Receive a Federal Safety Net Subsidy.* Paper prepared for the Financial Services Roundtable, May.

MARSHA J. COURCHANE

Kupiec, P. (2000). *What Exactly Does Credit VaR Measure?* working paper.

Jackson, P., & Perraudin, W. (2000). Regulatory Implications of Credit Risk Modeling. *Journal of Banking and Finance, 24*, 1–14.

Lopez, J., & Saidenberg, M. (2000). Evaluating Credit Risk Models. *Journal of Banking and Finance, 24*, 151–167.

Mingo, J., (2000). Policy Implications of the Federal Reserve Study of Credit Risk Models at Major US Banking Institutions. *Journal of Banking and Finance, 24*, 15–33.

PART III

THE ROLE OF A CAMEL DOWNGRADE MODEL IN BANK SURVEILLANCE

R. Alton Gilbert, Andrew P. Meyer and
Mark D. Vaughan

ABSTRACT

This article examines the potential contribution to bank supervision of a model designed to predict which banks will have their supervisory ratings downgraded in future periods. Bank supervisors rely on various tools of off-site surveillance to track the condition of banks under their jurisdiction between on-site examinations, including econometric models. One of the models that the Federal Reserve System uses for surveillance was estimated to predict bank failures. Because bank failures have been so rare during the last decade, the coefficients on this model have been "frozen" since 1991. Each quarter the surveillance staff at the Board of Governors provide the supervision staff in the Reserve Banks the probabilities of failure by the banks subject to Fed supervision, based on the coefficients of this bank failure model and the latest call report data for each bank. The number of banks downgraded to problem status in recent years has been substantially larger than the number of bank failures. During a period of few bank failures, the relevance of this bank failure model for surveillance depends to some extent on the accuracy of the model in predicting which banks will have their supervisory ratings downgraded to problem status in future periods. This chapter compares

Bank Fragility and Regulation: Evidence from Different Countries, Volume 12,
pages 265–285.
Copyright © 2000 by Elsevier Science Inc.
All rights of reproduction in any form reserved.
ISBN: 0-7623-0698-X

the ability of two models to predict downgrades of supervisory ratings to problem status: the Board staff model, which was estimated to predict bank failures, and a model estimated to predict downgrades of supervisory ratings. We find that both models do about as well in predicting downgrades of supervisory ratings for the early 1990s. Over time, however, the ability of the downgrade model to predict downgrades improves relative to that of the model estimated to predict failures. This pattern reflects the value of using a model for surveillance that can be re-estimated frequently. We conclude that the downgrade model may prove to be a useful supplement to the Board's model for estimating failures during periods when most banks are healthy, but that the downgrade model should not be considered a replacement for the current surveillance framework.

I. INTRODUCTION

Banking is one of the more closely supervised industries in the United States, reflecting the view that bank failures have stronger adverse effects on economic activity than other business failures. The federal government and the state governments grant authority to bank supervisors to limit the risk of failure assumed by banks. Supervisors impose sanctions on the banks that they have identified as being in poor financial condition. Effective bank supervision, therefore, requires accurate information about the condition of banks.

Bank supervisors use on-site examination and off-site surveillance to identify the banks most likely to fail. The most useful tool for identifying problem institutions is on-site examination, in which examiners travel to a bank and review all aspects of its safety and soundness. On-site examination is, however, both costly and burdensome: costly to supervisors because of its labor-intensive nature and burdensome to bankers because of the intrusion into their day-to-day operations. As a result, supervisors also monitor bank condition off-site. Off-site surveillance yields an ongoing picture of bank condition, enabling supervisors to schedule and plan exams efficiently. Off-site surveillance also provides banks with incentives to maintain safety and soundness between on-site visits.

Supervisors rely primarily on two analytical tools for off-site surveillance: supervisory screens and econometric models. Supervisory screens are combinations of financial ratios, derived from bank balance sheets and income statements, that have, in the past, given forewarning of safety-and-soundness problems. Supervisors draw on their experience to weigh the information content of these ratios.

One of the contributions of economists to bank supervision has been the estimation and simulation of econometric models designed to provide supervisors with early warning of the banks that are most likely to develop serious problems in the future. Econometric models use the information about the condition of banks in their financial statements to derive one number. In most early warning models, that number is the probability that a bank will fail in a future period. In a recent article the authors compared the accuracy of supervisory screens and econometric models in predicting which banks would fail in future periods, and in predicting which banks would have their supervisory ratings downgraded to problem bank status (Gilbert, Meyer & Vaughan, 1999). Our analysis and other research demonstrate that econometric models dominate supervisory screens as predictors of bank failure and downgrades of supervisory ratings.

The Federal Reserve System uses the System to Estimate Examination Ratings, or SEER model, as one of its principal off-site surveillance tools. Surveillance staff at the Board of Governors use one form of this model, the risk rank model, to compute a probability of failure for each bank. Because bank failures have been so rare during the last decade, the coefficients on this model have been "frozen" since 1991. Each quarter supervisors at each of the twelve Reserve Banks receive information from the surveillance staff of the Board of Governors about the probabilities of failure by the banks that are supervised by Federal Reserve staff. Probabilities of failure are calculated using the latest call report data for each bank and the "frozen" coefficients of the model estimated to predict bank failure.

This work investigates a practical issue in the use of econometric models in bank surveillance: the number of models that are relevant for surveillance. That is, does a model estimated to predict which banks are most likely to fail in future periods also provide accurate predictions of which banks are most likely to be downgraded to problem bank status? Or do supervisors need a different model to predict which banks they are most likely to rate as problem banks in future periods? Ability to predict downgrades of supervisory ratings, rather than failures, is especially relevant for surveillance during a period in which there are few failures, like most of the 1990s. We compare the performance of two econometric models in predicting which banks will have their supervisory ratings downgraded in future periods: the SEER risk rank model, which was estimated to predict bank failures, and another model that is estimated to predict downgrades of supervisory ratings.

II. ON-SITE AND OFF-SITE SURVEILLANCE:
A CLOSER LOOK

This section discusses the role of off-site surveillance and early warning models in bank supervision. Bank supervisors rely principally on regular on-site examinations to assess the condition of banks. Examinations ensure the integrity of bank financial statements and identify the banks that should be subject to supervisory sanctions.[1] During a routine exam, the examiners assess six components of safety and soundness – capital protection (C), asset quality (A), management competence (M), earnings strength (E), liquidity risk (L) and market risk (S) – and assign a grade of 1 (best) through 5 (worst) to each component. Examiners then use these six scores to award a composite rating, also expressed on a 1 through 5 scale.[2] Bank supervisors added the "S" component (market risk) in January 1997. Since examiners graded only five components of safety and soundness during most of our sample period, this paper refers to composite "CAMEL" ratings. Table 1 interprets the five composite CAMEL ratings.

Although on-site examination is the most effective tool for constraining bank risk, it is both costly to supervisors and burdensome to bankers. As a result,

Table 1.   Interpretation of CAMEL Composite Ratings.

CAMEL Composite Rating	Description
1	Financial institutions with a composite 1 rating are sound in every respect and generally have individual component ratings of 1 or 2.
2	Financial institutions with a composite 2 rating are fundamentally sound. In general, a 2-rated institution will have no individual component ratings weaker than 3.
3	Financial institutions with a composite 3 rating exhibit some degree of supervisory concern in one or more of the component areas.
4	Financial institutions with a composite 4 rating generally exhibit unsafe and unsound practices or conditions. They have serious financial or managerial deficiencies that result in unsatisfactory performance.
5	Financial institutions with a composite 5 rating generally exhibit extremely unsafe and unsound practices or conditions. Institutions in this group pose a significant risk the deposit insurance fund and their failure is highly probable.

Source: *Federal Reserve Commercial Bank Examination Manual.*

supervisors face continuous pressure to limit exam frequency. Supervisors yielded to this pressure in the 1980s, and many banks escaped yearly examination (Reidhill & O'Keefe, 1997). Congress mandated the frequency of examinations in the Federal Deposit Insurance Corporation Improvement Act of 1991, which requires annual examinations for all but a handful of small, well-capitalized, highly-rated banks, and even these institutions must be examined every 18 months. This new mandate reflects the lessons learned from the wave of bank failures in the late 1980s: more frequent exams, though likely to increase the up-front costs of supervision, reduce the down-the-road costs of resolving failures by revealing problems at an early stage.

Although changes in public policy have mandated greater exam frequency since the early 1990s, supervisors still have reasons to use off-site surveillance tools to flag banks for accelerated exams and to plan exams. Bank condition can deteriorate rapidly between on-site visits (Cole & Gunther, 1998; Hirtle & Lopez, 1999). In addition, the Federal Reserve now employs a "risk-focused" approach to exams, in which supervisors allocate on-site resources according to the risk exposures of each bank (Board of Governors, 1996). Off-site surveillance helps supervisors allocate on-site resources efficiently by identifying institutions that need immediate attention and by identifying specific risk exposures for regularly scheduled as well as accelerated exams. For these reasons, an interagency body of bank and thrift supervisors – the Federal Financial Institutions Examinations Council (FFIEC) – requires banks to submit quarterly Reports of Condition and Income, often referred to as the call reports. Surveillance analysts use the call report data to monitor the condition of banks between exams.

Supervisors have developed various tools for using call report data to schedule and plan exams, including econometric models.[3] A common type of model used in surveillance estimates the marginal impact of a change in a financial ratio on the probability that a bank will fail, holding all other ratios constant. These models can examine many ratios simultaneously, capturing subtle but important interactions. The Federal Reserve uses two models in off-site surveillance. One model, called the SEER risk rank model, combines financial ratios to estimate the probability that each Fed-supervised bank will fail within the next two years. Another model estimates a hypothetical CAMEL rating that is consistent with the financial data in the bank's most recent call report. Every quarter, economists at the Board of Governors feed the latest call report data into these models and forward the results to each of the twelve Reserve Banks. Surveillance analysts in the Reserve Banks then investigate the institutions that the models flag as "exceptions".

III. ESTIMATION OF THE SEER RISK RANK MODEL

The SEER risk rank model is a probit model of bank failure. The model uses call report data as of one point in time to estimate the probability of banks failing or becoming critically undercapitalized over the following two years. The estimation period spans the first quarter of 1985 to the last quarter of 1991. Table 2 lists the independent variables used in this failure prediction model. The actual SEER coefficient estimates, which are part of the official Federal Reserve monitoring system, are not reported here because they are confidential.

Because bank failures have been rare events since the early 1990s, the regression coefficients have been "frozen" since 1991, rather than being re-estimated in more recent years. Simulation of this model is relevant for bank surveillance during a period of few bank failures if the determinants of bank failure are also the determinants of CAMEL downgrades, and if the weights on the various determinants of distress in banks included in the model do not change much over time. This study investigates whether the ranking of banks by their estimated probabilities of failure (from the SEER risk rank model) provides reliable predictions of the banks most likely to have their CAMEL ratings downgraded in future periods.

IV. ESTIMATION OF THE DOWNGRADE MODEL

To facilitate a direct comparison between the performance of the two models in predicting CAMEL downgrades, we used the same independent variables in estimation of the SEER risk rank model and the downgrade equations, which are listed in Table 2. If we used different independent variables in estimating the two models, we would not know whether differences in the performance of the two models reflected different independent variables or the estimation of the models with different dependent variables (dummy variables for bank failures versus CAMEL downgrades).

We estimated the downgrade model for six separate years using probit regression analysis. Because there were considerably more CAMEL downgrades than failures in the 1990s, it was possible to re-estimate the downgrade model on a yearly basis. See Table 3 for the number of downgrades each year.

We chose the timing of CAMEL ratings and call report data for the estimation and simulation of the downgrade model to reflect the timing of the information that is available to supervisors in practice. Banks included in the sample for the first equation in Table 4 were rated CAMEL 1 or 2 as of March 1990. Call report data for the independent variables listed in Table 2 were as of the fourth quarter of 1989 because supervisors would not have access to the fourth quarter 1989 call report data for most banks until some time in March 1990. We assume that the supervisors would like to be able to rank these banks

Table 2. Regression Variables Used to Predict Bank Failures and CAMEL Downgrades.

This table lists the independent variables used in both the SEER risk rank model and the downgrade regression model. The signs indicate the hypothesized relationships between the variables and the likelihood of a safety-and-soundness problem. For example, the negative sign for the return-on-assets ratio indicates that other things equal, a higher ROA would reduce the likelihood of a failure or CAMEL downgrade.

Symbol	Description	Hypothesis about the sign of the coefficient for predicting failure or CAMEL downgrades (positive sign indicates positive correlation with probability of failure or rating downgrade).
ROA	Return on average assets.	−
COMMERCIAL-LOANS	Commercial and industrial loans as a percentage of total assets.	+
NET-WORTH	Total net worth (equity capital minus goodwill) as a percentage of total assets.	−
OREO	Other real estate owned as a percentage of total assets.	+
PAST-DUE–30	Loans past due 30–89 days as a percentage of total assets.	+
PAST-DUE–90	Loans past due 90+ days as a percentage of total assets.	+
NONACCRUING	Nonaccrual loans as a percentage of total assets.	+
SECURITIES	Book value of securities as a percentage of total assets.	−
LARGE-TIME-DEPOSITS	Deposits > $100M (jumbo CDs) as a percentage of total assets.	+
RESIDENTIAL-LOANS	Residential real estate loans as a percentage of total assets.	−
SIZE	Natural logarithm of total assets, in thousands of dollars.	−

currently rated CAMEL 1 or 2 by their probability of being downgraded during the year 1991. Supervisors also would like to have accurate information on the banks most likely to be downgraded in the remainder of 1990, but early intervention would require accurate information on the banks most likely to be downgraded in 1991.

The dependent variable of the first equation had a value of unity if a bank had its CAMEL rating downgraded from a 1 or 2 (satisfactory condition) to a CAMEL 3, 4 or 5 (problem bank status) in the calendar year 1991, zero otherwise. We limited the sample to banks that were examined at least once during the calendar year 1991 because supervisors generally change the CAMEL ratings of banks only after exams. We also excluded banks from the

Table 3.   Banks Rated CAMEL 1 or 2 that were Downgraded to CAMEL 3, 4 or 5.

This table shows the number of our sample banks that were downgraded from CAMEL 1 or 2 to 3, 4 or 5 in each year. We excluded from the sample any banks that received downgrades to problem status the same year as the CAMEL 1 or 2 observation. As overall banking performance improved in the mid–1990s, the percentage of banks suffering downgrades fell, but there was an upward trend in the late 1990s, and downgrades were still much more common than failures.

Date of Rating (Year of Downgrade)	CAMEL Rating	Number of Banks	Number of Banks Downgraded	Percentage Downgraded
March 1990 (1991)	1	2,057	79	3.84
	2	5,037	988	19.60
March 1991 (1992)	1	1,956	51	2.61
	2	4,987	670	13.43
March 1992 (1993)	1	1,978	17	0.86
	2	5,246	295	5.62
March 1993 (1994)	1	2,046	14	0.68
	2	5,040	185	3.67
March 1994 (1995)	1	2,363	13	0.55
	2	4,463	129	2.89
March 1995 (1996)	1	2,596	13	0.50
	2	3,964	136	3.43
March 1996 (1997)	1	2,655	13	0.49
	2	3,394	157	4.63
March 1997 (1998)	1	2,574	27	1.05
	2	2,803	194	6.92

Table 4.   In-Sample Fit of the Downgrade Model.

This table presents the estimated regression coefficients for the downgrade model. The model predicts in-sample downgrades ("1" represents a downgrade; "0" denotes no downgrade) for calendar year t with call report data for the fourth quarter of year $t - 2$. For example, observations on whether banks had their CAMEL ratings downgraded in 1993 were related to call report data for the fourth quarter of 1991. Standard errors appear in parentheses below the coefficients. Three asterisks denote significance at the one-percent level; two asterisks denote significance at the 5-percent level. Shading highlights coefficients that were significant with the correct sign in all six years. Overall, the evidence in this table suggests that the logit model predicted in-sample downgrades well.

Independent Variables	Years of downgrades in CAMEL ratings:		
	1991	1992	1993
Intercept	−1.452***	0.700	0.599
	(0.435)	(0.506)	(0.705)
COMMERCIAL-LOANS	0.018***	0.029***	0.025***
	(0.005)	(0.006)	(0.008)
RESIDENTIAL-LOANS	−0.006	−0.001	−0.004
	(0.004)	(0.005)	(0.007)
LARGE-TIME-DEPOSITS	0.035***	0.037***	0.041***
	(0.005)	(0.006)	(0.009)
NET-WORTH	−0.108***	−0.090***	−0.087***
	(0.020)	(0.022)	(0.029)
PAST-DUE–90	0.712***	0.583***	0.614***
	(0.075)	(0.078)	(0.101)
PAST-DUE–30	0.243***	0.281***	0.238***
	(0.041)	(0.043)	(0.058)
NONACCRUING	0.439***	0.255***	0.702***
	(0.056)	(0.065)	(0.079)
ROA	−0.529***	−0.598***	−0.375***
	(0.073)	(0.082)	(0.098)
SECURITIES	−0.040***	−0.045***	−0.037***
	(0.004)	(0.004)	(0.006)
OREO	0.300***	0.273***	0.241***
	(0.051)	(0.057)	(0.063)
SIZE	0.074**	−0.171***	−0.291***
	(0.030)	(0.038)	(0.057)
Number of Observations	7,121	6,975	7,257
-2 log likelihood testing whether all coefficients (except the intercept) = 0	4824.234***	3700.348***	2073.600***

COMMERCIAL-LOANS	Commercial and industrial loans as a percentage of total assets.	PAST-DUE–30	Loans over 30 days past due as a percentage of total loans.
RESIDENTIAL-LOANS	Residential real-estate loans as a percentage of total assets.	NONACCRUING	Loans on nonaccrual status as a percentage of total loans.
LARGE-TIME-DEPOSITS	Large denomination time deposit liabilities as a percentage of total assets.	ROA	Net income as a percentage of total assets.
NET-WORTH	Equity less goodwill as a percentage of total assets.	SECURITIES	Book value of securities as a percentage of total assets.
PAST-DUE–90	Loans over 90 days past due as a percentage of total loans.	OREO	Other real estate owned as a percentage of total assets.
		SIZE	Natural logarithm of total assets, in thousands of dollars.

Table 4.   (Continued) How Well Does the Downgrade Model Fit the CAMEL Downgrade Data?

Independent Variables	*Years of downgrades in CAMEL ratings:*		
	1994	**1995**	**1996**
Intercept	1.589	0.611	3.160***
	(0.865)	(0.991)	(1.116)
COMMERCIAL-LOANS	0.004	0.009	0.015
	(0.011)	(0.013)	(0.014)
RESIDENTIAL-LOANS	–0.013	–0.003	–0.037***
	(0.008)	(0.009)	(0.011)
LARGE-TIME-DEPOSITS	0.043***	0.063***	0.049***
	(0.011)	(0.012)	(0.013)
NET-WORTH	–0.107***	–0.037	–0.037
	(0.032)	(0.034)	(0.037)
PAST-DUE–90	0.477***	0.396***	0.634***
	(0.119)	(0.147)	(0.208)
PAST-DUE–30	0.317***	0.261***	0.254***
	(0.082)	(0.080)	(0.091)
NONACCRUING	0.322***	0.468***	0.482***
	(0.104)	(0.114)	(0.127)
ROA	–0.521***	–0.509***	–0.329**
	(0.112)	(0.126)	(0.134)
SECURITIES	–0.016**	–0.019***	–0.042***
	(0.006)	(0.008)	(0.008)
OREO	0.304***	0.345***	0.333***
	(0.096)	(0.098)	(0.143)
SIZE	–0.362***	–0.380***	–0.532***
	(0.073)	(0.087)	(0.095)
Number of Observations	7,121	6,853	5,935
–2 log likelihood testing whether all coefficients (except the intercept) = 0	1654.108***	1241.822***	1008.453***

sample if they were downgraded to problem bank status in April through December of 1990, since these banks would not be included among the banks downgraded during the year 1991. The other five equations in Table 4 involve banks that were downgraded in the calendar years 1992 through 1996, with the same timing of the observations on CAMEL ratings and call report data.

Using the same independent variables in the SEER risk rank model and this downgrade model tends to limit the predictive power of the downgrade model. It is likely that an attempt to estimate the optimal downgrade model would yield at least some independent variables not included in the SEER risk rank model. For instance, some of the independent variables with significant coefficients in the downgrade model in Gilbert, Meyer and Vaughan (1999) are not included as independent variables in the downgrade model in this chapter. Thus, the downgrade model is not designed to minimize the errors in predicting which banks will have their CAMEL ratings downgraded. Instead, it is designed to facilitate a comparison of the SEER risk rank model to a downgrade model.

Results in Table 4 indicate that the model fit for the downgrade regressions is very good. The coefficients on seven of the 11 variables are statistically significant at the 5% level in each of the six years, with the signs indicated in Table 2. The fit of the model declines gradually each year, however, with more variables becoming statistically insignificant later in the 1990s. For instance, the coefficients on the ratio of commercial and industrial loans to total assets were negative and statistically significant at the 5% level in the years 1991 through 1993, but insignificant in 1994 through 1996. The coefficients on equity to total assets were positive and statistically significant in the years 1991 through 1994, but insignificant in 1995 and 1996. The poorer fit of the downgrade model over time may reflect the decline in the number of downgrades throughout the 1990s.

V. OUT-OF-SAMPLE MODEL PERFORMANCE

While a good in-sample model fit is important for determining whether a model is statistically well specified, the real test for use in surveillance is its out-of-sample predictive performance. We use out-of-sample simulation to answer this question: Using a model estimated with existing information, how well can we distinguish the banks that will be downgraded in a future period from those that will not be downgraded?

The simulations are designed to reflect the information that supervisors could have used at the time for early warning of future CAMEL downgrades. The first out-of-sample simulation involved banks rated CAMEL 1 or 2 as of March 1992. We estimated the probabilities that these banks would be downgraded to problem bank status in 1993 by plugging their call report data as of the fourth quarter of 1991 into the equation estimated to predict downgrades in 1991. The other out-of-sample simulations of the downgrade model use the same lags for the other years. For instance, we used the coefficients on the sixth equation, estimated for banks downgraded in 1996, to estimate the probabilities that the banks rated CAMEL 1 or 2 as of March 1997 would be downgraded in 1998.

We used the following procedure to predict which banks would be downgraded to problem bank status with the SEER risk rank model. We ranked the banks in our sample by their probability of failing in 1993 by plugging their call report data as of the fourth quarter of 1991 into the SEER risk rank model and calculating the estimates of their probabilities of failing. We used this ranking by their probabilities of failing as a means of ranking these banks by their probabilities of being downgraded to problem bank status in 1993. To derive a ranking of banks by their probability of being downgraded in 1994, we plugged their call report data as of the fourth quarter of 1992 into the SEER risk rank model with its frozen coefficients. We followed this procedure for each year, using the model with the same coefficients and the new call report data.

In evaluating the out-of-sample performance of these models, we must consider the trade-off between type-1 and type-2 errors. The type-1 error rate is the percentage of downgrades that we fail to detect with the model, while the type-2 error rate is the percentage of healthy banks that we identify incorrectly as downgrade risks. In a traditional bank *failure* analysis, supervisors consider type-1 errors to be decidedly worse than type-2 errors. A bank failure imposes significant costs on society, including required payouts by the FDIC insurance fund (and possibly the taxpayers) and possible disruption to the bank's local community (Gilbert & Kochin, 1989). An early-warning system that misses a significant number of failures (i.e. has a high type-1 error rate) is highly undesirable. Errors in predicting CAMEL downgrades in future periods are considerably less serious than errors in predicting bank failures, but supervisors are interested in tools that provide accurate early warnings of CAMEL downgrades, which could enable them to provide added guidance to problem banks as early as possible.

On the other hand, a model that over-predicts failures and downgrades (i.e. has a high type-2 error rate) also imposes costs in the form of unnecessary resources devoted to the supervision of healthy banks. These costs range from a few extra examiner hours spent examining bank financial statements to the cost of stepped-up on-site examinations. Type-2 errors also *may* impose unnecessary costs on healthy banks. An explicit calculation of the costs of each type of error, which would involve certain arbitrary assumptions, is beyond the scope of this paper. We choose instead to focus on the "risk-return" trade-off along the entire range of errors by deriving type-1 vs. type-2 power curves for the two models, following closely the methods used by Cole, Cornyn and Gunther (1995). Each curve tells us the type-1 error we must accept for any given level of type-2 error. Looking at the entire power curve avoids setting an arbitrary cut-off for an acceptable level of type-1 or type-2 error.

To compute power curves for the SEER risk rank model and the downgrade model, we adjust the number of banks rated by each model as likely to be downgraded and observe the associated type-1 and type-2 errors. At one extreme, all banks are rated as unlikely to be downgraded. Our type-1 error rate would be 100%, since all of the downgrades would be recorded as errors. The type-2 error rate would be zero, since each bank that was not downgraded would be included among those not predicted to be downgraded. Next, we assume that the bank with the highest estimated probability of failing (from the SEER risk rank model) or being downgraded (from the downgrade model) is the one bank predicted to be downgraded in the future period. For each model we calculate the associated type-1 and type-2 errors. We continue adding the bank with the next highest estimated probability of failure or being downgrade to those already estimated to be downgraded, and calculating type-1 and type-2 errors, until we have traced out the entire power curve of type-1 and type-2 errors. At the other extreme position on the power curve, all banks are included among those estimated to be downgraded in the future; the type-1 error rate is 0%, and the type-2 error rate is 100%.

The curvature of the power curves provides a basis for comparing the performance of the two models. The greater the curvature of the power curve, the better the model. In other words, we can simultaneously achieve low type-1 and type-2 error rates using the model with the curve nearer the origin. A convenient way to express this curvature is to calculate the area under each power curve as a percentage of all of the area in the box where the power curves are presented. The smaller the area, the more accurate the model. A useful benchmark is the case in which the banks estimated to be downgraded in the future are selected at random, rather than through simulation of a model. This procedure would produce a power curve with a slope of approximately negative one, starting at the 100% type-1 error rate and extending to the 100% type-2 error rate. The area under this curve would be approximately 50% of the area in the entire box. The areas under power curves in Figs. 1 through 6 represent a clear improvement over a random selection of banks estimated to be downgraded.

The power curves in Fig. 1 are virtually on top of each other, with the downgrade curve slightly edging out the failure curve over most of the trade-off range in 1993. The area under the power curve in Fig. 1 for the downgrade model is 20.31%, only slightly better than the 21.47% for the SEER risk rank model. The similarity of these curves indicates the close relationship between the risk factors that cause failures and those that cause less significant deterioration in the condition of banks. Figure 2 shows a similar pattern for 1994 downgrades. The spread between the power curves starts to widen by 1995, however, and peaks at 5.12 percentage points in 1997. Table 5 summarizes the information about the areas under the power curves for each year.

The increase in the relative performance of the downgrade model over time has several implications. First, this pattern could indicate that the coefficients that assign weights to the various risk factors are not stable over time. If some variables were major predictors of bank performance in some years, but not others, a model with frozen coefficients would decline in usefulness over time. Evidence of coefficient instability over long periods indicates the value of re-estimating the model from time to time. During the 1990s, re-estimation has been possible for the downgrade model, but not for the failure model. A second implication is that the relative predictive power of the downgrade model increased over time even as its in-sample statistical properties deteriorated.

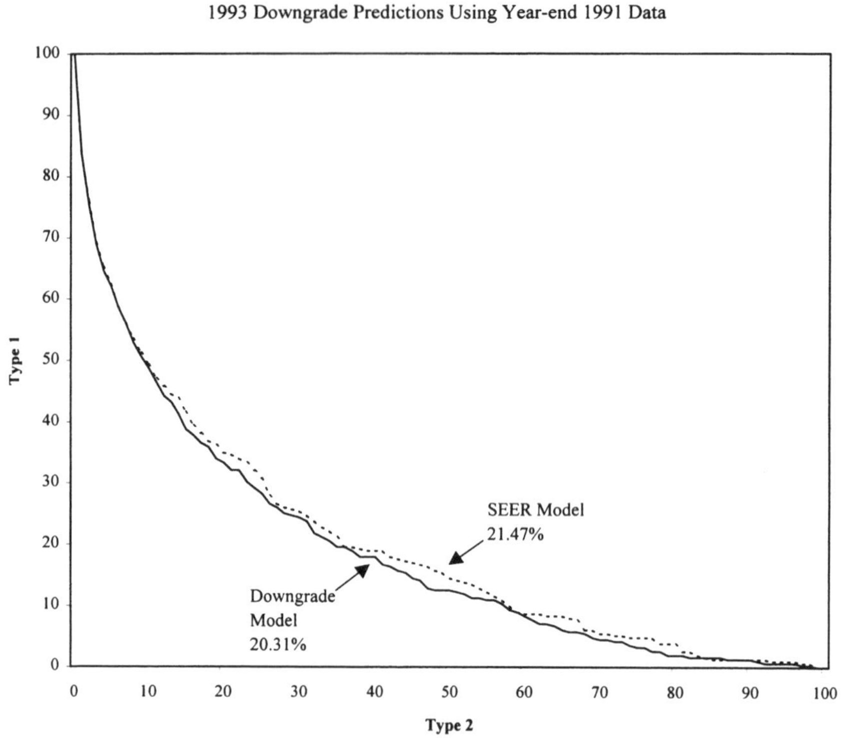

1993 Downgrade Predictions Using Year-end 1991 Data

This figure shows the trade-off between the type-1 error rate and the type-2 error rate. The type-1 error rate is the percentage of banks rated CAMEL-1 or -2 that were subsequently downgraded by supervisors but were not identified by the given model. The type-2 error rate is the percentage of banks rated CAMEL-1 or -2 that were not subsequently downgraded but were misidentified by the given model as a downgrade risk. A desirable early-warning system minimizes the level of type-2 errors for any given level of type-1 errors. This graph shows that for any type-1 error rate tolerated by supervisors, the downgrade model leads to slighly fewer type-2 errors than each curve. Smaller areas are more desirable because they imply simultaneously low levels of both types of errors. In the above graph, the downgrade model slightly edges our the SEER model by 20.31% to 21.47%.

Fig. 1. What is the Trade-Off Between False Negatives and False Positives in the Downgrade Prediction Model Compared to the SEER Model?

Re-estimation of the coefficients of the downgrade model over time enhanced the predictive power of the downgrade model, even with the deterioration over time of the in-sample statistical properties of the downgrade model. These results indicate that during long periods of economic expansion when there are few bank failures, a model estimated to predict the downgrades of CAMEL ratings can serve as a useful supplement to an early warning model estimated to predict bank failures.

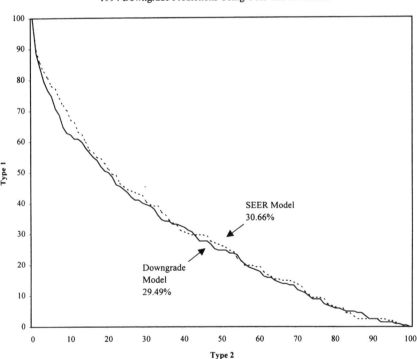

1994 Downgrade Predictions Using Year-end 1992 Data

This figure shows the trade-off between the type-1 error rate and the type-2 error rate. The type-1 error rate is the percentage of banks rated CAMEL-1 or -2 that were subsequently downgraded by supervisors but were not identified by the given model. The type-2 error rate is the percentage of banks rated CAMEL-1 or -2 that were not subsequently downgraded but were misidentified by the given model as a downgrade risk. A desirable early-warning system minimizes the level of type-2 errors for any given level of type-1 errors. This graph shows that for any type-1 error rate tolerated by supervisors, the downgrade model leads to slightly fewer type-2 errors than each curve. Smaller areas are more desirable because they imply simultaneously low levels of both types of errors. In the above graph, the downgrade model slightly edges our the SEER model by 29.49% to 30.66%.

Fig. 2. What is the Trade-Off Between False Negatives and False Positives in the Downgrade Prediction Model Compared to the SEER Model?

VI. CONCLUSIONS

This chapter demonstrates that the SEER risk rank model, which was estimated to predict which banks will fail, does a good job of identifying the banks that are likely to have their supervisory ratings downgraded in future periods.

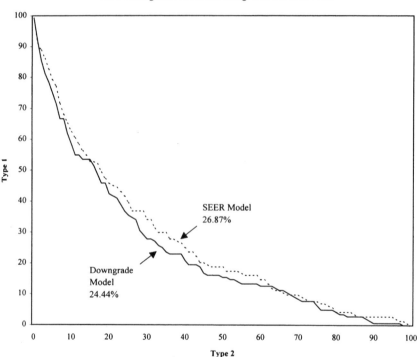

1995 Downgrade Predictions Using Year-end 1993 Data

This figure shows the trade-off between the type-1 error rate and the type-2 error rate. The type-1 error rate is the percentage of banks rated CAMEL-1 or -2 that were subsequently downgraded by supervisors but were not identified by the given model. The type-2 error rate is the percentage of banks rated CAMEL-1 or -2 that were not subsequently downgraded but were misidentified by the given model as a downgrade risk. A desirable early-warning system minimizes the level of type-2 errors for any given level of type-1 errors. This graph shows that for any type-1 error rate tolerated by supervisors, the downgrade model leads to slighly fewer type-2 errors than each curve. Smaller areas are more desirable because they imply simultaneously low levels of both types of errors. In the above graph, the downgrade model slightly edges our the SEER model by 24.44% to 26.87%.

Fig. 3. What is the Trade-Off Between False Negatives and False Positives in the Downgrade Prediction Model Compared to the SEER Model?

During a period with few bank failures, however, a model estimated to predict CAMEL downgrades could improve on the ability of the SEER risk rank model to predict downgrades. We must recognize, however, that our sample period is taken from the longest peacetime expansion in U. S. economic history. Consequently, a model designed to predict which healthy banks will become unhealthy may do a poor job of predicting which unhealthy banks will

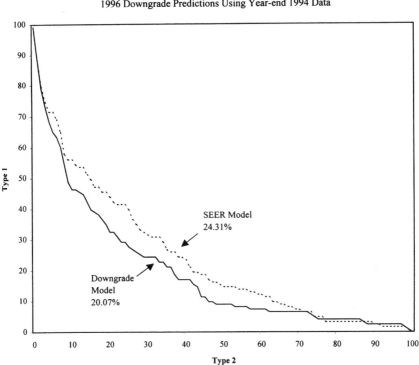

This figure shows the trade-off between the type-1 error rate and the type-2 error rate. The type-1 error rate is the percentage of banks rated CAMEL-1 or -2 that were subsequently downgraded by supervisors but were not identified by the given model. The type-2 error rate is the percentage of banks rated CAMEL-1 or -2 that were not subsequently downgraded but were misidentified by the given model as a downgrade risk. A desirable early-warning system minimizes the level of type-2 errors for any given level of type-1 errors. This graph shows that for any type-1 error rate tolerated by supervisors, the downgrade model leads to slighly fewer type-2 errors than each curve. Smaller areas are more desirable because they imply simultaneously low levels of both types of errors. In the above graph, the downgrade model slightly edges our the SEER model by 20.07% to 24.31%.

Fig. 4. What is the Trade-Off Between False Negatives and False Positives in the Downgrade Prediction Model Compared to the SEER Model?

ultimately fail. While a downgrade model may prove to be a useful supplement to the standard failure prediction model during good times, we should be careful to have all of our surveillance tools available to us during the next recession.

Use of both a bank failure model and a CAMEL downgrade model in bank surveillance may be better than choosing to use one of these models. Running

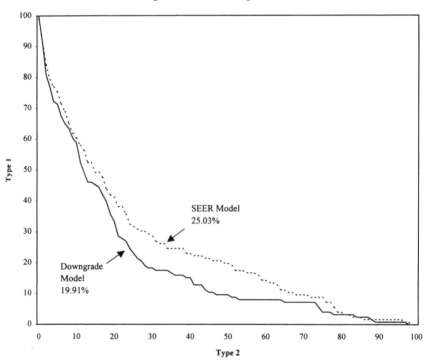

This figure shows the trade-off between the type-1 error rate and the type-2 error rate. The type-1 error rate is the percentage of banks rated CAMEL-1 or -2 that were subsequently downgraded by supervisors but were not identified by the given model. The type-2 error rate is the percentage of banks rated CAMEL-1 or -2 that were not subsequently downgraded but were misidentified by the given model as a downgrade risk. A desirable early-warning system minimizes the level of type-2 errors for any given level of type-1 errors. This graph shows that for any type-1 error rate tolerated by supervisors, the downgrade model leads to slighly fewer type-2 errors than each curve. Smaller areas are more desirable because they imply simultaneously low levels of both types of errors. In the above graph, the downgrade model slightly edges our the SEER model by 19.91% to 25.03%.

Fig. 5. What is the Trade-Off Between False Negatives and False Positives in the Downgrade Prediction Model Compared to the SEER Model?

more than one model in parallel could help us examine more closely the causes of bank downgrades that may be quite different from the causes of outright failure. Furthermore, while a downgrade model might serve admirably during periods of relative stability in the banking system, a failure model might be a more important tool for surveillance during a future period when the bank failure rate is higher than in recent years.

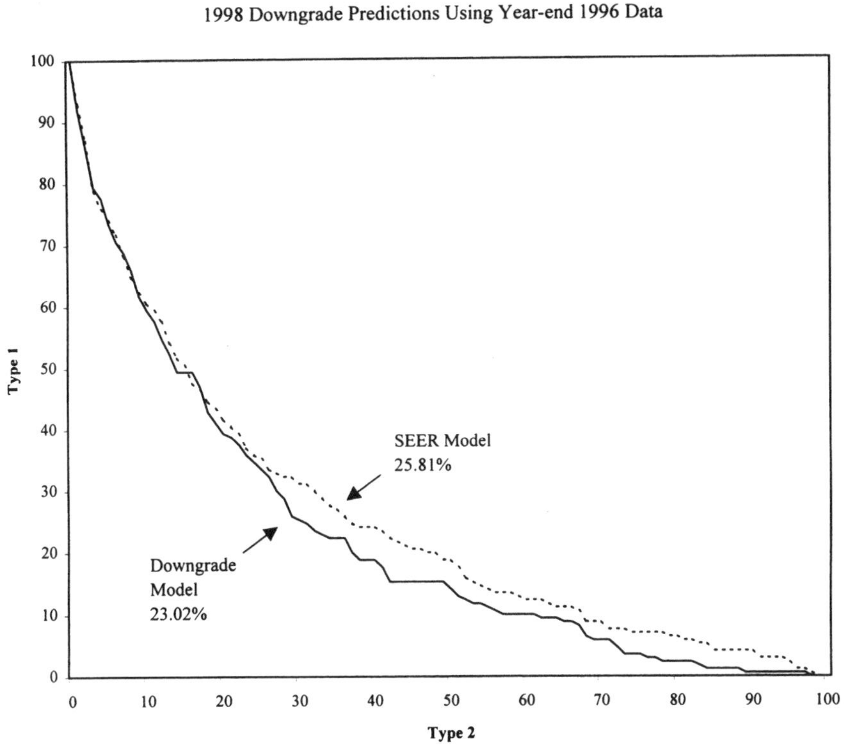

1998 Downgrade Predictions Using Year-end 1996 Data

This figure shows the trade-off between the type-1 error rate and the type-2 error rate. The type-1 error rate is the percentage of banks rated CAMEL-1 or -2 that were subsequently downgraded by supervisors but were not identified by the given model. The type-2 error rate is the percentage of banks rated CAMEL-1 or -2 that were not subsequently downgraded but were misidentified by the given model as a downgrade risk. A desirable early-warning system minimizes the level of type-2 errors for any given level of type-1 errors. This graph shows that for any type-1 error rate tolerated by supervisors, the downgrade model leads to slighly fewer type-2 errors than each curve. Smaller areas are more desirable because they imply simultaneously low levels of both types of errors. In the above graph, the downgrade model slightly edges our the SEER model by 23.02% to 25.81%.

Fig. 6. What is the Trade-Off Between False Negatives and False Positives in the Downgrade Prediction Model Compared to the SEER Model?

Table 5.   Out-of-Sample Predictive Performance of the SEER Risk Rank
Model and the Downgrade Model.

This table shows the areas under the "power curves" in Figures 1 through 6,
along with the percentage-point differences between the areas for the two
models. A power curve graphically illustrates the trade-off between type–1
errors (the percentage of missed downgrades) and type–2 errors (the percentage
of misidentified non-downgrades). A convenient way to compare curves is to
calculate the area under each curve. In this context, smaller is better because
smaller areas imply simultaneously lower error rates of both types. As shown
below, the difference in the areas increases slowly over time, indicating that the
downgrade model's performance, relative to the SEER risk rank model,
improves as the SEER coefficients become increasingly "stale".

Figure Number	Downgrade Year	Downgrade Model Area	SEER Failure Model Area	Percentage-point Difference
1	1993	20.31%	21.47%	1.16%
2	1994	29.49%	30.66%	1.17%
3	1995	24.44%	26.87%	2.43%
4	1996	20.07%	24.31%	4.24%
5	1997	19.91%	25.03%	5.12%
6	1998	23.02%	25.81%	2.79%

ACKNOWLEDGMENTS

The authors thank Robert Avery, Kevin Bertsch, Donald Conner, William
Francis, Michael Gordy, Jeffrey Gunther, James Harvey, Stephen Jenkins, Kim
Nelson and Joseph Turk for helpful comments. Boyd Anderson and Thomas
King provided excellent research assistance. The views expressed in this
chapter do not necessarily represent those of the Federal Reserve Bank of St.
Louis, the Board of Governors, or the Federal Reserve System.

NOTES

1. See Flannery and Houston (1999) for evidence that holding company inspections
help insure the integrity of financial statements. See Gilbert and Vaughan (1998) for a
discussion of the sanctions available to bank supervisors.

2. See Hall, King, Meyer and Vaughan (1999) for a more detailed discussion of the
factors used to assign individual and composite ratings.

3. See Putnam (1983) for a description of the use of supervisory screens in off-site
surveillance during the late 1970s and early 1980s.

REFERENCES

Board of Governors of the Federal Reserve System (1996). *Risk-Focused Safety and Soundness Examinations and Inspections.* SR 96–14, May 24.

Cole, R. A., Cornyn, B. G., & Gunther, J. W. (1995). FIMS: A New Monitoring System for Banking Institutions. *Federal Reserve Bulletin, 81,* 1–15.

Cole, R. A., & Gunther, J. W. (1998). A Comparison of On- and Off-Site Monitoring Systems. *Journal of Financial Services Research, 13,* 103–117.

Flannery, M. J., & Houston, J. F. (1999). The Value of a Government Monitor for U. S. Banking Firms. *Journal of Money, Credit, and Banking, 31,* 14–34.

Gilbert, R. A., & Kochin, L. A. (1989). Local Economic Effects of Bank Failures. *Journal of Financial Services Research, 3,* 333–345.

Gilbert, R. A., Meyer, A. P., & Vaughan, M. D. (1999). The Role of Supervisory Screens and Econometric Models in Off-Site Surveillance. *Federal Reserve Bank of St. Louis Review, 81,* 31–56.

Gilbert, R. A., & Vaughan, M. D. (1998). Does the Publication of Supervisory Enforcement Actions Add to Market Discipline? *Research in Financial Services: Public and Private Policy, 10,* 259–280.

Hall, J. R., King, T. B., Meyer, A. P., & Vaughan, M. D. (1999). *Do Certificate of Deposit Holders and Supervisors View Bank Risk Similarly? A Comparison of the Factors Affecting CD Yields and CAMEL Composites.* Supervisory Policy Analysis Working Paper, Federal Reserve Bank of St. Louis, October.

Hirtle, B. J., & Lopez, J. A. (1999). Supervisory Information and the Frequency of Bank Examinations. *Economic Policy Review,* Federal Reserve Bank of New York, 5, No. 1, 1–19.

Putnam, B.H (1983). Early Warning Systems and Financial Analysis in Bank Monitoring: Concepts of Financial Monitoring. Federal Reserve Bank of Atlanta *Economic Review,* November, 6–13.

Reidhill, J., & O'Keefe, J. (1997). Off-Site Surveillance Systems, *in History of the Eighties: Lessons for the Future,* volume I. Washington: Federal Deposit Insurance Corporation, 477–520.

CREDIT REGISTERS AND EARLY WARNING SYSTEMS OF BANK FRAGILITY

The Italian Experience

Paolo Marullo Reedtz and Maurizio Trapanese

ABSTRACT

A recent stream of literature has focused on the trade-off between the timeliness and effectiveness of information gathered from bank examinations and the costs of obtaining it. Given this trade-off, supervisors also monitor banks' condition off-site.

In Italy off-site supervision is based on a very detailed body of bank statistics provided to the supervisory authority on a bilateral basis and on a Credit Register collecting monthly data on individual loans granted to individual borrowers.

Nevertheless, the costs incurred by banks in recording the data and those connected with controlling their statistical reliability and preparing supervisory screens or econometric models for detecting problem banks may be substantial.

The problem is whether requesting banks to provide a larger amount of data than that publicly disclosed is justified by any gain in the quality of supervisory assessments. An empirical answer can be given by measuring

Bank Fragility and Regulation: Evidence from Different Countries, Volume 12, pages 287–302.
Copyright © 2000 by Elsevier Science Inc.
All rights of reproduction in any form reserved.
ISBN: 0-7623-0698-X

the improvement of early-warning techniques which derives from using Credit Register information.

The statistical methodology refers to a previous work in which a Cox PH model outperformed probit and logit techniques. First, the performance of a survival function is tested against a set of publicly available variables. Next, some information drawn from the Credit Register is considered in order to check whether it contributes to an ex ante distinction between sound and distressed banking firms.

Credit Register information makes it possible to improve the forecasting accuracy of the model, especially with reference to distressed banks. The so called Type I error (classifying a distressed bank as a healthy institution) falls from 14 to 7% in the in-sample exercise. The gap observed in the estimation exercise is confirmed out of the sample.

I. INTRODUCTION

Due to the increasing complexity of banking organizations, timely detection of a bank's crisis may have become more difficult than in the past.

Many initiatives have been taken in order to strengthen banking regulation and supervision. In the U.S. the 1991 Federal Deposit Insurance Corporation Act (FDICIA) has mandated annual on-site examinations for most commercial banks. The timely detection of problem banks has increased in importance in the supervisory process within the framework of so-called *prompt corrective action.*

On-site examinations are no doubt the most effective way of identifying banks likely to fail. At the close of each exam, the supervisor assigns a CAMELS rating which summarizes the bank's Capital adequacy, Asset quality, Management, Earnings, Liquidity, and Sensitivity to market risk. These ratings benefit both from publicly available information and from private information gathered during the inspections, first of all on the quality of individual loans.

However, on-site examinations are both costly in terms of supervisory resources and burdensome to bankers because of the intrusion into day-to-day operations.

In order to avoid too frequent inspections without loosing too much information, supervisors also monitor banks' condition off-site. The purpose of off-site supervision is twofold: to plan exams efficiently and maintain safety and soundness conditions between on-site inspections.

Nevertheless neither providing regulatory reporting data nor exploiting their informational content is costless. The amount of data requested for supervisory purposes may be much larger than that publicly disclosed. The costs connected with controlling their statistical reliability and preparing supervisory screens or econometric models for detecting problem banks may be substantial.

For this reason the informational content of supervisory information has to be constantly assessed in order to make its cost consistent with the benefits of contributing to financial stability.

In some ways the problem is similar to assessing the usefulness of on-site examinations. A recent stream of literature has compared the CAMEL ratings with various market assessments of banks' condition, in order to point out the value added of supervisory information with respect to the assessment that is already reflected in market prices.

With reference to call reports and other supervisory information, the question is whether requesting banks to provide a larger amount of data than that publicly disclosed is justified by any gain in the quality of supervisory ratings.

An empirical analysis focusing on the improvement of early-warning techniques that is possible as a result of supervisory private information is provided with reference to the Italian framework. The reference to Italy looks quite promising because in this country banks are requested to submit very detailed data on the activity they perform domestically and at their foreign branches, both on an individual and on a consolidated basis. Typically, a large bank submits around one million data a year.

Moreover a Credit Register is run by the Bank of Italy in order to collect on a monthly basis all loans above a given threshold granted by individual banks to individual borrowers. Bad debts are reported regardless of their size.

The methodology refers to a previous work in which alternative early warning models of bank fragility were compared in order to choose the best procedure. A Cox PH model showed the best classification accuracy in comparison with both probit and logit techniques.

First, the performance of a survival function is tested against a set of publicly available variables. Next, some information drawn from the Credit Register are introduced into the function in order to check whether it contributes to an ex ante distinction between sound and distressed banking firms.

II. OFF-SITE SUPERVISION AND EARLY-WARNING SYSTEMS OF BANK FRAGILITY IN ITALY

In the Italian institutional framework, the function of banking supervision is entrusted to the central bank. The assessment of the financial condition of banks is based on a combination of on-site examinations and off-site systems of bank monitoring relying on regulatory reports and qualitative information.

In contrast with the situation in the U.S., in Italy banking regulation does not mandate any periodical on-site exam. Inspections are mainly decided on the basis of the evidence provided by the whole set of information that is available to the supervisors. In the three years from 1997 to 1999 inspections were conducted at 517 banks out of around 900.

The overall assessment is mainly conducted within the framework of a monitoring system aimed at giving a systematic representation of the state of health of individual banks. The monitoring system provides support in the prioritization of the use of scarce supervisory resources, first of all to decide which banks to subject to on-site examinations (Bank of Italy, 1996).

The scheme focuses on five components of bank performance: capital adequacy (**PAT**rimonio); profitability (**R**edditività); credit risk (**R**ischiosità); organization (**O**rganizzazione); liquidity (**L**iquidità). This is the so-called PATROL rating system.

Moreover, a monitoring system for the interest rate risk stemming from the whole balance sheet has been set up. This system is similar to that underlying the standardized approach for trading securities within the Capital Accord.

Similar to the U.S. CAMEL system, the five aspects are rated on a scale from 1 to 5: the scores of 1 and 2 are for basically sound institutions which do not deserve any special intervention by the supervisory authority; 3 is for banks with some weaknesses which induce the authority to ask for initiatives aimed at avoiding any further deterioration; 4 and 5 are for a poor performance with a need for strong and timely corrective measures. Once the five component ratings have been assigned, an overall rating is derived, again on a scale from 1 to 5, which also includes both more recent quantitative information and qualitative information available to the analyst.

The scheme is mainly based on a large body of statistical information produced by banks on a bilateral basis and on qualitative information obtained through meetings with bank officers and on-site examinations.

On- and off- balance sheet data are provided on an end-of-month and monthly average basis; flows are reported on a monthly or quarterly or semi-annual basis; for a certain number of operations data on the residual maturity are also provided.

Bank deposits and lending are partitioned according to the area in which both the branches and the customers are located; total deposits and loans are also reported for individual towns. Semi-annual and annual data on profit-and-loss accounts are supplemented by quarterly information on the evolution of the main revenue and cost items.

Special sections make it possible to monitor compliance with capital requirements (solvency ratio and market risks) and with the regulations on large exposures and country risk. A special statistical source regarding credit relations is represented by the Central Credit Register. The minimum requirement for inclusion in this data set is that a firm or a household has borrowed more than 150 million lire (i.e. around 75,000 dollars) from an individual bank. For each borrower the Credit Register can compute the total bank debt he has taken on and the total size of the commitments which have been granted. Given the low level of the threshold, the Credit Register contains 1.7 million borrowers.

The participating banks can receive information about the total debt of each credit applicant and the number of lending banks before deciding whether to extend credit. For a sample of large banks, which represent about 75% of short-term bank lending, the interest rates charged on individual credit lines are also available.

By exploiting this data base, it is possible to get some valuable hints regarding the lending policy of each bank and the quality of individual credit portfolios. As an example, credit risk evaluation relies heavily on an aggregate of "adjusted bad debts": customers are included in this aggregate if their loans are classified among bad debts by the only lender, or by a lender granting at least 70% of the overall system exposure, or by at least two banks granting more than 10% of the overall exposure. If one of these conditions takes place the borrower is considered as insolvent irrespective of the individual bank's assessment; both stocks and flows of adjusted bad loans are computed. Some information regarding individual borrowers has recently been requested for doubtful loans as well.

A large body of evidence on the characteristics of Italian corporate firms comes from the loan registers operated by two companys. The first one, run by the Company Accounts Data Service, was created in 1983 by banks seeking to share standardized information about borrowers. The Register includes the accounts of around 40,000 medium-sized and large corporations.

The second data base, run by the Cerved company, is available for a shorter period. It represents the most comprehensive set of data on Italian corporations. Half a million sets of accounts are included according to a simplified reclassification scheme including 70 elementary entries and approximately 30 balance sheet ratios. However some statistical filters are required to select firms with high quality data.

Some research analysis has been conducted at the Bank of Italy by jointly focusing on the data included in the Credit Register and in the company accounts registers. The studies have dealt with the impact of credit relationships on loan term offered to borrowers (D'Auria, Foglia & Marullo Reedtz, 1998 and Sapienza, 1998) and on the effects of multiple banking relationships on the fragility of the corporate sector (Foglia, Laviola & Marullo Reedtz, 1999).

In order to study the quality of the assets of Italian banks and evaluate the application of internal rating methodologies to individual credit portfolios, the data included both in the Credit Register and in the company accounts registers have been used to classify bank borrowers according to their riskiness and compute the expected default frequency of internally rated firms (Marullo Reedtz, 2000).

As in other countries, attention is paid in Italy to the possibility of improving supervisors' ability to detect cases of bank distress well before the moment at which bank capital is depleted. Although the high quality of the off-site controls is constantly confirmed by the results of the inspections, the PATROL ratings do not constitute an early-warning system in the sense of forecasting the failure or the change of state in the financial condition of a bank for a given future period with a given likelihood. The scores provide an ex-post indication of the financial condition of individual banks which may remain relevant for relatively short periods of time.

In order to bypass the backward looking feature of financial ratio analysis, some resources have recently been devoted to a research project aimed at developing an early-warning technique on the basis of banks' regulatory reporting data.

III. SUPERVISORY INFORMATION AND EARLY WARNING SYSTEMS OF BANK FRAGILITY

As in the case of on-site results, the off-site evaluations can be ideally split into two components: the first is based on publicly-available financial data; the second relies on private information contained in the very detailed reporting schemes banks are mandated to provide only to the supervisory authority.

A recent stream of literature has dealt with the trade-off between the timeliness and completeness of the information gathered from bank inspections and the cost of obtaining it. A widely adopted approach has been that of comparing CAMEL ratings with various market assessments of banks' condition in order to check whether the information collected through bank examinations is already known to financial market participants.

Empirically, this consists in searching for contemporaneous or lagged relationships between supervisory ratings and stock or security prices or interest rates paid to large depositors. The evidence is rather mixed. On the basis of a significant contemporaneous correlation between exam ratings and stock returns, Hirschhorn (1987) argues that most supervisory information is not private.

With reference to bank holding companies Berger and Davies (1994) find a significant private information effect in the case of CAMEL downgrades. This result confirms that bank managers are more willing to release good news rather than bad news. Berger, Davies and Flannery (1998) find that lagged movements in supervisory ratings contribute significantly to explaining the 'additional' variation in bond ratings.

De Young, Flannery, Lang and Sorescu (1998) study the relationship between the private information known only to bank supervisors and the risk premium on the subordinated debt issued by bank holding companies. Their empirical results indicate that bank exams produce private information and that the market learns some of this information only a few months after the inspection.

A specific approach has been that of evaluating the rate of decay in the accuracy of the information collected during bank examinations. In fact, this is a fundamental piece of information for the purposes of deciding the timing and frequency of bank examinations.

By comparing the CAMEL ratings with the forecasts stemming from a probit model, Cole and Gunther (1998) find that the information content of on-site examination ratings begins to decay after two quarters. This result confirms the validity of statistical forecasting procedures based on call reports.

According to Hirtle and Lopez (1999) the private information component of examination information ceases to provide useful information about the current condition of a bank after six to twelve quarters. The rate of decay turns out to be greater for troubled banks and during the years in which the banking system experiences financial difficulties. In the case of very detailed reporting schemes and credit registers, the value added in terms of supervisory information cannot be evaluated using any external benchmark such as stock or bonds prices. The most straightforward way to proceede is to compare the accuracy of off-site supervisory evaluations formulated on the basis of publicly available information with the assessments assigned by exploiting private information as well. A substantial increase in the quality of supervisory assessment is expected as a result of the use of information that is provided to the supervisory authority on a bilateral basis.

Given the high performance of econometric models with respect to supervisory screens (Gilbert, Meyer & Vaughan, 1999), one way to proceed is to measure the contribution of supervisory statistics to the performance of early warning models of bank fragility.

As regards the Italian banking system, an earlier work showed that duration models significantly outperform other early-warning methodologies (Laviola, Marullo Reedtz & Trapanese, 1999). In that work, a sample of 427 troubled banks was defined for the 1990–97 period by including, year by year, all banks whose PATROL ratings worsened to 4 or 5; they had one third of total bank assets at the beginning of the nineties. A sample of sound institutions was also defined similar to the distressed banks in terms of size and geographical location. A set of indicators drawn from publicly disclosed information was used to characterize the financial position of each bank. A few variables were chosen to represent some demographic and economic features of the various geographical areas.

The performance of three models – *probit*, *logit*, and *survival* functions – was evaluated on the basis of their accuracy in identifying emerging problems in the two-year period after the date to which the PATROL scores referred. A Cox proportional hazard model (Whalen, 1991) produced the best results.

IV. FORECASTING BANK FRAGILITY IN ITALY: THE VALUE ADDED OF SUPERVISORY INFORMATION

As in the earlier work, a CPH model has been specified in order to classify the banks which became distressed or remained sound during the period 1995–96.

Table 1 shows the three sets of variables that have been used:

(1) 30 indicators have been used to characterize the financial position of each bank, mainly referring to bank size and to the five evaluation profiles which contribute to the PATROL rating; bank organization is proxied by efficiency and productivity variables. The information is obtained from the balance sheets and profit-and-loss accounts that are issued by each bank twice a year;

(2) three variables have been taken from the National Accounts to represent some demographic and economic features of the various regions;

(3) three more indicators have been drawn from the Central Credit Register to better describe the quality of bank credit portfolios. These variables are available only to the supervisors. In particular, the following variables have been considered:

  • the share of total loans that have already been recalled but are still in bank portfolios (QUOTARV). The effect of this variable on the fragility of individual banks is rather ambiguous: on the one hand it can be considered a proxy of doubtful loans; on the other it can signal active loan recovery behaviour on the part of the bank's management;

Table 1.   List of Variables.

Publicly Available Information

Staff Costs/Gross Income
Credit Losses/Operating Income
Operating Income/Average Credit Losses on a 3 years bases
ROE
ROA
Net Profit/Gross Income
Net Interest Margin/Gross Income
$\Delta\%$ Operating Costs
$\Delta\%$ Credit Losses
$\Delta\%$ ROA

Bad Debts/Total Loans
Bad and Doubtful Loans/Total Loans
Annual Flow of Bad Debts (t)/Bad Debts (t-1)
New Bad Loans (Capital Share)/Total New Bad Debts
Credit Losses (t)/Bad Debts (t-1)
(Loan-Bad Debts)/Total Assets
Corporate Loans/Total Loans
Total Loans/Own Funds
$\Delta\%$ Total Loans
$\Delta\%$ Bad Loans

Own Funds/Bad Debts
(Own Funds + Losses Reserves)/Total Assets
Credit Losses (t)/Own Funds (t-1)
Tier 1/Risk Weighted Assets

Ln (Total Assets)

Demand Deposits/Total Deposits
Liquid Assets/Total Deposits

Total Loans/Capital Base
Total Loans/N. of Employees

Herfindahl Index on Loans

Macroeconomic and Demographic Variables

GDP (Geographic Area)
Unemployment Rate (Geographic Area)
Population (Geographic Area)

Supervisory Information

Average Credit Quality
Revocated Loans
Loans with Tensions (if drawn/granted > 1.10)

Table 2. Duration Model. Specification Based on Public Information.

VARIABLE	MEDIAN		MEAN		MIN		MAX		STD	
	sound	failed	sound	failed	sound	failed	sound	failed	sound	failed
RE6 Staff Costs/Gross Income	36.55	41.07	36.47	41.21	14.37	16.91	56.68	69.42	6.27	9.89
RE9 ROE	8.41	3.14	9.10	2.27	1.09	−20.29	29.69	10.90	4.83	6.62
IRIS1 Bad Debts/Total Loans	3.99	13.76	4.84	14.77	0.07	2.11	20.43	31.82	3.55	7.89
IRIS10 Total Loans/Own Funds	368.02	427.69	392.06	441.45	67.22	239.48	812.59	783.14	150.29	151.00
IRIS12 Tier 1/Risk Weighted Assets	23.89	18.50	26.05	19.75	8.30	8.44	100.97	35.33	11.99	6.80
IRIS13 Ln (Total Assets)	12.52	11.87	12.91	12.46	10.00	10.54	18.40	16.62	1.58	1.69
DIS Unemployment Rate (Geographic Area)	6.90	21.20	9.20	17.25	6.90	6.90	21.20	21.30	4.58	5.97

SOUND BANKS = 256
FAILED BANKS = 28

- the share of overdraft facilities for which the amount of credit used is in excess of the credit line (QUOTATS), which has proved to be a useful indicator of stringent liquidity needs on the part of the borrower (positive expected sign);
- for the remaining loans, an indicator of the average probability of default of corporate borrowers (PCERV) (positive expected sign). For each bank this variable is a weighted average of a score proxying the probability of default of each borrower weighted by the share of loans to individual borrowers as a ratio of the bank's total credit portfolio. Bank borrowers are classified according to their riskiness on the basis of logit models run on financial ratios taken from the Cerved company accounts register (Borgioli, 1999). The distinction between insolvent and normally operating firms has been made on the basis of the classification of bad loans in the Credit Register: 3,343 firms were classified as bad borrowers for the first time in 1995 and 1996. The "bad" firms were divided according to 4 economic sectors and 4 geographic areas. A third of them were used for out-of-sample checks. For each set of distressed firms a matched sample of healthy firms was randomly drawn from the Cerved Register. The 16 estimated models made it possible to classify 162,500 companies, whose data look highly reliable by statistical standards. These firms account for around 60% of total bank loans to the corporate sector.

Both the banks' and the firms' accounts refer to 1994. Given the experience acquired in the earlier work, the estimation procedure has been run on unbalanced samples of distressed and sound banks: the in-sample exercise has regarded 28 distressed banks and 256 sound institutions. The holdout sample includes respectively 11 and 30 banks.

With reference to the exercise based on banks' balance sheets and on the macroeconomic variables, the specification which turned out to be the most satisfactory includes the variables shown in Table 2. Most of the variables present the expected sign (Table 3).

The overall correct classification rate is 82 and 84% for the 12 and 18-month time horizon; it peaks at 89% for a two-year interval (Table 4). These statistics are computed by taking into account what can be defined as an apparent error: as an example, a missclassification regarding banks predicted by the model to run into difficulties within a certain time period, but which actually became distressed in the subsequent period, signals that the model is able to identify situations of distress a long time in advance.

Table 3. Duration Model. Specification based on public information. Significant predictors for bank distress.

VARIABLE		expected	result
RE6	Staff Costs/Gross Income	+	−
RE9	ROE	−	−
IRIS1	Bad Debts/Total Loans	+	+
IRIS10	Total Loans/Own Funds	+	−
IRIS12	Tier 1/Risk Weighted Assets	−	−
IRIS13	Ln (Total Assets)	−	−
DIS	Unemployment Rate (Geographic Area)	+	+

Table 4. Duration Model on Italian Banks. Sound and Distressed Banks (1995–1996).

Specification based on public information

Months	Type I Error (1) (A)	Type II Error (2) (B)	Type II Error (3) (C)	Total Error (A + B)	Total Error (A + C)
12	15.8	18.5	15.8	18.3	15.8
18	9.5	16.7	12.5	16.2	12.3
24	14.3	10.1	5.5	10.6	6.5

Specification based on public and supervisory information

Months	Type I Error (1) (A)	Type II Error (2) (B)	Type II Error (3) (C)	Total Error (A + B)	Total Error (A + C)
12	15.8	15.1	12.8	15.1	13.0
18	9.5	14.8	10.3	14.4	10.2
24	7.1	11.7	5.9	11.3	5.9

(1) Type I Error calculated taking into account banks that improved their situation (Patrol ≤ 3) in the subsequent periods. (2) Type II Error calculated taking into account banks that failed and banks that deserved Patrol ≥ 4 in the subsequent periods. (3) Type II Error calculated taking into account banks that failed, banks that deserved Patrol ≥ 4 and banks with Patrol = 3 in the subsequent periods.

Table 5. Duration Model. Specification based on public and supervisory information.

VARIABLE		MEDIAN sound	MEDIAN failed	MEAN sound	MEAN failed	MIN sound	MIN failed	MAX sound	MAX failed	STD sound	STD failed
PCERV	Average Credit Quality	0.36	0.45	0.37	0.48	0.04	0.22	0.82	0.92	0.09	0.15
QUOTARV	Revocated Loans	1.02	10.59	2.32	18.26	0.00	0.00	57.95	100.00	5.50	22.28
QUOTATS	Loans with Tensions (if drawn/granted > 1.10)	0.93	1.47	1.54	3.39	0.00	0.00	16.42	15.56	2.13	4.24
RE6	Staff Costs/Gross Income	35.55	41.07	36.47	41.21	14.37	16.91	56.68	69.42	6.27	9.89
RE9	ROE	8.41	3.14	9.10	2.27	1.09	-20.29	29.69	10.90	4.83	6.62
IRIS1	Bad Debts/Total Loans	3.99	13.76	4.84	14.77	0.07	2.11	20.43	31.82	3.55	7.89
IRIS10	Total Loans/Own Funds	368.02	427.69	392.06	441.45	67.22	239.48	812.59	783.14	150.29	151.00
IRIS12	Tier 1/Risk Weighted Assets	23.89	18.50	26.05	19.75	8.30	8.44	100.97	35.33	11.99	6.80
IRIS13	Ln (Total Assets)	12.52	11.87	12.91	12.46	10.00	10.54	18.40	16.62	1.58	1.69
DELTA0	Δ% Total Loans	24.12	24.25	29.92	28.83	-54.61	-4.34	159.16	78.66	25.07	22.18
DIS	Unemployment Rate (Geographic Area)	6.90	21.20	9.20	17.25	6.90	6.90	21.20	21.30	4.58	5.97
LPOP	Population (Geographic Area)	3.61	3.07	3.54	3.24	3.07	3.07	3.61	3.61	0.17	0.25

SOUND BANKS=256
FAILED BANKS=28

The overall result implies an unsatisfactory performance of the model on distressed banks. This is the so called Type I error, which any supervisor fears most: classifying a distressed bank as a healthy institution. The error rate regards 16% of distressed banks on a 12-month horizon and 14% in a two-year interval.

The Type II error (a misclassification of sound institutions) is equal to 18.5% in one year's time and to 10% by the end of 1996. However, some of the banks considered as distressed by the model actually underwent a downgrading of the PATROL score over the observation period, although their score did not exceed 3. If one takes into account that these banks might also have called for a closer scrutiny by the supervisors, the Type II error falls to 5.5% on the 24-month time horizon. In this case the overall classification accuracy exceeds 93%.

As regards the model which also exploits the information contained in the Credit Register, the best specification includes the variables shown in Table 5. The actual sign of their contribution largely reflects a priori considerations (Table 6). In particular, the PCERVED indicator turns out to be one of the most powerful variables in the classification procedure, along with the return on equity, the ratio between bad loans and total loans, and the rate of unemployment at a local level.

The overall accuracy of the model turns out to be better than that of the specification not including the Credit Register information during the shorter observation periods. What is most important is the gain in accuracy with respect to distressed institutions: the Type I error is equal respectively to 16 and

Table 6.   Duration Model. Specification based on public and supervisory information. Significant predictors of bank distress.

VARIABLE		expected	result
PCERV	Average Credit Quality	+	+
QUOTARV	Revocated Loans	+/−	−
QUOTATS	Loans with Tensions (if drawn/granted > 1.10)	+	+
RE6	Staff Costs/Gross Income	+	−
RE9	ROE	−	−
IRIS1	Bad Debts/Total Loans	+	+
IRIS10	Total Loans/Own Funds	+	+
IRIS12	Tier 1/Risk Weighted Assets	−	−
IRIS13	Ln (Total Assets)	−	−
DELTA0	Δ% Total Loans	+	+
DIS	Unemployment Rate (Geographic Area)	+	+
LPOP	Population (Geographic Area)	+	+

9.5% for the 12 and 18-month time horizons; it reaches 7% (as against 14%) for a two-year interval.

The performance of both specifications is also high out of the sample, confirming the gap observed in the estimation exercise. The model using Credit Register data makes it possible to increase the overall correct classification rate by 5 percentage points.

V. CONCLUSION AND FUTURE WORK

According to the empirical results, the supervisory assessment of the risk profile of a banking institution can be made more effective by exploiting the information regarding individual credit relationships provided to the Supervisory Authority on a bilateral basis.

The effectiveness of supervisory evaluations can be increased further by adopting an internal ratings approach or credit risk models which allow the advantages of portfolio diversification to be taken into consideration. The information contained in Credit Registers may prove a fundamental input of such techniques.

Some statistical exercises have already been conducted in the Bank of Italy in order to compute the expected default frequency of a large proportion of bank borrowers and to measure capital at risk (Foglia & Laviola, 2000; Grippa, 2000; Marullo Reedtz, 2000).

As regards the EDFs, a first approach has involved establishing a link between internal evaluations and external ratings using the actual default rates to classify borrowers in the buckets identified on the basis of the default rates published by the agencies for each rating level.

An alternative approach relying on historical loss data allows more finely diversified rating scales to be obtained. In fact, internally rated firms can be grouped into classes of expected default frequency (EDF) according to their actual historical default rate record. This approach assumes the availability of a large historical data set on the rate of default recorded in lending to different sectors and regions, such as that provided by Credit Registers. The results of these exercises can be channeled into the early-warning procedures to make timely detection of problem banks more accurate.

ACKNOWLEDGMENT

The views expressed in this chapter are those of the authors and do not involve the Bank of Italy.

REFERENCES

Banca d'italia (1996). Economic Bulletin, No. 22, February.

Berger, A., & Davies, S. (1994). The Information Content of Bank Exams, Federal Reserve Bank of Chicago, Bank Structure and Competition, May.

Berger, A., Davies, S., & Flannery, M. (1998). *Comparing Market and Regulatory Assessments of Bank Performance: Who Knows What When*, Federal Reserve Board of Governors FEDS WP.

Borgioli, S. (1999). *An Exercise to Predict Corporate Insolvencies Using Balance Sheet Ratios and Credit Relationships Indicators*, Banca d'Italia, mimeo.

Cole, R., & Gunther, J. (1998). Predicting Bank Failures: A Comparison of On- and Off-Site Monitoring Systems. *Journal of Financial Services Research, 13*, 103–117.

D'Auria, C., Foglia, A., & Marullo-Reedtz, P. (1998). Bank Interest Rates and Credit Relationships in Italy. *Journal of Banking and Finance, 22*(10–11), 1441–1456.

De Young, R., Flannery, M., Lang, W., & Sorescu, S. (1998). *The Informational Advantage of Specialized Monitors: The Case of Bank Examiners*, Federal Reserve Bank of Chicago, WP 98–94, August.

Foglia, A., & Laviola, S. (2000). Probabilità di insolvenza individuali e rischio di portafoglio, Banca d'Italia, Modelli per la gestione del rischio di credito. I ratings interni, April.

Gilbert, A., Meyer, A., & Vaughan, M. (1999). The Role of Supervisory Screens and Economic Models in Off-Site Surveillance. *Federal Reserve Bank of St. Louis Reviews, 81*(6), 31–56.

Grippa, P. (2000). La misurazione del rischio di credito secondo l'approccio del capitale a rischio, Banca d'Italia, Modelli per la gestione del rischio di credito. I ratings interni, April.

Foglia, A., Laviola, S., & Marullo-Reedtz, P. (1998). Multiple Banking Relationships and the Fragility of Corporate Borrowers. *Journal of Banking and Finance, 23*(7), 1067–1093.

Hirschhorn, E. (1987). The Informational Content of Bank Examinations Ratings, Frderal Deposit Insurance Corporation. *Banking and Economic Review*, July/August, 6–11.

Hirtle, B., & Lopez, J. (1999). *Supervisory Information and the Frequency of Bank Examinations, Economic Policy Review*, Federal Reserve Bank of New York, vol. 5, No 1, April.

Laviola, S., Marullo-Reedtz, P., & Trapanese, M. (1999). Forecasting Bank Fragility. The Evidence from Italy. In: G. Kaufman (Ed.), *Research in Financial Services: Private and Public Policy* (Vol. 11, pp. 35–60). JAI Press.

Marullo-Reedtz, P. (2000). A comment to: Stephen, D., & Fischer, M., *On Internal Ratings, Models and the Basle Accord: Issues for Financial Institutions and Regulators in the Measurement and Management of Credit Risk*, IMF Conference on Financial Risks, System Stability, and Economic Globalization, Washington, June 5–8.

Sapienza, P. (1998). *The Effects of Bank Mergers on Loan Contracts*, working paper.

Whalen, G. (1991). *A Proportional Hazard Model of Bank Failure: An Examination of Its Usefulness as an early Warning Tool*, Federal Reserve Bank of Cleveland, Economic review, 1st Quarter, 21–31.

DEPOSIT INSURANCE FUNDING AND INSURER RESOURCE ALLOCATION: A PORTFOLIO MODEL OF INSURER BEHAVIOR UNDER UNCERTAINTY

Steven A. Seelig and John O'Keefe

ABSTRACT

In this chapter we develop an agency model of the deposit insurer whose decisions are made under uncertainty. The deposit insurer's bank supervision and monitoring activities are portrayed as resource allocations that endogenously determine two major components of the insurer's profits, deposit insurance premiums and failure-resolution costs. Using this framework we feel one can fairly represent the deposit insurer's resource allocation decisions as a portfolio choice problem. As a consequence, many of the results of portfolio theory can be applied to the deposit insurer. In particular, the availability of a deposit insurance fund that can be invested in riskless investment alternatives, and the availability of borrowing opportunities, necessarily influences the insurer's resource allocation decisions.

I. INTRODUCTION

Governments that are considering deposit insurance systems must begin by making several interrelated decisions. These include deciding upon the scope

Bank Fragility and Regulation: Evidence from Different Countries, Volume 12, pages 303–327.

Copyright © 2000 by Elsevier Science Inc.
All rights of reproduction in any form reserved.
ISBN: 0-7623-0698-X

of insurance coverage and methods of funding, loss control, and oversight of the insurer. This study is concerned with the method of funding and its potential influence on resource allocation by the insurer. The spectrum of possible funding methods is wide. At one end of the spectrum is a full federal-government guarantee of the insurance obligation which is financed on an as needed basis ("pay-as-you-go") with taxpayer funds, and at the opposite end of the spectrum is a completely privately financed deposit insurance fund that is solely responsible for protecting insured depositors. Clearly, there are many intermediate methods, in terms of the implied loss exposure for taxpayers. For example, one intermediate method is for the government to provide a "full faith and credit" guarantee of the insurance obligation as a "backstop" to the insurance fund. This was done in the United States in 1987 and required the government to use appropriated funds to deal with the savings and loan crisis.[1] Another intermediate method is for the government to replenish the deposit insurance fund when it drops below some predetermined critical level or becomes insolvent, as was done unsuccessfully with the Federal Savings and Loan Insurance Corporation (FSLIC) in 1987. In addition, prior to the advent of federal deposit insurance in the United States, many states sponsored public and private deposit insurance pools that were funded by insured institutions; most of these failed because of insufficient funds to handle their first failure.[2]

One of the critical issues surrounding the establishment of any deposit insurance system is the set of incentives created by the system. Researchers have written extensively on the issue of moral hazard and the role that the existence of deposit insurance plays in incentivizing management of insured institutions.[3] There is also extensive research on the incentives deposit insurance systems create for officials who are responsible for managing and overseeing the system. Much less research has been conducted, however, on the potential influence of alternative deposit insurance funding methods on the insurer's resource allocation decisions.

Governments that sponsor deposit insurance systems must also decide whether to fund the system's costs ex ante or ex post ("pay-as-you-go"). To simplify the discussion, consider a system where the insurer is not responsible for the cost of monitoring and supervising insured depositories. In this situation the insurer incurs no costs until an insured depository fails. Under an ex post funding approach, when an insured depository fails the government funds the deposit insurance costs either from general tax revenues or by borrowing in public markets.[4] An alternative is to create a deposit insurance fund prior to the failures and draw on that fund to pay deposit insurance costs. The fund can initially be capitalized by the government or by insured depositories (henceforth, banks) and funded on an ongoing basis by one or both groups.

This funding approach is referred to as ex ante because it occurs prior to the outlay of the funds.

Garcia (1999) examined international practices surrounding the two different forms of deposit insurance systems and found that the majority of the countries that had explicit deposit insurance systems in place had created a deposit insurance fund. Of the 68 countries with explicit deposit insurance systems, 58 had a fund and 9 relied solely on ex post assessments. Additionally, a number of countries, when faced with a crisis, have chosen to provide deposit guarantees on an ex post basis. Lindgren et al. (1999) describes the responses of the various Asian countries to the financial sector crisis of the late 1990s. Indonesia, Korea, Malaysia, and Thailand all guaranteed deposits in response to the crisis in their countries. In a recent study, Garcia (2000) strongly recommends an ex ante strategy for funding by recommending that countries establish an insurance fund in order to increase the flexibility to deal with banking problems.

In this study we examine the implications of alternative systems for funding deposit insurance on the behavior of the insurer and regulators that oversee the insurer, and examine the implications of these systems for the allocation of resources by the insurer. We seek to shed light on the incentives each system creates by developing an agency model of insurer behavior and analyzing whether the method of funding the insurer matters. Section II contains a brief review the agency cost literature on which our model is based. We model deposit insurer behavior when the insurer is faced with uncertain agency costs in Section III and summarize the equilibrium conditions in Section IV. In Section V we compare insurer decision making under different funding systems and in Section VI present overall conclusions.

II. AGENCY RELATIONSHIPS AND GOVERNMENT DEPOSIT INSURANCE FUNDING

This study examines how a government deposit insurer's sources of funding might affect its behavior, particularly its resource allocation decisions. The need for a deposit insurance fund is not clear in those instances where the government has indicated that it stands behind the insurance obligation, either by placing a "full faith and credit" guarantee on the obligation of the insurer or otherwise obligating itself to provide whatever funding the insurer needs. This "credit enhancement" is typically provided, at least in the U.S., with no explicit cost to the insured or the insurer.[5] Having government backing of a deposit insurance system should, in theory, eliminate the incentives for insured depositors to run on troubled banks. Additionally, having a liquid insurance fund makes it easier for the government to meet its deposit insurance obligations quickly without a protracted government appropriations process in the event of unanticipated failures.

The conflicts of interest between banks, bank depositors, deposit insurers, Congress and taxpayers are typically not an issue until the insurance system breaks down. Stigler (1971), Weingast (1984) and others examine the regulatory practices, political pressures and incentives facing typical government regulators but do not look at the issue of incentives related to deposit insurance. The savings and loan crisis and the subsequent insolvency of the FSLIC gave rise to subsequent examinations of what went wrong with the insurance system, however. In his examination of the savings and loan crisis, Kane (1989) identifies some of the incentives facing regulators that may have contributed to the failure of the FSLIC. He examines the political pressures brought to bear on regulators and develops a framework of agency costs to illustrate the potential misalignment of incentives among participants in the system. His analysis of the failures of two state sponsored deposit insurance plans (Kane, 1992), those in Ohio and Maryland, provides further descriptive support for his hypotheses about misalignment of incentives. Further work by Kane (1995), Kane and Hendershot (1996), and Kane and Kaufman (1992) examines the conflict of interest between the deposit insurer and taxpayers. They identify the potential or actual principal/agent problem in the regulatory structure surrounding deposit insurance in a variety of settings. However, none of this work, either the theoretical or the empirical, varies the mechanism for funding an insurance system. Rather the incentive conflict is posed as a principal/agent conflict where the end result was for the fund to become insolvent and for the taxpayers to pay the bill. Garcia (1999) suggests that a deposit insurance fund needs to be "well-funded" either ex post or ex ante to help avoid agency problems of the type described by Kane and others.

There is no research on deposit insurance of which we are aware that investigates the potential relationships between insurer funding and insurer behavior using portfolio choice models. This work does so by drawing upon the literature on optimal financial structure for firms and the theory of agency costs. Work by Stigler (1971, 1974) and Posner (1974) on the theory of government regulation sets the stage for models of deposit insurer behavior. Government agencies are by definition charged with acting on behalf of others – typically acting as agents for the public. This agency relationship necessarily involves the potential for conflicts of interest between the managers of government agencies and any "outside" group, including those whom agency managers are presumed to represent. Jensen and Meckling's (1976) well-known work on private firms' agency relationships uses the conflicts of interest associated with agency relationships to explain firm financial structure. They argue that a portion of the potential financial costs to a firm from its managers' self-seeking behavior can be limited by outside shareholders through monitoring and bonding of management. These activities are not costless, however. Nor, as Jensen and Meckling argue, can one eliminate all costly conflicts of interest. The net dollar cost to the firm of monitoring, bonding and unresolved conflicts of interest is defined as total "agency costs" by Jensen and Meckling. The most important feature of their model is the characteristic that firm managers' desires and abilities to impose agency costs upon a firm varies with the proportion of a firm's financing by "outsiders" or non-managers – both debt and externally held equity financing. Without detailing their results, suffice it to say that they show that agency costs help explain why firm financial structure matters in ways that affect the market value of the firm.

Kane (1995) refines the agency relationships for government deposit insurers and argues that these relationships are more complex than the bilateral, insurer–banker, relationship typically assumed in economic literature. He maintains that deposit insurance in the U.S. involves at least three primary agency relationships, insurer–banker–Congress, and that there are additional layers of agency relationships among the constituents within each of these three groups. The deposit insurance contract, Kane explains, is analogous to a surety where performance on the contract is contingent upon the surety/insurer maintaining safeguards against loss. At the conclusion of his article Kane offers a general comparative static model of the surety. However, he does not use the model to find its implied optimal decisions for resource use by the surety. More importantly from our perspective, Kane does not address how the surety's sources of funding might affect its decisions.

This article revisits the issues raised in Kane's (1995) surety model, and uses its agency relationships in a model that examines the importance of the deposit insurer's funding. We find that the deposit insurer's financial structure is a significant element in its decision making. The use of a simpler and more tractable model, as compared to the model developed by Kane, permits one to examine fundamental questions about the significance of a deposit insurer's financial structure. We believe the model presented below, while more tractable than Kane's, still maintains essential components regarding agency relationships. One improvement is that we introduce uncertainty into the deposit insurer's decision making, since all of the deposit insurer's major decisions involve uncertain outcomes. Hence, uncertainty is an essential characteristic of the deposit insurer's world and necessarily will affect its decisions. Because most of the literature on deposit insurance refers to government-sponsored deposit insurance, we focus entirely upon government deposit insurers.

III. A MODEL OF THE DEPOSIT INSURER WITH UNCERTAIN AGENCY COSTS

We use a one-period consumption-investment choice model to describe the deposit insurer's choice problem. Individuals that seek to maximize utility defined over expected deposit insurance agency profits, variance in profits, their perceived reputations as managers, and consumption of non-pecuniary agency resources (perquisites) are assumed to manage the government-sponsored deposit insurance agency (henceforth, agency).[6] The managers of the insurance agency (henceforth, agents) allocate beginning-of-period agency resources among alternative consumption and investment opportunities, subject to an initial resource constraint (agency net worth constraint). Some investment alternatives have uncertain outcomes, denoted by a superscript "~" tilde. These alternatives may also have several types of agency costs associated with them as will be explained. To simplify the presentation, time subscripts are not used. Unless otherwise stated, agents make all resource allocation or investment decisions at the start of the period. All rates of return or cost are one-period rates. The agent's maximization problem in mathematical form follows:

1. *Max $U(E(\tilde{\pi}), \sigma^2(\tilde{\pi}), J, E(\tilde{F}))$*
with respect to M^b, S^b, T, B

Such that

$$Y_0 - T + B - mM^b - sS^b - L(B) - E(\tilde{M}^C) - E(\tilde{M}^I) - E(\tilde{F}) = 0$$

Profits are defined as:

$$\tilde{\pi} = (r_T T - r_B B + \tilde{r}_A(M^b, S^b, \phi)D - \tilde{r}_C(M^b, S^b, \phi)D - mM^b - sS^b - L(B)$$
$$- \tilde{M}^C(B, \tilde{r}_A) - \tilde{M}^I(M^b, S^b, \tilde{r}_A) - \tilde{F}(\tilde{M}^C, \tilde{M}^I))$$

Variance in profits is given by:

$$\sigma^2(\tilde{\pi}) = (D^2\sigma^2(\tilde{r}_A) + D^2\sigma^2(\tilde{r}_C) + \sigma^2(\tilde{M}^C) + \sigma^2 {}^*\tilde{M}^I) + \sigma^2(\tilde{F}) - 2D^2 \operatorname{cov}(\tilde{r}_A, \tilde{r}_C)$$
$$- 2D \operatorname{cov}(\tilde{r}_A, \tilde{M}^C) - 2D \operatorname{cov}(\tilde{r}_A, \tilde{M}^I) - 2D \operatorname{cov}(\tilde{r}_A, \tilde{F})$$
$$+ 2D \operatorname{cov}(\tilde{r}_C, \tilde{M}^C) + 2D \operatorname{cov}(\tilde{r}_C, \tilde{M}^I) + 2D \operatorname{cov}(\tilde{r}_C, \tilde{F})$$
$$+ 2\operatorname{cov}(\tilde{M}^C, \tilde{M}^I) + 2\operatorname{cov}(\tilde{M}^C, \tilde{F}) + 2\operatorname{cov}(\tilde{M}^I, \tilde{F}))$$

Agents are also assumed to value their reputations as managers, where reputations are assumed to be a function of those job performance measures that prospective future employers might perceive as noteworthy. We assume that job performance is measured solely by agents' need to rely on government debt, B, to carry out insurance and regulatory responsibilities. This is based on the notion that the agency only needs to borrow if it needs additional funds to carry out its obligations (it has been unsuccessful in managing the insurance fund). The value that an agency manager places his or her self-perceived reputation as manager is given by the function $J(B)$. We assume reputation is a declining function of debt or that the first and second partial derivatives of $J(B)$ with respect to B have the following signs:

$$\frac{\partial J(B)}{\partial B} < 0 \quad and \quad \frac{\partial^2 J(B)}{\partial B^2} > 0$$

We also assume agents value profits, are risk averse and value their reputations as managers, hence:

$$\frac{\partial U}{\partial E(\tilde{\pi})} > 0 \quad and \quad \frac{\partial U}{\partial \sigma^2(\tilde{\pi})} < 0 \quad and \quad \frac{\partial U}{\partial J} > 0$$

Consumption of perquisites by agency managers, $\tilde{F}$, is assumed to be dependent upon the level of external monitoring of the agency by Congress and the banking industry. That is,

$$\tilde{F}(\tilde{M}^C, \tilde{M}^I)$$

We should mentioned that that level of external monitoring of the agency, upon which $\tilde{F}$ depends, is also assumed to be dependent upon the agent's allocation of resources to bank monitoring and supervision (more will be said about these allocations further on in this section.) Simply put, when the agent decides how to allocate resources to monitor and supervise banks, the agent indirectly determines the level of perquisite consumption, $\tilde{F}$. We also assume that increases in external monitoring reduce perquisite consumption or that the partial derivatives of F with respect to both types of monitoring are negative:

$$\frac{\partial \tilde{F}}{\partial \tilde{M}^C} < 0 \quad and \quad \frac{\partial \tilde{F}}{\partial \tilde{M}^I} < 0$$

Variable definitions follow:

B =Debt resulting from agency borrowing from the federal government. Alternatively, one can think of this as a central bank or taxpayer cash infusion.

M^b =Agency resources devoted to monitoring banks, where the unit cost of monitoring is assumed to be a constant, m. Bank monitoring consists of all on-site and off-site inspections of banks where the purpose is to assess the bank's safety and soundness. While in the U.S. the same individuals perform both bank monitoring and supervisory activities, we nevertheless divide these tasks in order to account for their potentially different effects on the agency's risks and returns.

S^b =Agency resources devoted to bank supervision, where the unit cost of supervision is assumed to be a constant, s. Bank supervision consists of all on-site and off-site activities by the agency intended to curtail risky practices by bank management and to limit deposit insurance losses.

ϕ =All factors that affect bank risk that are exogenous to the agency. These include factors such as the economic conditions in the markets to which banks lend.

T =Lending by the agency to the federal government or investment in federal government securities such as U.S. Treasury securities.

D =Bank deposits or the deposit insurance assessment base.

Y_0 =Beginning-of-period resource endowment of the agency, or net worth at the start of the period.

r_B =Nominal rate of interest on agency borrowings from the federal government.

r_T =Exogenous nominal rate of interest on agency lending to the federal government or yield on U.S. Treasury securities.

$\tilde{r}_A$ =Endogenously determined risk-related deposit insurance premium rate that is assumed to be dependent upon the level of bank monitoring and supervision by the agency as well as exogenous industry risk factors. That is:

$$\tilde{r}_A(M^b, S^b, \phi)$$

We further assume that insurance premium rates increase with bank monitoring due to the likelihood that more intense monitoring of banks will detect weaknesses sooner and perhaps uncover weaknesses that bank management and private auditors do not divulge. We also assume that bank supervision will limit risky behavior by bank management, which will result in the bank being charged lower insurance premium rates. Last, increases in bank risk due to factors outside the agency's control are assumed to increase assessment rates.

$$\frac{\partial \tilde{r}_A}{\partial M^b} > 0 \quad and \quad \frac{\partial \tilde{r}_A}{\partial S^b} < 0 \quad and \quad \frac{\partial \tilde{r}_A}{\partial \phi} > 0$$

$\tilde{r}_C$ =Endogenously determined loss rate to the agency on bank-failure resolutions, determined as a percentage of bank deposits. Resolution costs are assumed to depend on the level of bank monitoring and supervision by the agency, as well as exogenous industry risk factors. That is:

$$\tilde{r}_C(M^b, S^b, \phi)$$

Failure-resolution loss rates are assumed to decrease as bank monitoring increases due to the likelihood that more intense monitoring of banks will detect weaknesses sooner and permit closure of banks before severe losses accrue (e.g. limit moral-hazard problems). We also expect that effective bank supervision will limit risky behavior by bank management and, therefore, help reduce loss rates. Last, increases in bank risk due to factors outside the agency's control are also assumed to increase loss rates.

$$\frac{\partial \tilde{r}_C}{\partial M^b} < 0 \quad and \quad \frac{\partial \tilde{r}_C}{\partial S^b} < 0 \quad and \quad \frac{\partial \tilde{r}_C}{\partial \phi} > 0$$

$\tilde{M}^C$ = Endogenously determined Congressional monitoring or oversight costs for the agency that are assumed to depend upon the level of agency debt, B, plus, risk-related insurance assessment rates, $\tilde{r}_A$. That is:

$$\tilde{M}^C(B, \tilde{r}_A)$$

Congressional monitoring costs for the agency rise with the level of borrowing, B, since agency debt is perceived by Congress to represent an increased exposure of taxpayer loss. Monitoring costs are also assumed to rise with insurance premium rates, $\tilde{r}_A$. Moreover, as Kane (1992, 1995) points out, politicians respond to the interests of their industry constituents who will be affected by the level of premiums. Hence:

$$\frac{\partial \tilde{M}^C}{\partial B} > 0 \quad and \quad \frac{\partial \tilde{M}^C}{\partial \tilde{r}_A} > 0$$

$\tilde{M}^I$ = Endogenously determined banking industry monitoring or oversight costs for the agency that are assumed to depend upon the level of agency monitoring and supervision of banks plus risk-related insurance premium rates, r_A. That is:

$$\tilde{M}^I(M^b, S^b, \tilde{r}_A)$$

Since bankers incur additional costs from regulators' actions, including increased supervision and monitoring, the industry typically increases its level of monitoring and lobbying of regulators in response. This activity imposes costs on regulatory agencies. We assume banking industry monitoring or oversight costs on the agency rise as the agency increases its own supervisory and monitoring efforts, and also increase with any increase in insurance assessment rates. These changes may be viewed as industry efforts intended to reduce regulatory burden and insurance costs.

$$\frac{\partial \tilde{M}^I}{\partial M^b} > 0 \quad and \quad \frac{\partial \tilde{M}^I}{\partial S^b} > 0 \quad and \quad \frac{\partial \tilde{M}^I}{\partial \tilde{r}_A} > 0$$

$L(B)$ = Transactions costs the agency incurs when negotiating and obtaining debt financing from the federal government; assumed to depend upon the level of such debt obtained, B.

Since greater borrowings require that more staff resources devoted to explaining the need for the increased reliance on taxpayer funds, we assume transaction costs rise with the level of borrowing.

$$\frac{\partial L}{\partial B} > 0$$

IV. EQUILIBRIUM CONDITIONS

The agency model presented in Section III is fairly general and has features that characterize important aspects of the environment of the U.S. deposit insurance agency, the Federal Deposit Insurance Corporation (FDIC). For this reason we refer to that model as the "basic agency model." This section begins by describing the equilibrium conditions for the basic agency model. A step-by-step solution of the agent's utility maximization problem is contained in the Appendix.

The first-order conditions for utility maximization of the basic agency model require that the agent allocate resources such that the resulting risk-return trade-off agrees with the agent's own preferences. More specifically, agents must employ resources such that the marginal increase in risk that results from an increase in expected returns equals the agent's own marginal rate of substitution between risk and return. We next present these conditions for the major resource decisions that agents make. Interested readers can refer to the Appendix for detailed derivations.

The optimal use of bank monitoring resources is dictated by the following expression:

$$-\frac{U_{\tilde{\pi}}}{U_{\sigma^2}} = \frac{\Delta\sigma^2_{M^b} + \frac{U_{\tilde{F}}}{U_{\sigma^2}}(\Delta\tilde{F}_{M^b})}{\Delta\tilde{\pi}_{M^b} - r_T(m + \Psi_{M^b})}$$

The absolute value of the ratio of the marginal utility of expected profits to the marginal utility of variance in profits is the agent's marginal rate of substitution between risk and return (henceforth, MRS risk-return).

Bank monitoring results in two adverse consequences for the agent. The first is the change in the variance in profits that might result from an increase in bank monitoring, $\Delta\sigma^2_{M^b}$. This change consists of the resulting changes on the variances and covariances of stochastic returns and costs that are either directly or indirectly affected by bank monitoring. The second consequence is the adverse impact bank monitoring has on the agent's consumption of perquisites, $\Delta \tilde{F}_{M^b}$. The basic agency model we specified assumes increases in bank monitoring cause increases in oversight of the agency by both the Congress and banking industry which in turn reduces perquisite consumption. The change in perquisite consumption is in turn "translated" into its contribution to the risk-return trade-off by multiplying it by the agent's marginal rate of substitution between risk and perquisite consumption, U_F/U_σ. The sum of these two effects can be considered the total chance in "risk" associated with bank monitoring by the agent – risk to expected profits and risk to perquisite consumption.

The denominator of this quotient also needs an explanation. The first term is the change in expected profits due to expenditures on bank monitoring, $\Delta \tilde{\pi}_{M^b}$, which consists of a set of direct and indirect effects on profits. The direct effects are the expected increases in insurance assessment rates and decreases in loss rates on bank assets that are assumed to occur with additional bank monitoring, and the unit cost of monitoring, m. The indirect effects are the expected increases in Congressional monitoring of the agency and banking industry oversight of the agency in response to both the increase in insurance premiums and increased monitoring of banks. The agent's evaluation of the change in "expected returns" is not the same as the change in expected profits, however, and this difference is seen in the second term in the denominator, $-r_T(m + \Psi_{M^b})$. Agents have the option to invest a portion of the agency's wealth endowment in riskless government securities and earn a risk-free return, r_T. Therefore, any allocation of resources to risky investments (expenditures on monitoring and supervising banks that yield uncertain results) imposes an opportunity cost on the agent of foregoing the riskless alternative. Intuitively, risk-averse agents should not accept any risk unless the investment yields at least as much as the riskless alternative. Any risk accepted should be valued by its return over this riskless alternative since risky investments require the agent to bear risk. The result is that agents deduct the opportunity cost of what they could have earned by investing monitoring resources in riskless investments from the expected profit when valuing this "risky" use of resources. The term $(m + \Psi_{M^b})$ gives the total direct and indirect resource costs associated with an increase in bank monitoring, and r_T is the rate of return on the risk-free investment alternative. This result parallels that found among standard capital asset pricing models.

The optimal allocation of bank supervisory resources in dictated by essentially the same requirement:

$$-\frac{U_{\tilde{\pi}}}{U_{\sigma^2}}=\frac{\Delta\sigma_{S^b}^2+\dfrac{U_{\tilde{F}}}{U_{\sigma^2}}(\Delta\tilde{F}_{S^b})}{\Delta\tilde{\pi}_{S^b}-r_T(s+\Psi_{S^b})}$$

The interpretation of this marginal condition for optimal use of bank supervisory resources parallels that discussed above for bank monitoring; therefore, it is not repeated.

These necessary conditions for optimal use of bank monitoring and supervisory resources have the following implications for agents' behavior:

- Agents will balance bank monitoring and supervisory efforts using the same risk-return trade-off and will consider all direct and indirect consequences these activities have upon agency profits, the risks of these profits, their reputations and job perquisites.
- Resource allocations to bank monitoring and supervision are not independent of the riskless investment alternative. This very standard result is depicted in Fig. 1. The availability of riskless lending at a rate r_T allows agents to increase utility by first selecting an efficient set of risky investments, M, (monitoring and supervisory expenditures), and then lending to the federal government.

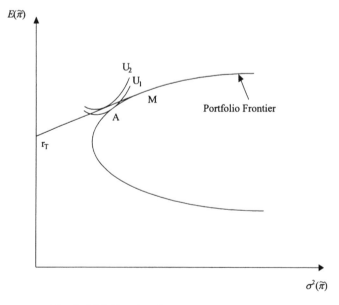

Fig. 1. Risk-Free Lending and Portfolio Choice.

The agency's use of "risky" debt, B, where no external limits are placed on the use of debt, is determined by the following expression:

$$-\frac{U_{\tilde{\pi}}}{U_{\sigma^2}} = \frac{\Delta\sigma_B^2 + \dfrac{U_J}{U_{\sigma^2}}(\Delta J_B) + \dfrac{U_{\tilde{F}}}{U_{\sigma^2}}(\Delta\tilde{F}_B)}{\Delta\tilde{\pi}_B + r_T(1 - \Psi_B)}$$

Debt financing results in three adverse consequences for the agent. The first is the change in variance in profits that might result in an increase in agency debt, $\Delta\sigma_B^2$. This change in variance consists of the resulting changes on the variances and covariances of stochastic returns and costs that are either directly or indirectly affected by agency debt. The second consequence is the adverse impact debt has on the agent's perceived reputation as a manager, ΔJ_B. That effect on reputation is "translated" by the agent into its contribution to the total risk-return trade-off by multiplying the effect, ΔJ_B, by the agent's marginal rate of substitution between risk and reputation, U_J/U_σ. The third is the adverse impact debt has on perquisite consumption, $\Delta\tilde{F}_B$. The effect on perquisite consumption is also translated into its contribution to the total risk-return trade-off by multiplying it by the marginal rate of substitution between risk and perquisite consumption, U_J/U_σ. The sum of these three effects can be considered the total change in "risk" associated with debt by the agent – risk to expected profits, risk to perceived reputation and risk to perquisite consumption.

The denominator of the above expression for the MRS risk-return also requires an explanation. The first term is the change in expected profits due to debt use, $\Delta\pi_{Mb}$, and consists of a set of direct and indirect effects of increased agency debt on expected profits. The direct effect is the nominal interest charge on debt, r_B, the indirect effects are the expected increases in transactions costs and Congressional oversight costs associated with the use of debt and the resultant reductions in perquisite consumption. As before, the agent considers the opportunity cost of debt. Each dollar of debt, B, results in non-interest costs associated with transactions costs, Congressional oversight and perquisite consumption, Ψ_B, but once debt is obtained these non-interest costs are not otherwise available for investment in riskless securities. As a result, the opportunity cost of a dollar of debt is computed net of these transaction costs.

An important question to raise at this point is what implication does the basic agency model have for the agency's capital structure? Since the basic agency model has many elements in common with that employed by Jensen and Meckling (1976), we also find that agency capital structure matters in ways that affect agency profits and value. Debt financing causes increased Congressional oversight of the agency thereby reducing perquisite consumption. This reduction in perquisite consumption increases profits; however, debt financing also has nominal interest costs, liquidity costs and direct Congressional oversight costs, which reduce profits. We do not have priors on the relative size of these costs; however, it is possible that in some situations agencies may find levels of debt that enhance profits. If, for example, very low levels of debt can be obtained relatively easily, it is possible that the enhanced oversight of the agency might reduce the use of perquisites enough to more than compensate for debt costs. If this were to occur, agency profitability might be higher than would occur with no debt or with large amounts of debt.

V. ALTERNATIVE AGENCY FINANCING AND AGENT PREFERENCES

As was stated at the start of Section IV, the basic agency model has many features we feel characterize the environment faced by the U.S. deposit insurance agency, the FDIC. Not all countries face the same institutional and political structures found in the U.S., however. Therefore, we next present an alternative environment and examine how this may change agency behavior. One alternative to the basic agency model is when the agency attempts to cover expected insurance costs on an ex ante basis entirely through risk-related insurance premiums. In this alternative we propose that the agent maximizes utility defined over expected profits and risk (variance) in profits, as previously. The agency does not have a net worth endowment nor the ability to invest in riskless government debt. Finally, the agency can not borrow funds ex ante. Monitoring and supervision costs, as well as expected failure-resolution costs are budgeted for by expected insurance assessments. Any unanticipated losses are covered by ex post government appropriations. The unconstraint maximization model follows:

2. *Max $U(E(\tilde{\pi}), \sigma^2(\tilde{\pi}))$*
with respect to M^b, S^b

Profits are defined as:

$$\tilde{\pi} = (\tilde{r}_A(M^b, S^b, \phi)D - \tilde{r}_C(M^b, S^b, \phi)D - mM^b - sS^b - \tilde{M}^C(\tilde{r}_A) - \tilde{M}^I(M^b, S^b, \tilde{r}_A))$$

Variance in profits is given by:

$$\sigma^2(\tilde{\pi}) = (D^2\sigma^2(\tilde{r}_A) + D^2\sigma^2(\tilde{r}_C) + \sigma^2(\tilde{M}^C) + \sigma^2(\tilde{M}^I) - 2D^2\,\mathrm{cov}(\tilde{r}_A, \tilde{r}_C)$$
$$- 2D\,\mathrm{cov}(\tilde{r}_A, \tilde{M}^C) - 2D\,\mathrm{cov}(\tilde{r}_A, \tilde{M}^I) + 2D\,\mathrm{cov}(\tilde{r}_C, \tilde{M}^C)$$
$$+ 2D\,\mathrm{cov}(\tilde{r}_C, \tilde{M}^I) + 2\,\mathrm{cov.}\,(\tilde{M}^C, \tilde{M}^I))$$

The pay-as-you-go agency's use of bank monitoring resources is dictated by the following MRS risk-return:

$$-\frac{U_{\tilde{\pi}}}{U_{\sigma^2}}=\frac{\Delta\sigma^2_{M^b}}{\Delta\tilde{\pi}_{M^b}}$$

Without the existence of the riskless lending alternative, or even the more costly borrowing alternative, the pay-as-you-go agent selects the efficient risky combination of bank monitoring and supervision that is in agreement with the agent's MSR risk-return. Changes in preferences for risk across agents will result in differences in the combinations of bank monitoring and supervision chosen. This can be seen in Fig. 2 by comparing preferences across agents A and B. Agent A can be considered more risk averse than Agent B (by comparison on MRS risk-return) and will, therefore, choose a lower risk-return portfolio combination than agent B. Both portfolios A and B could involve greater risk than the commonly chosen portfolio M in Fig. 1.

One consequence of the pay-as-you-go equilibrium is that when ex post realizations of losses exceed ex ante expectations, the pay-as-you-go agent may well have made riskier and more costly decisions than agents who can invest agency net worth in riskless assets. As a consequence, the pay-as-you-go agent could impose larger insurance losses upon the taxpayer than the basic agent would. The pay-as-go agency will also allocate resources depending upon the

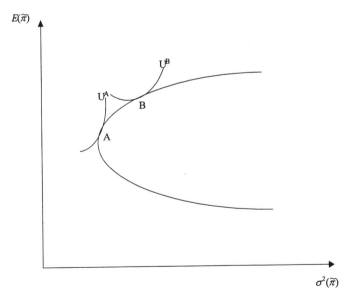

Fig. 2. Different Preferences with no Lending or Borrowing.

preferences of the agency's top managers (Fig. 2). If the same riskless borrowing and lending opportunities were available to the agent, however, agents would be able to select one common efficient allocation of resources, then borrow or lend based upon their risk preferences (Fig. 3). If the same borrowing and lending rates are not available to the agent, however, we return to a classic situation where resource allocation depends upon agent's preferences (Fig. 4). In the U.S. we anticipate that borrowing costs exceed lending costs for the insurance agency.

VI. CONCLUSIONS

In this chapter we develop an agency model of the deposit insurer that includes the agency relationships and associated costs that have become standard components of deposit insurance studies. Since uncertainty is a basic component of the deposit insurer's problem we model agents' decisions under uncertainty. In addition, the deposit insurer's bank supervision and monitoring activities are portrayed as resource allocations that endogenously determine two major components of the insurer's profits, deposit insurance premiums and failure-resolution costs. Using the agency preference functions and resource

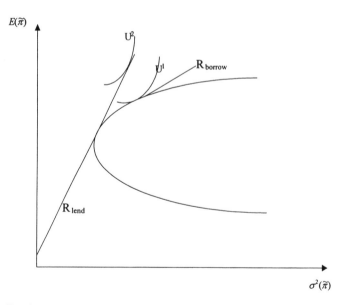

Fig. 3. Agent Utility when Borrowing Rates Exceed Lending Rates.

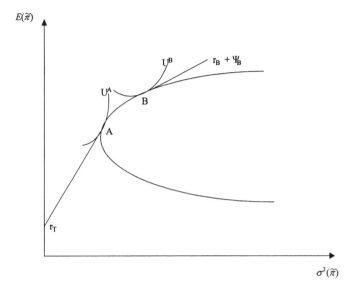

Fig. 4. Different Borrowing and Lending Rates.

constraints that result from this framework we feel one can fairly represent the deposit insurer's problem as a portfolio choice problem. As a consequence, we feel that many of the results of standard portfolio theory can be applied to the deposit insurer. In particular, the availability of a deposit insurance fund that can be invested in riskless investment alternatives, and the availability of borrowing opportunities, necessarily influences the insurer's resource alloca- tion or "investment" decisions. When the insurer can borrow or lend at the same rate of interest, resource allocations to "risky investments" in bank monitoring and supervision can be made independently of borrowing or lending decisions. If the borrowing rates do not equal lending rates available to the insurer, or the riskless investment is not available, or the insurer has no insurance fund, resource allocations to bank monitoring and supervision will depend upon the preferences of the insurance agency managers. In addition, when borrowing rates do not equal lending rates, resource allocations will be influenced by the rates of interest at which the insurer may borrow or lend.

An implicit assumption in the model is that the financial condition of the insurer is transparent to its constituents. If this is not the case, there clearly would be a temptation on the part of the agent responsible for an insurance fund that expected a negative net worth position at the end of the period, and therefore the need for taxpayer funding, to take greater risks than shown above.

This was clearly the case with the former Federal Savings and Loan Insurance Corporation (see Kane (1989)). Similarly, a pay-as-you-go insurer who faced the prospect of significantly greater than expected insurance losses might take actions that were not consistent with the taxpayers' interests.

While the model presented herein suffers the limitations associated with a one-period model and does not, therefore, allow for the kind of deterioration faced by the S&L industry, it suggests that there is a need for meaningful transparency regarding the financial condition of the insurer. This transparency serves as a means to constrain the agency costs associated with deterioration in the condition of the banking industry over time. Under generally accepted accounting standards the insurer's financial statements, where there is an insurance fund, will contain reserves for future insurance losses when such losses are estimable and probable. These financial statements should be subject to audit by independent auditors who are knowledgeable about the condition of the banking industry. Under many systems of government accounting, appropriated (pay-as-you-go) agencies do not have financial statements and thus rely on the willingness of the person in charge to disclose their expectations for the need for funds, usually in a political setting.

The model presented in this work is based on the agency cost work of previous researchers and does not contradict their findings. The results strongly suggest that for a government-sponsored deposit insurance system, the design and funding of the system matter and the choice of the person to manage the system, based on their risk preferences, is critical.

The existence of agency costs does not argue against implementing deposit insurance. Rather, as the results presented above suggest, the design of the system, the risk preferences of the person in charge of it, and the risk taking constraints imposed by transparency become critical. More research, especially the development of dynamic models, is necessary for a greater understanding of the linkages between institutional arrangements and management decisions that affect the risk to the taxpayer by the agent.

ACKNOWLEDGEMENTS

The authors thank David Greely and Rosalind Bennett of the Federal Deposit Insurance Corporation's Division of Research and Statistics, as well as the participants of the 2000 annual meetings of the Western Economic Association for helpful comments and suggestions. The views expressed in this chapter are those of the authors and do not necessarily reflect official positions of the International Monetary Fund or the Federal Deposit Insurance Corporation.

NOTES

1. The Competitive Equality Banking Act of 1987.
2. See Karp, Seelig and Voesar (1983).
3. See Hanc (1999) for a summary of the issue.
4. Whether the government uses tax revenues or issues debt to fund its deposit insurance responsibilities is not relevant for the purposes of this article. Nor is it relevant whether the government subsequently tries to recoup some of its outlay by a special tax on the industry, unless the ex post levy is known ex ante.
5. We recognize that there are implicit costs associated with the guarantee, such as the Community Reinvestment Act obligations, that insured banks face.
6. Implicitly we are imposing all the constraints of standard models of investor choice where utility is defined over the mean and variance of returns. That is, we employ a Von Neumann-Morgenstern utility index and assume portfolio returns are multi-normally distributed. In order to have utility defined over expected returns and expected perquisite consumption, we are assuming the agent's marginal rate of substitution between expected profits and perquisite consumption is constant.

REFERENCES

Garcia, G. (1999). *Deposit Insurance: A Survey of Actual and Best Practices*. International Monetary Fund. IMF Working Paper WP99/54.

Garcia, G. (2000). *Deposit Insurance and Crisis Management. International Monetary Fund.* IMF Working Paper WP00/57.

Gilbnert, A., Meyer, A., & Vaughan, M. (1999). *The Role of Supervisory Screens and Econometric Models in Off-Site Surveillance, Federal Reserve Bank of St. Louis Review*, Vol. 81, No. 6, November/December, 31–56.

Hanc, G. (1999). Deposit Insurance Reform: State of the Debate. *FDIC Banking Review, 12*(3), 1–26.

Jensen, M. C., & Meckling, W. H. (1976). Theory of the Firm: Managerial Behavior, Agency Costs, and Ownership Structure. *Journal of Financial Economics, 3*, 306–360.

Kane, E. J. (1989). *The S&L Insurance Mess: How Did it Happen?* Washington, D.C.: The Urban Institute Press.

Kane, E. J. (1992). How Incentive-Incompatible Deposit-Insurance Funds Fail. In *Research in Financial Services, Public and Private Policy vol. 4*, ed. George G. Kaufman, (pp. 51–91). Greenwhich, CT: JAI Press.

Kane, E. J. (1995). Three Paradigms for the Role of Capitalization Requirements in Insured Financial Institutions. *Journal of Banking and Finance. 19*: 431–59.

Kane, E. J., & Hendershott, R. (1996). The Federal Deposit Insurance Fund That Didn't Put a Bite on U.S. Taxpayers. *Journal of Banking and Finance. 20*: 1305–1327.

Kane, E. J., & Kaufman, G. G. (1992). Incentive Conflict in Deposit-Institution Regulation: Evidence from Australia. In: *Proceedings of the 28th Annual Conference on Bank Structure and Competition* (pp. 42–67). Chicago, IL: Federal Reserve Bank of Chicago.

Karp, J., Seelig, S. A., & Voesar, D. (1983). State Deposit Insurance Programs. In: *Deposit Insurance in a Changing Environment* (Appendix G). Washington, DC: Federal Deposit Insurance Corporation.

Lindgren, C-J., Baliño, T. J. T., Enoch, C., Gulde, A-M., Quintyn, M., & Teo, L. (1999). *Financial Sector Crisis and Restructuring: Lessons from Asia*. IMF Occasional Paper 188. Washington, D.C.: International Monetary Fund.

Posner, R. A. (1974). Theories of Economic Regulation. *Bell Journal of Economics, 3*, 335–358.

Stigler, G. (1971). The Theory of Economic Regulation. *Bell Journal of Economics, 2*, 3–21.

Stigler, G. (1974). Free Riders and Collective Action: An Appendix to Theories of Economic Regulation. *Bell Journal of Economics, 3*, 359–365.

Weingast, B. R. (1984). The Congressional-Bureaucratic System: A Principal Agent Perspective (with applications to the SEC). *Public Choice, 44*, 147–191.

APPENDIX

The constrained maximization choice problem for the basic agency model follows:

$$Max \ V = U(E(\tilde{\pi}), \ \sigma^2(\tilde{\pi}), \ J, \ E(\tilde{F})) + \lambda[Y_0 - T + B - mM^b - sS^b - L(B) - E(\tilde{M}^C) - E(\tilde{M}^I) - E(\tilde{F})]$$

with respect to M^b, S^b, T, B

Maximizing utility with respect to bank monitoring, M^b, yields:

$$\frac{\partial U}{\partial E(\tilde{\pi})} \frac{\partial E(\tilde{\pi})}{\partial M^b} + \frac{\partial U}{\partial \sigma^2(\tilde{\pi})} \frac{\partial \sigma^2(\tilde{\pi})}{\partial M^b} + \frac{\partial U}{\partial J} \frac{\partial J}{\partial M^b} + \frac{\partial U}{\partial E(\tilde{F})} \frac{\partial E(\tilde{F})}{\partial M^b}$$

$$+ \lambda \left[-m - \frac{\partial E(\tilde{M}^C)}{\partial \tilde{r}_A} \frac{\partial \tilde{r}_A}{\partial M^b} - \frac{\partial E(\tilde{M}^I)}{\partial M^b} - \frac{\partial E(\tilde{M}^I)}{\partial \tilde{r}_A} \frac{\partial \tilde{r}_A}{\partial M^b} \right.$$

$$\left. - \frac{\partial E(\tilde{F})}{\partial \tilde{M}^C} \frac{\partial \tilde{M}^C}{\partial \tilde{r}_A} \frac{\partial \tilde{r}_A}{\partial M^b} - \frac{\partial E(\tilde{F})}{\partial \tilde{M}^I} \left(\frac{\partial \tilde{M}^I}{\partial M^b} + \frac{\partial \tilde{M}^I}{\partial \tilde{r}_A} \frac{\partial \tilde{r}_A}{\partial M^b} \right) \right] = 0 \qquad (1)$$

Solving for the partial derivatives gives:

$$U_{\tilde{\pi}} \left\{ \frac{\partial E(\tilde{r}_A)}{\partial M^b} D - \frac{\partial E(\tilde{r}_C)}{\partial M^b} D - m - \frac{\partial E(\tilde{M}^C)}{\partial \tilde{r}_A} \frac{\partial \tilde{r}_A}{\partial M^b} - \frac{\partial E(\tilde{M}^I)}{\partial M^b} \right.$$

$$\left. - \frac{\partial E(\tilde{M}^I)}{\partial \tilde{r}_A} \frac{\partial \tilde{r}_A}{\partial M^b} - \frac{\partial E(\tilde{F})}{\partial \tilde{M}^C} \frac{\partial \tilde{M}^C}{\partial \tilde{r}_A} \frac{\partial \tilde{r}_A}{\partial M^b} - \frac{\partial E(\tilde{F})}{\partial \tilde{M}^I} \left(\frac{\partial \tilde{M}^I}{\partial M^b} + \frac{\partial \tilde{M}^I}{\partial \tilde{r}_A} \frac{\partial \tilde{r}_A}{\partial M^b} \right) \right\}$$

$$+ U_{\sigma^2}\left\{ D^2 \frac{\partial \sigma^2(\tilde{r}_A)}{\partial M^b} + D^2 \frac{\partial \sigma^2(\tilde{r}_C)}{\partial M^b} + \frac{\partial \sigma^2(\tilde{M}^C)}{\partial M^b} + \frac{\partial \sigma^2(\tilde{M}^I)}{\partial M^b} + \frac{\partial \sigma^2(\tilde{F})}{\partial M^b}\right.$$

$$- 2D^2 \frac{\partial \text{ cov}(\tilde{r}_A, \tilde{r}_C)}{\partial M^b} - 2D \frac{\partial \text{ cov}(\tilde{r}_A, \tilde{M}^C)}{\partial M^b} - 2D \frac{\partial \text{ cov}(\tilde{r}_a, \tilde{M}^I)}{\partial M^b}$$

$$- 2D \frac{\partial \text{ cov}(\tilde{r}_A, \tilde{F})}{\partial M^b} + 2D \frac{\partial \text{ cov}(\tilde{r}_C, \tilde{M}^C)}{\partial M^b} + 2D \frac{\partial \text{ cov}(\tilde{r}_C, \tilde{M}^I)}{\partial M^b}$$

$$+ 2D \frac{\partial \text{ cov}(\tilde{r}_C, \tilde{F})}{\partial M^b} + 2 \frac{\partial \text{ cov}(\tilde{M}^C, \tilde{M}^I)}{\partial M^b} + 2 \frac{\partial \text{ cov}(\tilde{M}^C, \tilde{F})}{\partial M^b}$$

$$\left. + 2 \frac{\partial \text{ cov}(\tilde{M}^I, \tilde{F})}{\partial M^b}\right\}$$

$$+ U_{\tilde{F}}\left\{ \frac{\partial E(\tilde{F})}{\partial \tilde{M}^C} \frac{\partial \tilde{M}^C}{\partial \tilde{r}_A} \frac{\partial \tilde{r}_A}{\partial M^b} + \frac{\partial E(\tilde{F})}{\partial \tilde{M}^I}\left(\frac{\partial \tilde{M}^I}{\partial M^b} + \frac{\partial \tilde{M}^I}{\partial \tilde{r}_A} \frac{\partial \tilde{r}_A}{\partial M^b}\right)\right\}$$

$$+ \lambda \left[-m - \frac{\partial E(\tilde{M}^C)}{\partial \tilde{r}_A} \frac{\partial \tilde{r}_A}{\partial M^b} - \frac{\partial E(\tilde{M}^I)}{\partial M^b} - \frac{\partial E(\tilde{M}^I)}{\partial \tilde{r}_A} \frac{\partial \tilde{r}_A}{\partial M^b} - \frac{\partial E(\tilde{F})}{\partial \tilde{M}^C} \frac{\partial \tilde{M}^C}{\partial \tilde{r}_A} \frac{\partial \tilde{r}_A}{\partial M^b}\right.$$

$$\left. - \frac{\partial E(\tilde{F})}{\partial \tilde{M}^I}\left(\frac{\partial \tilde{M}^I}{\partial M^b} + \frac{\partial \tilde{M}^I}{\partial \tilde{r}_A} \frac{\partial \tilde{r}_A}{\partial M^b}\right)\right] = 0$$

Maximizing utility with respect to bank supervision, Sb, yields similar looking results:

$$\frac{\partial U}{\partial E(\tilde{\pi})} \frac{\partial E(\tilde{\pi})}{\partial S^b} + \frac{\partial U}{\partial \sigma^2(\tilde{\pi})} \frac{\partial \sigma^2(\tilde{\pi})}{\partial S^b} + \frac{\partial U}{\partial J} \frac{\partial J}{\partial S^b} + \frac{\partial U}{\partial E(\tilde{F})} \frac{\partial E(\tilde{F})}{\partial S^b}$$

$$+ \lambda \left[-m - \frac{\partial E(\tilde{M}^C)}{\partial \tilde{r}_A} \frac{\partial \tilde{r}_A}{\partial S^b} - \frac{\partial E(\tilde{M}^I)}{\partial S^b} - \frac{\partial E(\tilde{M}^I)}{\partial \tilde{r}_A} \frac{\partial \tilde{r}_A}{\partial S^b} - \frac{\partial E(\tilde{F})}{\partial \tilde{M}^C} \frac{\partial \tilde{M}^C}{\partial \tilde{r}_A} \frac{\partial \tilde{r}_A}{\partial S^b}\right.$$

$$\left. - \frac{\partial E(\tilde{F})}{\partial \tilde{M}^I}\left(\frac{\partial \tilde{M}^I}{\partial S^b} + \frac{\partial \tilde{M}^I}{\partial \tilde{r}_A} \frac{\partial \tilde{r}_A}{\partial S^b}\right)\right\} = 0 \tag{2}$$

Solving for the partial derivatives gives:

$$U_\pi \left\{ \frac{\partial E(\tilde{r}_A)}{\partial S^b} D - \frac{\partial E(\tilde{r}_C)}{\partial S^b} D - m - \frac{\partial E(\tilde{M}^C)}{\partial \tilde{r}_A} \frac{\partial \tilde{r}_A}{\partial S^b} - \frac{\partial E(\tilde{M}^I)}{\partial S^b} \right.$$

$$\left. - \frac{\partial E(\tilde{M}^I)}{\partial \tilde{r}_A} \frac{\partial \tilde{r}_A}{\partial S^b} - \frac{\partial E(\tilde{F})}{\partial \tilde{M}^C} \frac{\partial \tilde{M}^C}{\partial \tilde{r}_A} \frac{\partial \tilde{r}_A}{\partial S^b} - \frac{\partial E(\tilde{F})}{\partial \tilde{M}^I} \left(\frac{\partial \tilde{M}^I}{\partial S^b} + \frac{\partial \tilde{M}^I}{\partial \tilde{r}_A} \frac{\partial \tilde{r}_A}{\partial S^b} \right) \right\}$$

$$+ U_{\sigma^2} \left\{ D^2 \frac{\partial \sigma^2(\tilde{r}_A)}{\partial S^b} + D^2 \frac{\partial \sigma^2(\tilde{r}_C)}{\partial S^b} + \frac{\partial \sigma^2(\tilde{M}^C)}{\partial S^b} + \frac{\partial \sigma^2(\tilde{M}^I)}{\partial S^b} + \frac{\partial \sigma^2(\tilde{F})}{\partial S^b} \right.$$

$$- 2D^2 \frac{\partial \, \text{cov}(\tilde{r}_A, \tilde{r}_C)}{\partial S^b} - 2D \frac{\partial \, \text{cov}(\tilde{r}_A, \tilde{M}^C)}{\partial S^b} - 2D \frac{\partial \, \text{cov}(\tilde{r}_a, \tilde{M}^I)}{\partial S^b}$$

$$- 2D \frac{\partial \, \text{cov}(\tilde{r}_A, \tilde{F})}{\partial S^b} + 2D \frac{\partial \, \text{cov}(\tilde{r}_C, \tilde{M}^C)}{\partial S^b} + 2D \frac{\partial \, \text{cov}(\tilde{r}_C, \tilde{M}^I)}{\partial S^b}$$

$$+ 2D \frac{\partial \, \text{cov}(\tilde{r}_C, \tilde{F})}{\partial S^b} + 2 \frac{\partial \, \text{cov}(\tilde{M}^C, \tilde{M}^I)}{\partial S^b} + 2 \frac{\partial \, \text{cov}(\tilde{M}^C, \tilde{F})}{\partial S^b}$$

$$\left. + 2 \frac{\partial \, \text{cov}(\tilde{M}^I, \tilde{F})}{\partial S^b} \right\}$$

$$+ U_{\tilde{F}} \left\{ \frac{\partial E(\tilde{F})}{\partial \tilde{M}^C} \frac{\partial \tilde{M}^C}{\partial \tilde{r}_A} \frac{\partial \tilde{r}_A}{\partial S^b} + \frac{\partial E(\tilde{F})}{\partial \tilde{M}^I} \left(\frac{\partial \tilde{M}^I}{\partial S^b} + \frac{\partial \tilde{M}^I}{\partial \tilde{r}_A} \frac{\partial \tilde{r}_A}{\partial S^b} \right) \right\}$$

$$+ \lambda \left[- s - \frac{\partial E(\tilde{M}^C)}{\partial \tilde{r}_A} \frac{\partial \tilde{r}_A}{\partial S^b} - \frac{\partial E(\tilde{M}^I)}{\partial S^b} - \frac{\partial E(\tilde{M}^I)}{\partial \tilde{r}_A} \frac{\partial \tilde{r}_A}{\partial S^b} - \frac{\partial E(\tilde{F})}{\partial \tilde{M}^C} \frac{\partial \tilde{M}^C}{\partial \tilde{r}_A} \frac{\partial \tilde{r}_A}{\partial S^b} \right.$$

$$\left. - \frac{\partial E(\tilde{F})}{\partial \tilde{M}^I} \left(\frac{\partial \tilde{M}^I}{\partial S^b} + \frac{\partial \tilde{M}^I}{\partial \tilde{r}_A} \frac{\partial \tilde{r}_A}{\partial S^b} \right) \right] = 0$$

Maximizing utility with respect to agency debt, B, yields:

$$\frac{\partial U}{\partial E(\tilde{\pi})} \frac{\partial E(\tilde{\pi})}{\partial B} + \frac{\partial U}{\partial \sigma^2(\tilde{\pi})} \frac{\partial \sigma^2(\tilde{\pi})}{\partial B} + \frac{\partial U}{\partial J} \frac{\partial J}{\partial B} + \frac{\partial U}{\partial E(\tilde{F})} \frac{\partial E(\tilde{F})}{\partial B}$$

$$+ \lambda \left[1 - \frac{\partial L}{\partial B} - \frac{\partial E(\tilde{M}^C)}{\partial B} - \frac{\partial E(\tilde{F})}{\partial \tilde{M}^C} \frac{\partial \tilde{M}^C}{\partial B} \right] = 0 \qquad (3)$$

Solving for the partial derivatives gives:

$$U_{\tilde{\pi}}\left\{-r_B - \frac{\partial L}{\partial B} - \frac{\partial E(\tilde{M}^C)}{\partial B} - \frac{\partial E(\tilde{F})}{\partial \tilde{M}^C}\frac{\partial \tilde{M}^C}{\partial B}\right\}$$

$$+ U_{\sigma^2}\left\{\frac{2\sigma^2(\tilde{M}^C)}{\partial B} + \frac{\partial \sigma^2(\tilde{F})}{\partial B} - 2D\frac{\partial \text{ cov}(\tilde{r}_A, \tilde{M}^C)}{\partial B} - 2D\frac{\partial \text{ cov}(\tilde{r}_A, \tilde{F})}{\partial B}\right.$$

$$+ 2D\frac{\partial \text{ cov}(\tilde{r}_C, \tilde{M}^C)}{\partial B} + 2D\frac{\partial \text{ cov}(\tilde{r}_C, \tilde{F})}{\partial B} + 2\frac{\partial \text{ cov}(\tilde{M}^C, \tilde{M}^I)}{\partial B}$$

$$\left. + 2\frac{\partial \text{ cov}(\tilde{M}^I, \tilde{F})}{\partial B} + 2\frac{\partial \text{ cov}(\tilde{M}^I, \tilde{F})}{\partial B}\right\} + U_J\left\{\frac{\partial J}{\partial B}\right\} + U_{\tilde{F}}\left\{\frac{\partial E(\tilde{F})}{\partial \tilde{M}^C}\frac{\partial \tilde{M}^C}{\partial B}\right\}$$

$$+ \lambda\left[1 - \frac{\partial L}{\partial B} - \frac{\partial E(\tilde{M}^C)}{\partial B} - \frac{\partial E(\tilde{F})}{\partial \tilde{M}^C}\frac{\partial \tilde{M}^C}{\partial B}\right] = 0$$

Maximizing utility with respect to agency lending to the federal government, or investment in risk-free U.S. Treasury securities, T, yields:

$$\frac{\partial U}{\partial E(\tilde{\pi})}\frac{\partial E(\tilde{\pi})}{\partial T} + \frac{\partial U}{\partial \sigma^2(\tilde{\pi})}\frac{\partial \sigma^2(\tilde{\pi})}{\partial T} + \frac{\partial U}{\partial J}\frac{\partial J}{\partial T} + \frac{\partial U}{\partial E(\tilde{F})}\frac{\partial E(\tilde{F})}{\partial T} + \lambda[-1] = 0 \qquad (4)$$

Solving for the partial derivatives gives:

$$U_{\tilde{\pi}}\{r_T\} + U_{\sigma^2}\{0\} + U_J\{0\} + U_{\tilde{F}}\{0\} - \lambda = 0$$

Our analysis of these results is greatly simplified if we use more compact notation. These four conditions are represented in matrix form below (for simplicity we assume the budget constraint has already been incorporated into these four simultaneous conditions.) The first rectangular matrix or "coefficient matrix" is composed of the partial derivatives of expected profits, variance in profits, job reputation and perquisite consumption with respect to the agent's four decision variables. The second matrix or column vector is composed of the agent's marginal utilities of expected profits, variance in profits, job reputation and perquisite consumption. The null column vector merely repeats the first-order conditions. Non-trivial solutions of the agent's problem requires the usual conditions that the coefficient matrix be non-singular and contain constant terms. In economic terms this requires that the four first-order conditions be linearly independent and that the cost and return generating processes contain elements that are proportional to the decision variables. For example, this requires that resolution-cost rates have one element that is proportional to bank monitoring resources.

If we put in our prior values for the values of terms we obtain:

$$
\begin{vmatrix}
\Delta\tilde{\pi}_{M^b} & \Delta\sigma^2_{M^b} & \Delta J_{M^b} & \Delta\tilde{F}_{M^b} \\
\Delta\tilde{\pi}_{S^b} & \Delta\sigma^2_{S^b} & \Delta J_{S^b} & \Delta\tilde{F}_{S^b} \\
\Delta\tilde{\pi}_{B} & \Delta\sigma^2_{B} & \Delta J_{B} & \Delta\tilde{F}_{B} \\
\Delta\tilde{\pi}_{T} & \Delta\sigma^2_{T} & \Delta J_{T} & \Delta\tilde{F}_{T}
\end{vmatrix}
\begin{pmatrix}
U_{\tilde{\pi}} \\
U_{\sigma^2} \\
U_{J} \\
U_{\tilde{F}}
\end{pmatrix}
=
\begin{pmatrix}
0 \\
0 \\
0 \\
0
\end{pmatrix}
$$

$$
\begin{vmatrix}
\Delta\tilde{\pi}_{M^b} & \Delta\sigma^2_{M^b} & 0 & \Delta\tilde{F}_{M^b} \\
\Delta\tilde{\pi}_{S^b} & \Delta\sigma^2_{S^b} & 0 & \Delta\tilde{F}_{S^b} \\
\Delta\tilde{\pi}_{B} & \Delta\sigma^2_{B} & \Delta J_{B} & \Delta\tilde{F}_{B} \\
\Delta\tilde{\pi}_{T} & 0 & 0 & \Delta\tilde{F}_{T}
\end{vmatrix}
\begin{pmatrix}
U_{\tilde{\pi}} \\
U_{\sigma^2} \\
U_{J} \\
U_{\tilde{F}}
\end{pmatrix}
=
\begin{pmatrix}
0 \\
0 \\
0 \\
0
\end{pmatrix}
$$

We now use these first-order conditions to learn how funding sources affects the agent's behavior. In particular, we would like to demonstrate how the agent's resource allocation decisions are decided. We begin with the agent's decisions regarding bank monitoring.

Equation (1) implies:

$$U_{\tilde{\pi}}(\Delta\tilde{\pi}_{M^b}) + U_{\sigma^2}(\Delta\sigma^2_{M^b}) + U_{\tilde{F}}(\Delta\tilde{F}_{M^b})$$

$$+\lambda\left[-m - \frac{\partial E(\tilde{M}^C)}{\partial\tilde{r}_A}\frac{\partial\tilde{r}_A}{\partial M^b} - \frac{\partial E(\tilde{M}^I)}{\partial M^b} - \frac{\partial E(\tilde{M}^I)}{\partial\tilde{r}_A}\frac{\partial\tilde{r}_A}{\partial M^b} - \frac{\partial E(\tilde{F})}{\partial\tilde{M}^C}\frac{\partial\tilde{M}^C}{\partial\tilde{r}_A}\frac{\partial\tilde{r}_A}{\partial M^b} \right.$$

$$\left. - \frac{\partial E(\tilde{F})}{\partial\tilde{M}^I}\left(\frac{\partial\tilde{M}^I}{\partial M^b} + \frac{\partial\tilde{M}^I}{\partial\tilde{r}_A}\frac{\partial\tilde{r}_A}{\partial M^b} \right) \right]=0$$

If we denote all non-wage costs associated with bank monitoring by a single term, ψ_{Mb}, we get:

$$U_{\tilde{\pi}}(\Delta\tilde{\pi}_{M^b}) + U_{\sigma^2}(\Delta\sigma^2_{M^b}) + U_{\tilde{F}}(\Delta\tilde{F}_{M^b}) = \lambda(m + \Psi_{M^b}) \qquad (1b)$$

Equation 4 gives us a value for λ, the shadow price of relaxing the budget constraint:

$$\lambda = r_T U_{\tilde{\pi}} \qquad (4b)$$

Combining (1b) and (4b) we get a value for the agent's marginal rate of substitution between the risk and return from bank monitoring:

$$-\frac{U_{\tilde{\pi}}}{U_{\sigma^2}} = \frac{\Delta\sigma^2_{M^b} + \dfrac{U_{\tilde{F}}}{U_{\sigma^2}}(\Delta\tilde{F}_{M^b})}{\Delta\tilde{\pi}_{M^b} - r_T(m + \Psi_{M^b})} \tag{6}$$

The same derivations can be used to obtain a similar expression for the marginal rate of substitution between risk and return from bank supervision:

$$-\frac{U_{\tilde{\pi}}}{U_{\sigma^2}} = \frac{\Delta\sigma^2_{S^b} + \dfrac{U_{\tilde{F}}}{U_{\sigma^2}}(\Delta\tilde{F}_{S^b})}{\Delta\tilde{\pi}_{S^b} - r_T(s + \Psi_{S^b})} \tag{7}$$

Equation 3 implies:

$$U_{\tilde{\pi}}(\Delta\tilde{\pi}_B) + U_{\sigma^2}(\Delta s^2_B) + U_J(\Delta J_B) + U_{\tilde{F}}(\Delta\tilde{F}_B)$$

$$= -\lambda\left[1 - \frac{\partial L}{\partial B} - \frac{\partial E(\tilde{M}^C)}{\partial B} - \frac{\partial E(\tilde{F})}{\partial \tilde{M}^C}\frac{\partial \tilde{M}^C}{\partial B}\right]$$

If we denote all non-interest costs associated with agency debt by a single term, ψ_B, we get:

$$U_{\tilde{\pi}}(\Delta\tilde{\pi}_B) + U_{\sigma^2}(\Delta\sigma^2_B) + U_J(\Delta J_B) + U_{\tilde{F}}(\Delta\tilde{F}_B) = -\lambda(1 - \Psi_B) \tag{3b}$$

By combining of equations 3.b and 4.b. we get an expression for the marginal rate of substitution between risk and return from agency debt:

$$-\frac{U_{\tilde{\pi}}}{U_{\sigma^2}} = \frac{\Delta\sigma^2_B + \dfrac{U_J}{U_{\sigma^2}}(\Delta J_B) + \dfrac{U_{\tilde{F}}}{U_{\sigma^2}}(\Delta\tilde{F}_B)}{\Delta\tilde{\pi}_B + r_T(1 - \Psi_B)} \tag{8}$$

COMMENT

Donald P. Morgan

For better or worse, banks in the U.S. and around the world are married to their governments through a complex structure of deposit insurance, regulation, and supervision. The three chapters in this session approach this Byzantine regulatory structure from very different angles. The one theoretical work considers how the funding of a deposit insurance program affects the behavior of the agents hired to manage the program. The two empirical studies are about bank supervision, and the statistical and empirical models used in the surveillance process. I will discuss the theory work first.

Sellig and O'keefe begin their chapter with a simple fact: most deposit insurance programs around the world are funded up front, or ex ante, and the agents managing the programs have some discretion in how to allocate the funds across competing uses, and across time. By contrast, there are a handful of countries around the world that use ex post funding, wherein the managing agents apply to the governing body for funds as needed. The authors' question is simple: under which mode of funding – ex ante or ex post-do the agents hired to manage the insurance program deliver the most "stable" outcomes? In particular, will one scheme lead to a more efficient allocation of supervisory and examination resources, and hence, a more stable banking system and a more solvent insurance program than the other?

The authors approach the question using portfolio theory in a principal-agent framework. Principals want an efficient insurance scheme with sufficient monitoring and supervision of banks (to prevent moral hazard at the bank level). Agents, i.e. the managers, want to maximize their own welfare. The managers choose a "portfolio" of supervisory (S) and monitoring (M) investments with random returns. Importantly, the agents also have the option

Bank Fragility and Regulation: Evidence from Different Countries, Volume 12,
pages 329–333.
2000 by Elsevier Science Inc.
ISBN: 0-7623-0698-X

of investing funds provided by the principal in the safe asset, which yields r. Agents are risk averse, so the expected utility depends on both the level and variance of the agency profits, as well as their reputation, and the level of perquisites they consume.

Funding does matter in their model. Giving the agents money upfront, the authors conclude, may lead to a more stable insurance agency where the level of supervisory and monitoring activity is invariant to the preferences of the agent hired to administer the fund. Given funds, and the discretion to invest them in the safe asset, all prospective insurance managers face the same opportunity cost when deciding to invest in another unit of S&M, or the safe asset. In equilibrium, all agents choose the same mix of S&M (see the figure in their paper). The agents' preferences only affect the choice of how much of the safe asset to hold.

Although this is a standard result in portfolio theory, it is surprising in this context. In essence, it says to loosen the purse strings on the bureaucrat and give them more discretion in investing the purse. This runs contrary to fiscally conservative instincts, which call for tight controls on bureaucrats and their use of funds. It also seems contrary to the "free cash flow" agency problem hypothesized by Michael Jensen in the corporate finance context. Absent pressure from shareholders, managers of firms with excess cash (i.e. more than needed to fund all positive present value projects) will squander the funds on perquisites or negative valued projects rather than distribute the funds to shareholders. Forcing a distribution of funds may take a tightening of the capital restructure with equity replaced by debt (as payments to debt holders are obligatory while dividends are optional).

The authors might consider a more formal contracting approach to the questions they raise. Contracting models, especially those used in the intermediation literature, are more explicit about agency problems between principal and agent, and they allow one to get closer to optimal financial structure. On the other hand, most contracting problems assume risk neutrality whereas the authors allow risk aversion, an important element in the story.

It was not entirely certain that ex ante funding, in fact, yield more stable outcomes. While the investment decisions of the agents are invariant to their own preferences when they have funds to invest, their portfolio *does* depend on interest rates. Agents will invest more or less in supervisory and monitoring resources, depending on whether interest rates are high or low. Comparative statics were not conducted in the paper, but I conjecture that higher interest rates lower the optimal mix of S&M. If so, the level of scrutiny applied to banks by regulators would be countercyclical (since interest rates are procyclical). Countercyclical exams and supervisions is not necessarily bad, but the point is that it changes over the cycle, which is another source of instability to the fund. Whether the principals want the agent's behavior to vary with the preferences or over the cycle is not clear.

The next two chapters, both empirical, are about statistical models of bank distress and their value in the bank supervision process. Alton Gilbert, Andrew Meyer and Mark Vaughan (GMV) shows that the out-of-sample predictive power of one such model may have deteriorated substantially as the model's parameters have aged. The particular model GMV investigate is the SEER model developed by staff at the Board. The model is a single logit equation that estimates the probability of failure given as a function of bank portfolio and performance measures (return on assets, capital-asset ratios, non-performing loans, etc.). In the days when bank failures were not altogether uncommon, the model's parameters were frequently reestimated. Since failures have now become rare, the parameters have been "frozen" since the early 1990s. The question GMV raise is whether these parameters are now obsolete, in the sense that the SEER model no longer reliably forecasts financial distress by banks. To test this, the authors ran a forecasting horse race; they compare the forecasting performance of the SEER model to an alternative model that uses the same set of vector independent variables but with reestimated parameters. To estimate the second model, the authors use an alternative measure of bank deterioration as the dependent variable: downgrades in a bank's CAMEL rating (from 1–2 to 3–5). Downgrades still occur with some regularity so the parameters in the downgrade model can be reestimated every quarter. They compare the out-of-sample predictive power of the SEER model (with frozen parameters) and the downgrade model (with reestimated parameters) to predict downgrades.

The results of the horse race clearly demonstrate the benefit of re-estimating the statistical models, as the SEER model with frozen parameters is easily outdone by the model with "fresh parameters." The power curves they use are a nice way to present their findings that allows for the possibility that supervisors are probably more concerned about type I forecast errors (i.e. false positives) than about type II (i.e. false negatives). Given the probability of a type I error, the probability of a type II error tends to be lower with the downgrade model. The differences between the power curves for each model widen with the forecast horizon.

While GMVs' point is well taken-that the relationships captured in the frozen SEER parameters may have gone stale-the particular horse race they run may exaggerate the problem. The SEER parameters were estimated using bank failures as the dependent variable, but the authors test the ability of the model to predict downgrades. Downgrades and failures are correlated, of course, but not perfectly, and not necessarily linearly; all failures are probably preceded by downgrades, but many downgrades are probably *not* followed by failures. Forcing the SEER parameters through the downgrades data must disadvantage that model relative to one fitted over downgrades. To see how much of the difference in the power curves was due to the switch in dependent variables (as opposed to stale parameters), they could also freeze the parameters in the downgrade model and see how the power curve for that model looks compared to a downgrade model with re-estimated parameters.

It would also be interesting to know *which* of the relationships in the SEER model had gone stalest. Was it the relationship between ROA and failure? Between liquidity and failure. The SEER model parameters are confidential, but the exercise just suggested (comparing the downgrade model with frozen parameters and with reestimated parameter) would allow them to address that point.

Whereas the GMV study highlights the gain for supervisors in having recently estimated parameters in the model, the paper by Reedtz and Trapanese (RT) demonstrates the gain to (Italian) supervisors of having detailed, but privately collected, bank loan data. The question they raise is whether these private data have any marginal value, given relatively detailed data on firm's balance sheets available from public sources akin to Computstat in the U.S. Although not the main question in the paper, I found the differences between the Italian and U.S. supervisory processes interesting. As in the U.S., Italian regulators rely on a combination of on-site examinations and off-site surveillance. Similar to our CAMEL rating system, the Italians have PATROL rating system, with 1–2 indicating basically healthy banks and 3–5 indicating problems. Exams are not as frequent in the U.S. however, so off-site surveillance figures more importantly in the Italian supervisory scheme. Surveillance is augmented there by considerably more detailed than what U.S. regulators collect in the call reports. Apart from detailed public data, the central bank maintains a Credit Register of private information on loan terms at banks. The three Credit Register variables the authors investigate are the share of distressed loans that banks have recalled, borrower overdrafts (relative to credit line limits), and the average probability of default of firms borrowing from each bank, weighted by the share of loans at each bank made to that firm.

These Credit Register variables do have marginal predictive value. Given the publicly available data, adding the detailed loan data reduced the probability of a Type I error (a false negative) from 14 to 7%. One puzzling result was the negative relationship between the probability of distress and the change in bad loans (RT Table 2), as one would obviously expect the opposite sign. A word about that from the authors would be helpful. The specific gain from the Registry variables also depended on the forecast horizon (RT Table 3). At shorter horizons (12–18 months), adding the loan variables reduced only the probability of Type II errors; the incidence of type I errors was the same with or without the loan variables. The reduction in Type II errors occurred only at the 24 month horizon, where the additional loan information reduced the probability of false negatives from 14.3% to 7.1%. That is indeed a sizable gain, but I was curious why it comes so far out on the time horizon.

I just have a few suggestions. As bank regulators are almost certainly more concerned about Type I errors than about Type II, they should avoid summing the probability of each. Plotting the power functions (as in the GMV paper) is a handy way to avoid this summing. I would also be interested to know *which* Register variables in particular added the most power; was it the quantity variables? Rates? Bad loans? Adding the variables incrementally and showing how the power functions shift would be capture the marginal gain from each variable. Which variables are most informative? Which are most subject to misinterpretation (i.e. carry the "wrong" regression coefficient)? Results of this sort might inform the initiative (in the U.S.) to increase disclosure by banks.

ACKNOWLEDGMENT

The authors' views do not necessarily represent those of the Federal Reserve System.